D1264646

THE REVELS PLAYS

Former general editors
David Bevington
Clifford Leech
F. David Hoeniger
E. A. J. Honigmann
J. R. Mulryne
Eugene M. Waith
Martin White

General editors
Karen Britland, Richard Dutton, Alison Findlay,
Rory Loughnane, Helen Ostovich and Barbara Ravelhofer

LOVE'S CURE, OR THE MARTIAL MAID

Manchester University Press

THE REVELS PLAYS

ANON   *Thomas of Woodstock or King Richard the Second, Part One*

BEAUMONT   *The Knight of the Burning Pestle*

BEAUMONT AND FLETCHER   *A King and No King*
The Maid's Tragedy   Philaster, or Love Lies a-Bleeding

CHAPMAN   *All Fools   Bussy d'Ambois*
An Humorous Day's Mirth

CHAPMAN, JONSON, MARSTON   *Eastward Ho!*

DEKKER   *Old Fortunatus   The Shoemaker's Holiday*

FORD   *The Lady's Trial   Love's Sacrifice*

HEYWOOD   *The First and Second Parts of King Edward IV*

JONSON   *The Alchemist   The Devil Is an Ass*
Epicene, or The Silent Woman   Every Man In His Humour
Every Man Out of His Humour   The Magnetic Lady
The New Inn   Poetaster   Sejanus: His Fall
The Staple of News   Volpone

LYLY   *Campaspe* and *Sappho and Phao   Endymion*
Galatea and *Midas   Love's Metamorphosis*
Mother Bombie   The Woman in the Moon

MARLOWE   *Doctor Faustus   Edward the Second*
The Jew of Malta   The Massacre at Paris
Tamburlaine the Great

MARSTON   *Antonio and Mellida*
Antonio's Revenge   The Malcontent

MASSINGER   *The Roman Actor*

MIDDLETON   *A Game at Chess   Michaelmas Term*
A Trick to Catch the Old One

MIDDLETON AND DEKKER   *The Roaring Girl*

MUNDAY AND OTHERS   *Sir Thomas More*

PEELE   *David and Bathsheba*
The Troublesome Reign of John, King of England

WEBSTER   *The Duchess of Malfi*

THE REVELS PLAYS

LOVE'S CURE, OR THE MARTIAL MAID

BY JOHN FLETCHER AND PHILIP MASSINGER

edited by José A. Pérez Díez

MANCHESTER
UNIVERSITY PRESS

The right of José A. Pérez Díez to be identified as the editor of
this work has been asserted by them in accordance with the
Copyright, Designs and Patents Act 1988.

This edition published by Manchester University Press
Altrincham Street, Manchester M1 7JA

www.manchesteruniversitypress.co.uk

British Library Cataloguing-in-Publication Data
A catalogue record for this book is available from the
British Library

ISBN   978 1 5261 3515 5   hardback

First published 2022

Typeset
by New Best-set Typesetters Ltd

Para Irma, y para David y Daniel

Contents

ILLUSTRATIONS   *page* viii

GENERAL EDITORS' PREFACE   ix

PREFACE   xii

LIST OF ABBREVIATIONS AND REFERENCES   xv

INTRODUCTION   1

    Date   6

    Authorship   14

    Sources   19

    Text   30

    Themes   36

    Performance   45

Love's Cure, or The Martial Maid   63

LONGER NOTES   224

APPENDICES

    1. Press variants in F   228

    2. Compositorial analysis and running titles   230

    3. Censorship in F   231

    4. Piorato's song   235

    5. Disputed narrative sources   238

INDEX   243

Illustrations

1. First page of *Love's Cure* in F (London, 1647), courtesy of Pennsylvania State University — 2

2. Detail from *Belägerung der Statt Ostende*, appendix (n.p., 1604–05), fo. 4^r, courtesy of the Staats- und Stadtbibliothek Augsburg (shelf mark: 2 Gs 68) — 27

3. Theatrical cut indicated in 5.3, F, sig. 5S5^r, courtesy of Pennsylvania State University — 31

4. 'The Persons Represented in the Play' from F2 (London, 1679), sig. ^{2}X3^r; personal copy — 35

5. Frontispiece of Gerard Langbaine's edition (London, 1711), personal copy — 48

6. Frontispiece of George Colman's edition (London, 1778), personal copy — 49

7. Final scene, British American Drama Academy, December 2013, production photograph © Simon Annand — 51

8. Typesetting problem in 1.3; F, sig. 5Q4^v, courtesy of Pennsylvania State University — 225

9. Piorato's song, edited by Jennifer Moss Waghorn — 236

General Editors' Preface

Clifford Leech conceived of the Revels Plays as a series in the mid-1950s, modelling the project on the New Arden Shakespeare. The aim, as he wrote in 1958, was 'to apply to Shakespeare's predecessors, contemporaries, and successors the methods that are now used in Shakespeare's editing'. The plays chosen were to include well-known works from the early Tudor period to about 1700, as well as others less familiar but of literary and theatrical merit. 'The plays included', Leech wrote, 'should be such as to deserve and indeed demand performance'. We owe it to Clifford Leech that the idea became reality. He set the high standards of the series, ensuring that editors of individual volumes produced work of lasting merit, equally useful for teachers and students, theatre directors and actors. Clifford Leech remained General Editor until 1971, and was succeeded by F. David Hoeniger, who retired in 1985.

Ever since then, the Revels Plays have been under the direction of four or five general editors: initially David Bevington, E. A. J. Honigmann, J. R. Mulryne, and E. M. Waith. E. A. J. Honigmann retired in 2000 and was succeeded by Richard Dutton. E. M. Waith retired in 2003 and was succeeded by Alison Findlay and Helen Ostovich. J. R. Mulryne retired in 2010, and David Bevington passed away in 2019. Published originally by Methuen, the series is now published by the Manchester University Press, embodying essentially the same format, scholarly character, and high editorial standards of the series as first conceived. The series now concentrates on plays from the period 1558–1642. Some slight changes have been made: for example, starting in 1996 each index lists proper names and topics in the introduction and commentary, whereas earlier indexes focused only on words and phrases for which the commentary provided a gloss. Notes to the introduction are now placed together at the end, not at the foot of, the page. Collation and commentary notes continue, however, to appear on the relevant pages.

The introduction to each Revels play undertakes to offer, among other matters, a critical appraisal of the play's significant themes and images, its poetic and verbal fascinations, its historical context, its characteristics as a piece for the theatre, and its uses of the stage for which it was designed. Stage history is an important part of the story. In addition, the introduction presents as lucidly as possible the criteria for choice of copy-text and the editorial methods employed in presenting the play to a modern reader. The introduction also considers the play's date and, where relevant, its sources, together with its place in the work of the author and in the theatre of its time. If the play is by an author not previously represented in the series, a brief biography is provided.

The text of each Revels play, in accordance with established practice in the series, is edited afresh from the original text of best authority (in a few instances, texts), in modern spelling and punctuation and with speech headings that are consistent throughout. Elisions in the original are also silently regularised, except where metre would be affected by the change. Emendations, as distinguished from modernized spellings and punctuation, are introduced only in instances where error is patent or at least very probable, and where the corrected reading is persuasive. Act divisions are given only if they appear in the original, or if the structure of the play clearly points to them. Those act and scene divisions not in the original are provided in small type. Square brackets are also used for any other additions to, or changes in, the stage directions of the original.

Rather than provide a comprehensive and historical variorum collation, Revels Plays editions focus on those variants which require the critical attention of serious textual students. All departures of substance from the copy-text are listed, including any significant relineation and those changes in punctuation which involve to any degree a decision between alternative interpretations. The collation notes do not include such accidentals as turned letters or changes in the font. Additions to stage directions are not noted in the collations, since those additions are already made clear by the use of brackets. On the other hand, press corrections in the copy-text are duly collated, as based on a careful consultation of as many copies of the original edition or editions as are needed to ensure that the printing history of those originals is accurately reported. Of later emendations of the text by subsequent editors, only those are reported which still deserve attention as alternative readings.

One of the hallmarks of the Revels Plays is the thoroughness of their annotations. Besides explaining the meanings of difficult words and passages, the annotations provide commentary on customs or usage, on the text, on stage business – indeed, on anything that can be pertinent and helpful. On occasion, when long notes are required and are too lengthy to fit comfortably at the foot of the page below the text, they are printed at the end of the complete text.

Appendices are used to present any commendatory poems on the dramatist and play in question, documents about the play's reception and contemporary history, classical sources, casting analyses, music, and any other relevant material.

Each volume contains an index to the commentary, in which particular attention is drawn to meanings for words not listed in the OED, and (starting in 1996, as indicated above) an indexing of proper names and topics in the introduction and commentary.

Our hope is that plays edited in this fashion will promote further scholarly and theatrical investigation of one of the richest periods in theatrical history.

KAREN BRITLAND
RICHARD DUTTON
ALISON FINDLAY
RORY LOUGHNANE
HELEN OSTOVICH
BARBARA RAVELHOFER

Preface

I have worked on this edition for virtually a decade, since Martin Wiggins mentioned this play to me as the most intriguing adaptation of a Spanish source in English Renaissance drama. I became fascinated with the difficulties in assessing its date of composition, its precise authorship, and, particularly, the processes by which a Spanish play that remained unpublished until the spring of 1625, within months of Fletcher's death, came to be refashioned into one of the most daring experiments on the performativity and malleability of gender to be seen on the English stage. I hope that my work of many years will help to dispel the persistent misconceptions around it, and that *Love's Cure* might be appreciated by new generations of readers, scholars, and theatre makers.

In many ways, and as the best of projects, this edition has been a labour of friendship. My first debt of gratitude is to the cast and crew who collaborated with me in workshopping and performing *Love's Cure* at the Shakespeare Institute, Stratford-upon-Avon, in 2012 using original staging practices, and especially to my dear friend Robert F. Ball (1968–2020), artistic director of FRED Theatre, who directed the production with his characteristic insight and gentle touch. Peter Malin, who played Álvarez, was a sharp-eyed and challenging textual advisor, and, as ever, an excellent friend. Red Smucker-Green, our costume designer, helped our cross-dressed male actors with their feminine movement. Jennifer Moss Waghorn arranged and performed the music in the production, and has kindly provided her annotated critical edition of the song in the play for this volume; as an expert in English Renaissance theatre music, her advice has been invaluable. Helen Osborne, our stage manager, remains one of my closest friends.

My general editor in the Revels Plays, Martin White, has been continuously encouraging and helpful, and I am enormously grateful for his wise advice and guidance, and the many hours we have spent talking about the play. I am also grateful to Matthew Frost, Paul Clarke, Lianne Slavin, and the staff at Manchester University Press for handling the process of publication with characteristic efficiency and understanding, and to Andrew Kirk for his outstanding copy-editing. This edition started as a doctoral project under the supervision of Martin Wiggins, to whom I owe more than I can say. He continues to be a crucial scholarly pillar of my work, and remains a dear friend. Gordon McMullan and John Jowett provided a wealth of useful feedback on that early version, as did Paul Edmondson, who kindly read the whole manuscript and commented on it with his characteristic insight and generosity. Martin Butler, who subsequently employed me in the Oxford Marston project, has further nurtured my editorial skills and scholarly rigour, and has also honoured me with his friendship. George Walton Williams produced in 1976 the magisterial old-spelling edition of the play that has been a constant guide and inspiration; his correspondence and encouragement was an unforeseen privilege. Finally, Graham Watts kindly invited me to see his insightful production of the play at the British American Drama Academy in 2013.

I would like to acknowledge as well the kind assistance of the staff of a number of libraries and archives in Europe and North America: the British Library; the Bodleian Library, Oxford; the Library of Birmingham (formerly Birmingham Central Library); the Cadbury Special Collections Library, University of Birmingham; the Brotherton Library, University of Leeds; Thomas Plume's Library, Maldon; the Biblioteca Nacional de España and the Real Biblioteca, in Madrid; the Houghton Library, Harvard University; the Harry Ransom Center, University of Texas at Austin; the Thomas Fisher Rare Book Library, University of Toronto; and the Biblioteca Palatina, Parma. In Stratford-upon-Avon, I would like to extend thanks to the librarians and archivists at the Shakespeare Centre and, very specially, to the wonderful staff of the Shakespeare Institute Library and their then librarian, Karin Brown. The Shakespeare Institute was my home for many years, and I would like to thank its director, Professor Michael Dobson, and its Fellows past and present for providing the perfect environment to grow as a scholar. I prepared the final text of the edition in the equally supportive School of English of the University of Leeds.

Among the friends who have been of crucial help, I need to single out John D. Langdon, and his family, Karen Nichols and Caelan Merrick Langdon, for their love and friendship, now in the inevitable distance; and also Will Sharpe, fellow editor, kindred spirit, and companion in many endeavours. I am also grateful for the friendship, support, and intellectual insights of Pascale Aebischer, C. K. Ash, Catherine Batt, Gareth Bernard, Matthew Blaiden, Claire M.

L. Bourne, Joyce Boro, Thea Buckley, Jason Burg, Lorna Burslem, John Curtis, Tom Disney, Gregory Doran, Fiona Douglas, Katherine Duncan-Jones, Richard Dutton, David Fairer, Ewan Fernie, Alison Findlay, Darren Freebury-Jones, Heather Froehlich, John Gallagher, Joy Leslie Gibson, David J. Graybill Jr, Brett Greatley-Hirsch, Huw Griffiths, Margaret Rich Greer, Paul Hammond, Lucy Holehouse, Jonathan Hope, Victoria Jackson, Kathleen Jeffs, Tim and Claire Johnson, David Lindley, Domenico Lovascio, Georgina Lucas, Jacqueline MacDonald, Harry R. McCarthy, Russ McDonald, Clare McManus, Melissa R. Machit, Laurie Maguire, Alison May, David McInnis, Richard Meek, Perry Mills, Nick Moon, Charles Morton, Lucy Munro, Harry Newman, Richard Nunn, Steve Orman, Eoin Price, Richard Proudfoot, Jane Rickard, Germán Rodríguez Balaguer, Abigail Rokison-Woodall, Alexander Samson, Héloïse Sénéchal, John Settle, Elizabeth Sharrett, Maria Shmygol, Emma Smith, Jodie Smith, Simon Smith, Clare Smout, Matthew Steggle, Joseph Stephenson, David and Ingrid Stevens, Erin Sullivan, Lucie Sutherland, Jonathan Thacker, Jesús Tronch Pérez, Yu Umemiya, and Sir Stanley Wells.

Nothing could have been possible without the love and unconditional support of my parents, Inmaculada and José Félix, of my brother Juan Luis, and of the rest of our extended family, and particularly of my aunt and uncle, Almudena and Miguel. My late and much-missed grandparents, José and María Luisa, and Celia, started it all. My wife, Irma, remains my constant and loving companion in life. Together we embarked on our biggest adventure when, while I was working on this edition, we got married and had our first child, David; our second-born, Daniel, came into this world during its revision. They make everything worthwhile.

Abbreviations and References

conj.	conjectured by
edn	edition
MS/S	manuscript/s
n.	commentary note
NS	New Style (Gregorian calendar)
OS	Old Style (Julian calendar)
Revels	The Revels Plays series
SD	stage direction
SP	speech prefix
SR	Stationers' Register
STC	Short-Title Catalogue number (1475–1640; http://estc.bl.uk/)
subst.	substantively
t.n.	textual note
Wing	Wing Short-Title Catalogue number (1641–1700; http://estc.bl.uk/)

EDITIONS OF *LOVE'S CURE* COLLATED
(IN CHRONOLOGICAL ORDER)

F	(First Folio) *Comedies and Tragedies Written by Francis Beaumont and John Fletcher Gentlemen* (London: Humphrey Robinson and Humphrey Moseley, 1647; Wing B1581)
F2	(Second Folio) *Fifty Comedies and Tragedies. Written by Francis Beaumont and John Fletcher, Gentlemen* (London: Printed by J. Macock, for John Martyn, Henry Herringman, and Richard Marriot, 1679; Wing B1582)
Langbaine	*The Works of Mr. Francis Beaumont and Mr. John Fletcher*, ed. Gerard Langbaine the younger, 10 vols (London: Jacob Tonson, 1711), VII

Q   (Quarto) *Love's Cure: or, the Martial Maid. A Comedy. Written by Mr. Francis Beaumont, and Mr. John Fletcher* (London: J. T., 1718)

TSS   *The Works of Mr. Francis Beaumont, and Mr. John Fletcher*, ed. Theobald, Seward and Sympson, 10 vols (London: J. Tonson, R. Tonson, and S. Draper, 1750), VII

Colman   *The Dramatic Works of Beaumont and Fletcher*, ed. George Colman the elder, 10 vols (London: Printed by T. Sherlock for T. Evans and P. Elmsley; J. Ridley; J. Williams; and W. Fox, 1778), VII

Weber   *The Works of Beaumont and Fletcher*, ed. Henry Weber, 14 vols (Edinburgh: Printed by James Ballantyne for F. C. and J. Rivington; Longman, Hurst, Rees, Orme, and Co.; White, Chrane, and Co.; W. Miller; J. Murray; R. H. Evans; R. Scholey; J. Mawman; and Gale and Curtis; John Ballantine and Co.; Doig and Stirling, 1812), VIII

Darley   *The Works of Beaumont and Fletcher*, ed. George Darley, 2 vols (London: Edward Moxon, 1839), II

Dyce   *The Works of Beaumont and Fletcher*, ed. Alexander Dyce, 11 vols (London: Edward Moxon, 1843–6), IX (1845)

Heath   Marginalia in a copy of TSS by George Craufurd Heath, quoted in Dyce

Battle   Guy A. Battle, 'Love's Cure, or The Martial Maid by Francis Beaumont and John Fletcher: A Critical Text with Comment', unpublished MA thesis, Duke University, 1947

GWW   *Love's Cure or, The Martial Maid*, ed. George Walton Williams, in Fredson Bowers, gen. ed., *The Dramatic Works in the Beaumont and Fletcher Canon*, 10 vols (Cambridge: Cambridge University Press, 1966–96), III (1976)

Mitchell   *Love's Cure, or The Martial Maid*, ed. Marea Mitchell (Nottingham: Nottingham Drama Texts, 1992)

GWW collated the text of four extant versions of the song in 3.2, set to music by John Wilson (see Appendix 4, 235–7). They are:

CA   John Wilson and others, *Cheerful Airs* (Oxford: Printed by W. Hall for Ric. Davis, 1659; Wing W2908), sig. T2^v–T3^r

MSB	Bodleian Library, Oxford, MS Mus b.1, fo. 28^v
MSE	University of Edinburgh, MS Dc 1, 69, fo. 44^v
MSR	Rosenbach Foundation, Philadelphia, MS 243/4, p. 55

I have collated the versions of the Epilogue and Prologue included in the following contemporary collection of poems:

Beaumont   'The Prologue to the *Martial Maid*' and '*The Epilogue*' in *Poems by Francis Beaumont, Gent.* (London: Printed for Laurence Blaiklock, 1653; Wing B1602), sigs. K7^v–K8^r

JOHN FLETCHER'S WORKS

For consistency, all plays by Fletcher and his collaborators are quoted from *The Dramatic Works in the Beaumont and Fletcher Canon*, gen. ed. Fredson Bowers, 10 vols (Cambridge: Cambridge University Press, 1966–96). All quotations have been silently modernised. The titles of the plays cited have been abbreviated as follows:

4Plays	*Four Plays, or Moral Representations, in One*
Barnevelt	*Sir John van Oldenbarnevelt*
Bush	*Beggars' Bush*
Chase	*The Wild-Goose Chase*
Corinth	*The Queen of Corinth*
Cupid	*Cupid's Revenge*
Double	*The Double Marriage*
Elder Brother	*The Elder Brother*
FalseO	*The False One*
FMI	*The Fair Maid of the Inn*
Fortune	*The Honest Man's Fortune*
Hater	*The Woman-Hater*
H8	*All Is True, or Henry VIII*
LC	*Love's Cure, or The Martial Maid*
LFrL	*The Little French Lawyer*
Lieut	*Demetrius and Enanthe, or The Humorous Lieutenant*
LP	*Love's Pilgrimage*
Malta	*The Knight of Malta*
Mill	*The Maid of the Mill*
Phil	*Philaster, or Love Lies a-Bleeding*
Pilgrim	*The Pilgrim*

Princess	*The Island Princess*
Prize	*The Woman's Prize, or The Tamer Tamed*
Progress	*The Lovers' Progress*
Prophetess	*The Prophetess*
Rollo	*Rollo, Duke of Normandy, or The Bloody Brother*
Sea V	*The Sea Voyage*
SpCur	*The Spanish Curate*
T&T	*Thierry, King of France, and his Brother Theodoret*
Val	*Valentinian*
Walkers	*The Night-Walkers, or The Little Thief*

Other editions of Fletcher cited are the following:

Bliss	*A King and No King*, ed. Lee Bliss, Revels (Manchester: Manchester University Press, 2004)
Lambarde MS	*The Woman's Prize*, ed. Meg Powers, Malone Society Reprints (Manchester: Manchester University Press, 2008)
Wiggins, *Sex Tragedies*	*The Maid's Tragedy* and *The Tragedy of Valentinian* in *Four Jacobean Sex Tragedies*, ed. Martin Wiggins, Oxford English Drama (Oxford: Oxford University Press, 1998)

PHILIP MASSINGER'S WORKS

All quotations from Massinger's solo plays are from *The Plays and Poems of Philip Massinger*, ed. Philip Edwards and Colin Gibson, 5 vols (Oxford: Clarendon Press, 1976). The text has been silently modernised. The titles of the plays cited have been abbreviated as follows:

Bashful	*The Bashful Lover*
BAYL	*Believe as You List*
Milan	*The Duke of Milan*
RA	*The Roman Actor*
Renegado	*The Renegado*

Another edition cited:

White	*The Roman Actor*, ed. Martin White, Revels (Manchester: Manchester University Press, 2007)

OTHER ENGLISH PLAYS

Plays by Thomas Dekker are quoted from *The Dramatic Works of Thomas Dekker*, ed. Fredson Bowers, 4 vols (Cambridge: Cambridge University Press, 1953–61). All quotations have been silently modernised. The titles of the plays cited have been abbreviated as follows:

Blurt	*Blurt, Master Constable*
PMHW	*The Patient Man and the Honest Whore* (with Thomas Middleton)
Shoe	*The Shoemakers' Holiday, or The Gentle Craft*
Untrussing	*Satiromastix, or The Untrussing of the Humorous Poet*

References to plays by Ben Jonson are from *The Cambridge Edition of the Works of Ben Jonson*, gen. ed. David Bevington, Martin Butler, and Ian Donaldson, 7 vols (Cambridge: Cambridge University Press, 2012). The titles of the plays cited have been abbreviated as follows:

Alch.	*The Alchemist*
Bart. Fair	*Bartholomew Fair*
EMI	*Every Man In his Humour*
Epicene	*Epicene, or The Silent Woman*
Volpone	*Volpone, or The Fox*

The plays by Thomas Middleton and his collaborators are quoted from the Oxford Middleton: Thomas Middleton, *The Collected Works*, gen. ed. Gary Taylor and John Lavagnino (Oxford: Oxford University Press, 2007). The titles of the plays cited have been abbreviated as follows:

Chang.	*The Changeling* (with William Rowley)
Chaste Maid	*A Chaste Maid in Cheapside*
Maiden's T	*The Maiden's Tragedy* (also known as *The Lady's Tragedy*)

All references to Shakespeare's plays are from *The Oxford Shakespeare: The Complete Works*, ed. Stanley Wells, William Montgomery, Gary Taylor and John Jowett, 2nd edn (Oxford: Oxford University Press, 2005). The titles of the plays cited have been abbreviated as follows:

A&C	*Antony and Cleopatra*
AYL	*As You Like It*
1H4	*The First Part of King Henry the Fourth*

2H4	*The Second Part of King Henry the Fourth*
H5	*King Henry the Fifth*
1H6	*The First Part of King Henry the Sixth* (with Thomas Nashe and Thomas Kyd)
JC	*Julius Caesar*
Lear H	*The History of King Lear* (1608 quarto)
Lear T	*The Tragedy of King Lear* (1623 folio)
MAdo	*Much Ado About Nothing*
MM	*Measure for Measure*
MND	*A Midsummer Night's Dream*
MV	*The Merchant of Venice*
Oth.	*Othello*
R2	*King Richard the Second*
R3	*King Richard the Third*
R&J	*Romeo and Juliet*
Tit.	*Titus Andronicus* (with George Peele)
TwN	*Twelfth Night*

All references to John Webster's plays are from *The Duchess of Malfi and Other Plays*, ed. René Weis, Oxford English Drama (Oxford: Oxford University Press, 1996). The titles of the plays cited have been abbreviated as follows:

Malfi	*The Duchess of Malfi*
Law Case	*The Devil's Law Case*
White Devil	*The White Devil*

Other plays cited:

Amends	Nathan Field, *Amends for Ladies*, in *Five Old Plays, forming a Supplement to the Collections of Dodsley and Others*, ed. J. Payne Collier (London: William Pickering, 1833)
Courtesan	John Marston, *The Dutch Courtesan*, ed. Karen Britland, Arden Early Modern Drama (London: Bloomsbury, 2018)
Fawn	John Marston, *Parasitaster, or The Fawn*, ed. David A. Blostein, Revels (Manchester: Manchester University Press, 1978)
Galatea	John Lyly, *Galatea*, in *Galatea and Midas*, ed. George K. Hunter and David Bevington, Revels (Manchester: Manchester University Press, 2000)

Jew	Christopher Marlowe, *The Jew of Malta*, in *Doctor Faustus and Other Plays*, ed. David Bevington and Eric Rasmussen, Oxford English Drama (Oxford: Oxford University Press, 1995)
Kindness	Thomas Heywood, *A Woman Killed with Kindness*, in *A Woman Killed with Kindness and Other Domestic Plays*, ed. Martin Wiggins, Oxford English Drama (Oxford: Oxford University Press, 2008)
Malcontent	John Marston, *The Malcontent*, ed. George K. Hunter, Revels (Manchester: Manchester University Press, 1975)
SpT	Thomas Kyd, *The Spanish Tragedy*, ed. Clara Calvo and Jesús Tronch, Arden Early Modern Drama (London: Bloomsbury, 2013)
'Tis Pity	John Ford, *'Tis Pity She's a Whore*, ed. Martin Wiggins, New Mermaids (London: A&C Black, 2003)
Zelotypus	*Zelotypus* [*The Jealous Man*], ed. and trans. Dana F. Sutton, Philological Museum, www.philological.bham.ac.uk/zelotyp/

GUILLÉN DE CASTRO'S WORKS

Arata	*Las mocedades del Cid*, ed. Stefano Arata, Biblioteca Clásica (Barcelona: Crítica, 1996)
Castro, *Habit*	*The Force of Habit*, ed. Melissa R. Machit and trans. Kathleen Jeffs, Aris & Phillips Hispanic Classics (Liverpool: Liverpool University Press, 2019)
Castro, *Segunda parte*	*Comedia de la fuerza de la costumbre*, in *Segunda parte de las comedias de don Guillem de Castro* (Valencia: Miguel Sorolla, 1625), sigs. 2C1^r–2E6^v
Juliá Martínez	*Obras de don Guillén de Castro y Bellvís*, ed. Eduardo Juliá Martínez, 3 vols, Biblioteca Selecta de Clásicos Españoles, 2nd series (Madrid: Real Academia Española, 1925–27)
Mesonero Romanos	*La fuerza de la costumbre* in *Dramáticos contemporáneos a Lope de Vega: Colección escogida y ordenada, con un discurso, apuntes biográficos y*

| | *críticos de los autores, noticias bibliográficas y catálogos*, ed. Ramón de Mesonero Romanos, Colección Biblioteca de Autores Españoles (Madrid: M. Rivadeneyra, 1857–8), XLIII, 347–66 |
| Oleza | *Obras completas*, ed. Joan Oleza (Madrid: Fundación J. A. Castro-Akal, 1997), I |

OTHER PRIMARY TEXTS

The titles of early printed books are given in modern spelling without regularising their capitalisation.

Annals	John Stow and Edmund Howes, *Annals, or a general chronicle of England* (London: Richard Meighen, 1632; STC 23340)
Bacon	Francis Bacon, *The Major Works*, ed. Brian Vickers (Oxford: Oxford University Press, 1996, 2002)
Bible	*Holy Bible: King James Version* (Cambridge: Cambridge University Press, [n.d.])
Carlell	Lodowick Carlell, *The deserving favourite* (London: Printed for Mathew Rhodes, 1629; STC 4628)
Cervantes, *Quijote*	Miguel de Cervantes, *Don Quijote de la Mancha*, ed. Francisco Rico, Instituto Cervantes (Barcelona: Círculo de Lectores/ Galaxia Gutenberg, 2004)
Chaucer	Geoffrey Chaucer, *The Riverside Chaucer*, ed. Larry D. Benson, 3rd edn (Oxford: Oxford University Press, 1987)
Cold Year	*The cold year* (London: W. W[hite] for Thomas Langley, 1615; STC 26091)
Contile	Luca Contile, *Comedia del Contile chiamata la Cesarea Gonzaga* (Milan: Francesco Marchesino, 1550)
Correas	Gonzalo Correas, *Vocabulario de refranes y frases proverbiales y otras fórmulas comunes de la lengua castellana* [1627], ed. Miguel Mir (Madrid: Real Academia Española, 1924)

Dante	Dante, *Comedia*, ed. and trans. José María Micó (Barcelona: Acantilado, 2018)
Diogenes	Diogenes Laërtius, *Lives of Eminent Philosophers, Volume II*, trans. R. D. Hicks (Cambridge, MA: Harvard University Press, 1931)
Finet	John Finet, *Finetti Philoxenis* (London: Printed by T. R. for Henry Twyford and Gabriel Bedell, 1656; Wing F947)
Gerardo	Gonzalo de Céspedes y Meneses, *Gerardo the unfortunate Spaniard*, trans. Leonard Digges (London: Printed [by George Purslowe] for Ed. Blount, 1622; STC 4919)
Grimeston	Edward Grimeston, *A true history of the memorable siege of Ostend* (London: Edward Blount, 1604; STC 18895)
Guzmán	Mateo Alemán, *Guzmán de Alfarache*, ed. Luis Gómez Canseco, Biblioteca Clásica de la Real Academia Española (Madrid: Galaxia Gutenberg, 2012)
Horace	Horace, *Satires, Epistles, and Ars Poetica*, trans. H. Rushton Fairclough (Cambridge, MA: Harvard University Press, 1942)
Jesuits	*The protestants and Jesuits up in armes in Gülich-land* (London: [printed by N. Okes] for Nicholas Bourne, 1611; STC 20449)
Langbaine, *Poets*	Gerard Langbaine, *An account of the English dramatic poets* (Oxford: Printed by L. L. for George West and Henry Clements, 1691; Wing L373)
Lazarillo	*Lazarillo de Tormes*, ed. Francisco Rico, Biblioteca Clásica de la Real Academia Española (Madrid: Galaxia Gutenberg, 2011)
Livy	Livy, *The Roman history*, trans. Philemon Holland (London: Printed by Adam Islip, 1600; STC 16613)
Lope XI	Félix Lope de Vega, *Oncena parte de las comedias de Lope de Vega Carpio* (Madrid: Alonso Martín de Balboa for Alonso Perez, 1618)
Mabbe, *Exemplary*	Miguel de Cervantes, *Exemplary novels in six books*, trans. James Mabbe (London: Printed

	by John Dawson, for R[alph] M[abbe], 1640; STC 4914)
Mabbe, *Rogue*	Mateo Alemán, *The rogue, or, The life of Guzman de Alfarache*, trans. James Mabbe (London: Printed for Edward Blount, 1622; STC 288)
Metam	Ovid, *Metamorphoses*, trans. Frank Justus Miller and G. P. Goold, 2 vols (Cambridge, MA: Harvard University Press, 1916, 2004)
Orlers	Jan Janszn Orlers, *The triumphs of Nassau*, trans. W. Shute (London: Printed by Adam Islip, 1613; STC 17676)
Perceval	Richard Harvey, *Plain Perceval the peace-maker of England* (London: Printed in [Eliot's Court Press for G. Seton, 1589]; STC 12914)
Pierce	Thomas Nashe, *Pierce Penniless his supplication to the devil* (London: Printed by Abel Jeffs, for J. B[usby], 1592; STC 18373)
Playford	John Playford, *The dancing master* (London: Printed by W. Godbid, 1670; Wing P2470)
Private combats	*A publication of His Majesty's edict and severe censure against private combats and combatants* (London: Robert Barker, 1613; STC 8498.5)
Proclamation, challenges	*A proclamation against private challenges and combats* (London: Robert Barker, 1614; STC 8497)
Proclamation, dags	*A proclamation against the use of pocket-dags* (London: Robert Barker, 1613; STC 8481)
Proclamation, duels	*A proclamation prohibiting the publishing of any reports or writings of duels* (London: Robert Barker, 1613; STC 8490)
Rowland	*The pleasant history of Lazarillo de Tormes, a Spaniard*, trans. David Rowland of Anglesey (London: Abel Jeffs, 1586; STC 15336)
Seneca	Seneca, *De Beneficiis*, in *Moral Essays, Volume III*, trans. John W. Basore (Cambridge, MA: Harvard University Press, 1935)
Suett	Richard Suett, *The female duellist: an afterpiece* (London: J. Owen and R. Baldwin, 1793)

Virgil

Virgil, *Eclogues. Georgics. Aeneid: Books 1–6*, trans. H. Rushton Fairclough, rev. G. P. Goold (Cambridge, MA: Harvard University Press, 1999)

OTHER REFERENCES

Apperson

G. L. Apperson, *English Proverbs and Proverbial Phrases: A Historical Dictionary* (London: Dent, 1929)

Astington

John A. Astington, *Actors and Acting in Shakespeare's Time: The Art of Stage Playing* (Cambridge: Cambridge University Press, 2010)

Bald

R. C. Bald, *Bibliographical Studies in the Beaumont and Fletcher Folio of 1647*, Supplement to the Bibliographical Society's Transactions (Oxford: Bibliographical Society, 1938)

Baum

Paull Franklin Baum, 'Judas's Red Hair', *The Journal of English and Germanic Philology*, 21.3 (1922), 520–9

Bellany

Alastair Bellany, 'Elwes, Sir Gervase', in *ODNB*

Bentley

G. E. Bentley, *The Jacobean and Caroline Stage: Vol. III, Plays and Playwrights*, 7 vols (Oxford: Clarendon Press, 1956)

Berek

Peter Berek, 'Cross-dressing, Gender, and Absolutism in the Beaumont and Fletcher Plays', *Studies in English Literature, 1500–1900*, 44.2 (2004), 359–77

Berggren

Paula Berggren, '"A Prodigious Thing": The Jacobean Heroine in Male Disguise', *Philological Quarterly*, 62 (1983), 383–402

Bond

R. Warwick Bond, 'On Six Plays in Beaumont and Fletcher, 1679', *Review of English Studies*, 11.43 (1935), 257–75

Bravo-Villasante

Carmen Bravo-Villasante, *La mujer vestida de hombre en el teatro español: siglos XVI–XVII*, 2nd edn (Madrid: Sociedad General Española de Librería, 1976)

Bruerton

Courtney Bruerton, 'The Chronology of the *comedias* of Guillén de Castro', *Hispanic Review*, 12.2 (1944), 89–151

Cal. Ven

Calendar of State Papers Relating to English Affairs in the Archives of Venice (London, 1864–1947), in *British History Online* (University of London, 2001–), www.british-history.ac.uk

Carson and Karim-Cooper

Shakespeare's Globe: A Theatrical Experiment, ed. Christie Carson and Farah Karim-Cooper (Cambridge: Cambridge University Press, 2008)

Chamberlain

The Letters of John Chamberlain, ed. Norman Egbert McClure, 2 vols (Philadelphia: American Philosophical Society, 1939)

Characters

Thomas L. Berger, William C. Bradford, and Sidney L. Sondergard, *An Index of Characters in Early Modern English Drama: Printed Plays, 1500–1660*, 2nd edn (Cambridge: Cambridge University Press, 1998)

Chelli

Maurice Chelli, 'Le drame de Massinger', thesis presented at the University of Paris, 1923

Chess, *MTF*

Simone Chess, *Male-to-Female Cross Dressing in Early Modern English Literature* (London: Routledge, 2016)

Chess et al., *Special Issue*

Simone Chess, Colby Gordon, and Will Fisher, eds, *Special Issue: Early Modern Trans Studies*, *Journal for Early Modern Cultural Studies*, 19.4 (2019)

Clark, '*Hic Mulier*'

Sandra Clark, '*Hic Mulier, Haec Vir*, and the Controversy over Masculine Women', *Studies in Philology*, 82.2 (1985), 157–83

Clark, *Plays*

Sandra Clark, *The Plays of Beaumont and Fletcher: Sexual Themes and Dramatic Representation* (New York: Harvester Wheatsheaf, 1994)

Collections

Collections IV & V, Malone Society (Oxford: Oxford University Press, 1911)

Collins

Collins Latin Dictionary and Grammar (Glasgow: HarperCollins, 1997)

Cressy

David Cressy, *Travesties and Transgressions in Tudor and Stuart England: Tales of Discord and*

Dissension (Oxford: Oxford University Press, 2000)

Cucala Benítez   Lucía Cucala Benítez, 'Hacia una caracterización genérica de *El español Gerardo* de Céspedes y Meneses: Entre la novela bizantina y la ficción sentimental', *Hesperia: Anuario de filología hispánica*, 13.1 (2010), 49–65

DB~e   *Diccionario biográfico español* (Madrid: Real Academia de la Historia, 2018), http://dbe.rah.es

Dollimore   Jonathan Dollimore, 'Subjectivity, Sexuality, and Transgression: The Jacobean Connection', *Renaissance Drama*, 17 (1986), 53–81

Doran   Gregory Doran, *Shakespeare's Lost Play: In Search of Cardenio* (London: Nick Hern, 2012)

DRAE   *Diccionario de la Real Academia Española*, 23rd edn (Madrid: Real Academia Española, 2014), http://www.rae.es

Duncan   Anne Duncan, 'It Takes a Woman to Play a Real Man: Clara as Hero(ine) of Beaumont and Fletcher's *Love's Cure*', *English Literary Renaissance*, 30.3 (2000), 396–407

Dustagheer   Sarah Dustagheer, *Shakespeare's Two Playhouses: Repertory and Theatre Space at the Globe and the Blackfriars, 1599–1613* (Cambridge: Cambridge University Press, 2017)

Dutton   Richard Dutton, *Shakespeare's Theatre: A History* (Oxford: Wiley Blackwell, 2018)

Edmond   Mary Edmond, 'Burbage [Burbadge], Richard', in *ODNB*

Embassy   *England and the North: The Russian Embassy of 1613–1614*, trans. Paul Bushkovitch, ed. Maija Jansson and Nikolai Rogozhin (Philadelphia: American Philosophical Society, 1994)

Erickson   Martin E. Erickson, 'A Review of Scholarship Dealing with the Problem of a Spanish Source for *Love's Cure*', in *Studies in Comparative Literature*, ed. Waldo F. McNeir (Baton Rouge, LA: Louisiana State University Press, 1962), 102–9

Finkelpearl, 'Beaumont, Francis'	Philip J. Finkelpearl, 'Beaumont, Francis', in *ODNB*
Finkelpearl, *Politics*	Philip J. Finkelpearl, *Court and Country Politics in the Plays of Beaumont and Fletcher* (Princeton, NJ: Princeton University Press, 1990)
Fischer	Sandra K. Fischer, *Econolingua: A Glossary of Coins and Economic Language in Renaissance Drama* (Newark, DE: University of Delaware Press, 1985)
Fitzmaurice-Kelly	James Fitzmaurice-Kelly, *The Relations between Spanish and English Literature* (Liverpool: University of Liverpool Press, 1910)
Fleay, *Chronicle*	F. G. Fleay, *A Biographical Chronicle of the English Drama, 1559–1642*, 2 vols (London: Reeves and Turner, 1891), I
Fleay, 'Chronology'	F. G. Fleay, 'On the Chronology of the Plays of Fletcher and Massinger', *Englische Studien*, 9 (1886), 12–35
Fleay, *Manual*	F. G. Fleay, *Shakespeare Manual* (London: Macmillan, 1876)
Fleay, 'Tests'	F. G. Fleay, 'On Metrical Tests Applied to Dramatic Poetry: Part II. Fletcher, Beaumont, Massinger', *Transactions*, 2 (1874), 51–84
Garber	Marjorie B. Garber, *Vested Interests: Cross-dressing and Cultural Anxiety* (London: Routledge, 1992)
García Lorenzo	Luciano García Lorenzo, *El teatro de Guillén de Castro* (Barcelona: Planeta, 1976)
Gerritsen	Johan Gerritsen, 'The Printing of the Beaumont and Fletcher Folio of 1647', *The Library*, series 5, 3, 4 (1949), 233–64
Grattan	Thomas Colley Grattan, *Holland: The History of the Netherlands* (New York: Cosimo, 2007)
Griffiths	Huw Griffiths, 'Trans* Historical Drama: Bodily Congruence in Beaumont, Fletcher, and Massinger's *Love's Cure* and Taylor Mac's *Hir*', *Comparative Drama*, 54.1 (2020), 31–53
Grimal	Pierre Grimal, *Dictionary of Classical Mythology*, ed. Stephen Kershaw (London: Penguin, 1990)

Gurr, *Company*   Andrew Gurr, *The Shakespeare Company 1594–1642* (Cambridge: Cambridge University Press, 2004)

Gurr and Ichikawa   Andrew Gurr and Mariko Ichikawa, *Staging in Shakespeare's Theatres*, Oxford Shakespeare Topics (Oxford: Oxford University Press, 2000)

Hammersmith, 'Section 5'   James P. Hammersmith, 'The Proof-Reading of the Beaumont and Fletcher Folio of 1647: Section 5, *8d, Πa, and Πg; Section 6 and Πd', *The Papers of the Bibliographical Society of America*, 83 (1989), 61–80

Hammersmith, 'Sections 7 and 8A-C'   James P. Hammersmith, 'The Proof-Reading of the Beaumont and Fletcher Folio of 1647: Sections 7 and 8A-C', *The Papers of the Bibliographical Society of America*, 83 (1989), 187–99

Heise   Ursula K. Heise, 'Transvestism and the Stage Controversy in Spain and England, 1580–1680', *Theatre Journal*, 44.3 (1992), 357–74

Helmers and Janssen   *The Cambridge Companion to the Dutch Golden Age*, ed. Helmer J. Helmers and Geert H. Janssen (Cambridge: Cambridge University Press, 2018)

Herbert   *The Dramatic Records of Sir Henry Herbert, Master of the Revels, 1623–1673*, ed. Joseph Quincy Adams (New Haven, CT: Yale University Press, 1917)

Hintze   Hannah Hintze, 'Gluttony and Philosophical Moderation in Plato's *Republic*', unpublished PhD thesis, University of Chicago, 2009

Holderness   Graham Holderness, *Shakespeare and Venice* (Farnham: Ashgate, 2010)

Howard   Jean E. Howard, 'Crossdressing, The Theatre, and Gender Struggle in Early Modern England', *Shakespeare Quarterly*, 39.4 (1988), 418–40

Hoy, 'Shares I'   Cyrus Hoy, 'The Shares of Fletcher and His Collaborators in the Beaumont and Fletcher Canon (I)', *Studies in Bibliography*, 8 (1956), 129–46

Hoy, 'Shares III'   Cyrus Hoy, 'The Shares of Fletcher and His Collaborators in the Beaumont and Fletcher Canon (III)', *Studies in Bibliography*, 11 (1958), 85–106

Hoy, 'Shares IV'   Cyrus Hoy, 'The Shares of Fletcher and His Collaborators in the Beaumont and Fletcher Canon (IV)', *Studies in Bibliography*, 12 (1959), 91–116

Hoy, 'Shares VI'   Cyrus Hoy, 'The Shares of Fletcher and His Collaborators in the Beaumont and Fletcher Canon (VI)', *Studies in Bibliography*, 14 (1961), 45–67

Ichikawa   Mariko Ichikawa, *Shakespearean Entrances* (Basingstoke: Palgrave Macmillan, 2002)

Israel   Jonathan Israel, *The Dutch Republic: Its Rise, Greatness, and Fall, 1477–1806* (Oxford: Clarendon Press, 1995)

Jardine   Lisa Jardine, *The Awful End of Prince William the Silent* (London: Harper, 2006)

Jowett   John Jowett, 'The Writing Tables of James Roberts', *The Library*, 20.1 (2019), 64–88

Kathman   David Kathman, 'Grocers, Goldsmiths, and Drapers: Freemen and Apprentices in the Elizabethan Theater', *Shakespeare Quarterly*, 55 (2004), 1–49

Koeppel   Emil Koeppel, *Quellen-studien zu den Dramen George Chapman's, Philip Massinger's und John Ford's* (Strassburg: K. J. Trübner, 1897)

Lamarca   Luis Lamarca y Morata, *El teatro de Valencia desde su origen hasta nuestros días* (Valencia: J. Ferrer de Orga, 1840)

Levine   Laura Levine, 'Men in Women's Clothing: Anti-theatricality and Effeminization from 1579 to 1642', *Criticism*, 28.2 (1986), 121–43

Lindley   David Lindley, *The Trials of Frances Howard: Fact and Fiction at the Court of King James* (London: Routledge, 1993)

Livak   Leonid Livak, *The Jewish Persona in the European Imagination: A Case of Russian Literature* (Stanford, CA: Stanford University Press, 2010)

Loftis	John Loftis, 'English Renaissance Plays from the Spanish Comedia', *English Literary Renaissance*, 14.2 (1984), 230–48
Low	Jennifer A. Low, 'Early Modern Audiences and the Pleasures of Cross-Dressed Characters', *Poetics Today*, 35.4 (2014), 561–89
Lucas	R. Valerie Lucas, '*Hic Mulier*: The Female Transvestite in Early Modern England', *Renaissance and Reformation / Renaissance et Réforme*, 12.1 (1988), 65–84
Martínez	Ramón Martínez, 'Mari(c)ones, travestis y embrujados: La heterodoxia del varón como recurso cómico en el Teatro Breve del Barroco', *Anagnórisis: Revista de investigación teatral*, 3 (2011), 9–37
Maxwell	Baldwin Maxwell, *Studies in Beaumont, Fletcher and Massinger* (Chapel Hill, NC: University of North Carolina Press, 1939)
McKendrick	Melveena McKendrick, *Woman and Society in the Spanish Drama of the Golden Age* (London: Cambridge University Press, 1974)
McMullan	Gordon McMullan, *The Politics of Unease in the Plays of John Fletcher* (Amherst, MA: University of Massachusetts Press, 1994)
Mérimée	Henri Mérimée, *Spectacles et comédiens à Valencia (1580–1630)* (Toulouse: Édouard Privat, 1913)
Motley, *Dutch Republic*	John Lothrop Motley, *The Rise of the Dutch Republic: A History*, 3 vols (Leipzig: Alphons Dürr, 1858), III
Motley, *United Netherlands*	John Lothrop Motley, *History of the United Netherlands*, 4 vols (London: John Murray, 1867), IV
Munro	Lucy Munro, 'Report of Francis Beaumont, John Fletcher and Philip Massinger's *Love's Cure* with the King's Players', *Research Opportunities in Renaissance Drama*, 41 (2002), 75–6
Nelsen	Paul Nelsen, 'Positing Pillars at the Globe', *Shakespeare Quarterly*, 48.3 (1997), 324–35
ODNB	*Oxford Dictionary of National Biography* (Oxford: Oxford University Press, 2004–), www.oxforddnb.com/

OED	*Oxford English Dictionary*, www.oed.com/
Oliphant	E. H. C. Oliphant, *The Plays of Beaumont and Fletcher: An Attempt to Determine their Respective Shares and the Shares of Others* (New Haven, CT: Yale University Press, 1927)
O'Malley	Susan Gushee O'Malley, ed., *'Custom Is an Idiot': Jacobean Pamphlet Literature on Women* (Urbana, IL: University of Illinois Press, 2004)
Opie	Iona Opie and Peter Opie, eds, *The Oxford Dictionary of Nursery Rhymes* (Oxford: Oxford University Press, 1951, 1983)
Orgel	Stephen Orgel, *Impersonations: The Performance of Gender in Shakespeare's England* (Cambridge: Cambridge University Press, 1996)
Palfrey and Stern	Simon Palfrey and Tiffany Stern, *Shakespeare in Parts* (Oxford: Oxford University Press, 2007)
Peltonen	Markku Peltonen, *The Duel in Early Modern England: Civility, Politeness and Honour* (Cambridge: Cambridge University Press, 2003)
Pérez Díez, 'Editing'	José A. Pérez Díez, 'Editing on Stage: Theatrical Research for a Critical Edition of John Fletcher and Philip Massinger's *Love's Cure, or The Martial Maid*', *Shakespeare Bulletin*, 34.1 (2016), 69–88
Pérez Díez, 'Quills'	José A. Pérez Díez, 'What the Quills Can Tell: The Case of John Fletcher and Philip Massinger's *Love's Cure*', *Shakespeare Survey 70: Creating Shakespeare* (2017), 93–102
Prak	Maarten Prak, *The Dutch Republic in the Seventeenth Century: The Golden Age* (Cambridge: Cambridge University Press, 2005)
Quarmby	Kevin A. Quarmby, *The Disguised Ruler in Shakespeare and his Contemporaries* (Farnham: Ashgate, 2012)
Rackin	Phyllis Rackin, 'Androgyny, Mimesis, and the Marriage of the Boy Heroine on the English Renaissance Stage', *PMLA*, 102.1 (1987), 29–41

Redworth   Glyn Redworth, *The Prince and the Infanta: The Cultural Politics of the Spanish Match* (New Haven, CT: Yale University Press, 2003)

Rico   Francisco Rico, *Tiempos del "Quijote"* (Barcelona: Acantilado, 2012)

Robinson   David M. Robinson, *Closeted Writing and Lesbian and Gay Literature: Classical, Early Modern, Eighteenth-Century* (Aldershot: Ashgate, 2006)

Sarmiento   Martín Sarmiento, *Onomástico etimológico de la lengua gallega*, ed. J. L. Pensado Tomé (La Coruña: Fundación Barrié, 1999)

Schevill   R. Schevill, 'On the Influence of Spanish Literature upon English in the Early 17th Century', *Romanische Forschungen*, 20.2 (1907), 604–34

Shapiro   Michael Shapiro, *Gender in Play on the Shakespearean Stage: Boy Heroines and Female Pages* (Ann Arbor, MI: University of Michigan Press, 1994)

Sharp   Iain Sharp, 'Wit at Several Weapons: A Critical Edition', unpublished PhD dissertation, University of Auckland, 1982

Shepherd   Simon Shepherd, *Amazons and Warrior Women: Varieties of Feminism in Seventeenth-Century Drama* (New York: St. Martin's Press, 1981)

Simoni   Anna E. C. Simoni, *The Ostend Story: Early Tales of the Great Siege and the Mediating Role of Henrick van Haestens*, Bibliotheca Bibliographica Neerlandica XXXVIII ('t Goy-Houten: HES & De Graaf, 2003)

Smith   Smith, David L., 'Herbert, Philip', in *ODNB*

Soyer   François Soyer, *Ambiguous Gender in Early Modern Spain and Portugal: Inquisitors, Doctors and the Transgression of Gender Norms*, Medieval and Early Modern Iberian World (Leiden: Brill, 2012)

SPD   *Calendar of State Papers Domestic: James I, 1603–1610*, ed. Mary Anne Everett Green (London, 1857–59), in *British History Online* (University of London, 2001–), www.british-history.ac.uk

SPF

Spink

Stallybrass and Jones

Statutes

Stiefel, 'Nachahmung' 1

Stiefel, 'Nachahmung' 2

Sykes

Thacker

Thomas

Tilley

Secretaries of State: State Papers Foreign, Holland and Flanders, c1560–1780 (National Archives, 2010), in *State Papers Online, 1509–171* (Cerngage, [n.d.]), www.gale.com/intl/primary-sources/state-papers-online

Ian Spink, 'Wilson, John', in *ODNB*

Peter Stallybrass and Ann Rosalind Jones, 'Fetishizing the Glove in Renaissance Europe', *Critical Inquiry*, 28.1 (2001), 114–32

Statutes at Large, of England and of Great-Britain from Magna Carta to the Union of the Kingdoms of Great Britain and Ireland, in Twenty Volumes, vol. IV, *From 1 Mary, A.D. 1553 – To 16 Charles I. A.D. 1642* (London: George Eyre and Andrew Strahan, 1811)

A. L. Stiefel, 'Die Nachahmung spanischer Komödien in England unter den ersten Stuarts', *Romanische Forschungen*, 5 (1890), 193–220

A. L. Stiefel, 'Die Nachahmung spanischer Komödien in England unter den ersten Stuarts', *Archiv für das Studium der neueren Sprachen und Literaturen*, 99 (1897), 271–310

Henry Dugdale Sykes, *Sidelights on Elizabethan Drama: A Series of Studies Dealing with the Authorship of Sixteenth and Seventeenth Century Plays* (London: Humphrey Milford, Oxford University Press, 1924)

Jonathan Thacker, *Role-Play and the World as Stage in the Comedia* (Liverpool: Liverpool University Press, 2002)

P. W. Thomas, *Sir John Berkenhead, 1617–1679: A Royalist Career in Politics and Polemics* (Oxford: Clarendon Press, 1969)

Morris Palmer Tilley, *A Dictionary of the Proverbs in England in the Sixteenth and Seventeenth Centuries: A Collection of the Proverbs Found in English Literature and the Dictionaries of the Period* (Ann Arbor, MI: University of Michigan Press, 1950)

Turner   Robert K. Turner, 'The Printers and the
                    Beaumont and Fletcher Folio of 1647, Section
                    2', *Studies in Bibliography*, 20 (1967), 35–59

Wiggins, *Catalogue* Martin Wiggins (in association with Catherine
                    Richardson), *British Drama 1533:1642: A
                    Catalogue*, 11 vols (Oxford: Oxford University
                    Press, 2011–)

Wiggins, 'Four'   Martin Wiggins, 'Signs of the Four', *Around
                    the Globe*, 57 (2014), 48–9

Wiggins, *Power*   Martin Wiggins, *Drama and the Transfer of
                    Power in Renaissance England* (Oxford: Oxford
                    University Press, 2012)

Wiggins, *Time*   Martin Wiggins, *Shakespeare and the Drama of
                    his Time* (New York: Oxford University Press,
                    2000)

Wilson, *Guillén*   Edward M. Wilson, *Guillén de Castro* (New
                    York: Twayne, 1973)

Wilson, 'Spanish'   Edward M. Wilson, 'Did John Fletcher Read
                    Spanish?', *Philological Quarterly*, 27 (1948),
                    187–90

Woudhuysen   H. R. Woudhuysen, 'Writing-Tables and
                    Table-Books', *Electronic British Library Journal*
                    (2004), Article 3, www.bl.uk/eblj/

Introduction

Love's Cure is one of the most memorable plays in John Fletcher's varied and extensive canon, and is among the most remarkable collaborations with his younger writing partner Philip Massinger. Their working relationship, which started in 1613 when Fletcher's earlier collaborators, Francis Beaumont and William Shakespeare, ended their careers as dramatists, continued until Fletcher's death during the plague of 1625. The play engages with a number of recurrent and characteristic Fletcherian tropes, including a playful handling of the theme of cross-dressing, an insightful exploration of the performativity of gender, and a meditation on the transformative power of love and (hetero)sexual desire. Fletcher is, in fact, the English dramatist of the period who included the greatest number of cross-dressers in his plays, exploiting the dramatic potential of the cross-dressed male actor as a female impersonator. Crucially, this play explores the difficulties that two essentially transgender characters encounter when forced to conform to the gender-normative expectations of a fiercely patriarchal society. In addition, Fletcher was also the English dramatist who engaged most often and most productively with Spanish contemporary literature, particularly the works of Miguel de Cervantes. In the case of *Love's Cure*, he modelled its two narrative lines on a number of Spanish literary sources, demonstrating the vibrant cultural transactions that were frequent in the pan-European context of the Renaissance.

The main drive of the plot is striking. Following an entrenched family feud, two siblings from Seville, a boy and a girl, were separated in their first infancy and were brought up as members of their opposite genders. The father took the girl, Clara, to the Spanish wars in Flanders where she would become a valiant soldier. Meanwhile, the mother stayed at home with the boy, Lucio, and educated him in the ways of domestic femininity. Twenty years later, a royal pardon granted as a recompense for Clara's heroic actions in battle enables the return of Don Fernando de Álvarez, the father, to Spain, and the family is reunited. The siblings are then commanded to revert to their expected gender identities: Clara is required to become a lady and Lucio has to learn the rough ways of a gentleman. On one

I

125

LOVES CURE
OR,
The Martial Maid.

Actus Primus——*Scæna Prima.*

Enter Vitelli, Lamorall, Anastro.

Vitelli.

Lvarez pardon'd?
Ana. And return'd.
Lamo. I saw him land
At St. *Lucars,* and such a generall welcome
Fame, as harbinger to his brave actions,
Had with the eaie people, prepard for him,
As if by his command alone, and fortune
Holland with those low Provinces, that hold out
Against the Arch-Duke, were again compel'd
With their obedience to give up their lives
To be at his devotion.
Vit. You amaze me,
For though I have heard, that when he fled from Civill
To save his life (then forfei ed to Law
For murthering *Don Pedro* my deer Uncle)
His extreame wants inforc'd him to take pay
In th'Army sat down then before O:tena,
'Twas never yet reported, by whose favour
He durst presume to entertain a thought
Of comming home with pardon.
Ana.' Tis our nature
Or not to hear, or not to give beliefe
To what we wish far from our enemies.
Lam. Sir 'tis most certaine the Infantas letters
Assisted by the Arch-Dukes, to King *Philip*
Have not alone secur'd him from the rigor
Of our Castillian Justice, but return'd him
A free man, and in grace.
Vit. By what curs'd meanes
Could such a fugitive arise unto
The knowledge of their highnesses? much more
(Though known)to stand but in the least degree
Of favour with them?
Lam. To give satisfaction
To your demand, though to praise him I hate,
Can yeild me small contentment, I will tell you,
And truly, since should I detract his worth,
'Twould argue want of merit in my selfe.
Briefly, to passe his tedious pilgrimage
For sixteene years, a banish'd guilty-man,

And to forget the stormes, th'affrights, the horrors
His constancy, not fortune overcame,
I bring him, with his little son, grown man
(Though 'twas said here he took a daughter with him)
To Ostends bloody seige that stage of war
Wherein the flower of many Nations acted,
And the whole Christian world spectators were;
There by his son, or were he by adoption
Or nature his, a brave Scene was presented,
Which I make choyce to speak of. since from that
The good successe of *Alvarez,* had beginning.
Vit. So I love vertue in an enemy
That I desire in the relation of
This young mans glorious deed, you'ld keep your self
A friend to truth, and it.
Lam. Such was my purpose;
The Town being ost assaulted, but in vaine,
To dare the prow'd defendants to a sally,
Weary of ease, *Don Inigo Peralta*
Son to the Generall of our Castile forces
All arm'd, advanc'd within shot of their wals,
From whence the muskateers plaid thick upon him,
Yet he (brave youth)as carelesse of the danger,
As carefull of his honor, drew his sword,
And waving it about his head, as if
He dar'd one spirited like himself, to triall
Of single valor, he made his retreat
With such a slow, and yet majestique pace,
As if he still cald low'd, dare none come on?
When sodainly from a posterne of the town
Two gallant horse-men issued, and o're-took him,
The army looking on, yet not a man
That durst relieve the rash adventurer,
Which *Lucio,* son to *Alvarez* then seeing,
As in the vant-guard he sat bravely mounted,
Or were it pity of the you'hs misfortune,
Care to preserve the honour of his Country,
Or bold desire to get himselfe a name,
He made his brave horse, like a whirle wind bear him,
Among the Combatants: and in a moment
Discha'd his Petronell, with such sure aime
That of the adverse party from his horse,
One tumbled dead, then wheeling round, and drawing
A faulchion swift as lightning, he came on

Upon

Figure 1 First page of *Love's Cure* in F (London, 1647), courtesy of Pennsylvania State University

level, then, this play is a fascinating exploration of the construction and performativity of gender, of the socially inevitable agency of heterosexuality, and of the cathartic power of human affection. But the roots of the old feud between the Álvarez family and that of the gallant Vitelli, whose uncle's murder prompted Don Fernando's banishment from Spain, problematise the generally light tone of the play by presenting it at the start as a revenge tragedy. Vitelli upholds his family's grudge against Álvarez for murdering his uncle Don Pedro two decades before, but he falls in love with the powerful Clara, the daughter of his enemy, when he sees her brandish a sword to defend him as he confronts the outnumbering enemy faction. The play, therefore, engages with Jacobean anxieties around sword fighting, which were particularly prominent in the mid-1610s due to a royal campaign against private duelling. It also presents a fascinating interpretation of stereotypically Spanish notions of family honour featured in the literature that Fletcher so obviously enjoyed.

In this respect, the play is immersed in the historical context of the wars between Habsburg Spain and the Dutch Republic in Flanders at the turn of the seventeenth century. The long and bloody siege of Ostend (1601–04) provides the backdrop to justify Álvarez's pardon: Clara's military prowess wins the Infanta's favour and grants the end of her father's exile. The Infanta alluded to in the opening scene is Isabella Clara Eugenia (1566–1633), daughter of Philip II of Spain and, with her husband, Archduke Albert VII of Austria (1559–1621), joint sovereign of the Spanish Netherlands. Her names inspired those of two of the play's female protagonists – the martial maid Clara and her mother, Eugenia – but these are not the only names that resonate with the specific historical context of the play. Álvarez is clearly named after Don Fernando Álvarez de Toledo y Pimentel, the 3rd Duke of Alba de Tormes (1507–82) mentioned in scene 1.1, who ruled the Spanish Netherlands with legendary ruthlessness between 1567 and 1573. The young male lead bears the name of Giovanni Luigi Vitelli, known as 'Chiappino' (i.e. 'bear') Vitelli, Marquis of Cetona (1519–75), an Italian aristocrat who served as general of the Spanish armies in Flanders. His associates, Lamoral and Anastro, are also named after relevant figures in that conflict. Lamoraal was the name of the Count of Egmont (1522–68), who fought for the independence of Flanders from Spain, and who was executed for high treason. Gaspar de Anastro was a Spanish merchant of Antwerp who was apparently commissioned to undertake the murder of William, Prince of Orange, in 1582. Even the comic lead, the cowardly steward Bobadilla, is named after a celebrated military commander who served under Alba, Francisco Arias de Bobadilla, 4th Count of Puñonrostro (1537–1610).[1]

Writing about *Love's Cure* in 1956, G. E. Bentley declared that 'nearly everything about the play is in a state of confusion'.[2] Analysing its Spanish indebtedness in 1962, Martin E. Erickson claimed that 'of all the problems involving questions of possible Spanish sources for Elizabethan [*sic*] plays, possibly none are beset with greater obscurity or controversy than those involving *Love's Cure*'.[3] Over the centuries since its first publication, scholars interested in Fletcher have sporadically analysed the genesis of this text, and have seldom come to an agreement. Tracing its narrative sources has proved to be elusive, determining the patterns of authorship and collaboration has been controversial, and the precise dating of the text has remained a matter of contention. The three problems – date, authorship, and sources – are, in fact, inextricable. The main plot of *Love's Cure* was taken from a Spanish play by Guillén de Castro: *La fuerza de la costumbre* (*The Force of Custom, c.* 1605–10). If the analysis of the two plays' thematic, structural, and verbal parallels makes the identification unequivocal, the precise historical processes by which one play came to be refashioned into the other is a case for a literary detective. In brief: the first known printing of the Spanish play appeared only a few months before Fletcher's death in August 1625. This means that he could not have secured a copy in time for him to rework his source into a new play. If, as the evidence suggests, he collaborated with Massinger in the composition of *Love's Cure* in the first half of 1615, we can only explain the adaptation by the presence of a manuscript copy of the Spanish *comedia* in London shortly after its premiere in Spain.

The authorship of the extant version of the text has also been under scrutiny. It was first printed in the 'Beaumont and Fletcher' folio of 1647, a collection of 34 plays, a masque, and some verses compiled by the royalist publisher Humphrey Moseley. In the middle of the English Civil War, and with the London theatres closed by the Parliamentary authorities, he had set out to offer the reading public every play attributed to the two famous collaborators that had not been printed previously. In fact, in addition to just two titles actually written by Beaumont and Fletcher in conjunction, the collection includes plays by Fletcher alone, plus collaborations with other dramatists including Massinger, Nathan Field, John Webster, and John Ford. It also includes at least two plays that were not written by either Beaumont or Fletcher.[4] The text of *Love's Cure* concludes, in that order, with an Epilogue that assigns the play to a single author, and a Prologue, 'At the reviving of this play', which attributes it to two, Beaumont and Fletcher. But by the end of the nineteenth century, the play was being studied as a product of collaboration and/or revision involving three dramatists: Fletcher, Beaumont, and Massinger. The authorship shares generally accepted were established by Cyrus Hoy in 1961, but Beaumont's retirement by 1613 makes Hoy's attribution of some scenes to him an impossibility. Establishing the date of composition with confidence is, therefore, the crucial factor in unravelling the authorial mystery.

Based on the most recent scholarship and a fresh examination of the internal evidence, it seems most likely that *Love's Cure* was originally written for the King's Men for a summer premiere at the Globe playhouse in 1615. With Shakespeare and Beaumont away from dramatic writing, the years 1614–15 heralded a new period in Fletcher's creative career. He had written *Valentinian* and *Bonduca* on his own following his collaborators' retirements. He was now about to embark on a long and fruitful writing partnership with Philip Massinger, which would last for the rest of his life. It seems that *Love's Cure* was their first extended collaboration after Massinger had contributed two small sections to *The Honest Man's Fortune* (*c.* 1613), which was otherwise authored by Field, with a small contribution from Fletcher. Despite Hoy's attribution of much of the dialogue to Massinger, *Love's Cure* addresses themes and uses techniques that are eminently and recognisably Fletcherian. It experiments with generic uncertainty in a way that his tragicomedies written with Beaumont had anticipated. The central concern of the play is also in line with Fletcher's frequent enjoyment of cross-dressing as a dramatic device. In addition, the play features two indomitable women – the manly and aggressive Clara and the formidable and entrepreneurial courtesan Malroda – who are part of a remarkable gallery of strong female characters in his plays who defy patriarchal conventions and masculine authority. In fact, the sudden comic resolution of the play is only brought about, in characteristic Fletcherian fashion, by the intervention of three of the women threatening to commit suicide in public if the men do not abandon their potentially fatal duel. The unflattering portrayal of the womaniser Vitelli, who ends up marrying the title heroine, and of other morally objectionable men – the corrupt Alguazir and his opportunistic associates, the violent and misogynistic Álvarez, the quick-tempered bully Lamoral, Clara's unwelcome suitor Sayave-dra, and the cowardly braggart Bobadilla – also presents a poignant critique of a male-dominated world. The Spanish setting and its historical context in the aftermath of the siege of Ostend add flavour to an engaging and superbly performable play that has remained unjustly neglected by the professional stage for four centuries.

DATE

The attribution of the play to Fletcher and Massinger, and not Beaumont, depends largely on whether it dates from after 1613, by which date Beaumont had stopped writing for the theatre.[5] In the absence of precise records of its licensing and performance, the date of composition can only be established indirectly. In this case, there are two ways to do this. On the one hand, the appearance of a group of five rogues in the comic subplot suggests that the play must have been in the repertory of the King's Men in the period between 1614 and 1618, when this kind of comic grouping can be traced across plays written for the company by different dramatists. On the other hand, and in addition to its linguistic and thematic proximity to Fletcher plays of the mid-1610s, the text features a number of topical allusions to contemporary events and cultural controversies that help narrow the date down to the first half of 1615. These topical references and the company requirements affect, respectively, the main plot and the picaresque subplot, which strongly suggests that both narrative strands were conceived at the same time. Even if it might have been revised for a later revival, as the added Prologue suggests, the play as a whole was composed as a coherent unity.

As Martin Wiggins has established, a number of plays written by different dramatists for the King's Men between 1613 and 1618 saw the appearance of 'distinct groups of four characters who interact primarily with one another and whose contribution to the play as a whole might not be felt to justify the deployment of quite so many actors'.[6] This 'Gang of Four' seems to have become a sort of running joke in the company across plays by different authors. It first emerged in the second half of 1613 after the fire that destroyed the Globe. In *The Two Noble Kinsmen* (*c.* autumn 1613) and *The Duchess of Malfi* (*c.* 1613) there are 'inserted set-pieces featuring dances recycled from recent court masques' in which 'four actors carry the main dialogue establishing the situation, and are then augmented by others for the dancing itself'. These are the four speaking Countrymen in 3.5 of *Kinsmen* and the four speaking madmen in 4.2 of *Malfi* (the mad Doctor, Priest, Lawyer, and Astrologer). Around the winter of 1614, Fletcher 'attempted to give the Gang a more integrated part in the narrative' as the four panders in *Valentinian* (Chilax, Balbus, Proculus, and Lycinius).[7] In his probable next play for the King's Men, *Bonduca* (*c*. 1614), a fifth character was added to the equation, turning the 'Gang of Four' into a 'Gang of Four Plus One'. This fifth member would invariably play the role of the leader of the other four, connecting them to the main plot. In *Bonduca* he was Judas, the merry corporal in command of the four hungry soldiers. In Middleton's *The Widow* (*c*. late 1615) he was Latrocinio, leader of a gang of four thieves (Occulto, Silvio, Stratio, and Fiducio). In *Rollo, Duke of Normandy* (*c*. 1617) he was Latorch, who subsequently leads two different groups, the kitchen staff (Cook, Yeoman of the Cellar, Butler, and Pantler) and the four astrologers (La Fiske, Russee, Norbret, and De Bube). In *The Loyal Subject* (November 1618) he was the Muscovite Ensign to Archas who leads a group of four discharged soldiers re-employed as street sellers.

After that date, the recurrent groups of subplot associates in plays for the King's Men were reduced to three, for example, 'the comedy executioners in *Sir John van Oldenbarnevelt*, or the male prostitutes, old before their time from their exertions, in the bawdy farce *The Custom of the Country*'.[8] The reason seems clear: one of its members had left the company or had died. Wiggins has identified that, apart from Richard Burbage himself, March 1619 saw the death of another actor of the company: Richard Cowley (active 1593–1619),[9] who was probably one of the four. Wiggins has identified two of the others from the cast list of *Malfi* as Nicholas Tooley (active 1603–23)[10] and John Underwood (*c*. 1587–1625).[11]

Wiggins argues that the detached member of the 'Four Plus One', at least in some of these plays, was an actor who had red hair. In *Bonduca*, Corporal Judas is described as having a 'red beard' (2.3.126), and Fletcher would have chosen the name following the received pictorial representation of the betrayer of Christ.[12] He would have appeared again as Latorch, whom Aubrey describes as a 'firebrand' (2.3.88). An actor who had joined the King's Men in the spring of 1614, just before the fifth associate started to make his appearance, was William Ecclestone (1590/1–1623),[13] who had worked previously with the King's Men, but who had spent two and a half years with Lady Elizabeth's Men from 1611, before returning to the company. During his time with Lady Elizabeth's Men, in mid-1613, Middleton wrote the only other role in the period outside the repertory of the King's Men specifically created for an adult actor with red hair: Sir Walter Whorehound in *A Chaste Maid in Cheapside*. It is unknown whether Ecclestone acted it, but, as Wiggins puts it, 'it would be a very curious coincidence that the decade's only red-haired adult roles were in plays written for just those companies at the time he was a member of them'.[14] In *Love's Cure*, Pacheco refers to the Alguazir's red beard (2.1.206), Malroda calls him a 'poisonous red-haired de'il' (3.1.58), and he is described as 'the ringleader of these / Poor fellows' (5.3.230–1; i.e. the four false watchmen). It is likely, then, that Ecclestone took on the role of the Alguazir.

Based on a systematic survey of the personnel, system of apprenticeship, and casting patterns of the King's Men from its foundation as the Lord Chamberlain's Men, Martin Wiggins, Héloïse Sénéchal, and Jodie Smith have suggested that Richard Cowley would have played Pacheco, while Robert Gough (active *c.* 1594–1624),[15] who usually took on roles requiring a physically small actor, would have appeared as Lazarillo. Given that Metaldi and Mendoza are diminutive parts that might have been played by hired men, they propose that, instead of completing the Gang of Four, on this occasion John Underwood would have played the romantic lead, Vitelli, and Nicholas Tooley, who, from what we know of his other roles, was good at fencing and singing, would have been cast as Piorato. Among the other sharers of the company, Richard Burbage (1568–1619)[16] or Henry Condell (1576–1627)[17] may have been given the role of Álvarez, while John Lowin (1576–1653)[18] could have played Lamoral. Richard Robinson (*c.* 1596–1648),[19] who created the title role in *The Duchess of Malfi* in 1613, but who had recently graduated to playing juvenile male roles, would have been cast as Lucio. The celebrated comic actor John Shank (*c.*1570–1636),[20] who had left the Palsgrave's Men to join the King's Men around this time, would have played Bobadilla, while his apprentice Thomas Pollard (1597–1653), who moved companies with him, may have taken on the leading apprentice role of Clara. Alternatively, Walter Haynes, who was playing leading apprentice roles at this time, could have played the martial maid instead. The second largest female role, Malroda, would have been taken on by George Birch (*c.* 1597–1625?),[21] who would play another courtesan, Doll Common, in the 1618 revival of *The Alchemist*. The other two apprentice parts would have been given, in order of seniority, to Michael Bedell as Eugenia and Nicholas Crosse as Genevora.[22] The rest of the roles are smaller and would have been entrusted to hired men.[23]

In addition to these company requirements, which fit the available actors and casting practices in 1615, the text features a number of allusions to historical circumstances that help narrow down the date of composition. One of the more distinct dating markers, already noted by Henry Weber in his 1812 edition, comes in 2.2 when, in response to Lucio's unmanly behaviour, his father angrily wonders whether his effeminacy is the result of a defect in his conception. Since effeminacy in a man was usually taken to be the result of an excess of wet and cold humours in the body, Álvarez asks whether Lucio is really the son of a foreigner from a cold climate: 'did the cold Muscovite beget thee, / That lay here lieger in the last great frost?' (2.2.155–6). Weber pointed out that this could be a reference to a resident ambassador (a 'lieger') from Russia staying in London in a particularly cold year. He traced two embassies to King James I in 1617 and 1622, the latter of which coincided with a frosty winter in which, according to John Stowe and Edmund Howes's *Annals*, 'the Thames was frozen all over so as the people went over the river in divers places'.[24] The conjunction of the presence of an embassy from the Tsar and a particularly severe winter seems to be persuasive. However, there is a fundamental problem with this dating if the lines were in the play when it premiered: in 1622 Fletcher was simply too busy, as he produced no fewer than three plays that year, and possibly four,[25] and in 1623 he wrote another three.[26] Dating *Love's Cure* to either year seems difficult. Moreover, the play does not feature on the list of plays licensed for performance from 1622 in the records of Sir Henry Herbert, Master of the Revels, which makes this particularly late ascription extremely unlikely.[27] In fact, the original licence for performance of *Love's Cure* must have predated Herbert's office-book, which Sir John Astley, his predecessor, had started on 10 May 1622.[28] If the play had premiered after that date, as George Walton Williams believed,[29] it would most probably have been registered in it. As for the 1617–18 embassy, it did not coincide with a particularly frosty period.[30]

There was, however, an earlier Russian embassy to the Jacobean court. Within months of his election on 7 February 1613, Tsar Michael I sent ambassadors to several foreign countries including England.[31] The ambassador, Aleksei Ivanovich Ziuzin, resided in

London for seven months between October 1613 and May 1614.[32] Although the chronicles do not record that that winter was particularly cold, the following winter, 1614–15, was especially severe. The *Annals* tell that in January 1615 'began a great frost, with extreme snow', with the freezing weather continuing until 7 March.[33] This weather anomaly is also attested in a dramatic dialogue published in 1615, *The Cold Year*.[34] *Love's Cure*, though set in Spain, was meant to be appreciated by a contemporary English audience, so that an allusion to recent events would add a touch of immediacy to the dialogue. A foreign dignitary from a faraway country proverbial for its cold climate, in conjunction with a bout of harsh wintry weather experienced by the original audience just months before the performance, would illustrate the point Álvarez is making by relating it to recent events. If we assume that the lines were originally in the premiere of the play, and were not inserted for a revival, then the references have to be to Ziuzin (1613–14) and the cold winter of 1614–15, made to blend into one fictitious allusion to real events from the immediate past. Here we have, therefore, an effective upper limit for the composition of *Love's Cure*: the frosty beginning of 1615.

In the same speech, a despairing Álvarez promises to find out whether his children's physiological sexes have not actually been modified by their unusual upbringing: 'I'll have you searched, I swear!' (2.2.159). The phrase may be reminiscent of a notorious episode in the 1613 legal process initiated by Frances Howard for the annulment of her marriage to Robert Devereux, 3rd Earl of Essex, who was reportedly unable to consummate the relationship. During the trial, a panel of matrons was commissioned to inspect the Countess's genitalia to verify whether she was capable of sustaining sexual intercourse and whether she was still a virgin, both of which were found to be so. The annulment from Devereux was granted on 25 September 1613, and Howard married the King's favourite, Robert Carr, 1st Earl of Somerset, at the chapel of Whitehall Palace on 26 December. Sir Thomas Overbury, who had been Carr's close friend but who had opposed the marriage, had died as a prisoner in the Tower on 15 September in mysterious circumstances. However, in September 1615 the case took an unexpected turn when it was discovered that Howard had arranged to have Overbury poisoned in prison. This murder, and her responsibility in it, was particularly topical in the autumn of 1615. On 10 September, the Lieutenant of the Tower, Sir Gervase Elwes, admitted to having known of the plot to poison Overbury, and his statement

> triggered the investigation and legal proceedings that eventually took four
> lives, destroyed the fortunes of Somerset, the royal favourite, and sup-
> plied the Jacobean public with a disturbing parade of scandalous revela-
> tions implicating the court in moral and political transgressions ranging
> from ambition, adultery, and sartorial excess to murder, witchcraft, and
> popery.[35]

The process resulted in several executions from late October, including that of Elwes, who was beheaded on Tower Hill on 20 November.[36]

What is relevant for the dating of *Love's Cure* to the summer of that year is that a joking reference to the 1613 panel of matrons would have been rather dangerous later in 1615 while the trials were taking place, especially since the episode with the matrons was, in a way, the trigger of the annulment, and subsequently of the new marriage, the imprisonment of Overbury, and later of his murder.[37] In addition, in the final scene of the play there is a likely allusion to Overbury and Carr, who had been close friends before the former was imprisoned. Álvarez moralises on the suspension of the duel by the intervention of the three women:

> Here may all ladies learn to make of foes
> The perfect'st friends, and not the perfect'st foes
> Of dearest friends, as some do nowadays.
>
> (5.3.261–3)

Overbury and Carr might have been the most perfect friends who 'nowadays' turned out to be the most perfect of foes through female agency (Howard's). Again, given his indirect implication in Over-bury's murder, a reference to Carr's enmity to the poisoned noble-man would have been toxic after September 1615. If these passages do indeed allude to Carr and Howard, this may be the lower limit for the composition of the play, suggesting the likelihood that the premiere took place in the summer season of 1615.

Beyond this notorious case, other recognisable cultural anxieties current in those years are evident in the play. Its plot relies heavily on reporting, deploying, and threatening violence, from the retelling of episodes from the siege of Ostend (1.1) to the skirmishes between the two enemy factions (1.3 and 4.3, for example). In particular, the play is immersed in the duelling culture of the period. The reparation of an affront to a gentleman's honour in a duel usually involved issuing a written or verbal challenge, the appointment of a time and a discreet place for the duel, and the actual fighting.[38] In addition, the assistance of two other gentlemen, the 'seconds', was normally required to guarantee that all formalities were observed and to provide succour in case of injury or death (see 5.3.27–8). Since duelling was illegal across Europe, duels were private and discreet affairs. Two scenes in Love's Cure feature duels, and in both cases some of the conventions are flouted. In 5.1 Lucio seeks to appoint a place for a duel against Lamoral, but events escalate and the fight takes place there with no seconds. In the final scene of the play, a duel is appointed between Vitelli and Álvarez, with Lamoral and Lucio as seconds, but it is a public occasion oddly prescribed by the King of Spain (a 'granted duel'; see 5.3.31). These two important moments in the play were responding to the legal campaign against duels promoted by James I between 1613 and 1614, which was prompted by a noticeable spike in the number of people killed while engaging in private duels.[39] Two royal proclamations were consecu- tively issued on 15 October 1613, prohibiting the printing of reports on duels,[40] and on 4 February 1614, banning private challenges and any duelling activity.[41] The royal printer, Robert Barker, also issued in 1613 a brief unsigned treatise, apparently written by the Earl of Northampton,[42] that extended the ideas that guided both proclama- tions.[43] If King James's campaign against duelling was channelled through these proclamations, the duel in 5.3 is also appropriately brought about by royal proclamation.[44] In addition, on 16 January 1613 King James also issued a proclamation to terminate the use of dags and pocket handguns on account of the fact that 'the use of them is suddenly grown very common'.[45] It is rather telling, then, that Lucio mistakes her sister's petronel (a large cavalry carbine, see 1.1.74 n.) for a dag (see 2.2.135 n.). The fact that the play is so heavily reliant on duelling culture, and is so specific as to the use of certain firearms, could hardly be a coincidence, and it seems to respond to the anti-duelling campaign of 1613–14.

Finally, the historical context of Anglo-Spanish politics also plays an important role through the references to the Infanta in 1.1 and 2.2. Isabella Clara Eugenia was at the time joint sovereign of the Spanish Netherlands with her husband Archduke Albert. Her name served as source for those of two female characters in Love's Cure, and her agency in the main plot is crucial: she is reported to have written to her half-brother, King Philip III, to secure a pardon for

Álvarez in recompense for Clara's deeds at the siege of Ostend, thus enabling his return to Seville and the reunion of his family. Her intervention, therefore, prompts Vitelli's revenge and sets the whole play in motion. A reference to the title of Infanta – the daughter of a King or Queen of Spain who is not the heir apparent – in connection with the siege of Ostend would have recalled immediately Isabella Clara Eugenia. But in 1615 there were two other living Infantas: her nieces Anne of Austria and Maria Anna of Austria, the daughters of Philip III. The former became Queen consort of France in November 1615 upon her marriage to Louis XIII, and the latter would come to play a crucial role in English foreign policy, as King James started negotiating with Spain a potential marriage between her and Charles, Prince of Wales. The long negotiations culminated in a politically fruitless, but culturally fascinating, journey to Madrid by the Prince and the Duke of Buckingham in 1623 that ultimately failed to secure her hand.

During the long negotiations, the title of Infanta was associated in English public discourse with Maria Anna, rather than her aunt. This shift must have occurred when the negotiations became public knowledge. According to Glyn Redworth, Diego Sarmiento de Acuña, Lord (and later Count) of Gondomar, the ambassador of Spain in London, initiated discreet discussions with King James about the marriage treaty shortly after the dissolution of the Addled Parliament of 1614.[46] The first draft of the treaty was sent to the English ambassador in Madrid in March 1615, still under diplomatic secret.[47] It was only on 2 March 1617 that the matter was taken to the Privy Council,[48] and after this date the issue became public knowledge, at least in courtly circles.[49] Thus the association of the title with a particular woman shifted from the sovereign of the Spanish Netherlands to her niece, who was, suddenly, the potential future Queen consort of England. After 1617 a reference to 'the Infanta' in an English play would have carried the wrong association.

In addition, the reference to the Archduke's political nemesis, Maurice of Nassau, in 1.2.35–6 had a particular poignancy on account of his having been awarded the Order of the Garter in January 1613.[50] In Love's Cure he is referred to as 'Graaf Maurice', as in 1615 he was still only Count (Graaf) of Nassau, and only became Prince of Orange in 1618, which is how the character is referred to in Fletcher and Massinger's 1619 tragedy Sir John van Oldenbarnevelt.

These allusions narrow down the composition of the main plot to 1615. Since the subplot was written for the 'Gang of Four Plus One' active in 1614–18, the play must have been first produced by the King's Men, and not any other company. This chronological coincidence, and the presence of the Alguazir connecting the two plots, suggest that the play as a whole was conceived and composed in the first half of 1615, possibly in the spring or early summer for a summer premiere, as Fletcher seems to have been busy writing *The Night-Walkers* for Nathan Field's company over the previous winter.[51] Contradicting the received authorship studies, this date eliminates any possibility that Beaumont had a hand in any of the scenes of the play, as he had stopped writing for the theatre by 1613. That leaves Fletcher and Massinger, and perhaps a third uncertain collaborator, as the authors of a play that was, perhaps, the first full-scale collaboration between the two in their long and fruitful writing partnership.

AUTHORSHIP

The lives of John Fletcher (1579–1625) and Philip Massinger (1583–1640) have been illustrated in other volumes of the Revels.[52] The two started collaborating around the summer of 1613, when Massinger supplied two short sections to the tragicomedy *The Honest Man's Fortune*, which Nathan Field (1587–1619/20) was writing for Lady Elizabeth's Men, with a small contribution from Fletcher, probably for a premiere in the Swan playhouse on Bankside. Fletcher already had a prolific career as a dramatist. He had written eight plays with Francis Beaumont for the King's Men, the Children of the Queen's Revels, and the Children of Paul's from around 1606.[53] Around 1612 he had collaborated as well with William Shakespeare on two plays for the King's Men – *All Is True* (*H8*) and *Cardenio* – possibly taking the lead in their plotting and composition. Around the time of *The Honest Man's Fortune* he was also working with Shakespeare on *The Two Noble Kinsmen*. Beaumont suffered a serious stroke in 1613, around the time of his marriage to an heiress, and he survived only three more years in a melancholic state. He never wrote anything else for the playhouse.[54] From that year, Shakespeare seems to have been spending most of his time in Stratford, and no other plays from his pen are known to have reached the stage. Fletcher worked for the next year or so on his own, dividing his labour between the King's Men – *Valentinian* and *Bonduca* – and Lady Elizabeth's Men at the Hope – *Wit without Money* and *The Night-Walkers*. The latter appears to date from early 1615, and the night-walking scene in *Love's Cure*, 4.3, is clearly related. The Children of the Queen's Revels had merged with Lady Elizabeth's Men in 1613, and Nathan Field, former member of the Children, became their leading figure, although he would defect to the King's Men around 1616.[55] Field and Fletcher wrote two plays together for Lady Elizabeth's Men around 1613 – *Four Plays in One* and *Fortune* – and would collaborate often after Field's defection. Massinger, a newcomer in *Fortune*, would continue to write with Fletcher and Field regularly after that time.

Love's Cure sits in this period of transition, at a moment when Fletcher was not yet writing exclusively for the King's Men, and when his working partnerships with Field and with Massinger were in their early stages. The play may have been, in fact, Massinger's first full-scale collaboration with Fletcher, although, as we will see, it is intriguing that so much of the extant text bears Massinger's imprint. George Walton Williams thought that Massinger's large share of the writing, and the remarkable stylistic and narrative unity of the play, could be explained if he had revised and reworked the text for the revival hinted at in the Prologue. This piece, subtitled 'At the reviving of this play', attributes it to Beaumont and Fletcher, the authors purportedly of the whole folio of 1647. By contrast, the Epilogue, printed immediately after Vitelli's final speech (sig. 5S5^v), refers to only one author. The Prologue, however, is bibliographically anomalous: it is the only prologue in the volume to appear on a whole new page (sig. 5S6^r) after the epilogue and the play's '*FINIS*', and we can question how attached it is to the play.[56] The publisher of F, Humphrey Moseley, confessed in his 'Postcript' [*sic*] that 'some prologues and epilogues here inserted were not written by the authors of this volume, but made by others on the revival of several plays' (sig. g2^r). Some of these pieces clearly became attached to a given play by generic similarity, rather than thematic content. This is also the case of the Epilogue, which, as Williams points out, 'sounds as if it might serve as epilogue to any comedy'.[57] In fact, a slightly different version of this Epilogue was used in another play in the repertory of the King's Men, the tragicomedy *The Deserving Favourite* (*c.* 1629) by Lodowick Carlell:

Our author fears there are some rebel hearts
Whose dullness doth oppose love's piercing darts;

These will be apt to say the plot was dull,
The language rude, and that 'twas only full
Of gross absurdities; for such as these
He cares not now, nor e'er will strive to please:
   For if yourselves as masters and love's friends
   Be pleased with this sad play, he hath his ends.[58]

The problem of the Epilogue and the Prologue has misled scholars, but in fact it is of little help in establishing the play's authorship. However, the revision hinted at in the Prologue, and the contradiction in the number of authors mentioned in the two pieces, prompted scholars to think that the play might not be simply a 'Beaumont and Fletcher' collaboration. F. G. Fleay declared in 1891 that Massinger was 'the reformer of the play for the revival', and that 'the Fletcher part is so worked over by Massinger, who was certainly the maker of the reformation, as to be inseparable, unless in detailed notes'.[59] His allocation of shares between Beaumont and Fletcher in the underlying text differs, but this is essentially the conclusion that Cyrus Hoy also reached in his own study. Hoy published a series of seven articles in *Studies in Bibliography* between 1956 and 1962, trying to ascertain the shares of collaboration in the 52-play canon traditionally ascribed to 'Beaumont and Fletcher', realising that 'less than twelve' are actually collaborations between the two dramatists, while 'some forty' represent Fletcher's collaborations with other dramatists, most importantly Philip Massinger.[60] Hoy's methodology was relatively straightforward: 'To distinguish any given dramatist's share in a play of dual or doubtful authorship, one must possess some body of criteria which, derived from the unaided plays of the dramatist in question, will serve to identify his work in whatever context it may appear.'[61] These criteria ranged from particular linguistic preferences to patterns of versification. For example, based on earlier scholarship, Hoy established that Fletcher seems to have preferred the use of *ye* over *you* for the second person pronoun, and in his solo plays there seems to be a tendency to use pentameters with double or feminine endings (i.e. with an extra unstressed syllable at the end of the line). Hoy claimed that distinguishing the work of Fletcher from that of Massinger was easier than with some of the other collaborators.[62] However, Beaumont's hand was more elusive on account of how few of his solo works survive: 'To distinguish, on the basis of linguistic evidence, the respective shares of the Beaumont–Fletcher collaborations is not always easy or possible.'[63] This may explain why some of Hoy's attributions to Beaumont are chronologically impossible. In fact, it has been convincingly proposed that the plays written around 1616–18 where he detected Beaumont's hand were actually co-authored with Nathan Field.[64]

For *Love's Cure*, Hoy identified the presence of different textual layers that would be the result of a superposition of collaboration and revision by Massinger:

> The play has been re-worked, in some degree, from beginning to end, but it has been re-worked much more extensively in some places than in others. Massinger's revision of the first and the last two acts has been so extensive as to amount to re-writing, though there are faint traces of the original in the prose of [1.2], and distinctly clearer ones in that of [5.3.200–63]. His handling of Acts II and III was much less thoroughgoing; there he has been content to stitch some of his favorite turns of phrase on to a textual fabric clearly not of his own devising.[65]

If we disregard Beaumont's hand, the shares that Hoy assigned are:[66]

1.1		Rewritten by Massinger
1.2		Fletcher revised by Massinger
1.3		Rewritten by Massinger
2.1		Fletcher and collaborator (?)
2.2	1–124	Fletcher
	125–74	Fletcher revised by Massinger
	174–265	Fletcher and collaborator (?)
3.1		Collaborator (?)
3.2		Fletcher revised by Massinger
3.3	1–17	Fletcher
	18–77	Collaborator (?)
	78–123	Fletcher revised by Massinger
3.4		Fletcher revised by Massinger
3.5		Fletcher
4.1		Rewritten by Massinger
4.2		Rewritten by Massinger
4.3	1–17	Rewritten by Massinger
	18–71	Fletcher lightly revised by Massinger
	71–132	Rewritten by Massinger
4.4		Rewritten by Massinger
5.1		Rewritten by Massinger
5.2		Rewritten by Massinger
5.3	1–199	Fletcher and collaborator (?) revised by Massinger
	200–63	Fletcher and collaborator (?)
	264–9	Massinger

Hoy's theory that the text is the product of a thorough revision by Massinger of the original version is persuasive and not without precedent. *The Lovers' Progress*, written by Fletcher and Massinger around 1623, was revised by Massinger a decade later as *The Tragedy of Cleander* (licensed afresh on 7 May 1634).[67] The fact that *Love's Cure* was printed in 1647 under two titles might support this supposition. Since the play is referred to by its F subtitle, *The Martial Maid*, in the only two documents that immediately predate its printing,[68] perhaps that was the title of the revised version in repertory by 1641, and *Love's Cure* was its original 1615 title. In fact, Massinger's revised *The Tragedy of Cleander* bears a character-focused and arguably more memorable title than the original *The Lovers' Progress*, which, like the title *Love's Cure*, is situational and rather unspecific. Massinger might have thought that Clara, perhaps the play's most memorable character, should feature in the revised title as *The Martial Maid*, a title that would give an audience a better sense of what to expect. The revision and retitling would have taken place before 1633 when the Master of the Revels, Sir Henry Herbert, required all old plays to be relicensed for revival, as the licence would presumably survive if he issued it after that date.[69]

We can safely establish that *Love's Cure* as printed was the work of Fletcher and Massinger, originally conceived as a whole in 1615 by Fletcher alone, or in collaboration with Massinger and/or another dramatist. The extant version is a more or less thorough revision by Massinger, who would have polished the text without eliminating the traceable dating markers from 1615. This revision would date perhaps from the early 1630s, before a revision for revival required a fresh licence for performance. If the case is indeed similar to that of *The Lovers' Progress*, in which Massinger reworked something that he had originally authored with Fletcher, then the underlying text of *Love's Cure* was already a Fletcher–Massinger collaboration: effectively their first full-scale piece of work.

The identity of the potential third collaborator that Hoy identified as Beaumont is not known, although chronologically and stylistically the most likely candidate is Nathan Field. Wiggins is unpersuaded that Field would have contributed to a play written in 1615 for the King's Men, a rival company to Field's Lady Elizabeth's Men. However, Fletcher and Field had worked together in 1613 for Field's troupe, and would do so again for the King's Men after Field's defection around 1616. Might their mutually supportive artistic relationship have transcended their commercial allegiances? Be that as it may, the alternative is to suppose that what Hoy took to be Beaumontisms in this and other post-1613 plays could be mere idiosyncrasies that Fletcher incorporated into his style after working with Beaumont for seven crucial years.

The theory of a revision is rendered perhaps more plausible by Massinger's anomalously large share in what was effectively his second extant play. In his other early collaborations with Fletcher, *Beggars' Bush* (c. 1616) and *The Queen of Corinth* (1617), his share was comparatively much smaller,[70] so Fletcher would have needed to place unprecedented trust in his less experienced colleague. But there are other aspects of *Love's Cure* that perhaps strengthen the case for a revision. From a tonal and narrative point of view, the play is noticeably more coherent than, for example, *Beggars' Bush*, in which the shifts in authorship between the different shares are more apparent and form a relatively incoherent whole. Massinger would have ironed out those tonal shifts to give the play a more unitary feel. In addition, Massinger usually attended more than Fletcher to political and historical issues in their collaborations, and the change of names from the main Spanish source to reso-nantly political names from the Hispano-Dutch wars might indi-cate that he revised the original *dramatis personae*. In fact, he did use the name 'Vitelli' for the juvenile lead of *The Renegado, or The Gentleman of Venice* in 1624. If we accept that Massinger revised the text, preserving, as I have shown, the two narrative strands from 1615 and substantial parts of the dialogue, what is difficult to imagine is why he considered that such thorough rewriting was necessary.

SOURCES

Guillén de Castro's play *La fuerza de la costumbre* (*The Force of Custom*) was identified as the source for the main plot of *Love's Cure* by the German scholar A. L. Stiefel in 1897.[71] Stiefel probably noticed the influence in the first place because of the recurrence of the word *custom* in the English play, recalling the word *costumbre* in the title of Castro's *comedia*.[72] In Fletcher and Massinger's text, *custom* is repeated no fewer than nine times across three of the five acts,[73] and it works as a kind of verbal leitmotif in the play, encapsu-lating its central theme: the exploration of the power of nurture over nature, and of gender as a social construct over the predetermina-tion of physiological sex. The term *costumbre* also recurs insistently in *La fuerza*. In 1984, John Loftis concluded that 'the resemblances to *La fuerza de la costumbre* in theme, in situations, and at times even in dialogue are striking', and dismissed all alternative theories.[74] Loftis traced the other three known cases of the adaptation of a Spanish *comedia* into an English play in the period: *The Renegado* (1624), partly based on Cervantes's *Los baños de Argel*, and two plays by James Shirley, *The Young Admiral* (1633), based on Lope de Vega's *Don Lope de Cardona*, and *The Opportunity* (1634), based on Tirso de Molina's *El castigo del penséque*.[75] If most English Renaissance plays based on Spanish sources took their material from works in prose, *Love's Cure* is, as far as we know, the earliest English play of this period to have been based on Spanish drama.

In a way, the other three English adaptations of *comedias* are less surprising, as the authors of the sources, Cervantes and Lope de Vega, are rather more canonical than Castro, and their reputation in popular culture and in print was, and is, much more widespread. The posthumous literary fame of Guillén de Castro y Bellvís (Valencia, 1569–Madrid, 1631)[76] rests mainly on his two-part historical play *Las mocedades del Cid* (*The Youthful Deeds of the Cid*),[77] which was subsequently adapted by Pierre Corneille as *Le Cid* (1636), and indirectly, via Corneille, by Joseph Rutter as *The Cid* (Beeston's Boys, 1637).[78] However, neither his *Cid* play nor the rest of his canon have been revived often.[79] His plays have not been reprinted regularly since they first appeared either. Apart from two plays included in an anthology of Valencian plays by various authors in 1608, the rest of his work was published in two quartos containing twelve plays each. The *Primera parte* appeared in 1618 (Valencia: Felipe Mey), and the *Segunda parte* in 1625, published and printed in Valencia by Miguel Sorolla. *La fuerza de la costumbre* was printed in the latter, although its date of composition can only be known approximately.[80] Courtney Bruerton, through a comparative metrical analysis of Castro's dramatic canon, concluded that *La fuerza* could be the earliest *comedia* in the *Segunda parte*, probably dating from 1610–15.[81] This is remarkably close to the date of composition of *Love's Cure*, which means that the play was known in London very soon after its premiere in Valencia.[82] This is not unimaginable nor unprecedented: the source for Fletcher's (and probably Field's) *Love's Pilgrimage*, Cervantes's *Las dos doncellas* (*The Two Maids*), was printed in Madrid in 1613 as part of the *Novelas ejemplares*, and the English adaptation dates approximately from just three years later.

The lateness of the first printing of *La fuerza*, which appeared within a few months of Fletcher's own death in August 1625, means that, necessarily, the play must have made its way into England in manuscript form. In fact, *La fuerza* survives in no fewer than four manuscripts, an unusually large number for a play from the Spanish Golden Age: three are in the Biblioteca Nacional in Madrid and one in the Biblioteca Palatina in Parma. As I have explained in 'What the Quills Can Tell: The Case of John Fletcher and Philip Massinger's *Love's Cure*',[83] at least three, if not all four, of those manuscripts predate the 1625 printing, which means that the play was probably in circulation in the early 1610s, and perhaps beyond Spain. In addition, as I concluded, 'the extraordinary degree of interrelation and interdependence between the four extant manuscripts, and the difficulty in establishing a definite stemma due to this genealogical complexity, seem to suggest that the number of intermediary manuscripts that could explain how these specific four variants originated must have been very great indeed'.[84] This wealth of textual witnesses reveals that the play was popular with its original audiences, as it was striking enough to be copied quite often for private reading and performance.[85] This makes it more likely that someone in Fletcher's circle of acquaintances could have alerted him to the existence of a Spanish play dealing with cross-dressed siblings that he would surely enjoy.

As it happens, the cross-dressing trope is frequent and productive in Spanish *comedias* of the period. In particular, the presence of a *mujer varonil* (a 'manly woman') in *La fuerza* is not a novelty, as breeches roles written for actresses in Spanish Golden Age drama are abundant and varied, as Carmen Bravo-Villasante, Melveena McKendrick, and Jonathan Thacker have shown.[86] By contrast, the figure of the *hombre femenil* (the 'feminine man') appeared infrequently, and has been less well investigated.[87] In Thacker's assessment, however, Castro's innovation was to chart 'the feminization of a *mujer varonil*, and the simultaneous masculinization of her effeminate brother, a less common *hombre femenil*'.[88] If other *comedias* featured cases of double cross-dressing,[89] it was usually a mere plot device, while in *La fuerza* it is the central theme that drives the whole story.

Fletcher clearly had an interest in the cross-dressing theme, and he became the English dramatist of the Jacobean period who employed the trope most frequently. It is not strange, therefore, that

Castro's play attracted his attention.[90] Even if critics have tended to question, or even dismiss, Fletcher's ability to read Spanish, and have therefore refused to give credit to direct adaptations from Spanish originals without an intermediary translation,[91] the evidence for his competence is strong and unsurprising: Fletcher was clearly fluent in Latin and French,[92] and he undoubtedly read Spanish well enough to understand the main plot of a play or a novel. Massinger read French and Spanish with some fluency as well.[93] It is also quite plausible that Fletcher had the recurring assistance of someone in his circle who kept him up to date with the latest developments in Spanish literature, and who could have helped him with the language. The likeliest candidate is James Mabbe (1571/2–1642?), a fellow of Magdalen College, Oxford, who had spent a few crucial formative years in Spain in 1611–13, and who translated into English Mateo Alemán's *Guzmán de Alfarache*, *La Celestina*, and half of Cervantes's 1613 *Novelas ejemplares* into English. Fletcher mined the latter for plots on no fewer than five occasions,[94] and the acquaintance is well attested.[95]

The parallels between *Love's Cure* and its main Spanish source are strong in thematic, structural, and verbal terms, and they suggest that a copy of *La fuerza* was at hand during the composition of the play, and that the authors had not merely heard about the Spanish original in a written or verbal summary. I will give here a brief account of the most salient similarities and differences between the two plays, although the interested English-speaking reader can easily compare the two texts by consulting Kathleen Jeffs's 2019 translation, the first available in English, which accompanies Melissa R. Machit's critical edition of the original.[96]

In *La fuerza*, the back story is in essence identical to that of *Love's Cure*. Pedro de Moncada (corresponding to Álvarez) committed a murder and had to flee for the wars in Flanders, and he has now returned to Spain after twenty years – to Zaragoza rather than Seville – bringing back with him the daughter who he took away as a baby, Hipólita (Clara). His wife, Costanza (Eugenia), remained at home pregnant with their second child, Félix (Lucio), and has brought him up at home. Hipólita, appropriately named after the warrior queen of the Amazons, has become a valiant soldier, while Félix has been educated in the ways of domesticity, and he has never been breeched: he still wears a long habit, like an infant. Unlike Lucio, Félix is not presented in female clothes, but just wears feminising attire: the long habit or cassock of a student.[97] Don Pedro immediately perceives these clothes to be inappropriately feminine, and draws up a plan for the re-education of his children:

Y a Hipólita le poned	And make Hipólita wear
largo vestido y tocado,	long gown and a headdress,
y en aposento y estrado	and in your bed- and sewing-room
para consuelo tened.	keep her for your comfort.
Yo a don Félix llevaré	I will have Don Félix
de ordinario al lado mío,	by my side every day,
porque aprenda a tener brío,	so that he may acquire some spirit;
y sí tendrá, yo lo sé;	and he will do it, well I know it,
pues mudará pareceres	because he will change his attitude
en ciñéndose la espada;	as soon as he wears a sword;
que la casa de Moncada	because the House of Moncada
no consiente hombres mujeres.	does not allow womanly men.
Y ansí podremos hacer,	And so we may make then,
para que el mundo se asombre	for the amazement of the world,
vos una mujer de un hombre,	you a woman out of a man,
yo un hombre de una mujer.	I a man out of a woman.
En los hombres cosa es cruel	In men it's a cruel thing
faldas largas de doncella;	to wear a long skirt like a maid;
id luego, y ponelde a ella	go now, and put on her
las que le quitais a él.	the skirt you take off him.
Quedaré con esperanza	I will remain in the hope
de trocar con el vestido	of changing with the dress
las costumbres que ha tenido.	the customs that he has had.[98]

(1.2.319–41)

This is the clearest verbal echo from the Spanish text in the English play, as 1.3 concludes with a strikingly similar declaration from Álvarez (see 1.3.178–84).

There are, however, substantial differences in the treatment of the revenge theme. Don Pedro, who had been having a secret affair with Costanza and had been climbing up to her bedroom at night by way of a rope ladder, was discovered by Costanza's brother Don Juan one night; a brawl ensued, and Pedro killed the brother in self-defence. Costanza's father discovered the stratagem and his daughter's relationship, and forced Pedro to flee with their baby girl Hipólita. Costanza now reports that, since her father has now died, she has recalled her husband from Flanders. The revenge plot, so prominent in *Love's Cure*, is here linked to a past that cannot interfere with the present. If Álvarez's murder of Vitelli's uncle perpetuates the young man's hatred in the present, the revenge plot in *La fuerza* dies with Costanza's father, and the comedy can flow free from the long shadow of the past: there are no consequences from Don Pedro's return to Spain, and no royal pardon is needed. Fletcher and Massinger developed instead the full-blown revenge plot that bookends and overshadows the play, and introduced the political tension between Vitelli's private right to see his honour satisfied, and the monarch's prerogative to grant a royal pardon for a murder.

The process of re-education of Hipólita and Félix is similar to that of Clara and Lucio. Hipólita complains of being forced to wear female clothes, while Félix feels confined in his *traje corto* (a close-fitting short doublet and breeches), and is given Hipólita's sword, to which the martial maid bids farewell in a long emotional speech (1.4.561–600). The first appearance of the siblings in their new clothes is interrupted by an offstage street brawl, as in scene 1.3 of *Love's Cure*, and Pedro and Hipólita rush out of the house, swords in hand. A fight ensues between Luis, the Vitelli figure, and Pedro, and then between Luis and Hipólita, who express mutual admiration at their skill with a sword. Luis's friends Otavio and Marcelo appear to stop the fight. It has all been a misunderstanding: Costanza identifies Luis and his sister, Leonor, as well-known relatives of the family, and Luis explains that the brawl started when some servants blocked the road and stopped his carriage, and were unpleasant to their driver. He declares that he would have avoided the fight if he had known that they served in Don Pedro's household, and they all go into the house in perfect amity. As a result of the episode, Luis falls in love with Hipólita, and Félix becomes infatuated with Leonor.

The reason for the brawl is entirely different in *Love's Cure*, but the faction that rushes in has the same composition: the young gallant followed by two other gentlemen, although with the addition of the gallant's sister (in *Love's Cure* Genevora does not appear until 4.1). In *La fuerza* the fight between the father figure and the young gallant is entirely fortuitous, and has no bearing on the rest of the play, but it clearly served as the basis for the expansion of the revenge plot in Fletcher and Massinger's version in the adjusting of the kinship of the murdered uncle from the cross-dressed siblings (Hipólita and Félix's late uncle Don Juan) to the young gallant (Vitelli's late uncle Don Pedro).

From this point, the Spanish play takes a different course, although a series of episodes, details of characterisation, and some verbal references were transferred to the English version. A passage from Act I of *La fuerza*, for example, could have provided the names of the two siblings in the adaptation, Lucio and Clara. Costanza declares:

Destas esperadas horas,	From these long-awaited hours
desta voluntad pagada,	from my own satisfied wishes,
destos logrados deseos,	from those accomplished desires,
destas tinieblas amadas,	from that beloved darkness,
una niña salió a *luz*,	a girl came out to light,
mas no para todos *clara*.	though not to everyone clear.

(1.1.109–14; my emphasis)

The occurrence of the words *luz* and *clara*, both related to luminosity, so close to the beginning of the play may have given Fletcher and Massinger a prompt for the related names of their cross-dressed siblings.

Apart from other minor verbal echoes, there are a number of noticeable parallel situations. Don Pedro instructs a Master at Arms to give Félix a fencing lesson in the second act of *La fuerza*, and Hipólita interrupts the lesson, recovers her sword from Félix, and attacks the Master at Arms (as Clara does with Piorato in 3.4). Don Pedro draws up a plan to awaken his son's bravery by arranging for a neighbour to distract Félix while he disguises himself and stages a nocturnal attack on his son. This was the inspiration behind the night-walking scene 4.3 in *Love's Cure*. Later in *La fuerza*, Leonor throws down a glove for Félix to pick up, but it is Otavio who snatches it away to wear in his hatband (as Lamoral does in 4.4). Don Pedro and Luis, aided by a Captain, try to arrange a duel between Félix and Otavio, but Félix protests that he must do this himself and leaves. He then surprises Otavio courting Leonor at her window, and challenges his rival to find a remote place to fight a duel. The duel takes place offstage while the Captain, who has followed Félix, narrates the events. Félix defeats Otavio and recovers Leonor's glove, just as Lucio does with Lamoral in 5.1. The duellists are surprised by the Alguacil and his watchmen; Félix kills one of the watches and the Captain comes forward to dispatch the rest.

In the meantime, Hipólita has been made to believe that Luis is marrying another woman, and, full of jealousy, challenges him to another duel. Luis appoints a nearby poplar grove for the encounter. Hipólita returns home, weeping, to report that, in the middle of the fight, Luis embraced her, they slipped on the grass, and they tumbled to the ground:

pero después de caer,	but after we fell,
hizo, ¡ay, madre!, cierta cosa,	he did, O mother, one thing,
que nunca la imaginé.	that I never could have imagined.
Revolvióme toda el alma	He stirred up all my soul
y mudóme todo el ser. [...]	and he changed all my being. [...]
Desde entonces soy mujer.	From then I am a woman.

(3.5.853–65)

It is unclear whether this violent sexual experience was consensual or whether Luis has raped Hipólita. Fletcher and Massinger transferred this sexual trope to Lucio: as part of his nocturnal plan, and in the event of coming across a woman, Álvarez commands his son to 'Take her away and use her like a man' (4.3.40). By contrast with Hipólita, Clara's transformation is brought about by the realisation that she is in love with Vitelli (2.2), and her jealousy – not prompted by the malicious report of an invented wedding, but by actually witnessing Vitelli's ongoing relationship with Malroda – does not generate the extreme rage that Hipólita displays in *La fuerza*.

Most of the episodes and circumstances that Fletcher and Massinger took from *La fuerza* occur in the early part of the *comedia*. They then developed these situations in their own distinct way by expanding the revenge plot, by augmenting the role of the Alguacil, by conflating some characters (Félix's tutor and the clown Galván into Bobadilla) and eliminating others (the Captain), by reducing the role of the gallant's sister (Leonor is a larger and more enterprising character than Genevora), and by downplaying the martial maid's transformation from a violent sexual experience to a sentimental awakening.[99]

Beyond the adaptation of the narrative framework, perhaps the other most meaningful alteration is the expansion of the historical context in which the play is set. In *La fuerza* Flanders remains a remote theatre of war, but no specific military actions are recalled or attributed to Hipólita, and no historical figures from the conflict are mentioned. By contrast, probably through Massinger's acute interest in international politics, the English version sets the play against the vivid backdrop of the Spanish campaign against the United Provinces in Ostend, filling the text with resonant historical pointers, and fleshing out the significance of Clara's military background. In fact, a major source for the character is an enigmatic

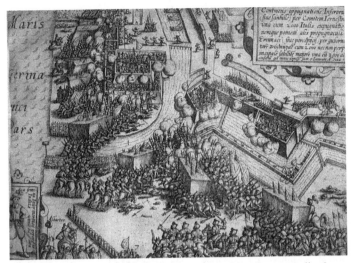

Figure 2 Detail from *Belägerung der Statt Ostende*, appendix (n.p., 1604–05), fo. 4ʳ, courtesy of the Staats- und Stadtbibliothek Augsburg (shelf mark: 2 Gs 68)

figure who appears in a number of reports from the siege of Ostend (5 July 1601–22 September 1604), one of the bloodiest campaigns in the Eighty Years' War in which some 60,000 people from both sides were killed.[100] On 7 January 1602, following a Spanish assault, the body of a young Spanish woman in masculine clothes was found among the dead, wearing a gold chain around her neck. Edward Grimeston's *A True History of the Memorable Siege of Ostend* (1604) contains the details that the dramatists would include:

> Searching among the dead, they found a young Spanish woman near unto Sandhill in man's apparel, the which (as they might guess by her wounds) had been slain at the assault; she had under her apparel a chain of gold set with precious stones, with other jewels and silver.[101]

The chain corresponds to the 'massy chain of gold' reportedly given to Clara as a reward for having saved the general's son from certain death (1.1.85–6). Nothing else is known about the mysterious woman who died in the siege, but, as Anna E. C. Simoni has traced, most accounts in Dutch, German, English, and French mention the sally of 1602 and the discovery of the slain cross-dressed Spanish woman.[102] A German report of the siege, *Belägerung der Statt Ostende* (1604–05), included the story and an engraving of the attack, with a sketch of the martial maid.[103] (See figure 2.) The description of the armed figure in the vignette on the lower left-hand corner, which shows female breasts under the doublet, reads *[Hispa]nica femina inter mortuos reperta induta virili habita*: 'A Spanish woman discovered among the dead, dressed in the habit of a man.' The anecdote was clearly known across Europe and provided a starting point for the main character in *Love's Cure* and a prompt to expand Hipólita's background in *La fuerza* by constructing the tale of her deeds at Ostend.

Apart from the historical sources that fleshed out the backdrop of the play and the names of many of its characters, and in addition to the main plot derived from *La fuerza*, the subplot of *Love's Cure* was also developed from existing literary sources. In particular, the character of the hungry knave Lazarillo was based on the eponymous anti-hero of *Lazarillo de Tormes*, the original picaresque novel, which first circulated in Spain in 1553,[104] and which David Rowland of Anglesey translated into English in 1586. The novella tells the story of a poor boy who serves a series of miserly masters who keep him in permanent starvation. In *Love's Cure*, the relationship between Lazarillo and his master, the cobbler Pacheco, recalls that between the Spanish *pícaro* and his master the Squire. Like Pacheco in 2.1, the Squire boasts of wearing a cloak and gentlemanly apparel in public to demonstrate a wealth that he does not possess, and neglects to feed his servant. Apart from this situational resemblance, two passages in the play are closely modelled on the novel. The Squire, like Pacheco in 2.1.9–15, defends the healthy properties of eating in moderation:

> 'Be then answered saying, it is a virtue to live soberly, therefore I commend thee much: pigs fill themselves, and wise men eat discretely what is only sufficient for them.' 'I now understand you well, sir', said I to myself. Evil luck light upon such virtue and goodness as these my masters do find in hunger.[105]

Although he does not take it to Pacheco's extreme in 2.1.22–4, the Squire also praises the virtue of not eating to prolong life:

> 'Sir', said I, 'take no care for me; I can pass over one night, and more if need be, without meat.' 'And that will be cause that thou shalt live longer', said he, 'for as wise men affirm, there is nothing that can make a man live longer than to eat a little.' 'If that be true', said I to myself, 'I shall never

die, for I have always been constrained to keep that rule, and I think I am fortuned to observe it as long as I live.'[106]

Lazarillo's propensity to insert comments to himself into the narrative, almost as private asides to the reader, is also reflected in the character's many asides to the audience in *Love's Cure*. Very much in line with the sharp social critique of Spanish society characteristic of the picaresque genre, Lazarillo's asides in 2.1 amount to a running satirical commentary on Pacheco's grandiloquent aspirations and those of his associates.[107]

In addition to Lazarillo, the character of the Alguazir in *Love's Cure* is recognisably based on the criminal exploits of another Spanish *pícaro*, the protagonist of *Guzmán de Alfarache* by Mateo Alemán.[108] Guzmán shares with the Alguazir the illegitimacy of his birth (see 2.1.168–70) and his dubious ancestry,[109] particularly with respect to their foreignness and their links with Islam and Judaism: the ancestors of Guzmán's Genoan father, a notorious swindler, were *levantiscos*, that is, Jews from the Levant who had converted to Christianity.[110] At one point he was taken captive to Algiers where he embraced the Muslim faith.[111] Both circumstances – the racial Jewishness of Guzmán's family and his father's conversion to Islam – are hinted at in the tale of the Alguazir's past: he can be identified as Jewish by his red hair,[112] and he is also accused of being 'descended o' the Moors', as well as of apostasy and perjury (being a false convert). Genoan men also had a reputation for effeminacy and homosexuality,[113] which recalls Mendoza's accusation in 2.1.196–7. Both characters also share a long record of criminal misdeeds, perpetrated alone or in association with others, as well as of serving a series of masters. The Alguazir was pressed to sail to the Spice Islands (2.1.175–9), which recalls Guzmán's extensive travels throughout the novel. Similarly to the Alguazir (2.1.170–1), Guzmán leaves Toledo fearing he will be whipped.[114] The Alguazir is reported to have served a term in the galleys for robbery (2.1.172–3), and at the end of the play he is threatened with being sent to them again (5.3.235); Guzmán is condemned in Seville to row in the galleys for theft towards the end of the book.[115] Apart from Guzmán's lack of direct involvement in prostitution, the Alguazir's main trade, the resemblance of all of the other episodes, circumstances, and locations is striking. In addition, Fletcher and Massinger borrowed the name of Sayavedra from *Guzmán*, who, rather than a gentleman, is a rogue whom Guzmán meets in Italy and who assists him in his misdeeds.[116] James Mabbe's English translation of *Guzmán* only appeared in 1622, and Fletcher contributed a prefatory poem to it, commenting on the novel's great popularity in Spain, Italy, and France before its publication in England. Clearly, he had already read the book by 1615.[117]

TEXT

The text printed in the 1647 folio is the only authoritative source for this play, and it is the copy-text for the present edition. It derives from a prompt book previously owned by the King's Men, rather than an authorial manuscript. There are numerous traces of this throughout the text. Generally, entrances are indicated a few lines earlier than they would usually be expected, which is where the book-keeper would have cued the actors to enter.[118] Other cues marked on the script, such as those calling for music and lighting instruments, also appear at a slightly earlier point than they would be required. For example, the stage direction at 1.3.38, '*Music*', would presumably accompany the entrance of Eugenia, Lucio, and the servants two lines later. Most notably, the marginal indication '*2 Torches ready*' (sig. 5S1^r, left column, 18–19), prompting their preparation at 3.4.76, anticipates their appearance on stage at the beginning of 4.1 by some 62 lines plus an act break.[119] In addition, there is only one missing entrance (Vitelli's in 4.2.24), while five exits are omitted,[120] which is also a sign that the manuscript was the book-keeper's copy: entrances needed to be cued in accurately, but exits were the actor's responsibility and would be recorded in his part script.[121] Finally, as Hoy observed, there seem to be two passages in 5.3 indicated for a theatrical cut: lines 140 to 153, and perhaps from 156 to 179, respectively 13 and 23 lines, 'which were never actually made in the prompt book, but the cues for which survive in the folio text in the otherwise inexplicable repetition of two speeches'.[122] (See figure 3.)

This prompt book would have been used by the King's Men in the decade leading up to the closing of the theatres, since the play was in their repertory by 7 August 1641, when it appears on a list of 60 plays in a letter addressed to the Company of Printers and Stationers by the Lord Chamberlain, the Earl of Essex. The letter requests that the Stationers were not to allow the printing of these plays without the consent of the King's Men. *Love's Cure* appears listed as '*The martiall maide*'.[123] The 27 'Beaumont and Fletcher'

Figure 3 Theatrical cut indicated in 5.3, F, sig. 5S5^r, courtesy of Pennsylvania State University

plays on that list, except *The Wild-Goose Chase*, were included by Humphrey Moseley and Humphrey Robinson in their entry in the Stationers' Register dated 4 September 1646. In that entry they registered for publication a total of 48 plays, including 29 that were marked as being 'by m^r Beamont and m^r fflesher [*sic*]'. *Love's Cure* is listed under the title '*Martiall maid*'.[124] Since the plays, except *The Mad Lover*, appear in the exact same order in both documents, both lists must be directly related in some way. R. C. Bald suggested that 'both the 1641 list and the entry were based on an inventory in the hands of the King's Men'.[125]

It seems almost certain that the manuscripts of most of these plays were sourced from the actors themselves. By 1646, when the publishers were in the last stages of assembling the collection, the surviving members of the King's Men had been virtually unemployed for over three years, as the London theatres had been closed by the Parliamentarian authorities in early September 1642.[126] For a group of impoverished actors, the income from Moseley and Robinson would have been most welcome. Moseley's prefatory note (sigs A4^{r-v}) relates his difficulties in chasing up the scattered manuscripts in order to assemble the collection during the ongoing Civil War, gleefully adding that 'They are now happily met in this book, having escaped these public troubles, free and unmangled.'[127] According to Bald, 'shortly before September 1646 Moseley had acquired the manuscripts of only twenty-four plays directly through the King's Men, and ... the ten remaining pieces in the volume came to him from other sources'.[128] Apart from the 29 plays in the 1646 entry, the six other pieces in F were not registered with the Stationers until the Restoration in an entry dated 29 June 1660.[129]

Love's Cure was among the plays that had been sourced from the actors, some of whom signed the dedication to Philip Herbert, Earl of Pembroke and Montgomery.[130] Despite its dedication to an aristocrat with anti-Royalist allegiances,[131] and the fact that one of the signatories, Eliard Swanston, had Parliamentarian sympathies,[132] the publication of F has been described as an act of royalist propaganda.[133] As Philip J. Finkelpearl has summarised, the evidence to support this view 'includes its production by the royalist publisher Humphrey Moseley, the apparent involvement of the cavalier propagandist Sir John Berkenhead, and the explicit sentiments of some of the prefatory poems, almost all of which were written by avowed loyalists'; these poets were 'largely cavalier literati who were disposed to see Beaumont and Fletcher from a partisan point of view'.[134] The majority of members of the King's Men – the royal company *par excellence* – evidently harboured royalist sympathies, and would have therefore collaborated with Moseley for political reasons, as well as monetary gain. Premeditated or not, the book was certainly making a political statement. First, it was offering the London readership a substitute for actual playgoing by printing many popular pieces of recent memory, in defiance of the Puritan loathing of the theatre. And second, it was vindicating the literary status of John Fletcher, a dramatist who had been associated with the King's Men for most of his career and who, despite his 'political resistance to absolutism', as Gordon McMullan has shown,[135] was clearly regarded as an eminently royalist writer.

The 1647 folio was printed in eight sections, each assigned to a different London printing house to speed up production. Six of these have been identified as Thomas Warren (section 1), William Wilson (2), Susan Islip (3 and possibly 7), Ruth Raworth (4 and the latter part of 8), Edward Griffin (5 and part of 8), and probably Moses Bell (6). The first three signatures of section 8 remain unassigned.[136] Johan Gerritsen reckoned that 'printing must have finished before 25 March [Lady Day] 1647', and he added that, 'assuming, as seems justified, that the title-page was the last part of the book to be printed, the occurrence of the 1646 date in some copies would argue that the publishers expected to sell a number of copies before the new year'.[137]

Love's Cure is the sixth play in Griffin's section 5, and occupies signatures 5Q3^r to 5S6^r; sig. 5S6^v is a blank page.[138] The play was, therefore, printed in three quires, the first two leaves of the first quire containing the last pages of *The Woman's Prize* (sigs 5Q1^r to 5Q2^r; 5Q2^v is a blank page). The first two quires (5Q and 5R) are in fours (two folded sheets, or eight pages per quire), which is the norm throughout the folio, while the final quire (5S) is in sixes (three sheets, or twelve pages). The play, like the rest of F, was printed in two columns, except for the Prologue (sig. 5S6^r), which was set in one column using a larger type and occupying a single page. Williams's analysis revealed that three compositors collaborated in typesetting the text, and that they did it seriatim, or continuously through following the manuscript, rather than by formes. Running titles are missing from the first page of the play (sig. 5Q3^r), which was the usual practice throughout F, and on signature 5S6. The recto of the leaf, 5S6^r – the unusual page containing the Prologue – was mis-paginated as 143, as the running title was removed from the frame to typeset the new page, but the page number was not.[139] The verso, S6[v], was left blank. Otherwise, running titles follow a regular pattern.[140]

The Second Folio of 1679 incorporated the plays that had been issued in quarto prior to the publication of F. As stated in the prefatory note 'The Book-Sellers to the Reader' (sigs A1[r–v]), the texts of the plays had been checked thoroughly by 'an ingenious and worthy Gentleman' who had 'taken the pains (or rather the pleasure) to read over' and annotate his own copy of F, 'wherein he had all along corrected several faults (some very gross)' (sig. A1[r]). This gentleman had sold his copy to the publishers – John Martin, Henry Herringman, and Richard Marriott – along with prologues and epilogues missing from F that he had preserved. The identity of this person is not revealed:

> His corrections were the more to be valued because he had an intimacy with both our authors, and had been a spectator of most of them when they were acted in their lifetime. (sig. A1[r])

The F2 text of *Love's Cure*, set from F, incorporated numerous corrections and emendations, but it also introduced some enduring misreadings. Guy A. Battle counted 2,453 variations between the two texts, including those 'in spelling, punctuation, capitalization, and italicization'.[141] F2 also included the first list of roles for the play (see figure 4).

The editions in the following century mainly used F2 as copy, adding further corrections and beginning to regularise spelling and punctuation. Gerard Langbaine's 1711 edition, the first new printing of the play in thirty-two years, made a number of sensible independent emendations. Seven years later, the Quarto appears to have been set from a copy of Langbaine's edition, rather than F or F2, as most individual readings suggest a near-complete coincidence. The first edition to reconsider both folios, and to comment on the difficult passages and textual cruxes, was Sympson and Seward's in 1750. Later in the century, George Colman's 1778 annotated text erroneously rendered all passages in prose as verse, the whole of scene 2.1 being the extreme case. Henry Weber's 1812 edition reprinted and expanded Sympson and Seward's commentary, while George Darley's 1839 edition reproduced the Weber text with virtually no variations.[142] Alexander Dyce was the first editor to collate all previous texts in his 1845 edition. He imaginatively reconsidered the censored

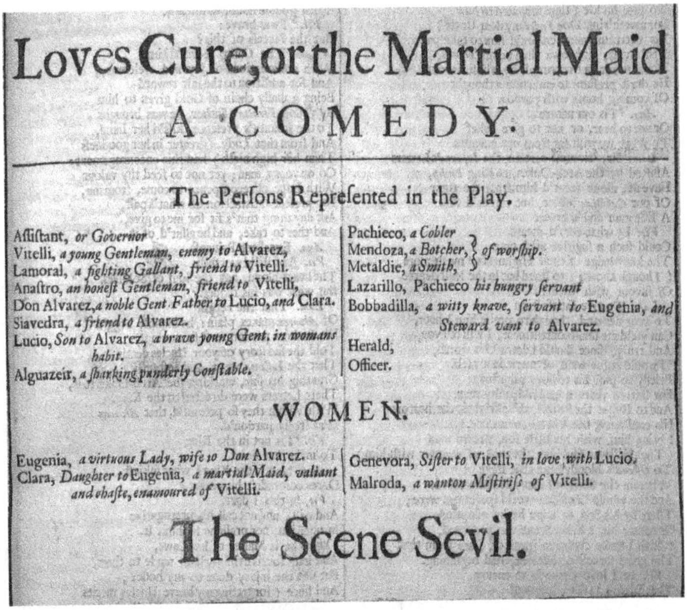

Loves Cure, or the Martial Maid

A COMEDY.

The Persons Represented in the Play.

Assistant, *or Governor*
Vitelli, *a young Gentleman, enemy to* Alvarez,
Lamoral, *a fighting Gallant, friend to* Vitelli.
Anastro, *an honest Gentleman, friend to* Vitelli,
Don Alvarez, *a noble Gent. Father to* Lucio, *and* Clara.
Siavedra, *a friend to* Alvarez.
Lucio, *Son to* Alvarez, *a brave young Gent, in womans habit.*
Alguazeir, *a sharking punderly Constable.*

Pachieco, *a Cobler*
Mendoza, *a Botcher,* } *of worship.*
Metaldie, *a Smith,*
Lazarillo, Pachieco *his hungry servant*
Bobbadilla, *a witty knave, servant to* Eugenia, *and Steward vant to* Alvarez.
Herald,
Officer.

WOMEN.

Eugenia, *a virtuous Lady, wife to Don* Alvarez.
Clara, *Daughter to* Eugenia, *a martial Maid, valiant and chaste, enamoured of* Vitelli.

Genevora, *Sister to* Vitelli, *in love with* Lucio.
Malroda, *a wanton Mistiriss of* Vitelli.

The Scene Sevil.

Figure 4 'The Persons Represented in the Play' from F2 (London, 1679), sig. ^{2}X3^r; personal copy

oaths, first investigated by Colman,[143] and carefully modernised and regularised the text, even rendering the Spanish phrases correctly.

A century later, Guy A. Battle completed a 'Critical Text with Comment' as a master's thesis at Duke University in 1947, which contributed a minute bibliographical study of F and F2, a list of suggested emendations to the F text, and four appendices of commentary. George Walton Williams used Battle's work as a main source for his own investigation of F and F2, although he did not include it in his historical collation.[144] Williams's 1976 edition was the only modern critical edition available prior to the present one. He included an excellent introduction, which, even if erroneous in some instances – most notably in its hypothesis as to the date of composition and the process of adaptation of the Spanish source – is the most solid scholarly approach to the play previously available. Marea Mitchell published her modernised version in the

Nottingham Drama Texts series in 1992. It was a worthy attempt at producing a modern-spelling text for a new generation of readers and critics,[145] although the annotation was sketchy and irregular, and the textual work did not give due consideration to the history of the text, mostly presenting Williams's version in modern spelling.

THEMES

Love's Cure is described in F2 as a comedy,[146] and features many situations that are broadly humorous and even farcical. Following the conventions of the genre, the play ends with several marriages: Vitelli and Clara, and Lucio and Genevora, plan to celebrate their weddings, while Piorato, the fencing master, is revealed to have married Malroda, the courtesan. Álvarez and Vitelli are reconciled after an enmity of decades in a happy ending that provides the logical generic conclusion. However, the tone of the opening scene is in no way that of a comedy. Lamoral's report of the return of Álvarez to Seville, following the pardon granted by the King in response to Clara's heroic deeds at Ostend, prompts in Vitelli a firm resolution: 'useless are all words / Till you have writ performance with your swords' (129–30). An unknowing spectator might easily take the play for a revenge tragedy: Vitelli, the revenger, sets off to seek reparation for his uncle's murder, and we might expect the play to end with Álvarez's death at the young man's hands. However, the second scene of the play, which introduces Lucio's unusual upbringing, is in marked contrast with the opening episode. The scene is full of Bobadilla's sexual innuendo and coarse language, and his ridiculing of Lucio's effeminacy is meant to be almost farcical. If, as Huw Griffiths has noted, 'the audience would have assumed that the actor playing [Lucio] was going to be playing the part of a woman for the duration of the play',[147] they gradually come to realise that the male performer is, in fact, playing a young man in drag. In addition, Clara's deployment of violence at various points in the play veers into farcical exaggeration. In 2.2, dressed in feminine clothes while incongrously carrying her weapons, she strikes Bobadilla and attempts to strangle him with his chain of office. In 3.4 she fails to restrain herself and ends up rejecting Sayavedra's amorous advances with yet more blows, and then she attacks Piorato in Lucio's defence during the subsequent fencing lesson.

This fusion of dramatic sub-genres – revenge tragedy, historical drama, romantic comedy, and farce – is a fundamental feature of the play's fabric, and has its origins in the experiments that Fletcher and Beaumont had attempted in their collaborative plays, particularly in tragicomedies such as *Philaster* and *A King and No King*, which toy with the audience's expectations as to how the plot will be resolved. In fact, the surprisingly sudden comic dénouement is only reached after an extended scene in which Clara, Eugenia, and Genevora manage to halt the duel between Álvarez and Vitelli, oddly granted as a public occasion by the King of Spain, over a space of no fewer than a hundred lines. The fatal resolution is delayed, and the tension builds up until the three women threaten to carry out an assisted triple suicide.[148] Up to this point the outcome of the scene seems irreversible: Eugenia will die by Bobadilla's pistol, Clara and Genevora will stab each other to death, and then Vitelli and Álvarez will engage in a mortal fight, causing the death of either or both of them. This fatal outcome would have been the natural resolution that the opening scene promised. The abrupt comic reversal, which may generate laughter in performance,[149] exposes the frail boundaries between genres, and, in a way, is not just a nod to traditional generic constraints – a comedy needs to end with reconciliation and marriage – but, rather, a playful questioning of the instability of such definitions.

Of course, the play is at its most experimental in its extraordinary engagement with the problematics of gender identity in the unusual upbringing and re-education of Lucio and Clara, and the memorable double case of cross-dressing at its heart. As generations of critics have appreciated, the cross-dressing trope was frequently exploited in late Elizabethan and Jacobean drama.[150] In particular, cross-dressers were extraordinarily frequent in the 1610s. This responded to an ongoing public controversy around people who were seen in public wearing the clothes of the opposite gender. The controversy played out in the decade leading up to the publication in 1620 of two frequently cited pamphlets, *Hic Mulier, or The Man-Woman* (STC 13375) and *Haec Vir, or The Womanish Man* (STC 12599), which condemned, respectively, the depravity of female and male cross-dressers. As Michael Shapiro has demonstrated, there were well-known real cases of cross-dressing in Renaissance London, particularly among women. Examples included aristocratic ladies, such as Arabella Stuart, a distant relative of James I who tried to escape house arrest by fleeing to France in male apparel in 1611, as well as women of more humble birth who, once accused of cross-dressing, were immediately branded for sexual promiscuity.

As Shapiro summarises, 'cross-dressing in and of itself was evidently considered a sexual misdemeanour, or evidence of such'.[151]

Apart from the occasional presence of cross-dressed patrons in the audience,[152] the relationship between cross-dressing and the English professional theatre was an obvious one: the most evident cross-dressers in the playhouses were the male actors playing the female roles, a persistent tradition that had gradually died out in other European countries, but that would remain current in England until the Restoration. Cross-dressing was the frequent target of anti-theatrical propaganda. In Jonson's *Bartholomew Fair* (1614), Busy interrupts the puppet show to protest against cross-dressing: 'my main argument against you is that you are an abomination: for the male among you putteth on the apparel of the female, and the female of the male' (5.5.77–9). As John Creaser comments, 'Busy paraphrases the source of a standard puritanical argument against the theatre: "The woman shall not wear that which pertaineth unto the man, neither shall a man put on woman's raiment: for all that do so, are abomination unto the Lord thy God" (Deuteronomy, 22.5).'[153] However, and beyond the theatre, *Hic Mulier* and *Haec Vir* were, as Shapiro states, part of 'an unorganised protest rather than a coherent movement, [in which] the issues involved the moral and spiritual equality of women and aspects of social freedom'.[154] Susan Gushee O'Malley has traced these social anxieties around cross-dressing in other books and pamphlets from the 1610s such as *The Curtain-Drawer of the World* (1612; STC 19298), in which William Parks condemned female cross-dressers as degenerates and their male counterparts as effeminate lechers, and *Mystical Bedlam, or The World of Mad Men* (1615; STC 124), in which Thomas Adams denounced cross-dressers as confusing entities. *Love's Cure* is inescapably immersed in this controversy, which, as O'Malley identifies, died out after 1620.[155]

The long and varied gallery of cross-dressers in English plays of the early 1610s include the title character of Jonson's *Epicene* (c. January 1610), Innogen in Shakespeare's *Cymbeline* (c. 1610), Ansaldo in female disguise in Middleton's *The Widow* (c. late 1615), and Wittipol disguised as a Spanish lady in Jonson's *The Devil Is an Ass* (1616). Perhaps most memorably of all, the real-life thief Mary Frith (1584/9–1659), also known as Moll Cutpurse, was dramatised in Field's *Amends for Ladies* (c. 1610) and in Middleton and Dekker's *The Roaring Girl* (1611). However, Fletcher is demonstrably the

Jacobean dramatist who engaged most frequently and most productively with cross-dressing: almost a third of his substantial canon of
plays – 15 out of 52 – feature cross-dressers in their *dramatis personae*.[156] Fletcher's interest in cross-dressing has been well studied, as
is attested, for instance, by the work of Peter Berek, Sandra Clark,
Jonathan Dollimore, Anne Duncan, and Jennifer A. Low.[157] In
particular, many female characters in his plays wear male apparel,
usually out of necessity. In *Cupid's Revenge* (*c.* 1607), Urania assumes
the persona of a page to escape an undesirable marriage, while in
Philaster (*c.* 1609), Euphrasia disguises herself as the page Bellario
to be closer to the title character, the object of her unrequited affection. In *The Maid's Tragedy* (*c.* 1611), Aspatia poses as her brother
in order to challenge Amintor to a duel, while Alathe is cross-
dressed throughout *The Night-Walkers* (*c.* 1615) as the witty boy
Snap. In *Love's Pilgrimage* (*c.* 1616), which has so much in common
with *Love's Cure*, Theodosia and Leocadia are in male disguise in
pursuit of the same womanising lover. In *The Pilgrim* (*c.* 1621),
Alinda and Juletta disguise themselves as boys, and in *The Maid of
the Mill* (1623), Aminta dresses up as a page. Male cross-dressers
are also plentiful in Fletcher: for example, Welford appears in drag
for comic effect in *The Scornful Lady* (*c.* 1610), Veramour disguises
himself as a maid and is accosted by La Verdine in *The Honest Man's
Fortune* (*c.* 1613), the title character of *Monsieur Thomas* (*c.* 1615)
dresses up as a lady, Alinda is really Archas's son in disguise in *The
Loyal Subject* (1618), and Cleremont in *The Little French Lawyer*
(1620) disguises himself in women's night-clothes. Since Massinger
seldom engaged with this theme in his extant solo plays, we must
assume that this was essentially a Fletcherian trait.[158]

  Love's Cure is, therefore, a quintessential example of Fletcher's
engagement with cross-dressing, but, at the same time, it is also an
anomaly. In all the cases mentioned above, cross-dressing is an
enabling disguise deployed for particular purposes. Crucially, these
disguises do not modify a character's actual gender identity. For
example, Euphrasia is a woman in male disguise, who poses as Bellario to be able to serve Philaster as a domestic page, but she reveals
herself to be a woman towards the end of the play. However, in the
opening act of *Love's Cure*, Clara and Lucio are not, strictly speaking, 'in disguise'. The two characters are wearing the clothes that
they have been wearing all their lives: Clara has been living as a man
named Lucio, and Lucio as a woman called Posthumia. As Griffiths

provocatively states, the play 'seems rather to pose the question: what happens when the disguises of the cross-dressing plot are adopted in earnest?'[159] From a modern perspective, we can argue that Lucio and Clara are, to all effects, transgender people, as the *OED* defines: 'a person whose sense of personal identity and gender does not correspond to that person's sex at birth, or which does not otherwise conform to conventional notions of sex and gender' (A *adj.* 1). The infant Lucio might have been disguised as a girl to protect him from his father's enemies – in fact, at the beginning of the play Eugenia still considers her son's feminine clothes to be a 'womanish disguise' (1.2.84) – but his identity as Posthumia has successfully conformed to the social expectations of the female gender: Posthumia is attentive to domestic matters such as her sewing work, the laundry, the care of domestic animals, and the management of servants (see 1.2.1–5), and she is stereotypically scared of physical violence. Clara might have been disguised as a male to enable her to live among soldiers, perhaps protected from sexual predation, but she has enjoyed a fulfilling life as a warrior and would not want to change her male identity: as she states, 'I could wish / I were what I appear' (1.3.37–8).

The siblings do not seem to have suffered from any kind of gender dysphoria, and they both demonstrate extraordinary resistance to the imposed abandonment of the gender identity that they have held all their lives. Arguably, the siblings' process of gender re-education, cruel and 'violently punitive' as it is,[160] particularly in Lucio's case, can only produce uncertain and potentially reversible results. As Griffiths argues, 'gender congruence between player and part shifts through the "cure" so that by the end of the play it is the Clara/Lucio part, rather than that of Lucio/Posthumia, that is the transvestite performance'.[161] Clara and Lucio's final gender identity – the former a demure lady and the latter a courageous fighter – is also a performative construction that is ridden with uncertainty. In fact, their re-education has produced two beings whose gender, as Simone Chess declares, is 'a genderqueer hybrid', rather than 'a seamlessly restored normative gender'.[162]

To consider that the siblings' new gender identity has effectively ceased to operate in terms of a heteronormative male/female binary divide is a useful way to investigate their transformation from a modern perspective. In this respect, we can suggest that Clara/Lucio and Lucio/Posthumia are, by the end of the play, non-binary people. Chess explores this hybridity by examining Lucio's female lover,

Genevora, and her expectations of his behaviour, particularly when she pleads that he abandon the duel in the final scene:

> Genevora not only shows her willingness to marry a man who has been, and to a certain degree will always be, a woman, but also her awareness that her own gender labor has not only normalized, eroticized and accepted his femininity but also now propped up his masculine presentation, begetting his valor with her eyes, tongue, and breast. Further, by insisting that Lucio's valor is not his own, Genevora shows that Lucio's femininity, his maiden's manners, are as authentic a gender presentation as his masculinity; both are performed, and of the two, she seems to prefer the former.[163]

Lucio's relationship with Genevora is a useful key to explore Lucio's masculinity. As Jonathan Dollimore states, the play's construction of masculinity relies on demonstrating 'sexual prowess and violence', both of which are encoded in Álvarez's two orders to his son: to fight another man and to rape a woman.[164] Seemingly unaware of what Álvarez meant by taking away the first woman that they come across and using her 'like a man' (4.3.40), instead of raping Genevora, he requests simply to kiss her. Sandra Clark has highlighted the importance of recognising this broken promise: 'Thus the equation Alvarez would make between manliness and violence is cancelled out', and Lucio subsequently develops 'his own notion of a masculine soul's instructions by defeating a rival [...] and then sparing his life'.[165] Given his upbringing and prior gender identity, Genevora expects that Lucio's re-crafted masculinity would be gentler and more reasonable than his father intended.

For her part, Clara displays a much more stereotypical and morally upright kind of masculinity: she even corrects her father's behaviour in scene 1.3 when he and Sayavedra violate their code of honour and the rules of hospitality to attack an outnumbered enemy near the family's own home. Anne Duncan argues that she

> is presented as the only 'real man' in the play. When she 'becomes' a woman, she performs equally well in that role, revealing that gender (and not just masculinity) is only a performance, and furthermore, in a reversal of English Renaissance stage practice, that a woman can perform a man best.[166]

Having failed to alter his children's gender by imposing socially appropriate clothes and behaviour on them, Álvarez expected that his son's masculinity would ultimately be awakened by a violent sexual experience with a woman. However, following the main title of the play, the siblings are 'cured' of their socially anomalous gender identity by a romantic experience: through falling in love with someone of the socially acceptable opposite sex. But the disconnection between the siblings' physiological sex and their gender identity is urgently important here: is it Lucio or Posthumia who falls in love with Genevora? Is it Clara or the soldier Lucio who becomes infatuated with Vitelli? As Griffiths summarises, beyond its focus on 'the existence of specifically sexed bodies', the play's dialogue 'delineates a possibility that "nature" can itself be rescripted. The trans★ possibilities that critics have seen in the play lie here: in the "body-becoming," and not in the understanding of staged manifestations of gender as only ever performative.'[167] Thinking about cross-dressing and emotional fulfilment in Love's Cure, David M. Robinson draws an interesting and useful connection with two plays from the repertory of the Children of Paul's. On the one hand, in John Lyly's Galatea (c. 1584), the title heroine and the maid Phyllida disguise themselves as boys, fall in love with each other before revealing their real identities, and then Venus agrees to transform one of them permanently into a male after the two young women get married. On the other hand, in The Maid's Metamorphosis (1600), the heroine Eurymine is physically transformed into a man with the curse that she will fall in love with another man. The difference is that 'unlike those earlier plays, Love's Cure magically transforms its characters' genders, not sexes'.[168] In Robinson's opinion, Fletcher and Massinger's comedy also deviates from those plays, and from Ovid's Metamorphoses, 'in almost completely avoiding the subject of homosexuality whether female or male'. And he goes a step further:

> At no point does the play suggest any possibility of erotic desire between women. As for erotic desire between men, it makes at most a fleeting, shadowy appearance when Clara and Vitelli first admire one another, before the secret of her true sex has been revealed, and before her gender change has begun [...] Moreover, the play does *not* allow us [...] to pursue such possibilities. No sooner has Cupid's arrow struck than it begins to work its unswervingly heterosexual magic.[169]

Robinson acknowledges the homoerotic element of the relationships between soldiers, as Dollimore had suggested, but is otherwise unpersuaded that Love's Cure addresses in any way the theme of same-sex desire. As he critiques, 'Deviant gender, not deviant sexuality, is the play's concern.'[170]

The homoerotic theme might seem absent from *Love's Cure*, as the play takes for granted the notion that heterosexuality is instinctive and 'natural', and that it can assist Lucio and Clara in overcoming their transformation. However, we can consider the implications of their transformation more closely. The play does not reveal how the siblings feel about the reality of their physiological sex – Lucio has 'a better needle' under his petticoat, after all (1.2.18) – but when the play comes full circle and reverses these 'monstrous metamorphoses' (5.3.268), it is only because Clara and Lucio have fallen in love with another pair of siblings, Vitelli and Genevora, who are almost stereotypical examples of the kind of people they have been all their lives. Clara is dazzled by Vitelli's dexterity with a sword and his courage in confronting his enemies: to her eyes, 'valour and true resolution / Never appeared so lovely' (1.3.100–1). Even witnessing his womanising habits in scene 4.2 does not ultimately put her off, as this is probably something that she expects from a young man. The awakening of her feelings towards these masculine characteristics coincides with the sudden discovery of her own femininity, a necessary step to make that love socially acceptable. But, even if she gives up her sword and former gender identity, Clara has fallen in love with a member of her own gender up until that point: a brave, boisterous young man.

For his part, Lucio is inescapably drawn by the feminine Genevora, a passive young woman who flees from danger in the middle of the street brawl in 4.3, and who is submissive to her brother and her suitor Lamoral (4.1 and 4.4). As a lady, she would have been expected to master all the domestic skills to which Posthumia has been applying herself all her life. They both share the same upbringing and social values. When Lucio feels an unexpected sexual arousal (4.4.12–14), he is responding to Genevora's external female attributes – her dress, her make-up, her smell, her voice – which are the kind of features that he has been trained to care about. In a way, just like his sister, he is falling in love narcissistically with an image of his former self, the person he would have preferred to remain: a demure young woman. Within the society of the play, the two heterosexual marriages are entirely acceptable, though I think there is more to them than meets the eye.

However, Jonathan Dollimore, who regarded *Love's Cure* as perhaps 'the most interesting theatrical containment of the transvestite challenge',[171] still finds this resolution unforgivably conservative and disappointing. In his opinion, it 'produces transgression precisely in order to contain it, and in the most insidiously ideological way [...] desire itself is transformed, not coerced, back from the perverse to the natural'.[172] By contrast, and unlike Dollimore, Clark problematises this perceived conservatism by vindicating the importance of the female intervention in the final scene to prevent a predictable bloodbath. She finds that the play ultimately 'does provide a critique of an influential concept of masculinity and a validation of the contribution of womanliness to the social order'.[173] Gordon McMullan also resists Dollimore's interpretation by attempting to distinguish between the two dramatists' shares. As he claims, 'it is Massinger, not Fletcher, who provides the words both for Clara's rejection of her erstwhile masculinity [...] and for Lucio's discovery of his "natural" sexual preferences [...] Fletcher's hand is present in [...] the scenes in which the gender inversion is presented', including 1.2 and 2.2.[174] In McMullan's opinion, this demonstrates that Fletcher is the progressive agent in the play, while Massinger's job was to contain the forces of subversion:

> Fletcher was fascinated by the setting-up of unlikely and transgressive political situations and effectively uninterested in the necessary process of resolving them, an obligation of writing for the Jacobean stage. *Love's Cure* may, as Dollimore suggests, ultimately offer a conservative resolution to the question of natural gender; John Fletcher, however, as coauthor cannot be held responsible for the resolution provided.[175]

This is a persuasive argument that vindicates the politically transgressive ideology that Fletcher's plays otherwise endorse. As he points out, we can assume that a Jacobean play might not have been allowed to end differently. Even in a comedy, a radical endorsement of transgenderism as an admissible possibility might not have been tolerated by the censoring authorities, or even perhaps the audiences. In fact, we can take the argument a step further by questioning again the suddenness of the ending: does the abrupt resolution, at the very brink of tragedy, actually undermine the conservativism that it upholds by its unlikely happy ending? If we read it in this way, the ending would be a mere formality that must be dealt with in a few lines, while the play as a whole, including Massinger's contribution, has been setting up an unresolvable problem. Thus *Love's Cure* as a whole would be doing what McMullan ascribes only to Fletcher: challenging the conservative values that it must reinforce publicly by featuring an ending that draws attention to its own implausibility.

PERFORMANCE

When in 2011 Gregory Doran was preparing his reimagined version of Fletcher and Shakespeare's lost *Cardenio* for the Royal Shakespeare Company, he came across a Renaissance stage version of the same story that had been written in Spain by Guillén de Castro. Unlike its English counterpart, Castro's *Don Quijote de la Mancha* is extant, and may have been the earliest stage adaptation of the Cervantian original, composed within a year of the publication of the First Part of the novel.[176] Doran became interested in the work of this obscure Valencian playwright who 'had written the play that inspired Corneille's *Le Cid*', and found a further connection between his work and English drama: 'Another of his works, *Fuerza de la Costumbre* [*sic*], tells the story of a young girl, who is brought up from birth as a boy, and of a boy who is brought up from birth as a girl. John Fletcher adapted it into an extraordinary play called *Love's Cure*.'[177] Reviewing the 2001 production of the play at King's College London, Lucy Munro found it to 'reveal itself in performance as witty, immediate and eminently stageable'.[178] The actors in the 2012 project that I led could not understand why this play has not been more popular in the theatre. If the play is so theatrically engaging, it is intriguing that it has not been produced professionally since 1642.

From a theatrical point of view, the F text was conceptualised for a playing space with two doors, probably a central opening or discovery space, and an above gallery. The two doors are used simultaneously, for example at the beginning of scene 3.3, whose opening stage direction prescribes '*Enter* VITELLI *and* [*the*] ALGUAZIR *at several doors*'. The previous scene ends with Malroda and Piorato's exit into her private apartment, which, assuming continuous action between 3.2 and 3.3, seems to indicate that they were meant to do so through the central opening, as the doors need to be clear for Vitelli and the Alguazir to enter. Another example of a simultaneous entrance at the two doors is that of the two combating factions in the final scene: '*Enter severally* ÁLVAREZ *and* LUCIO, VITELLI *and* LAMORAL.' The above gallery is used at two points in the play: Clara's overhearing of Vitelli's dealings with Malroda (4.2), and the appearance of the three women in the final scene.

The necessary blocking of the three groups of characters in 4.3 might suggest that the play was written for a stage with two pillars, such as the ones present in the second Globe.[179] The group of false watchmen hide somewhere on stage, while Álvarez, Lucio, and Bobadilla appear. They have to hide as well when Lamoral and Anastro make their entrance with Genevora, accompanied by two pages. The easiest way to do this would be to have the watchmen and Álvarez's faction standing apart at opposite sides of the stage, while Vitelli's friends appear – probably through the central opening, as the two sides of the stage are already busy – and take the centre. In the fiction of the play the scene happens in total darkness – as signified by the torches that the pages carry and as described in the dialogue – so the first two groups on stage could just be standing at some distance concealed by the assumed darkness. The scene is easier to play with two pillars on stage that can be used as hiding places. In any case, the company would have been able to transfer *Love's Cure* to the indoor Blackfriars playhouse in the winter, and perhaps the 'correction house hard by' with which Vitelli threatens Malroda in 3.3.93 was meant to be a reference to Bridewell, where prostitutes were socially re-educated, and which immediately adjoined the former monastic precinct. The line is in a section rewritten by Massinger, so perhaps the revival referred to in the added Prologue was envisaged for the indoor space.

In either playhouse, *Love's Cure* would have had four musical intervals between the acts, as indicated by some of the transitions: for example, the characters who left the stage at the end of act IV reappear at the beginning of scene 5.1.[180] As for the personnel required, the minimum number of actors needed to perform the play as it is written is 23: every character who has appeared during the play is present from line 5.3.230. That is, apart from the 19 speaking characters, the play requires at least four supernumeraries to perform the non-speaking Stefano and at least two other servants in 1.2, two pages with lights in 4.1 and 4.3, at least two watches in 4.3, and a minimum of two attendants and two guards in 5.3. There is no exit for the Herald after his last line in 5.3, but it is plausible that he might leave the stage and play one of the members of Pacheco's gang. Stefano might also plausibly be played by one of these.

We do not know how often the play was revived after 1615, although it was still technically in the repertory of the company according to the 1641 list. R. C. Bald suggested that the SR entry that Humphrey Moseley paid for the publication of F is also a sign of 'the successful conclusion a little earlier of an agreement with the King's Men, by which Moseley acquired rights in a large number of their plays'.[181] Moseley assumed that the agreement included the rights to performance. In a letter to Sir Henry Herbert, Master of the Revels, dated 30 August 1660, after the Restoration, he claims ownership of the rights to stage the plays that he had published: 'neither did I ever consent directly or indirectly, that he [the manager of the Cockpit playhouse, the Phoenix in Drury Lane] or any others should act any plays that do belong to me'.[182]

It is perhaps surprising, however, that this was not one of the popular plays from the 'Beaumont and Fletcher' canon that was revived in the Restoration, given the favourable taste for cross-dressing in the theatre after 1660. Perhaps there was not enough cross-dressing, or it was not particularly linked to disguise and confusion. Gerard Langbaine, who recorded the revival of these plays in his *Dramatic Poets*, does not report any productions,[183] though his 1711 edition includes the earliest image of a scene from the play, printed as its frontispiece (see figure 5). The engraving depicts the brawl in 1.3 (Álvarez and Sayavedra against Vitelli and Clara). The main street, receding into a vanishing point in the centre, is intersected by several perpendicular side streets that replicate the wings of a proscenium arch stage. This sense is strengthened by the framing of the image with an arch decorated with a classical acanthus leaf, with a piece of cloth draped over the corner suggesting a theatrical curtain. Apart from the realistic set, the characters are wearing early eighteenth-century costumes, which is consistent with the frontispieces of Nicholas Rowe's contemporary edition of Shakespeare (1709). The theatrical presentation of the scene, however, does not necessarily imply that it was taken from an actual performance.

Colman also included an image from the play as its frontispiece, in this case the moment at which Clara attempts to strangle Bobadilla with his own chain of office (2.2.122; see figure 6). The costumes are also contemporary with the edition (1778), and present a room in the house with, presumably, Álvarez's portrait hanging over the mantelpiece, and weapons arranged about the walls, with two pistols on a side table and the steward's staff of office broken on the floor after he has been hit on the head with it. It is also unlikely that the image replicates any actual performance.

In 1793 a short 'afterpiece' in two acts inspired by *Love's Cure* was printed as *The Female Duellist* in London as a small octavo.[184] The author was the comic actor and singer Richard Suett (baptised in 1755–d. 1805), who acknowledged his source in the prefatory

Love's Cure

Vol. 5. n. 2.681

Figure 5 Frontispiece of Gerard Langbaine's edition (London, 1711), personal copy

Figure 6 Frontispiece of George Colman's edition (London, 1778), personal copy

'Advertisement'. According to the title page, the play had been acted by the King's Company at the King's Theatre on Haymarket. It is the only vestige of *Love's Cure* to have been performed on a professional stage in almost four centuries, although, as the 'Advertisement' states, it was only loosely based on it. It retains some names and dramatic situations, but is otherwise a distinctly different work.

The first recorded production since the seventeenth century was staged in the Greenwood Theatre at King's College London on 22–24 March 2001. It was directed by Martha Crossley, who edited the text and played the role of Malroda, while Michael Caines composed the music and played Vitelli. Lucy Munro reviewed 'this stylish production' as 'a powerful reminder of the dramatic flair of some of Shakespeare's more underrated contemporaries'.[185] She was particularly impressed with Thea Gardner's and Rob Jessel's turn as Clara and Lucio, and described Crossley's performance as Malroda as 'memorable'. The text was cut 'for reasons of length and casting', doing away with the subplot involving Lazarillo and the three craftsmen, but retaining the Alguazir. In the absence of the hungry knave, James Healy's Bobadilla was the 'new comic centre' of the play, 'who was given a show-stopping and splendidly silly original song, "Beaumont and Fletcher," immediately before the interval'. The set was particularly impressive, 'with the stage being dominated by a huge needle, emblematic of both phallic power and the cultural constraints placed on women's behaviour by a patriarchal society'.[186]

In 2012, as part of the research for this edition, a team of professional and amateur actors under the direction of Robert F. Ball worked on the play for ten weeks, and then offered two script-in-hand performances at the Shakespeare Institute in Stratford-upon-Avon and at the University of Birmingham on 7 July.[187] The production was staged using 'original practices':[188] full Renaissance costume, period music, the use of a *frons scaenae* with a bare stage platform and no extra scenery, and an all-male cast that included nineteen actors, the youngest of whom was 19 and played Malroda. The two performances lacked the flow of a fully memorised production, but was enthusiastically received.[189]

A year later, on 12 December 2013, the students of the British American Drama Academy presented their production of the play at the Oval House theatre in London under the direction of Graham Watts, with an all-female cast of thirteen. The fixed set was dominated by a large central carpet painted with a geometric pattern, surrounded by four trellised doorways and two benches upstage. The costumes were perhaps more Caroline than Jacobean, but aimed at being consistent with the period in which the play is set. The pace of the show was vigorous, and there were some outstanding individual performances among the very young actors involved. Megan Hrabak was a nuanced Vitelli who was troubled by his inability to impose his will on the women who surrounded him, particularly with regard to Madison Gordon's powerful Clara, who perfectly captured the inner conflict of the character when commanded to switch her gender identity. Rachel Eskenazi-Gold, who also composed the music, gave two superbly differentiated performances as Anastro with an American accent, and as a Cockney Lazarillo, who revealed himself to be the comic heart of the play. Rosie Koocher's Bobadilla was appropriately coarse. The subplot was retained with some clever doubling – Anastro with Lazarillo, Eugenia with Mendoza, Sayavedra with Metaldi, and Piorato with Pacheco – and the Asistente's lines were reassigned to Sayavedra. The audience was overwhelmingly appreciative.

   The first professional revival of the play since the closing of the theatres in 1642 remains to be programmed.

Figure 7 Final scene, British American Drama Academy, December 2013, production photograph © Simon Annand

NOTES

1 All relevant dates for Spanish historical figures are from the *DB~e*. For English persons, dates have been checked with the *ODNB* and other sources, as detailed. For Anastro, see Jardine.

2 Bentley, 364.

3 Erickson, 102.

4 *Wit at Several Weapons* (*c.* 1613; Thomas Middleton and William Rowley) and *The Nice Valour, or The Passionate Madman* (*c.* 1622; Middleton). *The Laws of Candy* (*c.* 1620) has been attributed to Massinger and Ford, but there seem to be traces of Fletcher's hand (see Wiggins, *Catalogue*, 1932). All dates for the premieres of English plays are from Wiggins, *Catalogue*: dates are given if they are known precisely, or are preceded by *c.* to indicate that they are Wiggins's 'best guess' (for a more detailed time bracket, see the individual *Catalogue* entry). Citations to individual entries are given by their Wiggins number in the *Catalogue* sequence.

5 As Philip J. Finkelpearl relates, 'Beaumont suffered a seriously debilitating stroke' in the year of his marriage, 1613. The poet Thomas Pestell 'mentions that Beaumont wrote his last poem, the elegy to Lady Penelope Clifton (*d.* 1613) after he suffered the stroke'. The poem, 'A Funeral Elegy on the Death of Penelope Clifton', must have been written shortly after her death on 26 October 1613. After that date, he does not seem to have written anything else. See Finkelpearl, 'Beaumont, Francis'. The date of Lady Clifton's death is recorded on the funeral monument erected by her husband, Sir Gervase Clifton (1587–1666), in St Mary's Church, Clifton, Nottinghamshire.

6 Wiggins, 'Four', 48.

7 Ibid.

8 Ibid., 49.

9 Astington, 196.

10 Ibid., 220.

11 Ibid., 222. The composition of the Gang of Four does seem to vary in some plays, however, and Cowley, Tooley, Underwood, and Gough may have taken other roles, completing the four with hired men. In *LC*, for example, the parts of Mendoza and Metaldi would have been too small to employ two master actors such as Underwood and Tooley; see below.

12 See Baum. In Middleton's *Chaste Maid*, for instance, the First Puritan says, 'Sure that was Judas then with the red beard' (3.2.45).

13 Astington, 197, revised by Wiggins, private correspondence.

14 Wiggins, 'Four', 49. By contrast, Latrocinio and the Ensign are not described as having red hair, and might have been played by other members of the group.

15 Astington, 198, revised by Wiggins, private correspondence.

16 See Edmond.

17 Astington, 195.

18 Ibid., 205.

19 Ibid., 213.

20 Ibid., 214.

21 Ibid., 191.
22 For some details about the apprenticeships of Haynes, Birch, Bedell, and Crosse, see Kathman.
23 I am very grateful to Wiggins, Sénéchal, and Smith for sharing their casting ideas for the first performance of the play, emerging from their research project on the King's Men.
24 *Annals*, sig. 4L6ᵛ. The arrival of the 1621–22 Russian legation was reported at Whitehall on 5 October 1621 (*SPD* 14/123, 11), and Sir John Finet recorded its departure on or shortly after 13 June 1622; see Finet, sig. H4ʳ. All dates are in OS unless otherwise stated.
25 Certainly *Prophetess*, *SeaV*, and *SpCur.*, and probably *Double* as well.
26 *Mill*, *The Devil of Dowgate* (lost), and *Progress*, all licensed that year.
27 As Martin Wiggins states, '[Edmond] Malone found eleven licences for Fletcher plays [...] and transcribed ten [...] There was only one other Fletcher play licensed during the years 1622–5 [...] The strongest candidate for the eleventh "Fletcher" licence is *The Nice Valour* (2023), which was part of the received Fletcher canon in Malone's time, while the "missing" Fletcher play was probably *A Very Woman* (2043), which was not.' Wiggins, *Catalogue*, 1799, *Bush*.
28 *Herbert*, 23.
29 GWW, 7.
30 Finet records that the Russian legation arrived on 5 November 1617 (Finet, sig. D3v), and Piero Contarini, the Venetian ambassador, reported that they left in June 1618 (*Cal. Ven.*, 15, 570).
31 His coronation took place on 21 July the same year; see *Embassy*, 182.
32 Ibid., xxxi and 202. His arrival was recorded by John Chamberlain in a letter dated in London on 27 October 1613: 'Yesterday here arrived an ambassador from the newly elected emperor of Muscovy'; Chamberlain, I, 482. Within two days, he was taken to see the Lord Mayor's show, *The Triumphs of Truth*, scripted by Thomas Middleton. Ziuzin reported the spectacle to his master upon his return in his ambassadorial book; see the Oxford Middleton, 977.
33 *Annals*, sig. 4L1ʳ.
34 See *Cold Year*; and Wiggins, *Catalogue*, 1765.
35 See Bellany.
36 *Annals*, sig. 4L1ᵛ.
37 For further discussion, see Lindley. Middleton and Rowley referred to the matrons' examination in *The Changeling* (1622) when Beatrice-Joanna is trying to find out whether Diaphanta is a virgin; the maid exclaims: 'She will not search me, will she, / Like the forewoman of a female jury?' (4.1.102–3). By then the issue was perhaps less controversial, as the Somersets had been released in January 1622. See Annabel Patterson's introduction to *Chang.* in the Oxford Middleton.
38 As Markku Peltonen has summarised, 'These three aspects – a private or secret fight, caused by an insult and organised by a challenge in order to prove one's sense of honour rather than overcome one's opponent – gave the duel of honour its quintessential characteristics.' See Peltonen, 2.
39 Ibid., 82.
40 See *Proclamation, duels*.

41 See *Proclamation, challenges*.

42 Peltonen, 89.

43 See *Private combats*.

44 According to Baldwin Maxwell, 'King James, before coming to England, had in 1600 established a law in Scotland making it murder to kill one in a duel *held without royal sanction*'; Maxwell, 86, my italics. This legislation did not affect England, but it does reveal that King James had reserved the right to allow 'granted duels', at least in his other realm.

45 See *Proclamation, dags*.

46 Redworth, 15.

47 Ibid., 16.

48 Ibid., 17.

49 *SPD* 14/90, 122. John Chamberlain's correspondence records the gossip as early as 15 March 1617 in a letter to Sir Dudley Carleton, in which he claimed that the Spanish match was 'more than half made'; Chamberlain, II, 64.

50 *Embassy*, 6. He did not visit London, however, as it was Sir Raphe Winwood who travelled to the Hague to deliver the Order to Maurice; see Sir Raphe Winwood to James I, *SPF*, 84/69, ff. 7–10. In 1613 Adam Islip printed a translation of Jan Janszn Orlerls's hagiographic account of Nassau's heroic deeds under the title *The Triumphs of Nassau*, probably capitalising on his recent topicality (see Orlers).

51 Note that the play must have been titled *The Night-Walkers*, as its 1639 SR entry records, although it was printed as *The Night-Walker*, in the singular, by confusion with its alternative 1640 printed title *The Little Thief*, in the singular; the play does have, however, a number of 'night-walkers', and not just one.

52 For Fletcher, see the introduction to *King* in Bliss; for Massinger, see the introduction to *RA* in White.

53 Seven recognised collaborations, plus *Hater* (Children of Paul's, *c.* 1606), which is often attributed to Beaumont, but which bears traces of Fletcher's hand; see Wiggins, *Catalogue*, 1522.

54 See Finkelpearl, 'Beaumont, Francis'.

55 Astington, 197.

56 Quire 5S comprises six leaves rather than the usual four in most of the volume (except L2 and 7D which are in twos, and 6L, which is also in sixes). The compositors clearly calculated that the remainder of the play would take up ten pages, exceeding the eight available in a quire of four leaves. The final leaf would contain the space-filling Prologue on the recto in remarkably large type, and a blank page on the verso. The catchphrase at the bottom of sig. 5S6ʳ ('Queene of *Corinth.*') was originally placed there to link what was going to be the last play in F's section 5 to the first play in section 6 (*Corinth*); a last-minute readjustment of the contents of the volume must have required the moving of *Fortune* over from section 8. The catchphrase at the end of that play announces *4Plays*, which is the final work in section 8, and therefore in F. See Bald.

57 GWW, 3.

58 Carlell, sig. N3ᵛ.

59 Fleay, *Chronicle*, 180. Fleay had changed his mind about this from 1874, even considering William Rowley and Thomas Middleton as

collaborators in the play: see Fleay, 'Tests', 64; Fleay, *Manual*, 152; and Fleay, 'Chronology', 14. Among the various misjudged theories on the play's authorship, one of the strangest must be that formulated by H. D. Sykes, who found absolutely no trace of Fletcher or Beaumont, and assigned the authorship to Massinger, Webster, and Dekker without providing any evidence; see Sykes, 224. In an even more complicated theory, E. H. C. Oliphant considered *LC* 'as originally written by Beaumont for the Paul's boys not later than 1605, revised by Jonson and another in 1622 for the Lady Elizabeth's, and revised once again, this time by Massinger, when it came into the hands of the King's men, probably about the same time as *Love's Pilgrimage* and others'; see Oliphant, 415.

60 Hoy, 'Shares I', 129.

61 Ibid., 130.

62 Ibid.

63 Hoy, 'Shares III', 85.

64 For example, Hoy detected Beaumont's hand in about a third of *Bush* and *T&T*, when both plays conclusively post-date his retirement. See Hoy, 'Shares III', 85. Martin Wiggins has proposed Field as the most likely candidate to have written the shares that Hoy assigned to Beaumont; see Wiggins, *Catalogue*, entries for *Bush*, *Rollo*, and *T&T*, for example. Darren Freebury-Jones has stylometrically supported this theory; private correspondence.

65 Hoy, 'Shares VI', 49.

66 This table is adapted from GWW, 4.

67 Wiggins, *Catalogue*, 2077, based on Hoy's attributions.

68 A list of 60 plays in the company's repertory on 7 August 1641 and the Stationers' Register entry of 4 September 1646; see below, 30–2.

69 See *Herbert*, 20–1. For example, *LP* – which was originally performed around 1616 and shares with *LC* the Spanish setting, a plot involving a brother and a sister, and what Hoy took to be Beaumontisms – was relicensed on 16 September 1635 (*Herbert*, 36). The company might have just added the revised title to the licence on the original prompt book, which they would have kept as proof that the play was covered by the 1615 licence. Alternatively, it could have been the other way around, and *LC* might be the play's revised title: apart from Lyly's *Love's Metamorphosis* (*c.* 1590) and Fletcher's *LP*, a few other plays with '*Love's*' in their title do date from the early 1630s: *Love's Cruelty* (Shirley, November 1631), *Love's Sacrifice* (Ford, *c.* 1632), and *Love's Mistress* (Heywood, November 1634). Maybe Massinger was following this particular fashion, but in that case it is difficult to explain why *The Martial Maid* was the title by which the play was known by 1641, and the title that the company sought to protect from pirated printings at that point.

70 In *Bush*, he was responsible for the whole of the first act and the first 65 lines of the final scene, and in *Corinth* he contributed the first and fifth acts. See Hoy, 'Shares III', 87; and Hoy, 'Shares IV', 98.

71 Stiefel, 'Nachahmung' 2. R. Warwick Bond arrived at the same conclusion independently in 1905–06; see Bond, 263. Bond thought that he

was the first to make this discovery, but in 1908 a doctoral student informed him that Stiefel had anticipated it in his essay a decade before.

72 Note that the Spanish Golden Age term *comedia* is a false friend in English: it means 'play', and not 'comedy': tragedies and historical plays were also *comedias*, and were acted by *comediantes* ('players').

73 In 1.2.51; 1.3.21, 174, and 180; in 2.2.99 and 145; in 5.1.80; and in 5.3.93 and 265 (the final speech of the play).

74 Loftis, 243.

75 The first one was identified by Emil Koeppel; see Koeppel, 100. The other two were discovered and analysed by Stiefel in 'Nachahmung' 1.

76 For more details of his life, see Wilson, *Guillén*, 13–15, and Oleza, I, ix–xviii, as well as García Lorenzo.

77 The first part dates from '1612?–18 (probably 1612–15)' and the second from '1610–15'; see Bruerton, 127–8. Castro's paternal family claimed to be descended from Rodrígo Díaz de Vivar, the medieval hero known as the *Cid*, which may explain his interest in dramatising his life.

78 Corneille's play is also the basis of Jules Massenet's 1885 opera *Le Cid*.

79 Only five productions are recorded of *Las mocedades del Cid* since the seventeenth century: four at the Teatro Español in Madrid (1922, 1941, 1968, 1990, revived in 1997) and one in the Teatro de Cámara in Barcelona in 1954; see Arata. Apart from a staging of *Los malcasados de Valencia* (*The Ill-Mated Couples of Valencia*) by the Compañía Nacional de Teatro Clásico (Madrid, 1994) and a 2007 student production of *El curioso impertinente* (Brigham Young University, Provo, Utah, 2007), none of the other plays by Castro seems to have ever been revived, apart from two productions of *La fuerza* in the United States of America: in an English-language version as *The Force of Habit*, written and directed by Kathleen Jeffs (Magnuson Theatre of Gonzaga University, Spokane, Washington, February–March 2013); and in the original language, directed by Freddy Mancilla for Repertorio Español (New York City, August–September 2013).

80 *La fuerza de la costumbre* is the ninth play in Castro, *Segunda parte*, a large quarto of 562 pages (281 leaves), and occupies signatures 2C1^r to 2E6^v. The volume was ecclesiastically approved for publication by Fray Lamberto Novella on 20 December 1624, NS, and licensed to be printed by Martín de Funes, Vicar General of the diocese of Valencia, on 7 February 1625, NS. The volume might have taken at least two months to be ready for sale. For example, the First Part of *Don Quixote* was licensed in the Kingdom of Castile on 26 September 1604, but the printing was not completed until the last weeks of December, already bearing the date of 1605 on the title page; see Cervantes, *Quijote*, 1, 6, and Rico, 61.

81 Bruerton, 123.

82 The play probably premiered in the first Casa de Comedias de la Olivera, built in 1584 and completely refurbished in 1618. See Mérimée, 27; and Lamarca, 19.

83 See Pérez Díez, 'Quills'.

84 Ibid., 96.

85 In spite of its early reception, there are no records of any production of the play given in Spain since 1625, and it has only been revived twice in the USA; see above, n. 79.

86 See Bravo-Villasante; McKendrick; and Thacker.

87 See Martínez. There is a brief list of *comedias* with male cross-dressers in Bravo-Villasante, 76.

88 Thacker, 23.

89 For example, Lope de Vega's *El acero de Madrid* (*The Steel of Madrid*) includes a scene towards the end in which the *gracioso*, or clown, Beltrán, wears a feminine *manto* ('shawl') while the lady Belisa appears wearing '*capa, espada, sombrero, y vaquero*' ('cloak, rapier, hat, and tunic'); see *El acero de Madrid* in Lope XI, sig. G1^v.

90 For a comparison between the two theatrical traditions with respect to this theme, see Heise.

91 See, for example, Schevill, 616; and Fitzmaurice-Kelly, 23.

92 Fletcher's Latin can be sampled in the short prefatory poem that he contributed to Mabbe's translation of *Guzmán de Alfarache*; see Mabbe, *Rogue*, sig. A3^v. He used French translations and French original sources in many of his plays as well. See Wilson, 'Spanish'.

93 See Chelli, 42–3.

94 *LP* (*c.* 1616) based on *Las dos doncellas*; *The Chances* (*c.* 1617) on *La señora Cornelia*; *Corinth* (*c.* 1617) on *La fuerza de la sangre*; *RWHW* (1624) on *El casamiento engañoso*; and, posthumously, *FMI* (1626) on *La ilustre fregona*. Mabbe included the first three of these *novelas* in his 1640 translation, and may have brought them to Fletcher's attention; see Mabbe, *Exemplary*.

95 See Fletcher's prefatory poem to Mabbe's translation of *Guzmán de Alfarche*: I. F. [i.e. John Fletcher], 'To the exact Translator of the famous *History of infamous* GUZMAN', in Mabbe, *Rogue*, sigs A3^v–A4^r.

96 See Castro, *Habit*. Machit's text is the first printing of the play since the 1920s, and only the third since 1625. Before 2019 *La fuerza de la costumbre* had only ever been printed twice: in Mesonero Romanos, XLIII, 347–66, and in Juliá Martínez, III, 39–76.

97 Students at Spanish and Portuguese universities used to wear ecclesiastical robes in the period: a long dark *sotana* (cassock), a *manteo* (a dark cloak), and a *bonete* (academic bonnet).

98 The translations of the passages from *La fuerza* are mine and are meant to be as literal as possible to draw a useful parallel with the text of *LC*. Jeffs's excellent translation, based on her performance text for the 2013 production at Gonzaga University, is less literal for the sake of clarity.

99 For a table of correspondences between characters, see Stiefel, 'Nachahmung' 2, 288.

100 For more information on the Dutch Republic and the Spanish–Dutch wars, see, for example, Grattan; Helmers and Janssen; Israel; Motley, *United Netherlands*; and Motley, *Dutch Republic*.

101 Grimeston, sig. O2^v.

102 See Simoni, 98–103.

103 See Soyer, 7.

104 According to Francisco Rico, it might have been printed in late 1552, though it is known that there was an edition in 1553; the oldest extant printings, however, are from 1554. See *Lazarillo*, X.

105 Rowland, sig. E2^r.

106 Ibid., sig. E3ᵛ–E4ʳ.
107 The Lazarillo in *LC* is the most faithful stage version of the character in English drama. The first English stage Lazarillo was a Castilian braggart in Dekker's *Blurt* (a play referred to in 3.1.3 of *LC*), although the hunger theme does not apply to him, but to Blurt's hungry serving boy Pilcher (*LC* 2.1.51). In Beaumont and Fletcher's *Hater* (*c.* 1606), Lazarillo/ello is a gourmet courtier who spends the play chasing a delicacy, the head of an umbrana. The two post-1615 Lazarillos are also only loosely related to the anonymous novel: the Lazarillo/ello in William Rowley's *All's Lost by Lust* (*c.* 1619) is a scheming sycophantic minion, and in Dekker's *Match Me in London* (*c.* 1621) Lazarillo is a mercer's apprentice.
108 *Primera parte*, Madrid, 1599; *Segunda parte*, Lisbon, 1604.
109 See *Guzmán*, 50, I.i.2; all subsequent references are to the page, part, book, and chapter where each episode is narrated.
110 Ibid., 34, I.i.1.41 n., and 1172–3.
111 Ibid., 36, I.i.1.
112 As Leonid Livak summarises, 'English, German, French, Polish, and eastern Slavic popular cultures designate red hair and freckles as peculiar to Judas and "the Jews"'; Livak, 90.
113 *Guzmán*, 34, I.i.1.42 n.
114 Guzmán gets suspicious when an *alguacil* visits the inn where he is lodging to question the patrons; *Guzmán*, 233–4, I.ii.8.
115 Ibid., 727–9, II.iii.7 and 9.
116 Ibid., II.ii.4.
117 See I. F. [i.e. John Fletcher], 'To the exact Translator', in Mabbe, *Rogue*, sigs A3ᵛ–A4ʳ; see above.
118 Mariko Ichikawa has calculated that an actor would have taken between two and four pentameter lines to move from the *frons scaenae* to the front of the stage, and has observed that scripts from the period frequently have that delay written into them, with the length of the delay depending on the complexity of the move required; see Ichikawa, 43; and also Gurr and Ichikawa, 72–95 and 114–17.
119 This seems a remarkably early cue to prepare the props, since the torches would not have needed to be lit so long before being carried on stage. This kind of advance instruction for backstage preparation is not, however, uncommon or unprecedented: for example, in the extant prompt book of Massinger's *BAYL*, a marginal indication at 4.1.67 directs the actor playing Antiochus to place himself under the stage 45 lines before he speaks (see *BAYL* n.).
120 1.2.110, 1.3.84, 3.4.118, 5.3.189 and 253.
121 See Palfrey and Stern, 31.
122 Hoy, 'Shares VI', 55–6; see also 5.3.140 n.
123 The document survives in the Lord Chamberlain's Warrant Books in the National Archives, and was transcribed in 'Plays of the King's Men in 1641', ed. E. K. Chambers, in *Collections*, 364–9.
124 Bald, 5.
125 Ibid., 9. The order of the plays in F, however, is entirely different. Bald also speculated that Moseley might have been planning the publication of F from much earlier than 1646, suggesting that the project could have been in the making since at least 1643; see Bald, 5.

126 Wiggins, *Power*, 93. Many of the members of the King's Men fled to join the royalist forces in Oxford in 1642–43; see Gurr, *Company*, 203.

127 F, sig. A4^v.

128 Bald, 10.

129 These were *FalseO*, *The Nice Valour*, *Wit at Several Weapons*, *FMI*, Beaumont's *Masque of the Gentlemen of Gray's Inn and the Inner Temple*, and *4Pl*.

130 They were John Lowin, Richard Robinson, Eliard Swanston, Hugh Clark, Stephen Hammerton, Joseph Taylor, Robert Benfield, Thomas Pollard, William Allen, and Theophilus Bird; see F, sigs A2^{r-v}.

131 Smith.

132 Astington, 219.

133 See Thomas, 134.

134 Finkelpearl, *Politics*, 4. See also Thomas.

135 See McMullan, 260.

136 Based on Bald, corrected by Gerritsen; Hammersmith, 'Section 5'; Hammersmith, 'Sections 7 and 8A–C'; Sharp; and Turner.

137 Gerritsen, 248.

138 On the Epilogue and Prologue, see 15–16.

139 Williams detected another pagination mistake in one of the copies at the University of Texas, an error of verso for recto on 5Q4^r, giving the page number 128 for 127.

140 For a detailed table of press variants and a compositorial analysis, see Appendices 1 and 2, 228–30.

141 Battle, 8.

142 I have detected only one change in Darley: in the royal proclamation read out by the Herald, Weber's 'St. Jago' (the form in F) was expanded to 'Saint Jago' in Darley (5.3.29).

143 See Appendix 3, 231–4.

144 There was no point in including Battle's text, though, as it was simply a photocopied facsimile of F, with the folio pagination bizarrely made to coincide with that of the rest of the thesis.

145 For instance, Jonathan Dollimore cites her upcoming edition (in 1986) as providing much-needed access to a play he held in high esteem; see Dollimore, 78.

146 F2, sig. ^{2}X3r; see figure 4, 35.

147 Griffiths, 42.

148 The final scene in Fletcher's *LP*, a play written about a year after *LC*, also features the interruption of a duel by the intervention of three women. Note that in the final scene of Webster's *Law Case* (*c.* 1618) the situation is analogous, but the fight is not a duel: the initial SD specifies that it is a public joust: '*The lists [are] set up.*' (5.6.0 SD).

149 The sudden comic ending was received with laughs in the 2012 and 2013 productions.

150 Classic works on cross-dressing and the performance of gender include Berggren, Cressy, Garber, Howard, Levine, Lucas, Orgel, Rackin, Shapiro, and Shepherd.

151 Shapiro, 15–16.

152 As Shapiro suggests, 'theatergoers probably saw cross-dressed *Hic Mulier* women at playhouses, especially at the more expensive and fashionable so-called private theatres'; Shapiro, 23.

153 John Creaser, ed., *Bart. Fair* 5.5.77-9 n.
154 Shapiro, 21. The titles of the pamphlets were not original, but topical: a decade earlier, in Field's *Amends*, Seldom calls Moll 'Mistress *hic* and *haec*' (2.1, 23).
155 O'Malley, 252.
156 This count includes the partially extant *Cardenio* by Fletcher and Shakespeare.
157 See Berek; Clark, '*Hic Mulier*'; Clark, *Plays*; Dollimore; Duncan; and Low.
158 Massinger only included one cross-dresser in *Bashful* (1636). In *Milan* there is a woman in disguise, but she is not specifically cross-dressed.
159 Griffiths, 32.
160 Ibid., 49.
161 Ibid., 46.
162 Chess, *MTF*, 171.
163 Ibid., 172. For new directions in studies of transsexuality in English Renaissance literature, see Chess et al., *Special Issue*.
164 Dollimore, 74.
165 Clark, 71.
166 Duncan, 398.
167 Griffiths, 49.
168 Robinson, 212.
169 Ibid., 213.
170 Ibid., 215.
171 Dollimore, 72.
172 Ibid., 73.
173 Clark, 71.
174 McMullan, 152-3.
175 Ibid., 153.
176 Courtney Bruerton dated it to '1605-08 (probably 1605-06)'; see Bruerton, 116.
177 Doran, 19.
178 Munro, 76.
179 See Nelsen, 328; and Dustagheer, 24.
180 Intervals between acts were needed in indoor venues 'to allow the candelabra to be lowered and the wicks of the candles to be trimmed'; see Dutton, 300. From 1608, when the King's Men gained the use of the Blackfriars playhouse for their winter season, commercial plays in their repertory were written following a five-act structure to include these four intervals, as the plays needed to be transferable between their indoor and outdoor venues.
181 Bald, 4.
182 *Herbert*, 90.
183 Langbaine, *Poets*, sig. O2^r.
184 See Suett.
185 Munro, 75.
186 Ibid., 76.
187 Cast: Charles Morton (Lamoral), Jason Burg (Anastro), José A. Pérez Díez (Vitelli), John Curtis (Bobadilla), Hadley Brown (Lucio), James Parsons (Eugenia), Richard Ball (Stefano, Metaldi), Peter Malin

(Álvarez), Hefin Robinson (Clara), David Southeard (Sayavedra), Adrian McCarthy (Pacheco), Ryan Moir (Lazarillo), Robert Mrozek (Mendoza, Herald), Mark Spriggs (Alguazir), Callum Ashton (Malroda), Richard Nunn (Piorato), Liam Edwards (Genevora), Philip Hickson (Asistente), and Will Cotterill (Guard). Music arranged by Jennifer Moss Waghorn. Directed by Robert F. Ball. Costume design: Red Smucker-Green. Stage manager: Helen Osborne. Set design: Colin Judges. Set artwork: J. Sandelewski.

188 See Carson and Karim-Cooper.
189 For more information on the project, see Pérez Díez, 'Editing'.

LOVE'S CURE, or
THE MARTIAL MAID

[Characters in the Play

The ASISTENTE	*Governor of Seville*
Don Pedro de VITELLI	*A young gentleman of Seville*
GENEVORA	*His sister*
LAMORAL	*A duellist, friend to Vitelli*
ANASTRO	*A gentleman, friend to Vitelli*

5

Don Fernando de ÁLVAREZ	*A gentleman of Seville*
Doña EUGENIA	*His wife*
CLARA	*Their daughter, brought up as 'Lucio'*
LUCIO	*Their son, brought up as 'Posthumia'*
Don SAYAVEDRA	*A gentleman, friend to Álvarez*
Sancho Spindola BOBADILLA	*Servant and steward to the house of Álvarez*
Stefano	*A servant of the same household*

10

PACHECO Alasto	*A cobbler*
LAZARILLO	*Pacheco's hungry servant*
METALDI	*A smith*
MENDOZA	*A botcher*

15

The ALGUAZIR	*A corrupt constable*
MALRODA	*A courtesan from Madrid, maintained by Vitelli*
PIORATO	*A fencing master, in love with Malroda*

A HERALD

20

Servants, pages, watchmen, and guards]

TITLE (Loves Cure,or the Martial Maid / A COMEDY.)] *F2;* LOVE'S CURE / OR, / The Martial Maid.] *F.*

Characters in the Play] *F did not include a list of characters, so this one has been assembled from scratch. F2 included a list of 'The Persons Represented in the Play' (sig. ²X3ʳ; see figure 4, 35), which conventionally listed the female roles separately at the bottom and included frequently judgmental descriptions (Malroda is merely a 'wanton mistress of Vitelli' and the Alguazir is a 'sharking panderly constable', for example). The F2 lists have sometimes been used in modern editions of Fletcher plays, but they are Restoration documents from a different theatrical environment, and have no authority.*

---

1. *The ASISTENTE*] The *Asistente* (literally, the 'Assistant') was the civil authority directly appointed by the King to govern the city of Seville in his name and to preside over the municipal council, as well as to oversee the administration of justice. The office was commonly known elsewhere in Spain as the *Corregidor* ('vicegerent', as the Alguazir claims to be in 3.1.46). The Asistente of Seville is mentioned in Cervantes's *La española inglesa* (*The English Spanish Lady*), one of his *Novelas ejemplares* (Madrid, 1613), which Fletcher might plausibly have read in the original at the time of the composition of *Love's Cure*; the spelling of the name in F, *Assistente*, coincides with the old-spelling form given in that first edition of the *Novelas.* In F2, the character is described as 'Assistant, *or Governor*' (sig. ²X3ʳ; see figure 4, 35). Fletcher and Massinger used the title again in *SpCur.* (1622), in which the *Assistant* (list of roles, F2) is that '*which we call a Judge*' (sig. R2ᵛ). The correct Spanish modernisation of the name is *Asistente.*

2. *Don Pedro de VITELLI*] The name is the plural of the Italian *vitello*, 'lamb', which contrasts with the tempestuous personality of the character. *Pedro* recalls the name of the father figure in *La fuerza*, Don Pedro de Moncada, and derives from the Latin *petra*, 'stone', which may suggest firmness. Pedro is also the name of Vitelli's uncle in the play (see 1.1.12). Vitelli is a leading character in Massinger's *Renegado.* The inspiration for the name was probably 'Chiappino' Vitelli, Marquis of Cetona (1519–75), an Italian *condotiero* in the employ of Philip II of Spain who would rise to the rank of field marshal of the Spanish forces in the Netherlands, and who collaborated with the Duke of Alba in the capture of Lamoraal, Count of Egmont.

3. *GENEVORA*] In Ariosto's *Orlando furioso*, Canto V, Princess Ginevra is the daughter of the King of Scotland. Sections of that Canto were translated into English by Peter Beverley as *The history of Ariodanto and Jenevra* (London, *c.* 1570; STC 745.5), and a lost English play, *Ariodant and Jenevora*, based on the same story, played in the Merchant Taylors' School in 1582–83 (see Wiggins, *Catalogue*, 737). The name in *LC* is stressed on the second syllable, *Genévora.*

4. *LAMORAL*] Literally, 'the moral'. Lamoraal was the name of the Count of Egmont and Prince of Gavere (1522–68), general and statesman who, in defiance of Philip II, fought for the independence of Flanders from Spain, and whose execution for high treason ignited the long struggle that would eventually lead to the end of Habsburg rule in the Netherlands. 'Lamoral' is the standard anglicised spelling.

5. *ANASTRO*] Literally from the Greek, 'starless', carrying undertones of ill fate. Gaspar de Anastro was the name of a Spanish merchant of Antwerp who was involved in the attempted murder of William, Prince of Orange, in 1582.

6. *Don Fernando de ÁLVAREZ*] The first name, Fernando, is given by Pacheco in its more usual Spanish form (2.1.137), rather than the Italian form given by the Herald in 5.3.12. The surname scans as in Spanish, with the stress on the first syllable. The name is that of the 3rd Duke of Alba, Fernando Álvarez de Toledo y Pimentel (1507–82), who is mentioned in 1.1.114. The ancestral seat of that family is the town of Alba de Tormes in the present-day Spanish province of Salamanca; hence the modernised spelling, rather than the Anglicised *Alva*.

7. *Doña EUGENIA*] From the Greek ευγενία, 'well-born'. A recurrent Spanish name in the English drama of the period, including Fletcher's *LP* and Massinger's *Milan*. Her name and that of her daughter Clara was suggested by that of the Infanta referred to in 1.1: Isabella Clara Eugenia (1566–1633), daughter of Philip II of Spain and half-sister of Philip III, who was sovereign and governor of the Low Countries at the time of the siege of Ostend.

8. *CLARA*] Spanish name meaning 'clear' or 'luminous'. Sayavedra gets carried away with the darkness of her features in 3.4.41–4, perhaps because her complexion has been darkened by military service. Her hair is described as well as being dark. This darkness contrasts with her name. As with her mother, the source for her name was probably the Infanta Isabella Clara Eugenia.

9. *LUCIO*] Spanish derivation of the Latin *lux*, 'light'. It could be translated as 'luminous', establishing a semantic twinship with his sister Clara. Given the Spanish setting, the pronunciation of *-c-* as an 's' (/'lu.sɪ.əʊ/, 'lusio') seems preferable to the Italian pronunciation with a 'ch' (/'lu.tʃo/, 'lucho'). In modern peninsular Spanish, the name is pronounced with an interdental voiceless fricative: /'lu.θio/ ('luthio').

10. *Don SAYAVEDRA*] Friend to Álvarez, and perhaps a fellow soldier in the wars in Flanders, though this is not clear. Sayavedra was the name of Guzmán's criminal associate in Alemán's *Guzmán* (see Introduction, 29–30). The name means, literally, 'old tunic', and is a compound: *saya* ('a sort of tunic used by men', *DRAE*; my translation), from the vulgar Latin *sagia*, derived from *sagum* ('military cloak'; woollen mantle', *Collins*); *vedra* is a Galician word derived from the Latin *vetera*, 'old' (see Sarmiento). However, Dyce emended for *Saavedra*, probably thinking that it was an error for Miguel de Cervantes's second surname.

11. *Sancho Spindola BOBADILLA*] Sancho was a common name in Spain, well attested in medieval and Renaissance literature, and obviously popular as Don Quixote's squire. In F it is spelt 'Zancho', perhaps reflecting a contemporary pronunciation of the name in English with a voiced sibilant. Spindola is probably a jocular derivation, via 'spindle' (see 2.2.103), of the name of general Ambrogio Spinola Doria (1569–1630), 1st Marquis of Los Balbases and Grandee of Spain, who commanded the Spanish troops in the final year of the siege of Ostend referred to in 1.1. In addition, the name Bobadilla recalls that of Francisco Arias de Bobadilla, 4th Count of Puñonrostro (1537–1610), a celebrated Spanish military commander who

fought in many campaigns in the Netherlands under the Duke of Alba, and who was the chief military advisor to the Duke of Medina Sidonia in the failed invasion of England in 1588; in 1603 he was also briefly appointed as Asistente of Seville to prepare its defence against an Anglo-Dutch incursion. Bobadilla is the name of the cowardly braggart in Ben Jonson's *EMI*. He is described in *LC* as thin and ill-favoured.

12. *Stefano*] A servant in Eugenia's house, with an Italian name (the equivalent Spanish would be *Esteban*). Silent role in 1.2.

13. *PACHECO Alasto*] In all editions, *Pachieco*, although the correct form in Spanish is *Pacheco*. The verbose, grandiloquent language of the cobbler Pacheco is strongly reminiscent of Simon Eyre in Dekker's *Shoe*. (1599). They both share a tendency to draw from classical allusions, often to comic effect, and to elaborate on the nobility of their trade and its ancient origins. However, Pacheco is just a cobbler, or shoe-mender, while Eyre is a shoe-maker, a more skilled and better-regarded craft. He is, with his three associates, one of the 'Gang of Four' comic actors that recurs in other plays in the repertory of the King's Men in the period 1613–18 (see Introduction, 6–9).

14. *LAZARILLO*] Perhaps this is the most faithful stage version of the hungry anti-hero of the first picaresque novel, *Lazarillo de Tormes* (*c.* 1553), in English drama. The name is a diminutive of *Lázaro* ('Lazarus'), perhaps recalling the man whom Jesus raises from the dead in John 11:1–44.

15. *METALDI*] A smith bearing the appropriate surname 'de Forgia' ('of the Forge'; see 2.1.61 n.).

16. *MENDOZA*] A botcher, or mender of hose. His surname, according to Pacheco, is the ridiculous 'Pediculo de Vermini' (approximately 'Louse of the Vermin'; see 2.1.64 n.). The name was recurrent in Spanish literary sources and appears in many English plays of the period, including Marston's *Malcontent*, in which Mendoza is a villainous sycophant who aspires to usurp the Dukedom of Genoa.

17. *The ALGUAZIR*] An officer of justice, notorious for his corruption and his criminal activities, including stealing and pimping. In Spanish an *alguacil* is the 'inferior officer who executes the orders of the court of justice whom he serves' (*DRAE*, my translation). The *OED*, in its entry for *alguazil*, explains: 'Originally the same word as *vizier*, the meaning of which descended in Spain through that of *justiciary* or *justice*, to *warrant-officer* or *serjeant*.' The present English spelling is an adaptation of the etymological form of the Spanish *alguacil*, namely the Hispanic Arabic *alwazír*. In F and all previous editions the form is given as 'Alguazier', which recalls the etymological ending in English, -*zier*. The spelling of the word with a final -*l* is also attested in the English Renaissance, as given by Robert Barret in *The Theoric and Practic of Modern Wars* (London, 1598; STC 1500), *alguazil*, which is the form given in the *OED*. In the list of roles of the F2 text of *SpCur.*, there is a group of 'Algazeirs, *whom we call Serjeants*' (sig. R2ᵛ). According to *Characters*, it seems to be the only other commercial play to use either title for a character (17). The Alguazir is consistently referred to as being old and having red hair.

18. *MALRODA*] A courtesan who has given birth to Vitelli's illegitimate child. The name 'Mal' is a diminutive of Mary (which Vitelli uses in 3.3.32), and it means 'bad' or 'evil' in Spanish; 'roda', might perhaps suggest a 'road' (the sinful 'bad way' of a prostitute?). She is a characteristically Fletcherian

creation, in line with many other strong and outspoken female characters, particularly the domineering Bacha in *Cupid* (who also has a relationship with a young man, Leucippus, and is the mother to an illegitimate child, Urania).

19. *PIORATO*] A swordsman who is hired as fencing master to teach Lucio and who is in love with Malroda. The name only appears in one other play of the period, Dekker and Middleton's *PMHW* (1604), where Pioratto is a gentleman. The name is vaguely reminiscent of the English *pious*, but seems to have no clear etymology, unless it is a corruption of the Spanish *priorato*, 'priory'.

ACT I

SCENE I

Enter VITELLI, LAMORAL, [*and*] ANASTRO.

Vitelli. Álvarez pardoned?
Anastro.   And returned.
Lamoral.   I saw him land
  At Sanlúcar's, and such a general welcome
  Fame, as harbinger to his brave actions,
  Had with the easy people prepared for him,
  As if by his command alone and fortune   5
  Holland, with those Low Provinces that hold out

SCENE 1] *F (Actus Primus—Scæna Prima.).* 2. Sanlúcar's] *F (St.Lucars).*

1.1.0.] Location: Seville. Weber indicates '*A street*', but it could also be an indoor location. In Graham Watts's 2013 BADA production the scene was set in a tavern, signified by a small table, stools, and tankards, with Malroda smoking a pipe and serving drinks to Vitelli and his associates.

2. *Sanlúcar's*] the port of Sanlúcar de Barrameda in the present-day province of Cádiz in southern Spain, 97 km (60 miles) from Seville. Its location at the mouth of the navigable river Guadalquivir permitted easy communication with Seville, and its port was frequently used by Spanish military and commercial vessels in the sixteenth and seventeenth centuries. Despite its Spanish pronunciation with the primary stress on the second syllable, metrically it is stressed here on the first and third syllables ('Sánlucár's'); in F and all other editions it is given as two separate words, St Lucar's.

4. *easy people*] (a) the gullible populace; (b) specifically the women, perhaps easier to excite to acclamation than men.

5. *fortune*] arbitrary destiny operating in conjunction with his command.

6. *Holland ... Low Provinces*] The seven Protestant northern provinces of the Low Countries, including Holland, had declared independence from Habsburg Spain in 1581 and had established the Dutch Republic. The Spanish Monarchy, Europe's dominant Catholic power, retained the southern territories encompassing most of modern Belgium and Luxembourg, as well as areas in present-day northern France, western Germany, and the southern part of the Netherlands. The Spanish Netherlands, with its capital in Brussels, would remain under Spanish rule until the War of the Spanish Succession in the early eighteenth century.

Against the Archduke, were again compelled
With their obedience to give up their lives
To be at his devotion.
Vitelli.   You amaze me,
For though I have heard that when he fled from Seville   10
To save his life—then forfeited to law
For murdering Don Pedro, my dear uncle—
His extreme wants enforced him to take pay
In th' army sat down then before Ostend,
'Twas never yet reported by whose favour   15
He durst presume to entertain a thought
Of coming home with pardon.
Anastro.   'Tis our nature
Or not to hear or not to give belief
To what we wish far from our enemies.

10. Seville] *F* (Civill). 11. forfeited] *F2;* forfei ed *F.* 14. In th'] I' th'
F2. 14. Ostend] *F2;* Ostena *F.*

---

7. *Archduke*] Albert VII (1559–1621), Archduke of Austria and, jointly
with the Infanta Isabella Clara Eugenia, sovereign of the Spanish Netherlands
from 1598 until his death. He led the Spanish forces for most of the siege
of Ostend (1601–04).

10. *I have*] pronounced as monosyllabic, 'I've'.

Seville] stressed on the first syllable, as suggested by the F spelling, 'Civill';
plausibly punning on *civil*.

14. *sat ... before*] deployed in front of; the F reading is the *difficilior lectio*.
An alternative reading would be 'set down' (*OED* 1b), to be encamped, as
in *Coriolanus*: 'We will before the walls of Rome tomorrow / Set down our
host' (5.3.1–2).

Ostend] Flemish city on the west coast of the Netherlands that was
besieged by Spanish forces for over three years in 1601–04 in one of the
bloodiest episodes of the Dutch–Spanish wars of the early modern period.

15–17.] Cf. Flamineo in *White Devil*: 'How dares this banished count
return to Rome, / His pardon not yet purchased?' (3.3.54–5). Count Ludovico
was banished for crimes including murder and returned to the city before a
pardon had been granted. This is what Vitelli presumes that Álvarez has done;
Lamoral corrects him in lines 23–4.

17–19. *'Tis ... enemies*] 'It is in our nature not to want to hear or believe
what we do not wish to be recognised in our enemies.' Anastro expresses
that it is natural for Vitelli to be reluctant to listen to Lamoral's praise of
Álvarez's deeds of arms.

18. *or ... or*] either ... or.

Lamoral. Sir, 'tis most certain the Infanta's letters,   20
    Assisted by the Archduke's, to King Philip
    Have not alone secured him from the rigour
    Of our Castilian justice, but returned him
    A free man, and in grace.
Vitelli.   By what cursed means
    Could such a fugitive arise unto   25
    The knowledge of their highnesses? Much more,
    Though known, to stand but in the least degree
    Of favour with them?
Lamoral.   To give satisfaction
    To your demand—though to praise him I hate
    Can yield me small contentment—I will tell you,   30
    And truly, since should I detract his worth,
    'Twould argue want of merit in myself.
    Briefly to pass his tedious pilgrimage
    For sixteen years, a banished guilty man,

---

30. I] *F2;* 1 *F.*

20. *Infanta's*] The Infanta Isabella Clara Eugenia (1566–1633), daughter of King Philip II of Spain, was, jointly with her husband the Archduke, sovereign of the Spanish Netherlands until his death in 1621, and then on her own until her demise. See 2.2.137.

21. *King Philip*] In the historical period in which the play is set – the aftermath of the siege of Ostend – and during its first performances, the King of Spain was Philip III (1578–1621), who reigned from 1598 until his death. He is not to be confused with his father, Philip II (1527–98), who, as Queen Mary's husband, had been King consort of England, and who had launched the unsuccessful Armada against Elizabeth I in 1588.

22. *alone*] only.

23. *Castilian*] Until the early eighteenth century, Spain continued to be an amalgamation of administratively separate kingdoms and territories – with their own legal systems and institutions but under the rule of the same monarch – with Castile as its central dominant power.

29. *him I hate*] him whom I hate.

30–1. *I ... truly*] 'I will tell you the truth.'

33. *Briefly to pass*] 'Briefly to re-tell.'
tedious] (a) wearisome (*OED* 1a); (b) long (*OED* 1b).

34. *sixteen years*] Lamoral misremembers the number of years that Álvarez has been in exile: he left Seville twenty years before the play's action according to Bobadilla (1.2.24), Álvarez himself (1.3.47), and Clara (1.3.134 and 5.3.90). This kind of numerical inaccuracy is not uncommon in plays of the period, but the inconsistency is striking: since the other party clearly remembers that twenty years have passed, it seems odd that Lamoral, who

And to forget the storms, th' affrights, the horrors   35
His constancy, not Fortune, overcame,
I bring him, with his little son, grown man—
Though 'twas said here he took a daughter with him—
To Ostend's bloody siege, that stage of war
Wherein the flower of many nations acted,   40
And the whole Christian world spectators were;
There, by his son—or were he by adoption
Or nature his—a brave scene was presented,
Which I make choice to speak of, since from that
The good success of Álvarez had beginning.   45
Vitelli. So I love virtue in an enemy
That I desire in the relation of

---

44. make] made *Weber.*   48. you'd] *Weber;* you'ld *F*

---

provides the crucial back story in this opening scene from the point of view
of Vitelli's faction, gets this wrong; this might call into question the character's reliability as the play's main reteller of the past. However, the mistake
could have been an unintentional authorial inconsistency, perhaps due to
the play's multiple authorship, the product of inattentive revision, or a scribal
or compositorial error in the text's transmission from authorial draft to
playbook to print.

38.] This is the first reference to the cross-dressing theme: Álvarez was
thought to have taken his daughter with him into exile, though the news
arriving from Flanders reported that it was his son Lucio who accompanied
him to the wars (see line 67).

here] to Seville.

40. *many nations*] At the siege of Ostend, Archduke Albert commanded
around 20,000 Spanish, Walloon, and Italian soldiers from the *tercios.* The
city was defended by eighty-two companies of infantry garrisoned within its
walls, up to 8,000 men from six nations: English, Scottish, Dutch, Flemish,
French, and German soldiers. See Israel.

41. *Christian world*] a non-sectarian reference to the whole of Christendom,
presumably including the Protestant and Catholic nations of Europe.
Elsewhere in the play, Lucio and Sayavedra, for example, appeal to common
Christian values (see 2.2.49 and 5.3.42) which a Jacobean English audience
would share. However, note that, in the final scene, the faith of the Spanish
monarch and the characters in the play is specifically depicted as Catholic:
see 5.3.7 and 236.

42–3. *or ... Or*] either ... or.

were ... his] Since it was thought that Álvarez had taken a daughter with
him, Lamoral speculates that the son might have been adopted later or might
have been a natural child, perhaps engendered already in exile.

46. *So I*] 'So much do I.'

This young man's glorious deed you'd keep yourself
A friend to truth and it.
Lamoral.   Such was my purpose.
The town being oft assaulted but in vain,   50
To dare the proud defendants to a sally,
Weary of ease, Don Íñigo Peralta,
Son to the general of our Castile forces,
All armed, advanced within shot of their walls,
From whence the musketeers plied thick upon him;   55
Yet he—brave youth—as careless of the danger
As careful of his honour, drew his sword,
And waving it about his head as if
He dared one spirited like himself to trial
Of single valour, he made his retreat   60
With such a slow and yet majestic pace,
As if he still called loud 'Dare none come on?'.
When suddenly from a postern of the town
Two gallant horsemen issued, and o'ertook him,
The army looking on, yet not a man   65
That durst relieve the rash adventurer;
Which Lucio, son to Álvarez, then seeing

---

52. Íñigo] *F (Inigo).*   55. plied] *this edn;* plaid *F.*

49. *friend ... it*] to truth and to the 'glorious deed'.
51. *sally*] sudden rush out from a besieged place upon the enemy (*OED sally n.1* I.1a); Peralta wished to break the stalemate of the siege by daring the enemy to come forth.
52. *weary of ease*] 'tired of the idleness of waiting.'
Íñigo Peralta] A Spanish military officer, seemingly with no correspondence to any known historical figure.
53. *Castile forces*] the Castilian army; see line 23 n.
55. *musketeers*] a battalion carrying muskets.
plied thick] The musketeers employed themselves assiduously, shooting repeatedly on Peralta (*OED, v.²,* I.1.a).
59. *spirited*] animated with active properties; it scans as two syllables, 'sprited'.
59–60. *trial ... valour*] Sometimes a military dispute could be resolved by holding a single combat between two champions chosen to represent either side of the conflict, avoiding larger loss of life. Cf. David slaying Goliath, the champion of the Philistines, in 1 Samuel 17.
63. *postern*] concealed side exit.
67. *Lucio*] Clara's assumed masculine name is that of her actual brother. See earlier in the scene, lines 38 and 42–3.

As in the vanguard he sat bravely mounted,
Or were in pity of the youth's misfortune,
Care to preserve the honour of his country,   70
Or bold desire to get himself a name,
He made his brave horse like a whirlwind bear him
Among the combatants and in a moment
Discharged his petronel with such sure aim
That of the adverse party from his horse   75
One tumbled dead; then, wheeling round, and drawing
A falchion swift as lightning, he came on
Upon the other, and with one strong blow
In view of the amazèd town and camp
He struck him dead, and brought Peralta off   80
With double honour to himself.
Vitelli.   'Twas brave.
But the success of this?
Lamoral.   The camp received him
With acclamations of joy and welcome,
And for addition to the fair reward—
Being a massy chain of gold given to him   85
By young Peralta's father—he was brought
To the Infanta's presence, kissed her hand,
And from that lady—greater in her goodness

---

74. Discharged] *F2;* Dischar'd *F.*   80. struck] *F2;* strake *F.*

---

74. *petronel*] a large carbine particularly used by cavalry to shoot while
riding on horseback; see 2.2.74 SD and 2.2.136. The petronel seems to have
been an unusual prop weapon on the English Renaissance stage, as it only
appears twice in the whole extant corpus of plays and entertainments: here,
and in James Shirley's masque *The Triumph of Peace* (1634). Sir Petronel
Flash is a character in Jonson and Marston's *Eastward Ho!* (1605), and he
is referred to in Marston's *Histriomastix* (1600–3) and in *The Family of Love*
(attributed to Lording Barry; *c.* 1607).

76. *wheeling round*] turning around.

77. *falchion*] A broad single-edged sword with a curved blade, normally
carrying strong connotations of exoticism in the drama of the period. Cf.
Hieronimo to Balthazar in *SpT*: 'You must provide a Turkish cap, / A black
mustachio and a falchion' (4.1.138–9).

79. *town and camp*] in plain view of both warring contingents: the defend-
ers of Ostend and the attacking Spanish army.

82. *success*] outcome.

85. *massy*] made of pure solid gold (as opposed to hollow, alloyed, or
plated).

Than her high birth—had this encouragement:
'Go on, young man. Yet, not to feed thy valour   90
With hope of recompense to come from me
For present satisfaction of what's past,
Ask anything that's fit for me to give
And thee to take, and be assured of it.'

Anastro. Excellent princess.

Vitelli.   And styled worthily   95
The heart blood, nay, the soul of soldiers.
But what was his request?

Lamoral.   That the repeal
Of Álvarez makes plain: he humbly begged
His father's pardon, and so movingly
Told the sad story of your uncle's death   100
That the Infanta wept, and instantly
Granting his suit, working the Archduke to it,
Their letters were directed to the King,
With whom they so prevailed that Álvarez
Was freely pardoned.

Vitelli.   'Tis not in the King   105
To make that good.

Anastro.   Not in the King? What subject
Dares contradict his power?

Vitelli.   In this I dare,
And will; and not call his prerogative
In question, nor presume to limit it.
I know he is the master of his laws,   110

---

110. the] *F; not in F2.*

93–4. *Ask ... it*] a typical offer from a powerful figure as a gift. Cf. In *Cupid*, Dorialus recounts that Duke Leontius has sworn 'to grant his daughter anything she shall ask on her birthday' (1.1.8–9). Note, however, the Infanta's reservation in agreeing to grant only that which is proper.

96. *heart ... soldiers*] epithets applied to the Infanta by the troops; the historical sources record that the Infanta, who was encamped with the besiegers, was highly regarded by the Spanish troops at Ostend.

98–9. *he ... pardon*] In *La fuerza*, Hipólita, the martial maid, has no such direct intervention in her father's pardon to return to Spain, as no pardon is needed.

105. *freely*] (a) unreservedly; (b) generously.

105–6. *'Tis ... good*] As Vitelli subsequently explains, the King has no power to erase the injuries perpetrated against a gentleman's honour, even if, as the embodiment of the law, he can grant pardon to a murderer.

And may forgive the forfeits made to them,
But not the injury done to my honour.
And since, forgetting my brave uncle's merits
And many services under Duke d'Alba,
He suffers him to fall, wresting from Justice   115
The powerful sword that would revenge his death,
I'll fill with this Astraea's empty hand,
And in my just wreak, make this arm the King's.
My deadly hate to Álvar'z and his house,
Which, as I grew in years, hath still increased,   120
As if it called on time to make me man,
Slept while it had no object for her fury

---

114. d'Alba] *F* *(D' Alva)*.   119. Álvar'z] *F* *(Alvarz)*; Alvarez *F2*.

111–12.] The satisfaction of affronted honour was a general concern of Renaissance gentlemen and a rich literary trope in European literature. In this case, the murder of one of the members of Vitelli's family is inextricably linked to his sense of personal honour.

114. *Duke d'Alba*] Fernando Álvarez de Toledo y Pimentel (1507–82), 3rd Duke of Alba de Tormes, who belongs chronologically to the generation of Vitelli's uncle. He was governor of the Spanish Netherlands between 1567 and 1573, where he gained a long-lasting reputation for ruthlessness in the suppression of Protestantism and political dissidence. Vitelli's enemy, Fernando Álvarez, is named after the Duke of Alba (see 2.1.137 and 5.3.12).

115. *He … fall*] As the King has permitted the downfall of Don Pedro's honour by pardoning his murderer, even forgetting the military services to his country, Vitelli thinks that the dishonour affects the whole family and must be avenged.

wresting from] wrenching away from.

Justice] Rather than an actual judicial entity (as in 1.1.23), Justice is here personified as the Roman Iustitia, commonly represented as a blindfolded woman carrying a set of scales and a double-edged sword. The blindfold represents equanimity, the scales are used to measure opposing arguments, and the sword is to be used in punishing those found guilty. Since the King has deprived Justice of her sword, in Vitelli's opinion Don Pedro's murder remains illegitimately unpunished.

117. *this*] Vitelli's own sword.

Astraea's] Astraea, daughter of Zeus and Themis, was the Greek goddess of justice and virtue on which the Roman Iustitia was modelled; here the name is simply employed as a synonym for the personification of Justice in line 115.

118. *just wreak*] rightful revenge.

make … King's] Since the King's arm is the action of justice, Vitelli pledges to substitute it with his own and compensate for the King's neglect.

119. *Álvar'z*] Note that the contracted form in F, expanded in all later editions, is metrically correct.

122. *her*] Vitelli's hate, identified with his just revenge and, therefore, with Astraea.

But a weak woman and her talked-of daughter.
But now, since there are quarries worth her flight
Both in the father and his hopeful son,   125
I'll boldly cast her off and gorge her full
With both their hearts. To further which, your friendship
And oaths will your assistance. Let your deeds
Make answer to me; useless are all words
Till you have writ performance with your swords.   130

Exeunt.

SCENE 2

Enter BOBADILLA *and* LUCIO [*in women's clothes*].

Lucio. Go fetch my work. This ruff was not well starched,
So tell the maid; 't has too much blue in it.

124. flight] *TSS;* sight *F.*

SCENE 2] *F (Scæna Secunda.)*   0. SD] *this edn.*   2. 't has] *F2;* 'thas *F.*

---

123. *weak woman*] Eugenia.
talked-of] (a) publicly discussed; (b) reported to exist.
daughter] Posthumia (i.e., Lucio in disguise); see 1.2.66 n.
124. *quarries*] intended victims. In falconry, the quarry is the animal targeted by a bird of prey (*OED* n. 3).
her] Astraea's; see 122 n. Here her action is identified with that of a bird of prey.
flight] Although the F reading, 'sight', makes some sense of the hawking imagery (Mitchell annotates that it 'is consistent with the idea of a hawk being unhooded prior to flight'), Sympson's conjectured emendation for 'flight' makes this connection even clearer. It is also an easy compositorial mistake to make when setting F: 'fight' for 'flight'.
126. *cast ... off*] let her fly (a hawking term; *OED* 5).
gorge ... full] let her feed greedily (again, a term used in falconry; *OED* 1).
128. *will*] as a verb with full semantic value (a) ordain, impose the duty of (*OED v.*¹, I, 3a); (b) lend will to, affirm (*OED v.*¹, 1b).

1.2.0.] Location: Álvarez and Eugenia's house.
1–5.] Lucio's first speech deals exclusively with domestic affairs that were traditionally the concern of women of the household: embroidery, laundry, and tending to domestic animals.
1. *work*] needlework.
2. *blue*] powdered starch used by laundresses to whiten and stiffen the fabric of ruffs and other textiles; it whitened the cloth if diluted in water in the right amount, but dyed it blue if used in excess. In Jacobean England blue was a colour normally worn by servants (see 2.1.181 n.); Lucio may be protesting that it debases his social status.

And look you that the partridge and the pullen
Have clean meat and fresh water, or my mother
Is like to hear on't.   5

Bobadilla. O good Saint Jacques, help me! Was there ever such
an hermaphrodite heard of? Would any wench living, that
should hear or see what I do, be wrought to believe that
the best of a man lies under this petticoat, and that a
cod-piece were far fitter here than a pinned placket?   10

Lucio. You had best talk filthily; do. I have a tongue
To tell my mother, as well as ears to hear
Your ribaldry.

Bobadilla. Nay, you have ten women's tongues that way, I am
sure. Why, my young master, or mistress, madam, Don,   15
or what you will, what the devil have you to do with
pullen or partridge? Or to sit pricking on a clout all day?

---

6. Saint] *F2* (St.); Sir *F.*   7. an] a *Weber.*   hermaphrodite] Heramophrodite
TSS.   10. pinned placket] *F* (pind-Placket).   14. Nay] *F2;* May *F.*

---

3. *partridge ... pullen*] domestic fowls; *pullen* was the collective noun for
chicks (*OED* 2).

4. *meat*] fodder.

4–5. *my ... on't*] 'I will denounce you to my mother'; see 11–12 n.

6. *Saint Jacques*] Saint James the Apostle, or Santiago (derived in Spanish
from the Latin genitive 'Sancti Iacobi'), is the patron saint of Spain. His
grave and shrine are venerated in Santiago de Compostela, in north-western
Spain, a traditional centre of pilgrimage. In F, the name is given in the
archaic anglicised form 'Jaques', which usually puns with *jakes*, 'privy' (see
2.1.71); this is probably not the intention of this line, so the correct modernisation is the French form of the name. See also 5.3.213–14.

10. *pinned placket*] an apron or underskirt pinned to the front of a
woman's dress, with strong connotations of female genitalia (as a codpiece
is emblematic of the penis it covers). Cf. La-writ in *LFrL*: 'Keep thy hand
from thy sword and from thy laundress' placket, / And thou wilt live long'
(5.2.38–9).

11–12. *I ... mother*] Lucio threatens again to denounce Bobadilla.

14–15. *Nay ... sure*] Women were stereotypically said to be incapable of
remaining silent; Bobadilla implies that if Lucio were to denounce him to
Eugenia, he would be demonstrating the combined verbal excesses of ten
women. Cf. Rosalind in *AYL*: 'Do you not know I am a woman? When I
think, I must speak' (3.2.244–5).

17. *pricking ... clout*] embroidering a piece of cloth like a woman,
pejoratively.

You have a better needle, I know, and might make better
    work if you had grace to use it.
Lucio. Why, how dare you speak this before me, sirrah?   20
Bobadilla. Nay, rather, why dare you not do what I speak?
    Though my lady your mother, for fear of Vitelli and his
    faction, hath brought you up like her daughter, and has
    kept you this twenty year—which is ever since you were
    born—a close prisoner within doors, yet since you are a   25
    man, and are as well provided as other men are, methinks
    you should have the same motions of the flesh as other
    cavaliers of us are inclined unto.
Lucio. Indeed you have cause to love those wanton motions,
    They having holp you to an excellent whipping,   30
    For doing something—I but put you in mind of it—

---

23. has] *F2;* h'as *F;* hath *Q.*   24. this twenty year] *F* (this 20. year); these
20. years *F2.*   30. holp] *Q;* hope *F, F2;* helped *Mitchell.*

---

18. *better needle*] punning on Lucio's penis.

18–19. *better work*] better embroidery, i.e., sexual activity and the production of children.

19. *grace*] ironically, natural virtue (*OED* 4b).

24. *this twenty year*] Lucio's age; it was not unusual to find this construction in the singular. Cf. Bilioso in *Malcontent*: 'So have I [lived in the court]
this twenty year' (3.1.85). Twenty years have elapsed since Álvarez was
banished from Seville, leaving his wife pregnant with Lucio; see 1.3.47 and
134, and 5.3.90. However, Lamoral misremembered that number in 1.1.34
(see n.).

26. *provided*] sexually endowed.

27. *motions ... flesh*] (a) figuratively, sexual impulses; (b) literally, an erection; see line 29 ('wanton motions'). Cf. Bobadilla's advice to Vitelli against
'foolish hot motions' (2.2.166) and Lucio's sexual awakening with Genevora,
when he starts to feel 'strange new motions' (4.4.12).

30. *holp*] helped; Lucio uses the archaic form of the verb, in an unusual
form of the past participle, normally *holpen*; Bobadilla retorts with the same
verb in line 35.

31. *doing something*] getting her pregnant and giving the King a new
'subject' (see line 35).

I ... it] Puzzlingly, Lucio seems to claim that he suggested this idea to
Bobadilla. However, the speech is ironic: Bobadilla's love for the 'wanton
motions' towards the Indian maid only caused him to be whipped, presumably on Eugenia's command and not by the public authorities, on account
of having had an illegitimate child with a servant of lower standing within
the household.

With the Indian maid the Governor sent my mother
From Mexico.

Bobadilla. Why, I but taught her a Spanish trick in charity,
and holp the King to a subject that may live to take Graaf   35
Maurice prisoner, and that was more good to the state
than a thousand such as you are ever like to do. And I
will tell you (in a fatherly care of the infant I speak it) if
he live (as, bless the babe, in passion I remember him)
to your years, shall he spend his time in pinning, painting,   40
purling, and perfuming as you do? No, he shall to the
wars, use his Spanish pike, though with the danger of the
lash, as his father has done, and when he is provoked, as
I am now, draw his Toledo desperately, as—

[He draws his sword.]

---

35. Graaf] *this edn;* grave *F; Grave F2.*   44. SD] *this edn.*

32. *Indian*] a native of the West Indies, in this case an Aztec.

Governor] presumably not the Asistente of Seville, but a Spanish colonial governor.

33. *Mexico*] A colony under Castilian rule since the Aztec Empire was overthrown by Hernán Cortés in 1521 after a long campaign that culminated with the fall of its capital city, Tenochtitlan. There were numerous accounts of the Spanish colonisation of Mexico available in England; for instance, the influential treatise by Fray Bartolomé de las Casas, *Brevísima relación de la destrucción de las Indias* (*A Very Brief Account of the Destruction of the Indies*; Seville, 1552), had been translated into English as early as 1583.

35-6. *Graaf Maurice*] Maurice, Count (Graaf) of Nassau (1567–1625), Prince of Orange from 1618, who commanded the Dutch forces in several campaigns in the Dutch–Spanish wars in the early seventeenth century, and who was the head of the United Provinces during the siege of Ostend. The Dutch title 'Graaf' corresponds to that of a count or earl; the original spelling has misled most editors: Seward observed in TSS that F's 'grave' is an 'Epithet only'. Maurice of Nassau is the main antagonist to the title character in Fletcher and Massinger's controversial *Barnevelt*, which premiered in August 1619 and was quickly suppressed.

40-1. *pinning ... perfuming*] sticking pins into clothes (as dresses had to be pinned together when being put on), applying make-up, embroidering with purl (a cord made of twisted loops), and applying perfume; they are all activities usually associated with women.

42-3. *danger ... lash*] risk of being punished by flogging.

44. *Toledo*] A sword made in that Spanish city, famous for the high quality of its steel and the craftsmanship of its swordsmiths; Álvarez possesses an English 'old fox', rather than a sword from Toledo; see 3.4.70.

Lucio. You will not kill me? O!   45

Bobadilla. [*Aside*] I knew this would silence him. How he
hides his eyes! If he were a wench now, as he seems, what
an advantage had I drawing two Toledos, when one can
do this?

> *Enter* EUGENIA *and servants* [*including Stefano*].

But, O me, my lady! I must put up. [*He sheathes his sword.*   50
To Lucio] Young master, I did but jest. [*Aside*] O custom,
what hast thou made of him?

Eugenia. [*To Stefano*] For bringing this, be still my friend.
        No more
    A servant to me.

Bobadilla.   What's the matter?

Eugenia.   Here,
    Even here, where I am happy to receive   55
    Assurance of my Álvarez' return,

46–52.] *prose, TSS; F and F2 line* eyes? / advantage / this? / Master / him? /.
46. SD] *Dyce.*   47. hides] *F2;* hids *F.*   49. SD *including Stefano*] *this edn;*
Enter Eugenia, and Servants F, F2, Langbaine, Q; Enter Eugenia and Servant. |
Colman, TSS; Enter EUGENIA *and* STEPHANO | *Weber, Darley, Dyce; Enter*
Eugenia, [with Stephano*] and [other] Servants* | *GWW, Mitchell.*   50. SD] *this*
edn.   51. SD] *Dyce.*   53. SD] *this edn.*   56. Álvarez'] *Colman* (Alvarez');
Alvarez F, F2; Alvarez's *Mitchell.*

46–52.] This speech is set as verse in F, but it is clearly in prose, as TSS
recognised.
    46. *silence him*] If Lucio's 'O!' is loud enough, this is said ironically.
    49. SD] Colman, TSS, Weber, Darley, and Dyce assumed that there is
only one servant, Stefano; Dyce added that the plural form is 'a mistake for
"Servant"'.
    51. *custom*] (a) the behaviour that is 'widely practised and accepted (and
typically long established) in a particular society' (*OED* A.1.a), and (b) 'a
habitual practice or typical mode of behaviour' (A.2.b). It is phonetically
close and etymologically related to *costume*, the 'style of clothing, hairdress-
ing, and personal adornment typical of a particular place, period, group, etc.'
(*OED* 2a), which chimes with the play's focus on the performativity of the
male and female clothes that Lucio and Clara exchange. (See longer note.)
    53. *this*] the news of Álvarez's return to Seville, which might be materi-
alised as a letter, or might be a piece of verbal news imparted by Stefano
before the entrance.

I will kneel down. And may those holy thoughts

                                      [*She kneels.*]

That now possess me wholly, make this place

A temple to me, where I may give thanks

For this unhoped-for blessing heaven's kind hand   60

Hath poured upon me.

Lucio.   Let my duty, madam,

Presume, if you have cause to joy, to entreat

I may share in it.

Bobadilla. [*Aside*] 'Tis well. He has forgot how I frighted

    him yet.

Eugenia. Thou shalt. But first kneel with me, Lucio,   65

                                     [*Lucio kneels.*]

No more Posthumia now. Thou hast a father,

A father living to take off that name

Which my too credulous fears that he was dead

Bestowed upon thee. Thou shalt see him, Lucio,

And make him young again by seeing thee,   70

Who only hadst a being in my womb

When he went from me, Lucio. O, my joys

So far transport me that I must forget

---

57. SD] *this edn.*   64. SD] *Dyce.*   65. SD] *this edn.*   66. Posthumia] *F2;*
Posthumina *F.*

57, 65, 79. SDs] The placement of these indications to kneel and rise are approximate but necessary to make sense of the action; they may be reconsidered in rehearsal and performance. Eugenia might kneel at line 57, though the future tense implies that she might do it later. In any case, by line 66 they are both kneeling. They might get up at any point during the subsequent speeches, down to line 96, when it seems logical to assume that Eugenia is standing up to deliver the orders to her servants.

64. *yet*] so soon, already (*OED* 3b).

66. *Posthumia*] the only occurrence of the name given to Lucio when his father left for the Low Countries. Etymologically it implies that the child was born after the father's death, which is what Eugenia declares that she believed (lines 67–8) until the arrival of the good news of Álvarez's return. According to Livy, Postumia (in its classical Latin spelling) was a vestal virgin who was unjustly tried 'for incontinency and incest [...] by reason that she was suspected for her apparel and going more light and garish in her attire' (Livy, sig. P6ᵛ). This association with a character legally challenged for wearing inappropriate clothes connects the name with Lucio's dressing habits, and is preferable to the F reading, 'Posthumina', which seems to carry no ascertainable literary resonances.

The ornaments of matrons' modesty
And grave behaviour. But let all forgive me   75
If in th' expression of my soul's best comfort,
Though old, I do a while forget mine age
And play the wanton in the entertainment
Of those delights I have so long despaired of.

[They rise.]

Lucio. Shall I then see my father?
Eugenia.   This hour, Lucio,   80
Which reckon the beginning of thy life—
I mean that life in which thou shalt appear
To be such as I brought thee forth: a man.
This womanish disguise, in which I have
So long concealed thee, thou shalt now cast off,   85
And change those qualities thou didst learn from me
For masculine virtues. For which, seek no tutor,
But let thy father's actions be thy precepts.
And for thee, Sancho, now expect reward
For thy true service.   90
Bobadilla. Shall I? You hear, fellow Stefano? Learn to know
me more respectively. How dost thou think I shall become
the steward's chair, ha? Will not these slender haunches
show well with a gold chain and a nightcap after supper
when I take the accounts?   95

---

79. SD] *this edn.* 94. gold chain and a nightcap] *Colman (conj. Sympson);*
chaine, and a gold night-Cap *F, F2.* 95. accounts] *Colman;* accompts *F,*
F2.

77–9. *Though … of*] Eugenia's sexuality is awakened by the proximity of
an encounter with her husband after twenty years; cf. the 'second marriage'
predicted in line 100, and Bobadilla's inappropriate suggestion that she
should use an aphrodisiac (lines 103–4).

89. *expect reward*] Bobadilla assumes instantly that he is being appointed
steward of the house.

92. *respectively*] respectfully (*OED* 4).

93. *steward's chair*] office or dignity of a steward (*OED* 3b); alternatively,
chair may have been a misreading for *chain* in the MS that served as copy.

haunches] hips, buttocks.

94. *nightcap*] Bobadilla fantasises about wearing a gold chain, the emblem
of the steward's office, and about putting on a nightcap after supper when
preparing the domestic accounts before bedtime. The modern sense of
taking a last drink after supper does not apply here.

Eugenia. [*To her servants*] Haste, and take down those blacks
    with which my chamber
    Hath like the widow, her sad mistress, mourned,
    And hang up for it the rich Persian arras
    Used on my wedding night. For this to me
    Shall be a second marriage. Send for music,   100
    And will the cooks to use their best of cunning
    To please the palate.
Bobadilla. Will your ladyship have a potato pie? 'Tis a good
    stirring dish for an old lady after a long Lent.
Eugenia. Be gone, I say! [*Bobadilla walks slowly.*] Why, sir,
    you can go faster!   105
Bobadilla. I could, madam, but I am now to practise the
    steward's pace; that's the reward I look for. For every
    man must fashion his gait according to his calling. You,

---

96. SD] *this edn.* 105. SD] *this edn.*

96–100. *Haste ... marriage*] Eugenia has been acting as Álvarez's widow, since she believed he had died, and even her chamber is personified as mimicking the supposed widowhood of its mistress. This is most likely based on the opening speech of *La fuerza*, in which Don Félix (the Lucio figure) asks his mother why she has suddenly decided to have the house decorated with brocades and silks, changing 'mourning for fineries'. In *LC* the symbolism of the textile fineries hung in the house to celebrate the father's return is enriched with nuptial connotations absent from the original, both in terms of the particular location (Eugenia's private chamber) and in the choice of arras (the one used on her wedding night).
  96. *blacks*] black drapes, as in mourning.
  98. *for it*] instead of it.
  Persian] a particularly luxurious kind of silk, thin and soft (*OED* 4); Martin White annotates in his edition of Massinger's *RA*: 'Persia was widely associated with luxury goods, especially carpets and silk' (2.1.16–8 n.).
  101. *will*] command (see 1.1.128 n.).
  103–4. *potato ... Lent*] Bobadilla refers to the supposed aphrodisiac capacity of the potato, then still an exotic vegetable, to reawaken Eugenia's sexual desire. Weber annotates that 'potatoes were considered as strong provocatives'. In England sexual abstention was recommended by ecclesiastical authorities during Lent, the period of penance before Easter.
  105. *Why ... faster*] Bobadilla practises the slow and ceremonious pace of a steward, prompting Eugenia's impatience.
  108. *gait ... calling*] The phrase rings proverbial, but is not recorded in Tilley.

fellow Stefano, may walk faster to overtake preferment.
So, usher me.   [*Exeunt Bobadilla and servants.*]   110
Lucio. Pray, madam, let the waistcoat I last wrought
    Be made up for my father. I will have
    A cap and boot-hose suitable to it.
Eugenia.   Of that
    We'll think hereafter, Lucio. Our thoughts now
    Must have no object but thy father's welcome,   115
    To which thy help—
Lucio.   With humble gladness, madam.
                                                Exeunt.

SCENE 3

Enter ÁLVAREZ [*and*] CLARA [*in men's clothes*].

Álvarez. Where lost we Sayavedra?
Clara.   He was met
    Entering the city by some gentlemen,
    Kinsmen, as he said, of his own, with whom
    For complement sake—for so I think he termed it—
    He was compelled to stay. Though I much wonder   5

110. SD] *this edn.*   116. help] *F2*; helfe *F.*

SCENE 3] *F* (*Scæna Tertia.*).o. SD] *this edn.*   4. complement] *F*; compliment *F2.*

---

110. SD] Stefano probably opens the door and exits, ceremonially preceding Bobadilla, acting as usher for the newly appointed steward (see *OED steward v.* 2a).
    111. *wrought*] embroidered.
    112. *made up*] prepared, laid out.
    113. *boot-hose*] an over-stocking which covers the upper part of the leg.
    116. *help—*] Perhaps in view of his mother's indifference to his interest in clothes, Lucio interrupts her in mid-phrase. Colman repunctuated as 'To which, thy help!'

1.3.0.] Location: near Álvarez and Eugenia's house. Weber indicates '*A hall in the same*'. However, lines 91–2 seem to imply that the scene takes place somewhere in the house's vicinity, but not inside it.
    4. *complement*] The F reading was emended in F2 to 'compliment'; however, the joke here is that Clara, being unfamiliar with urban niceties, appears to mistake the word (adding immediately the confused 'for so I think he termed it').

A man that knows to do, and has done well
In the head of his troop when the bold foe charged home,
Can learn so suddenly to abuse his time
In apish entertainment. For my part—
By all the glorious rewards of war—   10
I had rather meet ten enemies in the field,
All sworn to fetch my head, than be brought on
To change an hour's discourse with one of these
Smooth city fools or tissue cavaliers,
The only gallants, as they wisely think,   15
To get a jewel or a wanton kiss
From a court lip, though painted.
Álvarez   My love, Clara—
For Lucio is a name thou must forget
With Lucio's bold behaviour—though thy breeding
I'th' camp may plead something in the excuse   20
Of thy rough manners, custom having changed,
Though not thy sex, the softness of thy nature,
And Fortune—then a cruel step-dame to thee—

---

15. The] *F2;* Then *F.*   gallants] *F2;* Gallans *F.*   17. love] *F, F2;* lov'd
TSS; lovd *GWW;* loved *Mitchell.*

---

6. *man ... do*] man of action.

9. *apish*] silly, in bad imitation of a human being.

14. *tissue*] rich cloth embroidered with gold or silver; here applied as an adjective to gentlemen who enjoy ostentation.

16. *jewel*] perhaps with a sexual connotation; cf. Vitelli about Malroda and her confederates: 'I am gulled; / First cheated of my jewels, and then laughed at' (4.2.138–9).

17. *court lip*] by metonymy, a courtesan.

painted] wearing make-up.

17–34.] Álvarez's speech is syntactically convoluted and laborious, perhaps meaning to give the impression that the old commander has prepared it carefully. The main clause is the vocative 'Clara' repeated twice (17 and 28) followed by a gentle command, 'Entertain' (28); lines 18–28 are a long preamble. Clara interrupts the long utterance with an immediate expression of submission to paternal authority, and, arguably, to a military superior.

17. *My love, Clara*] Seward and Sympson suggested that this vocative is inappropriately applied to a daughter, and they emended for 'loved'; Williams and Mitchell accepted the emendation. Dyce supported this view in his annotation, but refrained from emending the dialogue. Social propriety seems an insufficient reason to justify the alternative reading.

21. *custom*] see 1.2.51 n.

Imposed upon thy tender sweetness burdens
Of hunger, cold, wounds, want, such as would crack   25
The sinews of a man not born a soldier,
Yet now she smiles, and like a natural mother
Looks gently on thee, Clara. Entertain
Her proffered bounties with a willing bosom.
Thou shalt no more have need to use thy sword;   30
Thy beauty—which even Belgia hath not altered—
Shall be a stronger guard to keep my Clara
Than that has been, though never used but nobly;
And know thus much—
Clara.   Sir, I know only that
It stands not with my duty to gainsay you   35
In anything. I must and will put on
What fashion you think best, though I could wish
I were what I appear.
Álvarez.   Endeavour rather   *Music.*
To be what you are, Clara, entering here
As you were born: a woman.

            Enter EUGENIA, LUCIO, [*and*] *servants.*

Eugenia.   Let choice music   40
In the best voice that e'er touched human ear—
For joy hath tied my tongue up—speak your welcome.
Álvarez. My soul (for thou giv'st new life to my spirit),

---

25. hunger] *F2;* hunder *F.*   38. SD] *placement, F; placed before 40 SD, Weber; placed after 40 SD, Mitchell; placed after 40, GWW.*   40. SD EUGENIA] *F2* (Eugenia*); Eugnia F.*

---

31. *Belgia*] the Spanish Netherlands, the southern territories in the Low Countries where Ostend is located (in present-day Belgium).

31–3.] Álvarez compares the power of Clara's beauty to fend off enemies (presumably the unwanted advances of men) with that of her sword.

33. *that*] your sword.

37. *fashion*] garments, but also behaviour.

37–8. *though ... appear*] Clara expresses her wish to continue to live as the (male) soldier that she has become. This might be an aside.

38. SD] The F placing of the music cue two lines before the entrance of Eugenia, Lucio, and the servants makes sense theatrically, as it announces the entrance of the maternal party in advance.

43. *My soul*] in vocative sense.

Myriads of joys, though short in number of
Thy virtues, fall on thee. O my Eugenia,   45
Th' assurance that I do embrace thee makes
My twenty years of sorrow but a dream,
And by the nectar which I take from these
I feel my age restored, and, like old Aeson,
Grow young again.   [*They kiss.*]

Eugenia.   My lord, long-wished-for welcome;   50
'Tis a sweet briefness, yet in that short word
All pleasures which I may call mine begin,
And may they long increase before they find
A second period. Let mine eyes now surfeit
On this so-wished-for object, and my lips   55
Yet modestly pay back the parting kiss
You trusted with them when you fled from Seville
With little Clara, my sweet daughter. Lives she?
Yet I could chide myself, having you here,
For being so covetous of all joys at once,   60
T'enquire for her, you being alone to me

---

44. joys] *F;* joy *Colman.*   50. SD] *this edn.*   57. Seville] *F (Civill).*   61.
T'enquire] *F;* To enquire *Weber.*

---

46. *Th' assurance*] the certainty (*OED* II.6).
embrace thee] Álvarez and Eugenia have obviously embraced at this point,
perhaps before he says 'O my Eugenia', as in the 2012 Shakespeare Institute
production. The actors in the 2013 BADA production did it as Álvarez said
'O my Eugenia'.
48. *nectar*] as a restorative taken from Eugenia's lips ('these'), akin to
Medea's potion; see below.
49. *old Aeson*] Medea drained all of Aeson's blood before giving him a
rejuvenating potion, as recounted in Ovid's *Metamorphoses* (VII, 285–93).
50. *My ... welcome*] alternative modernisation: 'My lord, long-wished-for,
welcome' (Dyce).
54. *period*] full stop, ending.
56. *parting kiss*] Eugenia may kiss Álvarez again. In the 2012 production,
the actor playing Eugenia chose to kiss Álvarez again after 'my sweet daughter', and then returned quickly to Clara.
58. *Lives she?*] The question, a genuine one since Eugenia does not rec-
ognise her daughter until later in the scene (line 161), capitalises on the
masculine clothes that Clara is wearing.
61–3. *you ... world*] The sense is that Álvarez is more than himself to
Eugenia: he contains the whole family and her entire universe.

My Clara, Lucio, my lord, myself—
Nay, more than all the world.
Álvarez.   As you to me are.
Eugenia. Sit down, and let me feed upon the story
    Of your past dangers. Now you are here in safety,   65
    It will give relish and fresh appetite
    To my delights, if such delights can cloy me.
    Yet do not, Álvarez. Let me first yield you
    Account of my life in your absence, and
    Make you acquainted how I have preserved   70
    The jewel left locked up within my womb
    When you, in being forced to leave your country
    Suffered a civil death.   *Within clashing swords.*
Álvarez.   Do, my Eugenia,
    'Tis that I most desire to hear.
Eugenia.   Then know—
Sayavedra. (Within) If you are noble enemies,   75
    Oppress me not with odds, but kill me fairly.

---

71. within] *TSS; in F, F2.*   75. SP] *F2; not in F.*   SD *(Within)] placed here in F, F2; moved to SP, TSS; Sayavedra [calls] within | GWW; Sayavedra [calls] | Mitchell.*

---

64. *Sit down*] Eugenia may indicate to the servants to bring on one or more seats. When they are interrupted at line 73 by the fight offstage the servants may clear the space quickly, maybe after Bobadilla's entrance. It is not certain, however, that there is enough time before the interruption for the order to be carried out.

67. *cloy*] satisfy my appetite (*OED v.*[1], 7).

71. *jewel*] the embryo of the unborn babe; usually, as earlier in line 16, a term alluding to a woman's virginity or the access to her sexual favours. The line in F is metrically imperfect (hence the emendation of 'in' for 'within' in TSS).

73. *civil death*] the cessation of his status as a citizen, losing his freedom to reside in his home town with his family.

73–8.] The sequence as it appears in F is confusing; the present rearrangement of the order of the speeches justifies the F reading 'voice' (77) while making sense of the action. (See longer note.)

76. *Oppress ... fairly*] Sayavedra protests against being ignobly and unfairly outnumbered.

Álvarez. What voice is that?

Vitelli. (Within) Stand off; I am too many of myself.

Enter BOBADILLA.

Bobadilla. Murder, murder, murder! Your friend, my lord,
    Don Sayavedra, is set upon in the streets by your enemies,   80
    Vitelli and his faction. I am almost killed with looking on
    them.

Álvarez. I'll free him, or fall with him. [*To Clara*] Draw thy
    sword,
    And follow me.   [*Exit.*]

Clara.   Fortune, I give thanks
    For this occasion once more to use it.   *Exit.*   85

    [*Eugenia restrains Bobadilla from following them.*]

Bobadilla. Nay, hold not me, madam; if I do any hurt, hang
    me.

Lucio. O, I am dead with fear! Let's fly into
    Your closet, mother.

Eugenia.   No hour of my life
    Secure of danger? Heav'n be merciful,
    Or now at once dispatch me.

Enter VITELLI *pursued by* ÁLVAREZ *and* SAYAVEDRA,
[*and*] CLARA *beating off* ANASTRO [*and* LAMORAL].

77. voice] *F, GWW, Mitchell;* noise *F2 and all other eds.*   78. SP] *F2; not in
F.*   SD (*Within*)] *placed marginally next to line 75 in F, F2; not in Q; moved to
SP, TSS and all other eds.*   80. enemies] Enemy *TSS.*   83. SD] *this edn.*
84. SD] *Colman.*   85. SD2] *this edn.*   90. SD1 *and* LAMORAL] *this edn.*

---

    78. *I ... myself*] Vitelli instructs his associates, Lamoral and Anastro, to
leave him alone to fight against Sayavedra. Perhaps reminiscent of the
Gerasene demoniac in Mark 5:9, 'And he asked him, What *is* thy name? And
he answered, saying, My name *is* Legion: for we are many' (also in Luke
8:30). A man has been possessed by a multitude of devils, and Jesus cures
him by allowing them to leave his body and possess a herd of swine, which
then run down a slope, fall into the sea, and drown. Vitelli is metaphorically
possessed by devils in pursuing his revenge by forcing his entry into his
enemy's house.

    80. *set upon*] attacked, assailed.

    84. *Fortune*] cf. the 'cruel step-dame' of line 23.

    88. *closet*] private room, inner chamber.

    90. SD1] As well as Anastro's, Lamoral's presence seems to be demanded
by the text, as Clara uses the plural to refer to her opponents, 'Leave me to
keep *these* off' (91, my emphasis).

    SD1 *beating off*] driving away, repelling.

Clara. [*To Álvarez and Sayavedra*] Follow him;   90
    Leave me to keep these off.
    [*Clara attacks Anastro and Lamoral, and makes them flee.*]
Álvarez. [*To Vitelli*]   Assault my friend
    So near my house?
Vitelli.   Nor in it will I spare thee,
    Though 'twere a temple. And I'll make it one,
    I being the priest, and thou the sacrifice
    I'll offer to my uncle.
Álvarez.   Haste thou to him,   95

---

90. SD2] *this edn;* [*to Alvarez*] *GWW.*   91. SD1, SD2] *this edn.*   91. my] *F2*;
by *F.*   92. will I spare] *this edn;* will spare *F, F2.*

91. *him*] Vitelli.
91. *these*] Anastro and Lamoral.
91–2. *Assault ... thee*] Perhaps an instance of *hamesucken*, the assault on
a man's house, which was a capital offence in ancient Anglo-Saxon law
(*hamesucken, OED*); however, note that the scene seems to be set outdoors,
near the house (line 92), rather than inside.
91. *my friend*] Sayavedra.
92. *will I spare*] The emendation provides a subject for Vitelli's sentence,
which is otherwise syntactically incomplete. It also regularises the slightly
odd metre of the line, allowing a stress on the verb 'spare', semantic centre
of the line, and rendering a feminine ending on 'thee'. It is likely to have
been a simple typesetting mistake: the compositor might have overlooked or
accidentally omitted the capital 'I' between the double 'l' in *will* and the long
's' at the beginning of the next word, mistaking the number of consecutive
ascenders required in the sequence 'will I ſpare'.
93. *temple*] implying that Álvarez would not avoid punishment even if he
claimed right of sanctuary: criminals could traditionally seek protection in a
church or monastery if persecuted by the civil justice. This ancient law, still
in the statute book at the time of the play's premiere, was finally repealed
in England in 1623 (*Statutes* 21 James I. c. 28). Cf. in *Phil.*, the titular character threatens to kill Pharamond, Prince of Spain, in Arethusa's bedroom:
'but were't the church, / Ay, at the altar, there's no place so safe / Where
thou darest injure me, but I dare kill thee' (1.2.182–4).
93–5. *And ... uncle*] Vitelli shifts from the initial Christian legal imagery
to that of a pagan temple where he is to act as priest to offer a human sacrifice
in memory of his uncle (or perhaps, literally, to his uncle as the god of his
revenge).

And say I sent thee.
     [*Álvarez and Sayavedra attack Vitelli.*]
Clara. [*Aside*]   'Twas put bravely by.
 And that! And yet comes on, and boldly rare!
 In the wars, where emulation and example
 Join to increase the courage and make less
 The danger, valour and true resolution   100
 Never appeared so lovely. Brave again!
 Sure he is more than man, and if he fall
 The best of virtue, fortitude, would die with him.
 And can I suffer it? Forgive my duty.
 So I love valour as I will protect it   105
 Against my father and redeem it, though
 'Tis forfeited by one I hate.
Vitelli. [*To Álvarez and Sayavedra*] Come on,
 All is not lost yet. You shall buy me dearer
 Before you have me.   [*Clara takes Vitelli's side.*]
     Keep off!
Clara.   Fear me not.
 Thy worth has took me prisoner, and my sword 110
 For this time knows thee only for a friend,
 And to all else I turn the point of it.
Sayavedra. Defend your father's enemy?
Álvarez.   Art thou mad?

---

96. SD1] *GWW;They fight* | *Weber.*   SD2] *this edn;apart* | *GWW.*   97. And
yet] *F;* yet he *TSS.*   107. SD] *this edn; to Clara* | *GWW.*   109. SD] *this
edn; She joins* Vitelli. | *GWW, at line 107.*

96–7. *'Twas ... that!*] Clara comments on the various manoeuvres of the
fight between her father and Sayavedra against Vitelli, admiring the skill that
the latter demonstrates.

97. *yet comes on*] he advances yet again.

103. *fortitude*] one of the classical cardinal virtues, alongside temperance,
prudence, and justice.

109. SD] Clara seems to take Vitelli's side at this point, rather than
earlier, while Vitelli's lines seem to be directed at the foes he is fighting
against. Williams interpreted the opposite: Vitelli speaks to Clara after she
has taken his side at line 107.

Clara. Are you men, rather? Shall that valour which
   Begot you lawful honour in the wars   115
   Prove now the parent of an infamous bastard,
   So foul, yet so long lived, as murder will
   Be to your shames? Have each of you, alone
   With your own dangers only, purchased glory
   From multitudes of enemies, not allowing   120
   Those nearest to you to have part in it,
   And do you now join and lend mutual help
   Against a single opposite? Hath the mercy
   Of the great King but newly washed away
   The blood that with the forfeit of your life   125
   Cleaved to your name and family like an ulcer,
   In this again to set a deeper dye
   Upon your infamy? You'll say he is your foe,
   And by his rashness called on his own ruin.
   Remember yet he was first wronged, and honour   130
   Spurred him to what he did. And next the place
   Where now he is, your house, which by the laws
   Of hospitable duty should protect him;
   Have you been twenty years a stranger to it
   To make your entrance now in blood? Or think you   135
   Your countryman, a true-born Spaniard, will be
   An off'ring fit to please the genius of it?
   No, in this I'll presume to teach my father,
   And this first act of disobedience shall
   Confirm I am most dutiful.
Álvarez. [*Aside*]   I am pleased   140
   With what I dare not give allowance to.
   [*To Clara*] Unnatural wretch, what wilt thou do?
Clara.   Set free

---

140. SD] *Weber.*   142. SD] *this edn.*

114–18. *Shall … shames?*] The metaphor implies that valour can generate
a legitimate child (lawful honour) or a bastard (murder). A death caused in
an act of bravery for a rightful cause is honourable, while committing a
murder against an outnumbered fighter is shameful.

137. *genius*] The genius of the house, akin to the Roman household deities
(e.g., the manes or the lares).

140–1. *I … to*] This aside expresses Álvarez's secret approval of his daughter's honourable judgement.

A noble enemy.   [*Álvarez advances towards her.*]
        Come not on, by heaven!
You pass to him through me. [*To Vitelli*] The way is open;
Farewell. When next I meet you, do not look for   145
A friend, but a vowed foe. I see you worthy,
And therefore now preserve you for the honour
Of my sword only.
Vitelli. [*Aside*]   Were this man a friend,
How would he win me that being a vowed foe
Deserves so well? [*To Clara*] I thank you for my life.   150
But how I shall deserve it, give me leave
Hereafter to consider.   *Exit.*
Álvarez. [*To Eugenia*]   Quit thy fear,
All danger is blown over. I have letters
To the Governor in the King's name to secure us
From such attempts hereafter. Yet we need not,   155
That have such strong guards of our own, dread others;
And to increase thy comfort, know this young man
Whom with such fervent earnestness you eye
Is not what he appears, but such a one
As thou with joy wilt bless: thy daughter Clara.   160
Eugenia. A thousand blessings in that word.
Álvarez.   The reason
Why I have bred her up thus, at more leisure
I will impart unto you. Wonder not
At what you have seen her do, it being the least
Of many great and valiant undertakings   165
She hath made good with honour.
Eugenia.   I'll return
The joy I have in her with one as great
To you, my Álvarez. You in a man
Have given to me a daughter. In a woman,
I give to you a son. This was the pledge   170

---

143. SD] *this edn.* by heaven] *Colman* (by Heaven); by — *F, F2.* 144.
SD] *GWW.* 148. SD] *Dyce.* 150. SD] *this edn.* 152. SD] *GWW.*

143. *Come not on*] do not advance any further (with a hostile intent; *OED*
1).
154. *the Governor*] the Asistente of Seville.
156. *dread*] fear greatly.

You left here with me, whom I have brought up
Different from what he was, as you did Clara,
And with the like success: as she appears,
Altered by custom, more than woman, he,
Transformed by his soft life, is less than man.   175
Álvarez. Fortune in this gives ample satisfaction
     For all our sorrows past.
Lucio.   My dearest sister.
Clara. Kind brother.
Álvarez.   Now our mutual care must be
     Employed to help wronged Nature to recover
     Her right in either of them, lost by custom.   180
     To you I give my Clara, and receive
     My Lucio to my charge. And we'll contend
     With loving industry who soonest can
     Turn this man woman, or this woman man.

                                                        Exeunt.

173–5. *as ... man*] This statement assumes a valuation of a person's worth based on their gender: a man is more than a woman. In this respect, a masculine woman is compared positively to women in general, while an effeminate man is less valuable than a truly masculine man.

174. *custom*] see 1.2.51 n.

176. *satisfaction*] compensation (*OED* 1b); Álvarez seems to express his joy at the family's reunion, rather than at the fact that his son is effeminate, for which he will express his subsequent outrage (by contrast, note that he regards his daughter's manliness positively; see lines 140–1).

180. *custom*] see 1.2.51 n.

182. *contend*] endeavour; Álvarez implies that there will be a competition between the feminising and masculinising parties in seeing who will succeed in altering the siblings' gender behaviour.

ACT 2

SCENE I

Enter PACHECO *and* LAZARILLO.

Pacheco. Boy, my cloak and rapier. It fits not a gentleman of
   my rank to walk the streets in *cuerpo.*

Lazarillo. [*Aside*] Nay, you are a very rank gentleman. [*Aloud*]
   Señor, I am very hungry; they tell me in Seville here I
   look like an eel with a man's head. And your neighbour   5
   the smith, here hard by, would have borrowed me th'
   other day to have fished with me because he had lost his
   angle-rod.

Pacheco. O, happy thou, Lazarillo, being the cause of other
   men's wits as in thine own. Live lean and witty still.   10

SCENE 1] F *(Actus secundus. Scæna prima.) Colman relineated this scene in
verse, as well as all prose speeches throughout the play.* 1. my cloak] F; and
Cloak F2. 2. cuerpo] F *(Querpo).* 3. SD1 *and* SD2] *this edn.* gentle-
man] F *(Gent.).* 4. Señor] F *(Signior).* Seville] F *(Civill).*

2.1.0.] Location: '*A street*' (Weber).

2. *cuerpo*] The Spanish expression *a cuerpo* (literally, 'in body') applies to
someone who is not wearing 'any external item of warm clothing' (*DRAE*,
my translation). Pacheco thinks it is improper for a gentleman not to wear
his cloak and rapier, the symbols of his social status, in the street.
Etymologically, 'rapier' is related, through Middle French, to its Spanish
equivalent, *espada ropera*, literally a 'dress sword', the weapon a gentleman
would necessarily wear as part of his outfit (*OED*).

3. *rank*] (a) impressive due to his social dignity (*OED* 3a); (b) arrogant,
haughty (*OED* 1a); (c) festering, rotting (*OED* 12). Lazarillo often uses the
aside to comment on the character of his associates, and especially to deride
his master, the cobbler Pacheco.

4. *Señor*] Spanish modernisation of the Italian form printed in F, 'Signior'.
In this period words from both languages were frequently confused and
interchanged. Since the play is set in Spain, the modern Spanish form has
been adopted.

5–6. *neighbour the smith*] Metaldi.

8. *angle-rod*] fishing rod.

9–10. *cause ... wits*] Echoing Falstaff in *2H4*: 'I am not only witty in
myself, but the cause that wit is in other men' (1.2.9–10).

96

Oppress not thy stomach too much. Gross feeders, great
sleepers; great sleepers, fat bodies; fat bodies, lean brains.
No, Lazarillo: I will make thee immortal, change thy
humanity into deity, for I will teach thee to live upon
nothing.   15

Lazarillo. 'Faith, señor, I am immortal then already, or very
near it, for I do live upon little or nothing. Belike that's
the reason poets are said to be immortal, for some of
them live upon their wits, which is indeed as good as little
or nothing. But, good master, let me be mortal still, and   20
let's go to supper.

Pacheco. Be abstinent; show not the corruption of thy generation. He that feeds shall die; therefore he that feeds not,
shall live.

Lazarillo. Ay, but how long shall he live? There's the   25
question.

Pacheco. As long as he can without feeding. Didst thou read
of the miraculous maid in Flanders?

Lazarillo. [*Aside*] No, nor of any maid else, for the miracle
of virginity nowadays ceases ere the maid can read   30
'virginity'!

Pacheco. She that lived three year without any other sustenance than the smell of a rose?

Lazarillo. I heard of her, señor, but they say her guts shrunk

---

11–12. great sleepers; great sleepers] *F;* great sleepers *F2.*   14. deity] *F2;*
dietie *F.*   16. señor] *F (Signior).*   29. SD] *GWW.*   32. year] *F;* years
F2.   34. señor] *F (Signior).*

13–15. *No ... nothing.*] The purifying and spiritual qualities of a moderate
life are here taken to the extreme. See Introduction, 27–9.

14. *deity*] The F reading, 'dietie', perhaps reflective of the early pronunciation, may indicate a pun linking Lazarillo's diet with the godly status he
would aspire to.

23–4. *He ... live*] Cf. John 6:58, 'not as your fathers did eat manna, and
are dead: he that eateth of this bread shall live for ever'.

28. *miraculous ... Flanders*] This may refer to the case of 'Eva Fliegen of
Meurs in the Rhenish duchy of Clèves, said to have supported life for sixteen
years by smelling sweet flowers' (Bond, 266). A 1611 pamphlet, *Jesuits*, also
gives an account of her life; it reports that she had not consumed any food
or drink since 1597.

34. *heard*] Pacheco had asked Lazarillo if he has read about the maid,
rather than having had a verbal account; Lazarillo's answer may imply that
he is illiterate.

all into lute-strings, and her nether parts clinged together   35
like a serpent's tail, so that, though she continued a
woman still above the girdle, beneath yet she was a
monster.

Pacheco. So are most women, believe it.

Lazarillo. Nay, all women, señor, that can live upon the smell   40
of a rose.

Pacheco. No part of the history is fabulous.

Lazarillo. I think, rather, no part of the fable is historical. But
for all this, sir, my rebellious stomach will not let me be
immortal. I will be as immortal as mortal hunger will   45
suffer. Put me to a certain stint, sir, allow me but a red
herring a day.

Pacheco. ¡Ah de Dios! Wouldst thou be gluttonous in thy
delicacies?

Lazarillo. He that eats nothing but a red herring a day shall   50
ne'er be broiled for the devil's rasher. A pilchard, señor,
a sardine, an olive, that I may be a philosopher first, and
immortal after.

Pacheco. Patience, Lazarillo; let contemplation be thy food

---

37. beneath yet] *F;* yet beneath *TSS;* beneath that *GWW.*   40. señor] *F*
(Signior).   48. ¡Ah de Dios!] *F (O' de dios).*   51. señor] *F (Signior).*   52.
sardine] *Mitchell;* surdiny *F;* sardina *TSS.*

35–6. *her ... tail*] The 1611 pamphlet (see line 28 n.) mentions the 'nether
parts' of one of the fasting maids of the period, Joan Ballam, as being dry
and clean of any secretion: 'She voided nothing forth, nothing at all she ate;
/ Her privy parts were clean, thence nothing fell to ground' (*Jesuits*, sig. B1ʳ).

36–8. *though ... monster*] Echoes *Lear,* 'Down from the waist / They are
centaurs, though women all above' (*Lear T* 4.5.121–2).

42. *fabulous*] fictional, untrue.

46–7. *red herring*] a smoked herring, a kipper; a fish diet was acceptable
during the period of abstinence at Lent.

48. *¡Ah de Dios!*] Spanish expression that denotes a mild invocation to
God. Note here and elsewhere the correct Spanish modern punctuation
marking the exclamatory clause between ¡ and !

51. *ne'er ... rasher*] shall never go to hell; the image of the soul in hell
roasting like a rasher of bacon, presumably to be consumed by the Devil,
does not seem to have been proverbial.

pilchard] the European pilchard (*sardina pilchardus*) is a type of sardine;
in *Blurt,* Lazarillo de Tormes is a Castilian soldier whose hungry serving boy
is named Pilcher.

52. *sardine*] the entire genus to which pilchards belong.

philosopher] Plato, for example, said that the philosopher should exercise
moderation in the nourishment of the body (see Hintze, 3).

awhile. I say unto thee one pease was a soldier's provant   55
a whole day at the destruction of Jerusalem.

Enter METALDI *and* MENDOZA.

Lazarillo. [*Aside*] Ay, an it were anywhere but at the destruction of a place, I'll be hanged.
Metaldi. Señor Pacheco Alasto, my most ingenious cobbler of
Seville, the *buenas noches* to your signory.   60
Pacheco. Señor Metaldi de Forgia, my most famous smith,
and man of mettle, I return your courtesy tenfold and do
humble my bonnet beneath the shoe-sole of your congee.
The like to you, Señor Mendoza Pediculo de Vermini, my
most exquisite hose-heeler.   65

---

57. SD1] *this edn.*   an] *Colman;* and *F.*   59. Señor] *F (Signior).*   60. Seville]
F (Civill).   *buenas noches*] *Dyce;* bonos noxios *F;* buenos noches *Weber.*
61. Señor] *F (Signior).*   Forgia] *this edn; forgio* F; *Forgio* F2.   64. Señor] *F*
(Signior).   Vermini] *TSS; vermim* F; *Vermim* F2.

---

55. *pease*] pea.
   provant] allowance of food.
   56. *destruction ... Jerusalem*] During Nebuchadnezzar's siege and destruction of Jerusalem in 589 BC the besieged population were famously
famished.
   57. SD] This aside is not marked in any previous edition, but it is consistent with Lazarillo's previous asides.
   an it were] if it were.
   60. *buenas noches*] Spanish for 'good night', literally, or, in this context,
'good evening' as a salutation.
   signory] signorship; a more radical modernisation would be the Spanish
equivalent, *señoría.*
   61. *Metaldi de Forgia*] Spanish-Italian hybrid for 'Metal of the Forge'; the
correct modernisation in Italian is 'Forgia', as a feminine noun, rather than
the F reading, 'Forgio'.
   62. *mettle*] courage, spirit (*OED* 2a), with a pun on Metaldi's profession
and on his name.
   63. *congee*] ceremonious leave-taking (*OED* 2a).
   64. *Pediculo de Vermini*] a comical form, approximately equivalent to
'Louse of the Vermin'; from the Spanish *pediculo* ('louse') and an Italianate
form of the English *vermin.* Cf. In Dekker's *Untrussing* (1601), Captain Tucca
insults Horace using a similar collocation: 'You must have three or four suits
of names when, like a lousy, pediculous vermin, thou'st but one suit to thy
back' (1.2.309–11).
   65. *hose-heeler*] Mendoza is a botcher specialised in mending or re-heeling
hose; this is the only instance of the term recorded in the *OED.* The term
botcher carried connotations of clumsiness and unskilfulness (*OED* 1), as well
as of being a second-rate professional: if a tailor makes clothes, the botcher
only mends them (see 66 n.).

Lazarillo. [*Aside*] Here's a greeting betwixt a cobbler, a smith, and a botcher. They all belong to the foot, which makes them stand so much upon their gentry.

Mendoza. Señor Lazarillo.

Lazarillo. [*To Mendoza*] Ah, señor, sí. [*Aside*] Nay, we are all   70
señors here in Spain, from the jakes-farmer to the Grandee or Adelantado. This botcher looks as if he were dough-baked: a little butter now, and I could eat him like an oaten cake. His father's diet was new cheese and onions when he got him: what a scallion-faced rascal 'tis!   75

Metaldi. But why, Señor Pacheco, do you stand so much on the priority and antiquity of your quality, as you call it, in comparison to ours?

Mendoza. Ay, your reason for that.

---

66. SD] *GWW.* Here's] *F2;* Her's *F.*   69. Señor] *F* (*Signior*).   70. SD1 and SD2] *this edn.*   señor] *F* (*Signior*).   sí] *TSS;* see *F, F2.*   71. señors] *F* (*Signiors*).   72. were] *F2;* w're *F.*   76. Señor] *F* (*Signior*).

66–8.] Lazarillo comments on the social inappropriateness of the ceremonious salutations of the three craftsmen, who can hardly claim to be members of the gentry. They all 'belong to the foot' in that they work with objects that are worn on the lower limbs: the cobbler mends shoes, the botcher mends hose to be worn on the legs, and the smith fixes shoes on to horses' hooves.

66. *cobbler*] A craftsman who mends shoes, rather than making them. His secondary professional status to that of a shoemaker is similar to that of a botcher with respect to a tailor. In *Plain Perceval* (1590), Richard Harvey declares that 'in every trade and occupation, there is a better and a worse [...] there is a shoemaker, there is a cobbler; a tailor and a botcher' (*Perceval,* sig. C3ᵛ).

70–1. *Nay ... Spain*] Lazarillo comments on the oddity of Mendoza's address to him as an equal when he is Pacheco's servant; again, an aside seems to be preferable.

71. *jakes-farmer*] the person in charge of cleaning the privy or jakes; i.e., someone employed in the lowliest of menial jobs.

72. *Grandee*] The highest distinction among the Spanish aristocracy (*Grande de España*), only granted by the monarch to a select elite.

Adelantado] In seventeenth-century Spain, the 'president or chief justice of a certain realm, province or district, and captain-general in times of war' (*DRAE,* my translation).

73. *dough-baked*] insufficiently baked, raw, which Lazarillo finds appetising if butter were added.

74–5. *cheese and onions*] foods proverbially associated with the Welsh.

75. *scallion-faced*] with a face like a chibol or Welsh onion.

77. *quality*] social status.

Pacheco. Why, thou iron-pated smith. And thou, woollen-witted   80
    hose-heeler. Hear what I will speak indifferently—and
    according to ancient writers—of our three professions.
    And let the upright Lazarillo be both judge and moderator.

Lazarillo. [*Aside*] Still am I the most immortally hungry that
    may be.   85

Pacheco. [*To Metaldi*] Suppose thou wilt derive thy pedigree
    like some of the old heroes—as Hercules, Aeneas,
    Achilles—lineally from the gods, making Saturn thy
    great-grandfather and Vulcan thy father. Vulcan was a
    god.   90

Lazarillo. [*Aside*] He'll make Vulcan your godfather by and
    by.

Pacheco. Yet, I say Saturn was a crabbed blockhead, and
    Vulcan a limping horn-head, for Venus, his wife, was a
    strumpet, and Mars begat all her children; therefore,   95

---

84. SD] *this edn.*   86. SD] *this edn.*   87. Aeneas] *F2; Æeas F.*   91. SD]
GWW.   94. Vulcan] *F2; Vulgan F.*   95. begat] *F;* begot *F2.*

---

80. *iron-pated*] iron-headed, obstinate.
woollen-witted] soft-headed, foolish.
81. *indifferently*] without bias.
82. *ancient writers*] authorities to support his argument.
87–8. *Hercules, Aeneas, Achilles*] heroes of classical antiquity descended
from the gods. The three of them were the offspring of an immortal god or
goddess and a mortal: Hercules was the son of the supreme god Jupiter/Zeus
and the mortal Alcmene, and accomplished the Twelve Labours; the Trojan
hero Aeneas was the son of the goddess Venus/Aphrodite and prince
Anchises, and was the legendary founder of Rome after the fall of Troy; and
the Greek hero Achilles was the son of the immortal sea nymph Thetis and
the mortal prince Peleus, and is the principal hero of the *Iliad*. (For classical
allusions in this scene, see Grimal.)
88. *Saturn*] Roman version of the Greek Titan Cronos, sometimes said
to be the father of Hephaestus/Vulcan.
89. *Vulcan*] Roman deity identified with the Greek fire god Hephaestus.
He was lame due to having been thrown down from Olympus by his father
in a rage. He was married to the goddess Aphrodite (the Roman Venus),
who was unfaithful to him with Ares (the Roman Mars), thus making him
a proverbial cuckold (see lines 93–5).
93. *crabbed blockhead*] irritable dullard.
94. *limping horn-head*] see 89 n.
94–5. *Venus … strumpet*] see 89 n.; Venus/Aphrodite was the goddess of
love.
95. *Mars … children*] see 89 n.; Mars/Ares was the god of war.

however, thy original must of necessity spring from bas-
tardy. Further, what can be a more deject spirit in man
than to lay his hands under everyone's horse's feet to do
him service, as thou dost? [*To Mendoza*] For thee, I will
be brief. Thou dost botch, and not mend. Thou art a   100
hider of enormities; *videlicet*, scabs, chilblains and kibed
heels. Much prone thou art to sects and heresies, disturb-
ing state and government; for how canst thou be a sound
member in the commonwealth that art subject to stitches
in the ankles? Blush and be silent, then, O ye mechanic.   105
Compare no more with the politic cobbler. For cobblers—
in old time—have prophesied. What may they do now,
then, that have every day waxed better and better? Have
we not the length of every man's foot? Are we not daily
menders? Yea, and what menders? Not hose-menders—   110
Lazarillo. [*Aside*] Nor manners-menders.
Pacheco. But soul-menders. O divine cobblers. Do we not, like
the wise man, spin our own threads, or our wives for us?

---

97. be] *F;* shew *Colman.*   99. SD] *GWW.*   101. *videlicet*] *F (viz.).*   105.
mechanic] *F;* Mechanicks *F2.*   110. hose] *this edn;* horse *F.*   111. SD]
GWW.   112. soul-menders] *F state 2;* soule-members *F state 1.*   113. spin]
F; spin out *F2.*

96. *however*] in any case.
101. *videlicet*] Latin for 'that is to say', often abbreviated as *viz.*
scabs] diseases of the skin, such as tinea or eczema, that produce itching
scales or pustules.
chilblains] inflammations of the skin produced by extreme cold.
101–2. *kibed heels*] feet affected by chilblains.
102. *sects and heresies*] In Thomas Nashe's *The Unfortunate Traveller*
(1594; STC 18380), botchers and tailors are criticised as ignorant schismat-
ics, as the tailor John of Leiden had been the leader of the Anabaptist upris-
ing in Münster in 1534.
104. *commonwealth*] body of people constituting a nation.
105. *mechanic*] tradesman, manual worker.
106–7. *cobblers ... prophesied*] Probably a reference to Robert Wilson's play
The Cobbler's Prophecy (c. 1592).
108. *waxed*] (a) thrived; (b) waxed the thread to mend shoes.
112. *soul-menders*] repairers of souls, but punning on the homophone *sole*
of a shoe; cf. the Cobbler in Shakespeare's *JC*: 'A trade, sir, that I hope I
may use with a safe conscience, which is indeed, sir, a mender of bad soles'
(1.1.12–13).
112–13. *Do ... us*] The phrase rings proverbial, but is not recorded.

Do we not, by our sewing the hide, reap the beef? Are
not we of the gentle craft, whilst both you are but crafts- 115
men? [*To Metaldi*] You will say you fear neither iron nor
steel, and what you get is wrought out of the fire; I must
answer you again, though: all this is but forgery. [*To
Mendoza*] You may likewise say a man's a man that has
but a hose on his head; I must likewise answer that man 120
is a botcher that has a heeled hose on his head. To conclude, there can be no comparison with the cobbler, who
is all in all in the commonwealth, has his politic eye and
ends on every man's steps that walks, and whose course
shall be lasting to the world's end. 125

Metaldi. I give place. The wit of man is wonderful. Thou hast
hit the nail on the head, and I will give thee six pots for't,
though I ne'er clinch shoe again.

Enter VITELLI *and* [*the*] ALGUAZIR.

---

116. SD] *this edn.* 118. is] *not in TSS.* SD] *this edn.* 126. SP] *F2; Net.*
F. 128. clinch] *F2;* clinth *F;* clench *Weber.*

---

114. *sewing ... beef*] 'By stitching the leather to make shoes, we earn our
sustenance', punning on 'sewing' and 'sowing'; cf. Galatians 6:7 'whatsoever
a man soweth, that shall he also reap'.

115. *gentle craft*] A phrase commonly applied to shoemakers, as in the title
of Thomas Dekker's *The Shoemakers' Holiday, or The Gentle Craft.* In this
passage Pacheco appropriates the phrase for a profession that is not strictly
shoemaking, as cobblers only mend shoes but do not make them. His self-
aggrandising diction and the tendency to weave proverbs into his speech are
reminiscent of Simon Eyre, the protagonist of Dekker's city comedy.

118. *forgery*] falsehood, counterfeit; punning on the forge where Metaldi
works as a smith, as well as on his name, 'de Forgia' (see 61 n.).

119–20. *You ... head*] Mitchell suggests the paraphrase 'a man is still a
man even if he wears his hose on his head i.e., the wrong place?' If this is
so, then a botcher can be distinguished from other men in that he would
wear patched-up hose.

123. *all in all*] everything.
eye] the eye of his needle, which has sewn shoes (and is therefore 'on every
man's steps that walks')

124. *course*] his path in life, and, by extension, the path trodden by every
man whose shoes he has mended.

126. *I give place*] I concede that you are right.

127. *six pots*] six drinks, presumably in metal containers (as he is talking
in terms of his trade as a smith).

128. *clinch shoe*] fix nails into a horse's hoof.

Pacheco. [*Apart*] Who's this? O, our Alguazir. As arrant a
    knave as e'er wore one head under two offices. He is one   130
    side Alguazir—
Metaldi. [*Apart*] The other side sergeant.
Mendoza. [*Apart*] That's both sides carrion, I am sure.
Pacheco. [*Apart*] This is he apprehends whores in the way of
    justice, and lodges 'em in his own house in the way of   135
    profit. He with him is the grand Don Vitelli, 'twixt whom
    and Fernando Álvarez the mortal hatred is. He is indeed
    my Don's bawd, and does at this present lodge a famous
    courtesan of his, lately come from Madrid.
Vitelli. [*To the Alguazir*] Let her want nothing, señor, she
    can ask.   140
    What loss or injury you may sustain,
    I will repair, and recompense your love.
    Only that fellow's coming I mislike,
    And did forewarn her of him. Bear her this
            [*He gives him a gift for Malroda.*]
    With my best love; at night I'll visit her.   145

---

129. SD] *GWW.*   130. one head] *F2;* ont head *F.*   132. SD] *GWW.*
133. SD] *GWW.*   134. SD] *GWW.*   139. Madrid] *F2;* Madrill *F.*   140.
SD] *this edn.*   señor] *F (Signior).*   144. SD] *this edn.*

129–39.] The three craftsmen obviously discuss the Alguazir and Vitelli
out of earshot, hence the SD *Apart.*
   130. *wore ... offices*] wearing two hats, performing a double office.
   130–3. *He ... sure*] The description is suggestive of an anamorphic portrait of the period in which an image was seen differently when looked from
opposing points of views. Cf. Cleopatra in Shakespeare's *A&C:* 'Though he
be painted one way like a Gorgon, / The other way's a Mars' (2.5.117–18).
   133. *carrion*] corrupt, figuratively rotten like a decomposing corpse.
   134. *he*] he who.
   136. *grand*] the eminent, the renowned; an augmentation of the title.
   137. *Fernando Álvarez*] Clara and Lucio's father, who is named by the
Herald with the expanded form 'Don Ferdinando de Álvarez' in 5.3.12,
probably perceived to be a more formal version of the same name. Since the
character is named after the Duke of Alba, the form given here, 'Fernando
Álvarez', is correct (see 1.1.114 n.).
   138. *my Don*] the Don I'm currently talking about.
   140. *she ... ask*] that she can ask.
   143. *that fellow's coming*] Piorato's visits to Malroda, with a probable pun
on the swordsman's orgasm (see *OED*, 'come', *v.*, 22); obviously the two
characters have not yet appeared on stage.
   144. SD *gift*] The SD cannot be more specific, as the prop is not named;
it could be a jewel or money, or any other small portable item of some value.

Alguazir. I rest your lordship's servant.
Vitelli. [*To the others*]   Good ev'n, señors.
    [*Aside*] O Álvarez, thou hast brought a son with thee
    Both brightens and obscures our nation;
    Whose pure strong beams on us shoot like the sun's
    On baser fires. I would to heaven my blood   150
    Had never stained thy bold unfortunate hand,
    That with mine honour I might emulate,
    Not persecute, such virtue. I will see him,
    Though with the hazard of my life. No rest
    In my contentious spirits can I find   155
    Till I have gratified him in like kind.   *Exit.*
Alguazir. I know you not. What are ye? Hence, ye base
    bisognos.
Pacheco. Marry, *cazzo*! Señor Alguazir, do ye not know us?
    Why, we are your honest neighbours, the cobbler, smith,   160

---

146. SD] *this edn.*   señors] *(Signiors);*signior *Dyce.*   147. SD *Aside*] *Dyce;*
apart | *GWW.*   148. brightens] *F2;* brightnes *F.*   157. you not] ye not
Colman.   159. Marry] *F (Mary).*   Señor] *F (Signior).*   do ye] *F (*do'ye*);*
d'ye *F2;* d'you *Colman;* do you *Weber.*

146. *señors*] The correct Spanish would be *señores*, but the metre dictates
that it should be anglicised to a two-syllable word. Dyce emended for
'signior', interpreting that Vitelli bids farewell to the Alguazir before leaving.
It seems unnecessary to emend the F reading, though, as implies that Vitelli
acknowledges the presence of the craftsmen and Lazarillo, and salutes them
before directing his aside to the audience.

147–56.] This is an important soliloquy for the understanding of Vitelli's
motivations. From his point of view, Álvarez's son (i.e., Clara) has contributed to advance Spain's military reputation with his deeds in battle, but he
has also brought infamy to the country by securing that a murderer, Álvarez,
might remain unpunished. Vitelli, impressed by the honourable conduct of
the youth, laments that his uncle's blood inevitably stains, by generational
transference, the hands of him who should have been a model of conduct
and not the target of revenge. Despite his conflicted emotions, Vitelli
acknowledges his indebtedness to the young man for saving his life (in 1.3)
and he prepares to risk a return to his enemy's home to pay him a visit (2.2).

148. *Both*] who at the same time.

150. *my blood*] my family's blood, i.e., the blood of his murdered uncle
Don Pedro (see 1.1).

156. *gratified*] (a) expressed my gratitude; (b) offered some service in
return; cf. 2.2.195.

158. *bisognos*] raw soldiers, inexpert beginners.

159. *Marry*] a mild oath ('by Mary').

cazzo] Italian swearword, literally 'penis'.

and botcher, that have so often sat snoring cheek by jowl
with your señory in rug at midnight.

Lazarillo. [*To Pacheco*] Nay, good señor, be not angry. You
must understand a cat and such an officer see best in the
dark.   165

Metaldi. By this hand, I could find in my heart to shoe his
head.

Pacheco. [*To the Alguazir*] Why then, we know you, señor, thou
mongrel begot at midnight at the jail gate by a beadle on
a catchpole's wife: are not you he that was whipped out   170
of Toledo for perjury?

---

162. señory] *F* (signiorie); Signior *Langbaine.*   163. SD] *this edn.*   señor]
F (Signior).   168. SD] *this edn.*   we] *TSS; not in F.*   señor] *F* (Signior).

---

161. *cheek ... jowl*] proverbial (Tilley, C263).

162. *your señory*] your worship; the correct Spanish *señoría* would be a
more radical modernisation.

in rug] wearing a coarse woollen garment or blanket.

163. *be not angry*] calm down; a commonplace expression (see 2.2.1).

164–5. *cat ... dark*] The Alguazir, like a cat, is active during the night.

166–7. *hand ... heart ... head*] an interesting alliterative succession of
body parts.

166. *to shoe*] to nail a horseshoe to his head.

168–70. *thou ... wife*] Pacheco implies that, by his supposed illegitimate
and adulterous parentage, the Alguazir is prone to abuse his legal duties.

169. *mongrel*] By identification with dogs, the offspring of parents of dissimilar circumstances.

midnight] with the aggravation of night.

beadle] a warrant officer of justice.

170. *catchpole's wife*] the adulterous wife of an unpopular catchpole, a
petty officer of justice.

170–97.] This sequence is an augmentation of the exchange between
Robin Goodfellow and the Fairy in *MND*: 'Are you not he / That frights the
maidens of the villag'ry [...] Are you not he?' (2.1.34–42).

170–1. *whipped ... perjury*] Perhaps the Alguazir was a converted Jew (as
suggested by his red hair) who was banished for his false conversion (see
line 206, and 3.1.3–4 and 58). Toledo had a significant Jewish population
until the expulsion in 1492. In *Guzmán* the eponymous *pícaro* leaves Toledo
when, after being extorted of some gold, he finds an *alguacil* in the inn where
he is staying, and decides to run away from the city (I, II, 8); the juxtaposition of the *alguacil*, Toledo, and petty crime indicate that Guzmán is probably
the source for the Alguazir (see Introduction, 29–30).

Mendoza. Next condemned to the galleys for pilfery, to the
    bull's pizzle?
Metaldi. And after called to the Inquisition for apostasy?
Pacheco. Are not you he that, rather than you durst go an   175
    industrious voyage, being pressed to the Islands, skulked
    till the fleet was gone and then earned your royal a day
    by squiring punks and punklings up and down the city?
Lazarillo. Are not you a Portuguese-born descended o' the
    Moors, and came hither into Seville with your master, an   180

---

172. pilfery] pilfery, there *TSS.*   180. Seville] *F* (Civill).

172. *galleys*] Being sentenced to row in the King's galleys was a Spanish
punishment for major offences. Even a strong man would not typically
survive such strenuous physical activity for more than a few years. Mendoza's
accusation is reminiscent of Guzmán's punishment towards the end of
Guzmán, in which the *picaro* is sent off to the galleys for stealing from a lady
whom he served (II, III, 7). Cf. the Asistente's sentence on the Alguazir and
his associates in 5.3.235.
    pilfery] petty robbery.
    173. *bull's pizzle*] a whip made from a stretched bull's penis, particularly
associated with its use on galleys to flog rowers.
    174. *Inquisition ... apostasy*] If the Alguazir was a false convert from
Judaism, the Inquisition would have tried him for perjury and for abandon-
ing the true Catholic faith, i.e., for apostasy. The Tribunal of the Holy Office
of the Inquisition was established in Castile and Aragón by the Catholic
Monarchs (see 5.3.7 n.) in 1478 to uphold Catholic orthodoxy in their kingdoms, and was not abolished completely until 1834.
    176. *industrious*] profitable.
    pressed] conscripted to service on a ship.
    Islands] perhaps the Spice Islands, now the Maluku archipelago, where
Fletcher's *Princess* is set.
    skulked] sneaked away, hid out of sight.
    177. *royal a day*] A Spanish silver *real* was worth 5 English shillings (or
60 pence; see Fischer, 115); Pacheco implies, therefore, that the Alguazir's
business as a pander was very profitable.
    178. *squiring*] escorting, accompanying (*OED* 1).
    punks ... punklings] small and large prostitutes, or adult whores and pros-
tituted children; this is the only instance of the coinage *punkling* in the *OED*
(defined as 'A small or young prostitute'). Cf. Sir Epicure Mammon in *Alch.*:
'You shall start up young viceroys / And have your punks and punketees, my
Surly' (2.1.22–3).
    179–80. *Portuguese-born ... Moors*] An instance of racial, national, and
religious prejudice. On the one hand, he seems to be implicitly accused of
having Jewish ancestry, as many expelled Spanish Jews emigrated to Portugal
after 1492 (cf. lines 170–1). On the other hand, he is accused of being a

errant tailor, in your red bonnet and your blue jacket,
lousy; though now your blockhead be covered with the
Spanish block, and your lashed shoulders with a velvet
pee?

Pacheco. Are not you he that have been of thirty callings, yet   185
ne'er a one lawful? That, being a chandler first, professed
sincerity, and would sell no man mustard to his beef on
the Sabbath, and yet sold hypocrisy all your lifetime?

Metaldi. Are not you he that were since a surgeon to the stews,
and undertook to cure what the church itself could not,   190

Morisco, a descendant of Spanish Muslims who had converted to the
Christian faith; the Moriscos were officially expelled from Spain in stages
between 1609 and 1614, so the issue was topical. For an English audience
this might have presented a multiple layer of prejudice: the Alguazir is not
only Spanish, but also Portuguese and Moorish.

181. *errant tailor*] itinerant tailor; tailors were regarded as puny; cf. the
proverb 'Nine tailors make a man' (Tilley, T23).

red ... jacket] In Jacobean England blue was worn by servants and prostitutes in houses of correction; a red bonnet carries connotations of
Jewishness. In *Valentinian* the poet Paulus wants to wear blue to a state
occasion, earning Lycippus' mockery for its inappropriateness (see Wiggins,
Sex Tragedies, 5.4.14 n.). It was well-known that Jews in Renaissance Venice
were required to wear red hats to distinguish them from Christians (see
Holderness, 45–6).

183. *Spanish block*] a hat in the Spanish fashion; the block was the wooden
piece used to mould hats (*OED* 4b). The Alguazir dresses in the Spanish
fashion but is still a despised foreigner.

lashed shoulders] The Alguazir's back is scarred from being flogged (with
the bull's pizzle) in the galleys (see lines 172–3).

184. *pee*] coat of coarse fabric.

185. *callings*] professions, vocations; in the early modern picaresque
novel, the *pícaro* was usually employed in a series of professions, which
provided the conventional episodic structure of the narrative.

186. *chandler*] grocer (*OED* 3a).

187–8. *sell ... lifetime*] The Alguazir is accused of having pretended to be
a Sabbatarian, a man who observed strict restraint on the Christian Sabbath
(Sunday); on that day, adding mustard to a dish of beef would be a frivolous
sophistication.

189. *since*] specifically after being a chandler.

surgeon ... stews] a surgeon who assists syphilitic women in brothels.

190. *church*] in the context of the play, the Roman Catholic Church.

strumpets; that ris to your office by being a great Don's
bawd?

Lazarillo. That commit men nightly, offenceless, for the gain
of a groat a prisoner, which your beadle seems to put up
when you share threepence?   195

Mendoza. Are not you he that is a kisser of men in drunkenness, and a berayer in sobriety?

Alguazir. [*Aside*] *¡Diablo!* They'll rail me into the galleys
again.

Pacheco. Yes, señor, thou art even he we speak of all this while.   200
Thou may'st by thy place now lay us by the heels. 'Tis
true. But take heed, be wiser, pluck not ruin on thine own
head. For never was there such an anatomy as we shall
make thee then. Be wise therefore, O thou child of the
night! Be friends and shake hands; thou art a proper man,   205

---

191. ris] *Dyce (*riss*); rise F   197. berayer] Betrayer *Langbaine.*   198. SD]
Dyce. Diablo] *Weber; Diabolo F, F2.*   200. señor] *(*Signior*).*   204. O] *not
in F2.*

191–2. *ris ... bawd*] If the Don in question is Vitelli, then the implied story
is that the gallant procured him the office of Alguazir when he agreed to
keep Malroda in his own house.

191. *ris*] archaic form of the past tense of *rise*, rose, sometimes spelled
risse.

193–5. *That ... threepence*] The Alguazir illegally arrests blameless people
at night and charges four pence (a groat) for each of them; of these, three
are given to a complicit beadle while he keeps a penny, making a small profit.

194. *to put up*] to tolerate knowingly, to accept an illegal share (*OED* 9b).

196–7. *kisser ... drunkenness*] The long list of insulting charges against the
Alguazir concludes with an accusation of homosexuality.

197. *berayer*] beshitter, one who defecates in his own breeches; the simultaneous accusation of homosexuality and self-defecation may imply that the
Alguazir has committed sodomy, presumably resulting in the loosening of
the anal sphincter.

198. *¡Diablo!*] Spanish for 'devil'. The F reading is in Italian, '*Diabolo*';
Weber emended for the Spanish form, as it recurs in 2.2.2.

198–9. *They'll ... again*] 'If anyone overhears this, I will be charged and
sent to the galleys again.'

201. *lay ... heels*] arrest us.

203. *anatomy*] corpse, normally supplied by the gallows, which was publicly dissected in an anatomy theatre, usually in front of a paying audience.

205. *proper man*] Pacheco uses the language of moral value in an inverted
way, suggesting that a morally wicked person is the better for the criminal
business, and thus 'proper'.

if thy beard were redder. Remember thy worshipful function, a constable; though thou turnst day into night, and
night into day, what of that? Watch less, and pray more.
Gird thy bear's skin—*videlicet*, thy rug gown—to thy
loins, take thy staff in thy hand, and go forth at midnight.   210
Let not thy mittens abate the talons of thy authority, but
grip theft and whoredom wheresoever thou meet'st 'em.
Bear 'em away like a tempest, and lodge 'em safely in
thine own house.

Lazarillo. Would you have whores and thieves lodged in such   215
a house?

Pacheco. They ever do so. I have found a thief or a whore there
when the whole suburbs could not furnish me.

Lazarillo. But why do they lodge there?

209–10. Gird ... midnight] *not in F2.*   209. bear's skin] *F* (beares skin);
bear-skin *Colman.*   videlicet] *F (viz.).*   210. loins] *Colman;* loyes *F; not in*
F2.

---

206. *if ... redder*] Judas Iscariot, the ultimate malefactor as the betrayer
of Jesus Christ, was traditionally thought to have had a red beard; the
Alguazir's red beard qualifies him as a proverbial criminal, as well as a Jew.
See 3.1.58.

206. *worshipful*] respectful on account of his civic rank (*OED* 2a).

207–8. *turnst ... day*] He is on duty (and up to his criminal activities) at
night, and rests during the day.

208. *Watch*] He watches in two senses: at night he is a watchman and he
stays awake.

209–10. *Gird ... midnight*] Missing passage in F2. As Battle points out,
'the omission might have been made because of the Biblical parody (see 1
Kings 20:32, Job 12:18, Proverbs 31:17)' (Battle, 9). Other obvious biblical
parodies in the text, however, were not censored (e.g., see 1.3.78 n.).

209. *rug gown*] a coat made of rug (see line 162 n.).

210. *staff*] staff of office.

211. *mittens*] gloves, figuratively as a hindrance to someone's sense of
touch, but also punning on 'mittanes', birds of prey (*OED*); the mittens were
also the handcuffs used to arrest people.

talons] the claws of a bird of prey, figuratively the Alguazir's grip; cf.
4.2.127–8.

217–18. *I ... me*] This makes the Alguazir's house a good place in which
to find potential accomplices for criminal deeds.

218. *suburbs*] as the typical haunt of criminals.

219.] Lazarillo responds naively to the situation.

Pacheco. That they may be safe and forthcoming. For in the   220
　　morning usually the thief is sent to the jail, and the whore
　　prostrates herself to the Justice.

Mendoza. Admirable Pacheco.

Metaldi. Thou cobbler of Christendom.

Alguazir. [*Aside*] There is no railing with these rogues. I will   225
　　close with 'em till I can cry quittance. [*Aloud*] Why,
　　señors, and my honest neighbours, will you impute that
　　as a neglect of my friends which is an imperfection in me?
　　I have been sand-blind from my infancy. To make you
　　amends, you shall sup with me.   230

Lazarillo. Shall we sup with ye, sir? [*Aside*] O' my conscience,
　　they have wronged the gentleman extremely.

Alguazir. And after supper, I have a project to employ you in
　　shall make you drink and eat merrily this month. I am a
　　little knavish. Why, and do not I know all you to be   235
　　knaves?

Pacheco. I grant you, we are all knaves, and will be your
　　knaves. But O, while you live take heed of being a proud
　　knave.

Alguazir. On then, pass. I will bear out my staff, and my staff   240
　　shall bear out me.

Lazarillo. [*Aside*] O Lazarillo, thou art going to supper!
　　　　　　　　　　　　　　　　　　　　　　　　　　Exeunt.

---

221. jail] *F* (Goale). 225. SD] *Weber.* 226. SD] *Dyce.* 227. señors]
F (Signiors). you] ye *Colman.* 231. SD] *this edn.* 242. SD] *this edn.*

---

222. *prostrates herself*] (a) kneels down before the Justice; (b) offers him
sexual services.
　　Justice] Justice as an institution, or the specific local authority.
　　226. *close*] make a deal.
　　cry quittance] say we are even, terminate the arrangement.
　　229. *sand-blind*] dim-sighted; cf. Old Gobbo in *MV*: 'Alack, sir, I am
sand-blind. I know you not' (2.2.70).
　　231–2.] Lazarillo seems to take the Alguazir's invitation to be one to a
lawful merry gathering, when they are really being invited to partake in the
gains of crime; cf. the Asistente's invitation at the end of the play (5.3.226).
　　234. *this month*] for this entire month.
　　238–9. *proud knave*] overconfident knave; this is a subtle form of black-
mail, as Pacheco is implying that they will use what they know of the
Alguazir's activities if he behaves in a supercilious way.
　　240–1. *I ... me*] everything he shall do will seem legitimate because of his
office, as symbolised by his staff.

SCENE 2

Enter LUCIO [*in men's clothes*] *and* BOBADILLA

Lucio. Pray, be not angry.

Bobadilla. I am angry, and I will be angry, *diablo*. What should
you do in the kitchen? Cannot the cooks lick their fingers
without your overseeing? Nor the maids make pottage
except your dog's head be in the pot? Don Lucio, Don   5
Cotquean, Don Spinster, wear a petticoat still and put on
your smock o' Monday. I will have a baby o' clouts made
for it, like a great girl. Nay, if you will needs be starching
of ruffs, and sewing of black work, I will of a mild and
loving tutor become a tyrant. Your father has committed   10
you to my charge, and I will make a man or a mouse on
you.

SCENE 2] *F (Scæna Secunda.).*   o. SD] *this edn.*   2. SP] *F2; not in F.*
7. o'] *F (a').*   baby] *F2;* badie *F.*

2.2.0.] Location: Álvarez and Eugenia's house. Weber indicates '*A room
in Álvarez's house. Arms hanging on the wall.*'

  1. *be not angry*] commonplace expression (see 2.1.163).

  2. *diablo*] Spanish for 'devil', used here as an expletive, not in vocative
sense.

  4. *pottage*] either a broth with vegetables or oatmeal porridge.

  6. *Cotquean*] a contemptuous term for man who busies himself with tasks
normally allocated to women or who generally behaves like a woman (*OED*
3); a compound of *cot* (mean house, hut) and *quean* (a coarse, vulgar woman,
especially a prostitute).

  Spinster] in the sense of one who busies himself in spinning (as Lucio does
with his needlework), but also, from around this time, an unmarried woman.

  6–7. *put ... Monday*] Also given as 'Put on your/thy smock a Monday'; is
the title of a well-known English dance tune of the period. It appears for
the first time in the fourth edition of John Playford's *The Dancing Master*
(1670) as 'Put on thy Smock a Munday. *A Round Dance for six*' (Playford,
sig. I3ᵛ). In Heywood's *Kindness*, Nicholas refers to it in 2.41. Bobadilla's
sense is 'put on your skirt and go out dancing like a girl'.

  7–8. *I ... girl*] Bobadilla uses baby talk with Lucio, addressing him as *it*
as if he were a child.

  7. *baby o' clouts*] a rag doll in the shape of a baby.

  8–9. *starching of ruffs*] see 1.2.2 n.

  9. *black work*] a type of embroidery that used black silk threads on white
cloth, especially popular in the Elizabethan period; see 3.4.38.

  of] from being.

  11–12. *I ... you*] remaining a woman is not an alternative.

  11. *on*] of.

Lucio. What would you have me do? This scurvy sword
 So galls my thigh, I would 'twere burnt. Pish, look:
 This cloak will ne'er keep on. These boots, too
  hidebound,   15
 Make me walk stiff as if my legs were frozen,
 And my spurs jingle like a Morris-dancer.
 Lord, how my head aches with this roguish hat.
 This masculine attire is most uneasy.
 I am bound up in it. I had rather walk   20
 In folio again, loose, like a woman.
Bobadilla. In 'foolio', had you not? Thou mock to heav'n, and
 nature, and thy parents; thou tender leg of lamb. [*Lucio
 walks.*] O, how he walks as if he had bepissed himself,
 and fleers! Is this a gait for the young cavalier Don Lucio, 25

22–30.] *prose in this edn; F and all eds line* not? / Parents, / walkes / fleares! / Cavalier, / *Alvarez?* / conscience, / wayes, / *Vitelli*, / advance, / sword. /.
23. SD] *this edn.*

---

13. *burnt*] perhaps indicating that it is a wooden sword for practice (or a theatrical prop), and not one made of metal and obviously impossible to burn. However, Clara's comment later ("'Tis a reasonable good one', line 126) may indicate that it is an actual metal sword, and thus Lucio might mean to see it melted out of use. Alternatively, see Ezekiel 39:9–10.

15. *too hidebound*] The leather (hide) is too tight (see Tilley, H454).

17. *Morris-dancer*] Morris-dancers wear bells on their legs.

19. *This ... uneasy*] Cf. Phillida disguised as a boy in Lyly's *Galatea*: 'I neither like my gait nor my garments, the one untoward, the other unfit, both unseemly' (2.1.14–15).

21. *In folio*] Feminine clothes, including skirts with wide farthingales (like the one Clara is wearing later in this scene) are here likened to books printed in large folio format; tighter masculine clothes are analogous to a smaller binding (as Lucio is 'bound up' in them; see line 20).

22–30.] This speech was erroneously typeset as eleven lines of verse in F (and every subsequent edition), resulting in a sequence of irregular, predominantly non-iambic lines. Bobadilla speaks in prose in the rest of this scene (except in his next speech, for a justifiable reason; see lines 32–5 n.). His speech patterns, however, vary from scene to scene: he speaks in prose in 1.2, 1.3, 2.2, and 5.3, but he uses only verse in 3.2, 3.4, 4.3, and 5.2. These patterns seem to have no correspondence with Hoy's authorship shares.

25. *fleers*] (a) he grimaces or distorts his face with grins (*OED* 1); (b) he laughs in an unbecoming manner (*OED* 2)

gait] manner of walking, bearing (*OED* 1).

son and heir to Álvarez? Has it a corn? Or does it walk
on conscience, it treads so gingerly? Come on your ways;
suppose me now your father's foe, Vitelli, and spying you
i'th' street, thus I advance, I twist my beard, and then I
draw my sword.   [He draws.]   30

Lucio. Alas.

Bobadilla. And thus accost thee: 'Traitorous brat,
How durst thou thus confront me? Impious twig
Of that old stock dewed with my kinsman's gore,
Draw, for I'll quarter thee in pieces four.'   35

Lucio. Nay, prithee, Bobadilla, leave thy fooling,
Put up thy sword. I will not meddle with ye.
Ay, jostle me, I care not. I'll not draw.
Pray be a quiet man.

Bobadilla. Do ye hear? Answer me as you would do Don   40
Vitelli, or I'll be so bold as to lay the pommel of my sword
over the hilts of your head.
'My name's Vitelli, and I'll have the wall.'

---

30. SD] *this edn.*   36. leave] leaving *Langbaine.*   37. ye] you *Weber.*   40. Do
ye] *F* (Do'ye)*; D'ye *F2;* Do you *Dyce.*   43.] *verse, TSS; prose, F.*

---

26. *it*] as in lines 7–8, *it* is indicative of baby talk.
corn] horny induration of the cuticle caused by excessive pressure on the
feet from wearing tight footwear (*OED n.*[2] 1a).
27. *on conscience*] self-consciously.
gingerly] daintily, effeminately (*OED* A.a).
29. *twist my beard*] Weber annotates that 'to twist one's own beard was
an insult intended to provoke the choler of the adversary, a mark of indignity
similar to biting the thumb [as in Shakespeare's *R&J,* 1.1]'.
30. SD *He draws.*] If Lucio is carrying a wooden practice sword, a staging
possibility would be for Bobadilla to use his staff of office as a weapon.
32–5.] Bobadilla shifts to blank verse to impersonate Vitelli, perhaps
adjusting his voice and physicality to mimic that of the actor playing the
gallant.
32. *Traitorous*] scans as bisyllabic, 'trait'rous'; the speech is bombastic,
verging on the mock heroic.
38. *jostle me*] push me.
39. *quiet*] calm.
43.] a single line of verse, again impersonating Vitelli.
43–4. *wall … kennel*] The space closest to the walls of adjoining buildings
was the cleanest area in a street, while the kennel – the gutter that ran in
the middle of streets – is where waste was usually dumped. A gallant would
defend his right to walk by the wall, ascertaining his social superiority, and
perhaps his masculinity, over another. Lucio quickly surrenders his place,

Lucio. Why then, I'll have the kennel. What a coil you keep!
   'Señor, what happened 'twixt my sire and your   45
   Kinsman was long before I saw the world,
   No fault of mine; nor will I justify
   My father's crimes. Forget, sir, and forgive.
   'Tis Christianity. I pray, put up your sword;
   I'll give you any satisfaction   50
   That may become a gentleman. However,
   I hope you are bred to more humanity
   Than to revenge my father's wrong on me
   That crave your love and peace.' La you now, Sancho,
   Would not this quiet him were he ten Vitellis?   55
Bobadilla. O craven chicken of a cock o' th' game! Well, what
   remedy? Did thy father see this, o' my conscience, he
   would cut off thy masculine gender, crop thine ears, beat
   out thine eyes, and set thee in one of the pear-trees for a
   scarecrow. As I am Vitelli, I am satisfied; but as I am   60
   Bobadilla Spindola Sancho, steward of the house, and thy
   father's servant, I could find in my heart to lop off the
   hinder part of thy face, or to beat all thy teeth into thy

---

45. Señor] *F (Signior).*   54. La] *Dyce;* law *F.*   59. of] off *Q.*

---

and prefers to walk in the dirty gutter. In addition, in a street brawl a wall
provides extra protection to a fighter who has his back against it, while the
kennel is the most exposed position, open to opponents on all sides. Cf.
Bergetto in *'Tis Pity:* 'As I was walking just now in the street, I met a swag-
gering fellow would needs take the wall of me' (2.6.69–70).
   44. *coil*] noisy disturbance.
   45–54. *Señor ... peace*] Lucio, following Bobadilla's role play, addresses
the steward as if he were Vitelli.
   46. *long ... world*] A slightly misleading statement: according to Eugenia,
she was pregnant with Lucio when Álvarez was forced to leave Seville after
killing Vitelli's uncle (see 1.3.68–73).
   48. *Forget ... forgive*] proverbial (Tilley, F597); cf. 'Pray now, forget and
forgive.' *Lear H,* 21.83.
   49. *Christianity*] forgiveness is a fundamental Christian value; cf. 5.3.42.
See also 1.1.41 n.
   50. *satisfaction*] scans as five syllables.
   56. *craven chicken*] beaten coward.
   cock o' th' game] cock o' th' walk (Vitelli).
   58. *gender*] genitalia; however, this use is not recorded in the *OED.*
   62. *lop off*] cut off.

mouth. O thou whey-blooded milksop, I'll wait upon thee
no longer, thou shalt ev'n wait upon me. Come your   65
ways, sir, I shall take a little pains with ye else.

> *Enter* CLARA [*in women's clothes, carrying her weapons.*
> LUCIO *and* BOBADILLA *stand apart.*]

Clara. Where art thou, brother Lucio? Ran tan tan ta ran tan
    ran tan tan, ta ran tan tan tan. O, I shall no more see those
    golden days! These clothes will never fadge with me. A
    pox o' this filthy farthingale; this hip-hap! Brother, why   70
    are women's haunches only limited, confined, hooped in,
    as it were, with these same scurvy farthingales?
Bobadilla. Because women's haunches only are most subject
    to display and fly out.

> [*Clara aims her petronel at Lucio.*]

---

65. ev'n] even *Weber.*   66. ye] you *Colman.*   SD] *this edn.*   68. tan, ta]
F; tan ta, ta *F2.*   69–70. A pox] *Colman;* a — *F.*   70. farthingale] *F* (var-
dingale*).*   hip-hap] *F* (hip hape*).*   72. farthingales] *F* (vardingales*).*   74.
SD] *this edn.*

---

64. *whey-blooded milksop*] thin-blooded effeminate boy (*milksop, OED* 1a);
a milksop is also an infant who is still not weaned (*OED* 1b).
    66. SD *weapons*] The effect of the staging is the grotesque appearance of
a woman wearing feminine clothes (including a bulky farthingale), while she
carries a number of weapons. Clara must come on stage with three items,
since she discusses or uses them in the course of the scene: her sword, her
large petronel, and her father's truncheon or staff of command.
    67–8. *Ran ... tan*] Clara imitates the sound of a drum in battle. Cf. Juletta
pretending to be a page boy in *Pilgrim*: 'I am a drum, sir, / A drum at midnight; ran tan tan tan tan, sir. / Do you take me for Juletta? I am a page, sir'
(5.6.103–5).
    69. *fadge with me*] suit me (fadge, *OED* 1).
    70. *farthingale*] a hooped petticoat or underskirt to increase the bulk of
a skirt; the F spelling, *vardingale*, is closer to the Spanish etymology of the
word, *verdugado*, through a corruption of the French *verdugal*. In *La fuerza*,
Doña Costanza prescribes that her daughter Hipólita must wear a *verdugado*.
    hip-hap] a covering for the hips; the *OED* cites this passage as the only
recorded instance of the use of this term.
    73. *haunches*] hams.
    74. *display ... out*] In Bobadilla's opinion, if unconfined by a farthingale
and hip-hap, women's legs would have a natural tendency to be perpetually
apart, inviting sexual intercourse.

Clara. Bobadilla, rogue, ten ducats I hit the prepuce of thy   75
   cod-piece.
Lucio. Hold if you love my life, sister! I am not Sancho
   Bobadilla; I am your brother Lucio. What a fright you put
   me in!
Clara. Brother? And wherefore thus?   80
Lucio. Why, Master Steward here, Señor Sancho, made me
   change. He does nothing but misuse me, and call me
   coward, and swears I shall wait upon him.
Bobadilla. Well, I do no more than I have authority for. [*Aside*]
   Would I were away, though. For she's as much too   85
   mannish, as he too womanish. I dare not meddle with
   her, yet I must set a good face on't—if I had it. [*To Clara*]
   I have like charge of you, madam: I am as well to mollify
   you as to qualify him. What have you to do with armours,
   and pistols, and javelins, and swords, and such tools?   90
   Remember, mistress: nature hath given you a sheath only,
   to signify women are to put up men's weapons, not to

---

76. cod-piece] *F2;* Cod-peicu *F.*   81. Señor] *F (Signior).*   84. SD] *Weber.*
87. SD] *this edn.*   88. of you] of *F2.*

75–9.] This moment is the most interesting staging crux in the play. As
Williams explained, 'This is a difficult passage to visualize. In both of her
speeches [lines 67–72 and 75–6], Clara addresses one man and the other
answers' (94). The confusion may be explained if a frightened Bobadilla
hides behind Lucio when he hears Clara enter while replicating the sound
of the drum (2012 Shakespeare Institute production), or if Clara has her
vision temporarily impaired by a veil (2013 BADA production). See Pérez
Díez, 'Editing on stage'.
   75–6. *ten ... cod-piece*] 'I bet ten ducats I can shoot at and hit the end of
your codpiece.'
   75. *prepuce*] the foreskin of the penis; here, figuratively, the codpiece's
point (the lace fastening the codpiece) or simply its end.
   76. *cod-piece*] the protruding appendage on the front of a pair of breeches,
often conspicuous and ornamented (*OED* a).
   82. *misuse*] mistreat.
   87. *if ... it*] Bobadilla self-deprecatingly admits that he is ill-favoured.
   88–9. *mollify you*] soften you, tame you.
   89. *qualify him*] to bring him into a normal (i.e., masculine) condition
(*OED* 13).
   91–3. *nature ... them*] Bobadilla implies, quite explicitly, that women have
been given a vagina ('a sheath', following the Latin etymology of *vagina*) to
be penetrated ('to put up') by men's penises ('men's weapons').

draw them. [*Clara moves.*] Look you now: is this a fit trot
for a gentlewoman? You shall see the court's ladies move
like goddesses, as if they trod air; they will swim you their   95
measures like whiting-mops as if their feet were fins, and
the hinges of their knees oiled. Do they love to ride great
horses as you do? No, they love to ride great asses sooner.
'Faith, I know not what to say to ye both. Custom hath
turned nature topsy-turvy in you.   100

Clara. Nay, but master steward—

Bobadilla. You cannot trot so fast but he ambles as slowly.

Clara. Señor Spindle, will you hear me?

Bobadilla. He that shall come to bestride your virginity, had
better be afoot o'er the dragon.   105

Clara. Very well.   [*She walks towards Lucio.*]

Bobadilla. Did ever Spanish lady pace so?

Clara. [*To Lucio*] Hold these a little.

[*She offers Lucio her weapons.*]

Lucio.   I'll not touch them, I.

[*Clara leaves them aside.*]

---

93. SD] *this edn.*   99. say to ye] *F* (say to'ye*); say t'ye *F2;* say't ye *Q.*
103. Señor] *F* (Signior).   106. SD] *this edn.*   108. SD1, SD2, SD3] *this
edn.*

---

93. *a fit trot*] an appropriate way of walking.

96. *whiting-mops*] a type of young fish; Weber annotates that it is equivalent to 'young whitings, commonly used as a term of endearment'.

98. *great asses*] They would sooner have sex ('ride') with stupid courtiers.

99. *Custom*] see 1.2.51 n.

102. *You ... slowly*] Lucio moves like an ambling horse, in a smooth way,
which contrasts with Clara's brisk trot.

103. *Señor Spindle*] punning on Bobadilla's middle name, Spindola (see
line 61), and alluding to his lean figure (cf. his 'slender haunches'; 1.2.93).

104–5. *He ... dragon*] Bobadilla compares the man who might attempt to
take Clara's virginity to a warrior fighting a dragon. Unusually, this metaphorical knight will not fight the dragon on horseback, but by actually
mounting it (i.e., trying to penetrate Clara sexually). Later in the scene he
will advise Vitelli that she is like 'Bel the Dragon' (see line 170 n.). Cf.
Petronius in *Prize*, advising his son-in-law, Petruccio, before entering the
bedchamber on his wedding night: 'Will you to bed, son, and leave talking?
/ Tomorrow morning we shall have you look, / For all your great words, like
Saint George at Kingston, / Running a-foot back from the furious dragon /
That with her angry tail belabours him / For being lazy' (1.3.17–22).

108. *these ... them*] Clara offers Lucio her weapons; the cowardly Lucio
objects to holding them.

Clara. [*To Bobadilla*] First do I break your office o'er your pate—
    [*She takes Bobadilla's staff of office, and hits him with it.*]
    You dogskin-faced rogue, pilchard, you poor John—   110
    Which I will beat to stockfish!
Lucio.   Sister!
Bobadilla.   Madam!
Clara. You cittern-head, who have you talked to, ha?
    You nasty, stinking, and ill-countenanced cur?
Bobadilla. By this hand, I'll bang your brother for this when
    I get him alone.   115
Clara. How? Kick him, Lucio. He shall kick you, Bob,
    Spite o' the nose, that's flat. Kick him, I say,
    Or I will cut thy head off!
Bobadilla. Softly, you'd best.   [*Lucio kicks Bobadilla.*]
Clara. Now, thou lean, dried, and ominous-visaged knave,   120
    Thou false and peremptory steward, pray,
    For I will hang thee up in thine own chain.
    [*She tries to strangle Bobadilla with his chain of office.*]
Lucio. Good sister, do not choke him!   [*She releases him.*]
Bobadilla. Murder, murder!   *Exit.*

---

109. SD1, SD2] *this edn.*   117. the] thy *TSS.*   118. cut] kick *Weber.*   119. you'd] *Dyce;* y' had *F;* you had *Colman.*   SD] *this edn.*   122. SD] *this edn.*
123. SD] *this edn.*

---

109. *office*] Bobadilla's staff of office as steward of the house.
    110. *dogskin-faced*] a further comment on Bobadilla's ill-favoured complexion (see line 87 n.) *pilchard*] see 2.1.51 n.
    poor John] another type of fish.
    111. *stockfish*] a type of fish that is mashed up before consumption.
    112. *cittern-head*] the cittern, a musical instrument of the lute family, had a grotesque head carved at the end of its pegbox; it was a usual term of abuse (the *OED* records this instance).
    117. *Spite … nose*] A phrase commonly used as intensifier. Cf. Bergetto's defiance to his uncle in *'Tis Pity*: "'Sfoot, I will have the wench, if he were ten uncles, in despite of his nose' (3.1.4–5).
    120. *ominous-visaged*] with an awful or unsettling face; another reference to Bobadilla's ill-favoured features (see lines 110 and 112).
    122. SD] This moment is depicted in the frontispiece of Colman's 1778 edition (see figure 6, 49).

Clara. Well, I shall meet with ye. Lucio, who bought this?   125
    'Tis a reasonable good one; but there hangs one
    Spain's champion ne'er used truer. With this staff
    Old Álvarez has led up men so close
    They could almost spit in the cannon's mouth,
    Whilst I with that and this, well mounted, skirred   130
    A horse troop through and through, like swift desire,
    And seen poor rogues retire, all gore and gashed
    Like bleeding shads.
Lucio.   Bless us, sister Clara.
    How desperately you talk. What do ye call
    This gun? A dag?   135
Clara. I'll give't thee. A French petronel.
    You never saw my Barbary the Infanta
    Bestowed upon me as yet, Lucio?
    Walk down and see it.
Lucio.   What, into the stable?

---

125. with ye] *F* (with 'ye); w' ye *TSS;* with you *Dyce.*   130. skirred] *TSS;*
scurr'd *F;* scour'd *F2.*   134. do ye] *F* (do'ye); d' ye *F2;* do you *Dyce.*

125–33.] In this speech Clara retells some of the military deeds that she
and her father have accomplished by showing Lucio a collection of weapons:
her sword, her father's truncheon, and her petronel. For reasons of economy
of staging, she is probably carrying all of them; see 66 SD n. Alternatively,
they may be pre-set on stage (as per Weber's indication for a realistic staging
at the beginning of the scene; see 2.2 Location n.).

    125. *this*] Lucio's sword.

    126. *there hangs one*] Clara's sword, which may be hanging from her belt
(or could be hanging somewhere on stage).

    127. *this staff*] Álvarez's truncheon, which she is probably carrying.

    130. *that and this*] her sword and her petronel.

    skirred] repelled, made to flee.

    132. *seen*] have seen.

    133. *shads*] allices or river herrings, a type of fish.

    134. *desperately*] hopelessly (*OED* 3).

    135. *dag*] a kind of heavy but small handgun (*OED n.*[2]; see Introduction,
12).

    136. *petronel*] see 1.1.74 n.; a large carbine such as a petronel would be
unmistakably much larger than a dag, which betrays Lucio's ignorance of
weaponry.

    137. *Barbary*] a Barbary horse; horses from the north coast of Africa were
much appreciated across Europe.

    Infanta] see 1.1.20 n.

Not I; the jades will kick. The poor groom there   140
Was almost spoiled the other day.
Clara.   Fie on thee!
Thou wilt scarce be a man before thy mother.
Lucio. When will you be a woman?

              Enter ÁLVAREZ *and* BOBADILLA.

Clara.   Would I were none.
But nature's privy seal assures me one.
                                    [*They talk apart.*]
Álvarez. Thou anger'st me. Can strong habitual custom   145
Work with such magic on the mind and manners
In spite of sex and nature? Find out, sirrah,
Some skilful fighter.
Bobadilla.   Yes, sir.
Álvarez.   I will rectify
And redeem either's proper inclination,
Or bray 'em in a mortar, and new mould 'em.   150

---

144. SD] *GWW.*

---

140. *jades*] horses of inferior breed (*OED jade n.1* 1a), but also a term of
reprobation applied to a woman, sometimes playfully, like *hussy* or *minx* (2a).

141. *spoiled*] injured, crippled.

142. *before*] in the presence of.

144. *nature's ... one*] 'nature's decree unavoidably makes me a woman';
Clara is aware that her biological sex predetermines her socially expected
gender behaviour. The 'privy seal' was the sign that authenticated the royal
provenance of government documents; its metaphorical use here refers to a
legal document issued by nature as the highest authority.

145. *strong habitual custom*] see 1.2.51 n.; in this case, custom is presented
as an intense driving force that is generated by habit, i.e., through the repetition of received behavioural patterns. The polysemic *habitual* refers to these
patterns, as well as, or particularly, to clothing as a powerful signifier of
gender. The phrase, by semantic proximity between *strength* and *force*, is
reminiscent of the title of Castro's play, which can be translated as *The Force
of Habit* (as in Kathleen Jeff's translation).

149. *proper*] appropriate.

150. *bray ... mould 'em*] beat them to a pulp and remake them from their
component matter; cf. Proverbs 27:22: 'Though thou shouldest bray a fool
in a mortar among wheat with a pestle, *yet* will not his foolishness depart
from him.' Braying his children (pounding, crushing them into powder) in
a mortar is reminiscent of the fate of the Greek philosopher Anaxarchus,
who was 'pounded to death with iron pestles' at the command of Nicocreon,
tyrant of Cyprus (Diogenes, IX, '10. Anaxarchus', 59). Álvarez repeats this

Bobadilla. Believe your eyes, sir. I tell you, we wash an
    Ethiop.   *Exit.*
Clara. [*To Lucio*] I strike it for ten ducats.
Álvarez.   How now, Clara,
    Your breeches on still? And your petticoat
    Not yet off, Lucio? Art thou not gelt?
    Or did the cold Muscovite beget thee,   155
    That lay here lieger in the last great frost?
    Art thou not, Clara, turned a man indeed
    Beneath the girdle? And a woman thou?

---

152. SD] *this edn.*   155. did] did not *TSS.*   156. lieger] leger *Colman.*

---

same threat to Lucio alone in 4.3.26 and, using a baking metaphor, in 3.4.90.
Cf. in *Prize*, Maria sets off to reform Petruccio's misogyny: 'Yet would I
undertake this man, thus single, [...] Turn him and bend him as I list, and
mould him / Into a babe again' (1.2.170–3).

   151. *wash ... Ethiop*] proverbially, we attempt a futile task (Tilley, E186),
like trying to wash off the colour of a black Ethiopian's skin; cf. Petruccio
in *Prize*: 'so I did, / But to no end: I washed an Ethiop' (3.3.10–11).

   152. *I ... ducats*] Perhaps Clara is referring again to the money she would
bet to shoot at Bobadilla's codpiece, threatening him upon return (cf.
2.2.75).

   152–4. *How ... gelt?*] Given the briefness of his appearance, Álvarez may
not actually notice that the man in front of him is Lucio and the woman
Clara, if they have simply exchanged clothes (2012 Shakespeare Institute
production). Alternatively, Álvarez may be speaking of breeches and petticoat in a metaphorical sense (2013 BADA production).

   154. *gelt*] in a metaphorical sense, castrated.

   155–6. *Muscovite ... frost?*] In Renaissance humoral theory, coldness and
wetness in the body was associated with an excess of phlegm that could
generate effeminacy: a man with an excess of cold and wet humours would
only produce female children or, alternatively, effeminate boys (for example,
Falstaff in *2H4* accuses young men who do not consume strong drink of
being only able to 'get wenches' due an overcooling of their blood; 4.2.91).
Álvarez jokes here with the possibility that his son might have been conceived
in a cold climate by a foreigner from a cold country. This, most probably,
is a topical reference to Aleksei Ziuzin, ambassador of Tsar Michael I, who
resided in London from June 1613 to May 1614. In that context, the 'last
great frost' was the winter of 1614 to 1615, months before the play premiered.
(See Introduction, 9–10.)

   156. *lieger*] an ordinary or resident ambassador, as opposed to extraordinary or temporary.

I'll have you searched, I swear! I strongly doubt.
We must have things mended. Come, go in.   *Exit.*   160

Enter VITELLI *and* BOBADILLA.

Bobadilla. With Lucio, say you? There is for you.
                              [*He points at Lucio.*]
Vitelli. And there is for thee.
                              [*He gives Bobadilla some money.*]
Bobadilla. I thank you. You have now bought a little advice of
    me: if you chance to have conference with that lady there,
    be very civil, or look to your head. She has ten nails and   165
    you have but two eyes. If any foolish hot motions should
    chance to rise in the horizon under your equinoctial
    there, qualify it as well as you can, for I fear the elevation

---

159. I swear] *this edn;* by— *F;* by Heaven *Colman.*   161. is] he's *TSS;* he
is *Weber.*   SD] *this edn.*   162. SD] *this edn.*   163–70.] *prose, TSS; F lines*
advice / that / has / foolish / horizon / as / will / constitution: / you. /; *Colman
lines* bought / chance / there, / head! / eyes: / chance / there, / fear / not /
constitution: / you. /.

---

159. *I'll ... searched*] Perhaps reminiscent of the episode in the 1613
process for the annulment of Frances Howard's marriage to Robert Devereux,
Earl of Essex, in which a panel of matrons verified that she was still a virgin
and that the marriage had not, therefore, been consummated, thus allowing
her to remarry. (See Introduction, 10–11.)

160. *things*] 'these matters', but perhaps also punning on his children's
genitalia.

Come, go in] Álvarez may not notice that his children do not follow him.

161. *With ... you?*] 'You want to speak with Lucio?'

166–70. *If ... constitution*] Bobadilla's warning to Vitelli against attempting sexual advances on Clara is phrased in planetary and astrological terms.
The 'hot motions' of Vitelli's sexual arousal are personified by the sun rising
above the horizon at dawn, occurring figuratively under his 'equinoctial', or
below his waistline (i.e., in his genitalia). Bobadilla advises Vitelli to control
his erection (the elevation of his celestial pole) as it will not be willingly
received (it will not be agreeable to Clara's horoscopic disposition).

165. *nails*] fingernails to scratch Vitelli's eyes.

166. *hot motions*] lusty movements, sexual arousal; cf. Lucio's 'wanton
motions' (1.2.29).

167. *equinoctial*] region adjacent to the terrestrial equator; figuratively, the
area near a man's waist (his equator), i.e., his genitalia.

168. *qualify it*] mitigate it, control it.

168–9. *elevation ... pole*] Vitelli's erection; the reference is to the celestial
pole, but punning on Vitelli's penis.

of your pole will not agree with the horoscope of her
constitution. She is Bel the Dragon, I assure you. *Exit.*   170
Vitelli. Are you not the Lucio, sir, that saved Vitelli?
Lucio. Not I indeed, sir, I did never brabble.
    There walks that Lucio, metamorphosèd.
Vitelli. Do ye mock me?   *Exit* [*Lucio*].
Clara.   No, he does not. I am that
    Supposèd Lucio that was, but Clara   175
    That is, and daughter unto Álvarez.
Vitelli. Amazement daunts me. Would my life were riddles,
    So you were still my fair expositor.
    Protected by a lady from my death!
    O, I shall wear an everlasting blush   180
    Upon my cheek from this discovery.
    O you, the fairest soldier I e'er saw,
    Each of whose eyes, like a bright beamy shield,
    Conquers, without blows, the contentious.
Clara. Sir, guard yourself: you are in your enemy's house,   185
    And may be injured.
Vitelli.   'Tis impossible:
    Foe, nor oppressing odds, dares prove Vitelli

---

170. Bel the] *F* (Bell the*)*; Bell and the *Langbaine.*   174. SD] *GWW.*

169. *horoscope*] configuration of the planets at a certain moment that
governs with its influence the personality and fate of human affairs; the phrase
implies that Clara has an intrinsic predisposition against the sexual advances
of men caused by her artificial manliness, rather than this being a temporary
characteristic that may revert to its natural state, as her father interprets.
    170. *constitution*] disposition.
    Bel the Dragon] Bobadilla confuses the name of the Babylonian idol Bel
and the dragon that the Babylonians also worshipped. Both stories are
recounted in the extended book of Daniel, chapter 14, which was not
included in the Geneva Bible or the King James Version, but was available
in the Bishop's Bible of 1568. Daniel destroyed the dragon when he stuffed
its mouth with a mixture of pitch, fat, and wool. Langbaine silently emended
for 'Bel and the Dragon', but this misses the joke at Bobadilla's expense,
ridiculing his lack of biblical knowledge.
    172. *brabble*] quarrel, brawl about trifles.
    173. *metamorphosèd*] transformed; this is, of course, the central theme of
the play.
    178. *expositor*] expounder of the riddles that Vitelli wishes his life would
have retained.
    187. *prove*] test in combat.

If Clara side him, and will call him friend.
I would the difference of our blood were such
As might with any shift be wiped away;   190
Or would to heaven yourself were all your name,
That having lost blood by you, I might hope
To raise blood from you; but my black-winged fate
Hovers aversely over that fond hope;
And he, whose tongue thus gratifies the daughter   195
And sister of his enemy, wears a sword
To rip the father and the brother up;
Thus you, that saved this wretched life of mine,
Have saved it to the ruin of your friends.
That my affections should promiscuously   200
Dart love and hate at once, both worthily!
Pray, let me kiss your hand.

Clara.   You are treacherous
And come to do me mischief.

Vitelli.   Speak on still:
Your words are falser, fair, than my intents,
And each sweet accent far more treacherous; for   205

---

188. *side*] join forces with.

189. *difference ... blood*] enmity between our families.

190. *shift*] small change.

192-3. *That ... you*] 'having been injured (in my honour) by your family, I might hope to engender children with you'.

193. *black-winged fate*] Perhaps one of the classical fates that governed people's destiny, the Greek Moirai (Clotho, Lachesis, and Atropos). However, these were not depicted as having wings; perhaps Vitelli is transferring the appearance and ability to fly from the unfriendly harpies. Alternatively, *fate* here is not a mythological reference but an unspecific personification of destiny as a bird of prey with ominous black wings.

194. *Hovers*] circles like a bird of prey.

aversely] A possible emendation would be *adversely*, expressing a more active enmity towards Vitelli in the black-winged personification of fate, rather than the blander aversion or distaste that the F reading implies.

fond] pretentious.

195. *gratifies*] expresses gratitude, gives thanks. Sympson suggests that the authors might have meant 'glorifies', as it is not clear what gratification 'does *Vitelli* make *Clara* here'; but Vitelli has come to thank Clara for saving his life (see 2.1.154-6).

204. *fair*] as a vocative.

Though you speak ill of me, you speak so well
I do desire to hear you.
Clara.   Pray be gone;
Or kill me, if you please.
Vitelli.   O, neither can:
For to be gone were to destroy my life,
And to kill you were to destroy my soul.   210
I am in love, yet must not be in love.
I'll get away apace. Yet, valiant lady,
Such gratitude to honour I do owe,
And such obedience to your memory,
That if you will bestow something that I   215
May wear about me, it shall bind all wrath,
My most inveterate wrath, from all attempts
Till you and I meet next.
Clara.   A favour, sir?
Why, I will give ye good counsel.
Vitelli.   That already
You have bestowed. A ribbon or a glove.   220
Clara. Nay, those are tokens for a waiting maid
To trim the butler with.
Vitelli.   Your feather.
Clara.   Fie;
The wenches give them to their servingmen.
Vitelli. That little ring.
Clara.   'Twill hold you but by th' finger
And I would have you faster.
Vitelli.   Anything   225
That I may wear and but remember you.

---

208. can] *F; can I F2.* 212. apace] a pace *F.* 213. honour] *F2 (honor);*
hononr *F.* 223. their] the *TSS.* 225. have] have have *F2.*

---

208. *neither can*] 'I can do neither.'
211–12. *I am ... apace*] This may be an aside.
218. *favour*] a lady's personal property that a gentleman might wear publicly as a token of her esteem or affection.
222. *trim*] decorate.
224–5. *'Twill ... faster*] Clara's first expression of a romantic interest in
Vitelli?

Clara. This smile, my good opinion, or myself.
    But that it seems you like not.
Vitelli.   Yes, so well.
    When any smiles I will remember yours.
    Your good opinion shall in weight poise me   230
    Against a thousand ill. Lastly, yourself
    My curious eye now figures in my heart,
    Where I will wear you till the table break.
    So, whitest angels guard you.   [*He starts to go.*]
Clara.   Stay, sir. I
    Have fitly thought to give what you as fitly   235
    May not disdain to wear.
Vitelli.   What's that?
Clara.   This sword.
    [*Aside*] I never heard a man speak till this hour.
    His words are golden chains, and now I fear
    The lioness hath met a tamer here.
    Fie, how this tongue chimes. [*Aloud*] What was I saying? 240
    O, this favour I bequeath you, which I tie

---

234. SD] *this edn.*   237. SD] *Weber.*   240. this] *Dyce;* his *F.* SD] *this edn.* saying] a saying *TSS.*

    227. *myself*] also in the sense of 'my being'.
    230. *poise*] ballast, add moral weight against ill opinions.
    232. *My ... heart*] 'my eye draws your image on my heart'.
    233. *wear ... break*] Vitelli will metaphorically wear Clara's image drawn on his own heart (the table-book where his eye has engraved it) until his death (when this metaphorical cardiac notebook will break). A table-book or writing-table was a pocket notebook, usually in octavo, which might contain a printed calendar and a set of astronomical tables, followed by some ten white leaves made of ass-skin coated with gesso or plaster of Paris, on which the owner could make notes in pencil or ink, or by scratching the treated surface with a brass stylus; if used in this way, the scratched marks could be erased by using a wet sponge to restore the smooth gesso surface (see Jowett and Woudhuysen). The marks that Vitelli envisages are, however, permanent.
    238-9. *His ... here*] Clara pictures herself as a fierce lioness that has been tamed with gold fetters. The line echoes the subtitle and the main theme of Fletcher's *The Woman's Prize, or The Tamer Tamed.*
    240. *this tongue*] 'my tongue'; Dyce emended the F reading as suggested by Heath: 'i.e., her own tongue, which had just uttered two *chiming* or rhyming verses' (quoted in Dyce).

In a love-knot, fast, ne'er to hurt my friends;
Yet be it fortunate 'gainst all your foes—
For I have neither friend, nor foe, but yours—
As e'er it was to me. I have kept it long,   245
And value it next my virginity.

[She gives him her sword.]

But, good, return it, for I now remember
I vowed who purchased it should have me too.
Vitelli. Would that were possible. But, alas, it is not.
Yet this assure yourself, most honoured Clara: 250
I'll not infringe an article of breath
My vow hath offered to ye, nor from this part
Whilst it hath edge or point, or I a heart.   *Exit.*
Clara. O, leave me living! What new exercise
Is crept into my breast that blancheth clean   255

---

245. I have] I've *F2.*   kept it] *F2;* kepit it *F.*   246. SD] *this edn.*   251. an article] a particle *F2.*

---

242. *love-knot*] an intricate ornament in the shape of a knot given as a love token; figuratively, a bond of affection and an implicit promise of fidelity. In this case, the sword is exchanged with the promise that it will never be used to hurt Clara's relatives (see 5.3.159–62).

246. *value ... virginity*] Clara is naturally determined to remain chaste until her marriage. This contrasts with Hipólita's violent sexual transformation in *La fuerza*.

247. *good*] as a vocative.

247–8. *I ... too*] This is a martial variant of the tradition that a gentleman who secured a lady's ring would be able to marry her. It is interesting that Clara has changed the token in this tradition from a ring – a symbol of femininity as well as a frequent bawdy term for the vagina – for a sword, a phallic object associated with men. In handing over her sword to her chosen sexual partner, she is obviously giving up her virginity as well, having drawn a psychological bond between the two in line 246.

248. *purchased*] acquired.

251. *article ... breath*] verbal oath that will be as binding as clauses in a legal written agreement.

252. *from this*] from this sword.

254. *leave ... living*] Uncertain meaning, perhaps implying that she would prefer to die rather than live in the anguish of the love that she is discovering. It plays with the conventional effects of love as a source of pain; cf. lines 259–60.

exercise] (a) habitual behaviour (*OED* 3); (b) distress, state of anxiety (*OED* 6c); (c) military drill (*OED* 5a).

255. *blancheth clean*] whitewashes, erases.

My former nature? I begin to find
I am a woman, and must learn to fight
A softer, sweeter battle than with swords.
I am sick methinks, but the disease I feel
Pleaseth and punisheth. I warrant, love   260
Is very like this that folks talk of so;
I skill not what it is, yet sure, even here,
Even in my heart, I sensibly perceive
It glows and riseth like a glimmering flame,
But know not yet the essence on't nor name.   *Exit.*   265

---

256. *my former nature*] 'my masculine personality'; note, however, that she regards her former masculine gender as a primary natural identity, not as an artificial product of custom: she is discovering a second nature, not assuming that her former one was not real.

260. *Pleaseth and punisheth*] This paradoxical juxtaposition of the effects of love as simultaneously painful and pleasurable was commonplace in the European literature of the period.

262. *skill*] understand, comprehend (*OED* 4a).

ACT 3

SCENE I

Enter MALRODA *and* [*the*] ALGUAZIR.

Malroda. He must not, nor he shall not? Who shall let him?
　You, politic diego, with your face of wisdom?
　Don Blurt, the pox upon your aphorisms,
　Your grave and sage ale-physiognomy!
　Do not I know thee for the Alguazir　　　　　　　　　　5
　Whose dunghill all the parish scavengers
　Could never rid? Thou comedy to men,
　Whose serious folly is a butt for all

SCENE I] *F (Actus tertius, Scæna prima.).* 3. Don Blurt] *F (Don-blirt).*
the pox] *Colman;* the — *F.* upon] *TSS;* on *F* 4. sage ale-physiog-
nomy] *Weber;* sage Ale physiognomy *F;* Sage-Ale Physiognomy *F2.* 5.
Alguazir] *F2 (Alguazier); Alquazier F.* 8. butt] *F2;* but *F*

3.1.0.] Location: '*A room in the Alguazir's house*' (Weber).
　1. *He*] i.e., Piorato.
　let] hinder, stop.
　2. *diego*] common name for a Spaniard.
　3. *Don Blurt*] Reference to the title role of Dekker's *Blurt;* that play also
contains a character based on *Lazarillo de Tormes;* see Introduction, 28–9.
　3–4. *the pox ... ale-physiognomy*] 'a curse upon your sentences, and your
stern and wise drunken face'. The word *ale* seems to be semantically attached
to the Alguazir's *physiognomy* rather than the preceding *sage.* The expression
'grave and sage' is meant as an ironic comment on the Alguazir's 'face of
wisdom'. Presumably the Alguazir has the reddened face of a drunkard,
which coincides with his hair colour (see 2.1.206 and 3.1.58). F2's reading,
'sage-ale physiognomy', referring to a kind of beer flavoured with sage,
destroys the collocation 'grave and sage'.
　the pox upon] See Appendix 3, 233.
　6. *parish scavengers*] officers of a parish employed to clean the streets,
including ridding them of the piles of rubbish and waste left by town dwellers
in front of their houses; metaphorically, the Alguazir's dunghill is enormous
due to his corruption.
　7. *rid*] get rid of, clear away.
　8. *butt*] target.

130

To shoot their wits at, whilst thou hast not wit
Nor heart to answer or be angry.
Alguazir.   Lady—   10
Malroda. Peace, peace, you rotten rogue supported by
    A staff of rottener office. Dare you check
    Any's accesses that I will allow?
    Piorato is my friend and visits me
    In lawful sort to espouse me as his wife;   15
    And who will cross, or shall, our interviews?
    You know me, sirrah, for no chambermaid
    That cast her belly and her waistcoat lately.
    Thou thinkst thy constableship is much. Not so:
    I am ten offices to thee. Ay, thy house,   20
    Thy house, and office is maintained by me.
Alguazir. My house of office is maintained i'th' garden.
    Go to, I know you, and I have connived.
    You're a delinquent, but I have connived;

---

13. Any's accesses] *TSS*; *Anys accesses F*; Any accesses *F2*; Any's access
Mitchell.   14. friend] Frinnd *TSS.*   16. interviews] *Colman*; enter-viewes
F.   23, 24. connived] *Dyce*; contriv'd *F.*

8–10. *for … angry*] This is precisely what happened in the long exchange
with the craftsmen in 2.1.168–99, when the Alguazir was unable to make
any reply to the abuse directed at him.
   12. *check*] interfere with.
   13. *Any's*] anyone's.
   16. *will*] implying human intention.
   shall] implying definitive action.
   17–18. *You … lately*] Malroda states that she is not a naïve girl, who has
been made pregnant recently out of inexperience.
   18. *cast her belly*] vomit with morning sickness in the early stages of
pregnancy.
   waistcoat] used by low-class women of ill-repute (*OED* 4a); the waistcoat
was also a child's first garment (*OED* 1d), with the implication that a young
woman who has recently cast her waistcoat is still inexperienced (metaphorically in her first infancy).
   20. *I … thee*] 'I earn ten times more than you do.'
   20–1. *Ay … me*] 'I pay for the upkeep of your house and your office.'
   22. *house of office*] outside privy, located in the garden.
   23. *connived*] overlooked, tolerated. Dyce based his emendation of F on
Heath, who, finding the reading of the folios to be 'stark nonsense', suggested that, if emended, the lines might be paraphrased as 'You are a delin-
quent, you are a poison, yet I have connived at all this'; he added that 'the

A poison, though not in the third degree.   25
I can say black's your eye, though it be grey.
I have connived at this, your friend and you.
But what is got by this connivency?
I like his feather well: a proper man,
Of good discourse, fine conversation,   30
Valiant, and a great carrier of the business,
Sweet-breasted as the nightingale or thrush.
Yet I must tell you, you forget yourself:
My lord Vitelli's love and maintenance
Deserves no other Jack-i'-th'-box but he.   35

---

26. black's] *F* (blacks).   29. feather] feature *TSS*.

---

correction is confirmed by the next line but one [line 27]' (quoted in Dyce). The F reading *contrived* ('plotted or conspired with you') does not seem to agree with the rest of the Alguazir's argument: he has turned a blind eye on Malroda's dealings rather than actively planning them with her. The collocation in F of *conniv'd* near *connivency* in lines 27 and 28 suggests that the earlier occurrence of *contriv'd* in lines 23 and 24 might have been the result of a confusion during typesetting between *conniv'd* (the presumed MS reading) and *contriv'd* (the compositor's choice), with the second -*n*- confused with the digraph -*tr*-.

25. *A ... degree*] 'you are a poison, but not a lethal one'. The 'third degree' was regarded as the most intense stage in any succession: cf. Olivia in Shakespeare's *TwN*: 'he's in the third degree of drink, he's drowned' (1.5.130–1).

26. *black's ... grey*] 'I can accuse you of wrongdoing, I can find fault in you'; it was a common catchphrase. Black eyes were generally regarded as proverbially attractive in women. The Alguazir is implying that Malroda's eyes are not so attractive (grey, not black), and yet he can lie about their colour and appeal, and accuse her of being morally faulty.

27. *this*] your relationship.

29. *his feather*] figuratively, his plumage, his attire, his outward appearance (*OED* 2a); Sympson's emendation makes good sense of the speech, but seems unnecessary.

32. *Sweet-breasted ... thrush*] sweet-voiced, like the nightingale and the thrush, two birds renowned for their beautiful singing; Piorato is the only character who sings in the play (see 3.2.118–25).

35. *Jack-i'-th'-box*] mechanical toy consisting of a puppet actioned by a spring that leaps out of a box when opened. The *OED*'s first record is from 1659, but this seems to be the sense: a gull kept in the box (Malroda's establishment at the Alguazir's house). As Weber notes, it might also be 'another name for Jack of the clock', the automaton that comes out of a clock's case to strike the hours on the bell with a hammer; in this sense, Malroda's visitors come in and out of the house with great frequency (figuratively once every hour).

What, though he gathered first the golden fruit,
And blew your pig's coat up into a blister
When you did wait at court upon his mother?
Has he not well provided for the bairn?
Beside, what profit reap I by the other?   40
If you will have me serve your pleasure, lady,
Your pleasure must accommodate my service;
As good be virtuous and poor, as not
Thrive by my knavery. All the world would be
Good, prospered goodness like to villainy.   45
I am the King's vicegerent by my place,
His right lieutenant in mine own precinct.
Malroda. Thou art a right rascal in all men's precincts.
Yet now, my pair of twins, of fool and knave:

---

37. pig's coat] *F* (pigges-coat*).   40. by] be *Langbaine.*   47. own] *F2;*
owe *F.*

---

36. *gathered ... fruit*] had first access to her sexual favours, took away her
virginity.

37. *blew ... blister*] 'impregnated you'; in this case, the coat or petticoat,
a garment suspended from the waist, could have been made from a pig's
hide; figuratively it could be the skin on Malroda's belly, swollen by pregnancy, said to belong to a pig as an insult to her. An alternative modernisation is the homophonous phrase 'pigs' cote', in general use in the period to
refer to a small shed used to house swine, figuratively Malroda's womb.

blister] a swollen vesicle on the skin containing serum produced by a burn
or an injury; in this sense, the expanded skin of Malroda's belly (or her skirt)
when pregnant, containing amniotic fluid and the baby.

39. *bairn*] child of either sex; Vitelli has fathered a child with Malroda,
which he maintains by paying her an allowance (see 4.2.44).

40. *the other*] Piorato.

45. *prospered ... villainy*] 'if goodness were as prosperous as villainy.'

46. *the King's vicegerent*] the King's deputy, his officer (*OED* 1a); in the
city of Seville, as portrayed in the play, the King's deputy is, in reality, the
Asistente (see Characters in the Play, 1 n.).

place] office in the crown's service (*OED* 14a).

47. *right lieutenant*] legitimate representative.

precinct] administrative district (*OED* 2a).

48. *precincts*] by extension, particular areas of concern (*OED* 2b),
opinions.

49. *Yet ... knave*] Perhaps referring to the two-faced Alguazir (as commented on by the craftsmen in 2.1.129–33). It does not seem to refer to
Vitelli and Piorato: if the first may be the fool they both want to gull, the
second is the subject of Malroda's affections.

Look, we are friends. There's gold for thee. [*She gives*
      him gold.] Admit   50
Whom I will have and keep it from my Don,
And I will make thee richer than thou art wise.
Thou shalt be my bawd, and my officer.
Thy children shall eat still, my good night owl,
And thy old wife sell andirons to the court,   55
Be countenanced by the Dons, and wear a hood,
Nay, keep my garden-house; I'll call her mother,
Thee father, my good poisonous red-haired de'il,

---

50. SD] *this edn.*   52. thou art] thou'rt *F2.*   58. de'il] *this edn;* Dill *F;*
Deel *TSS;* devil *Weber.*

51. *keep it*] conceal it.
my Don] Vitelli.
52.] The F2 reading suggests that, to fit the pentameter, 'thou art' is
pronounced as one syllable, 'thou'rt'; alternatively, 'I will' could scan as a
monosyllable, 'I'll'.
53. *my officer*] In a way, Malroda declares that she is taking the place of
the King, paying for the Alguazir's services.
55. *andirons*] fire-dogs, pairs of horizontal iron bars supported by decorated vertical columns that are placed in the hearth to support and oxygenate
a fire.
to the court] to courtiers, presumably in Madrid.
56. *countenanced*] looked upon, admired.
hood] a hood was worn by civic officials and members of other professions
as a mark of their dignity (it survives in English academic dress).
57. *garden-house*] perhaps a quip on the Alguazir's earlier statement that
his house of office was in the garden, i.e., the outside privy (22); quoting
this passage, the *OED* defines it as 'a house kept for immoral purposes' (2b).
58. *poisonous*] pronounced as two syllables, 'pois'nous'.
red-haired] see 2.1.206 n.
de'il] contraction of *devil* (as Weber emended). Dyce left the text un-
emended but suggested that it might have been a misprint for *drill*, 'a
Baboon, or overgrown Ape'. Williams suggested that the meaning of *dill* as
a girl or wench (*OED n.*[2]) is spurious, and that *devil* is the likeliest meaning.
The noun *devil* applied to the Alguazir recurs later in this scene (62 and 66).
In their Arden 3rd Series edition of *Hamlet*, Ann Thompson and Neil Taylor
modernised the Q2 reading *deale* for *de'il* in: 'The spirit that I have seen / May
be a de'il, and the de'il hath power / T'assume a pleasing shape' (2.2.533–5).

And gold shall daily be thy sacrifice,
Wrought from a fertile island of mine own   60
Which I will offer like an Indian queen.
Alguazir. And I will be thy devil, thou my flesh,
With which I'll catch the world.
Malroda.   Fill some tobacco
And bring it in. If Piorato come
Before my Don, admit him. If my Don   65
Before my love, conduct him, my dear devil.
Alguazir. I will, my dear flesh. First come, first served. Well
        said.   *Exit [Malroda].*
O equal heaven, how wisely thou dispossessed
Thy several gifts! One's born a great rich fool
For the subordinate knave to work upon;   70
Another's poor with wit's addition,

---

67. SD] *this edn.*   68. dispossessed] *F (disposest).*

59–61. *gold ... queen*] A startling colonial image: Malroda presents herself
as a native queen in the Indies who will offer gold to the evil spirit of the
island as a sacrifice. The possession of gold in abundance was commonly
associated with the inhabitants of the Indies. Fletcher would develop the
theme later in his career in *Sea V* (1622), and particularly in *Princess* (1621),
in which he fully exploited the figure of the Indian queen in its female protagonist, Princess Quisara.

60. *fertile ... own*] presumably the assets of her trade as a courtesan, i.e.,
her charm and sexual appeal. Piorato will refer to her in similarly economic
terms as 'the most wealthy mine of Spain / For beauty and perfection'
(3.2.60–1); see also 4.2.88 n.

61. *Indian queen*] possibly (and perhaps unwittingly) punning on *quean*,
'whore'.

62–3. *devil ... flesh ... world*] The world, the flesh, and the Devil are the
enemies of the soul according to Christian theology, as in Ephesians 2:1–3.

63. *fill*] fill a pipe with.

65–6. *admit ... conduct*] Piorato needs no ushering as he belongs to a lower
class than Vitelli, who would need to be shown in.

67. *First ... served*] proverbial (Tilley, C530).

68.] The line is metrically anomalous, and could only be a pentameter if
'heaven' is pronounced as one syllable ('heav'n') and 'dispossessed' is
emended to 'disposed', which may make better sense.

dispossessed] disbursed, bestowed; the verb is employed in an unusual sense
(not recorded in the *OED*).

69–73. *One's ... descends*] A rich man, such as Vitelli, is rich and foolish
by birth, while one born lowly is often congenitally wiser.

71. *Another's poor*] another who is poor.

Which, well- or ill-used, builds a living up,
And that too from the sire oft descends.
Only fair virtue by traduction
Never succeeds and seldom meets success.   75
What have I then to do with 't? My free will,
Left me by heaven, makes me or good or ill.
Now, since vice gets more in this vicious world
Than piety, and my stars' confluence
Enforce my disposition to affect   80
Gain, and the name of rich, let who will practise
War, and grow that way great; religious,
And that way good. My chief felicity
Is wealth, the nurse of sensuality;
And he that mainly labours to be rich   85
Must scratch great scabs, and claw a strumpet's itch.

                                              Exit.

---

74. *traduction*] inheritance; pronounced as four syllables.

75. *succeeds*] passes down from generation to generation; virtue, unlike poverty and wit, is not inherited.

76. *free will*] The defence of free will was associated with Roman Catholicism, which traditionally teaches that salvation of the soul in the afterlife depends on a person's choice to do good or bad actions (see also 5.3.236). By contrast, Lutheranism preaches salvation by faith alone, and Calvinism advocates spiritual determinism: human beings are predestined to attain salvation or damnation.

77. *Left me*] granted to me.

or ... or] either ... or.

79. *my stars' confluence*] my horoscope; astrological determinism is in direct opposition to the free will that the Alguazir had just invoked.

81. *let who will*] let who is so inclined.

84. *nurse*] fosterer, nurturer (originally the noun was associated with the activity of a wet-nurse breastfeeding babies).

sensuality] the pleasures of the senses, particularly lasciviousness (hence lines 85–6).

86. *scabs*] see 2.1.101 n.

claw ... itch] scratch, and figuratively satisfy her sexual need; cf. Alfonso's reaction to his daughter Alinda's escape in *Pilgrim*: 'Some pelting rogue has watched her hour of itching, / And clawed her, clawed her' (2.1.4–5).

itch] (a) irritation of the skin produced perhaps by venereal disease; (b) sexual urges (*OED* 2).

SCENE 2

Enter PIORATO *and* BOBADILLA *with letters.*

Piorato. To say, sir, I will wait upon your lord
    Were not to understand myself.
Bobadilla.   To say, sir,
    You will do anything but wait upon him
    Were not to understand my lord.
Piorato.   I'll meet him
    Some half-hour hence, and doubt not but to render   5
    His son a man again. The cure is easy;
    I have done divers.
Bobadilla.   Women do ye mean, sir?
Piorato. Cures I do mean, sir. Be there but one spark
    Of fire remaining in him unextinct,
    With my discourse I'll blow it to a flame,   10
    And with my practice into action.
    I have had one so full of childish fear
    And womanish-hearted sent to my advice,
    He durst not draw a knife to cut his meat.
Bobadilla. And how, sir, did you help him?
Piorato.   Sir, I kept him   15
    Seven days in a dark room by candlelight,
    A plenteous table spread with all good meats
    Before his eyes, a case of keen broad knives
    Upon the board, and he so watched, he might not
    Touch the least modicum, unless he cut it;   20

SCENE 2] *F (Scæna secunda.)*.   7. ye] you *Colman*.   16. by] by a *F2*.

3.2.0.] Location: '*A street before the house of the Alguazir*' (Dyce).

0. SD *letters*] from Clara to Vitelli.

7. *I ... divers*] 'I have cured various people with similar maladies on other occasions'; Bobadilla mistakes it for (or puns upon) having 'done' several women, in a sexual sense.

10. *blow ... flame*] the cure will rekindle Lucio's dormant manliness, perhaps also his sexual desire. This sense will be developed in 4.4.12–4 and 24–5.

15–21. *Sir ... knife*] In Webster's *Law Case* (5.4.17–26), Julio reports the similar case of a fencer (like Piorato) who was hired to make a cowardly Welshman fight.

20. *the least modicum*] the smallest morsel.

And thus I brought him first to draw a knife.
Bobadilla. Good.
Piorato.   Then for ten days did I diet him
    Only with burnt pork, sir, and gammons of bacon;
    A pill of caviary now and then,
    Which breeds choler adust, you know?
Bobadilla.   'Tis true.   25
Piorato. And to purge phlegmatic humour and cold crudities,
    In all that time he drank me aquafortis,
    And nothing else but—
Bobadilla.   Aqua-vitae, señor,
    For aquafortis poisons.
Piorato.   Aquafortis

---

28. señor] *F (Signior).*

---

23. *gammons of bacon*] smoked ham, which consumed in conjunction with the burnt pork would contribute to provide the body with heat and dryness, and to excite the choler or yellow bile (the hot and dry humour that caused irritability), causing the pusillanimous to fight. As with Lucio, an effeminate man would lack yellow bile, as he would naturally have an excess of phlegm, the cold and wet humour that Álvarez lamented earlier (see 2.2.155–6 n.). A diet based on certain foods would regulate the imbalance of humours in the body.

24. *pill of caviary*] a mouthful of caviar, perhaps moulded into a sphere. The choice of word, *pill*, suggests that the food is being used as humoral medicine.

25. *choler adust*] The adjective *adust* described any of the four humours when an abnormal concentration occurred in the body, producing a darkening of its colour. This excess was associated with a state of hotness and dryness in the body, and was therefore particularly applied to choler. In conjunction with the hot foods mentioned, Piorato tried to cause a darkening of the choler with the caviar, hoping in that way to provoke the desired anger in his patient.

26. *phlegmatic humour*] phlegm, the cold and wet humour (see line 23 n.).
   crudities] imperfect concoctions of the bodily humours producing an imbalance (*OED* 2a), cold in this case.

27. *aquafortis*] nitric acid, a powerful corrosive that would certainly supply the desired heat to the patient. A solution for a similar malady is proposed by Leontius in *Lieut.*: 'Then will I have thee blown with a pair of smith's bellows, / [...] Filled full of oil o' devil, and aquafortis, / And let these work; these may provoke' (3.3.41–4). This passage may be based on Field's *Amends*, in which Master Welltried has promised Lord Feesimple to overcome his fear and teach him 'to endure to look upon a naked sword' (2.1, 26); he takes him to a tavern in Turnbull Street to visit a band of ruffians, so that drinking finally excites him to fight against them.

28. *Aqua-vitae*] any strong distilled spirit.

I say again. What's one man's poison, señor,   30
  Is another's meat or drink.
Bobadilla.   Your patience, sir;
  By your good patience, he'd a huge cold stomach.
Piorato. I fired it, and gave him then three sweats
  In the artillery yard, three drilling days.
  And now he'll shoot a gun, and draw a sword,   35
  And fight with any man in Christendom.
Bobadilla. A receipt for a coward. I'll be bold, sir,
  To write your good prescription.
Piorato.   Sir, hereafter
  You shall, and underneath it put 'probatum'.
  Is your chain right?
Bobadilla.   'Tis both right and just, sir,   40
  For, though I am a steward, I did get it
  With no man's wrong.
Piorato.   You are witty.
Bobadilla.   So, so.
  Could you not cure one, sir, of being too rash
  And over-daring? There now's my disease:
  Foolhardy as they say, for that in sooth   45
  I am.

---

30. señor] *F* (*Signior*).   32. he'd] *this edn;* h'ad *F;* h'had *F2;* he'ad *Langbaine;* he had *Weber.*   40. 'Tis] It is *TSS.*   42. You are] You're very *TSS.*

30–1. *What's ... drink*] cf. Middleton and Rowley's *Chang.* 1.1.111 and 127–8.

31. *meat*] food, sustenance, not just animal flesh.

32. *he'd*] he must have had.

33. *fired it*] put fire in his stomach.

34. *artillery yard*] The Artillery Yard was an area east of Bishopsgate (now called Artillery Lane) 'used after 1610 by the newly formed Honourable Artillery Company for practising' (Holland and Sherman, eds, Jonson's *Alch.*, 1.1.31 n.).

37. *receipt ... coward*] medical prescription to cure cowardice.

39. *'probatum'*] a demonstrated fact, a remedy found to be effective (*OED* 1).

40. *Is ... right?*] 'Is your chain made of pure gold?' (Sympson; *OED* 13c); Piorato changes the subject after his medical advice.

45. *foolhardy*] Bobadilla declares he is rashly daring, while he regularly behaves like a coward (see 1.3.85, 2.2.124, and 5.3.185–6).

Piorato.   Most easily.

Bobadilla.   How?

Piorato.   To make you drunk, sir,
      With small beer once a day, and beat you twice
      Till you be bruised all over: if that help not,
      Knock out your brains.

Bobadilla.   This is strong physic, señor,
      And never will agree with my weak body.   50
      I find the medicine worse than the malady,
      And therefore will remain foolhardy still.
      You'll come, sir?

Piorato.   As I am a gentleman.

Bobadilla. A man o'th' sword should never break his word.

Piorato. I'll overtake you. I have only, sir,   55
      A complimental visitation
      To offer to a mistress lodged hereby.

Bobadilla. A gentlewoman?

Piorato.   Yes, sir.

Bobadilla.   Fair and comely?

Piorato. O, sir, the paragon, the nonpareil
      Of Seville, the most wealthy mine of Spain   60
      For beauty and perfection.

Bobadilla.   Say you so?

---

49. señor] F (*Signior*).   51. medicine] *F2*;   medcine   *F*.   57. hereby]
Langbaine; here by *F.*   60. Seville] *F (Civill).*

---

46. *easily*] pronounced as two syllables, 'eas'ly'.

47. *small beer*] weak beer or beer of poor quality.

51. *I ... malady*] Francis Bacon expressed the same idea in 'Of Seditions
and Troubles' in the 1625 augmented edition of his *Essays*: 'the remedy is
worse than the disease' (Bacon, 371). As recorded by Apperson, the idea
echoes Seneca's *De Beneficiis*: 'Ungrateful is Lucius Sulla, who healed his
fatherland by remedies that were harsher than her ills' (V, 16.3). The idea
recurs in Massinger's *The Bondman*, where Cleon declares: 'The cure / Is
worse than the disease' (1.3.222–3). The phrase is also proverbial in Spanish
('Es peor el remedio que la enfermedad', although it is not recorded in
Correas), but it does not seem to have been in proverbial use in English.

54. *man ... word*] A general commonplace, rather than a particular
recorded proverb.

55. *I'll overtake you*] I'll catch up with you later (*OED* 2a); also, in fighting
terms, reach you with a blow (*OED* 1a).

60. *mine*] Figuratively, a rich source of beauty and perfection (see 3.1.60);
ore of precious metal, treasure (*OED* 2a).

Might not a man entreat a courtesy
To walk along with you, señor, to peruse
This dainty mine, though not to dig in't, señor?
Ha! I hope you'll not deny me being a stranger;   65
Though I am steward, I am flesh and blood,
And frail as other men.

Piorato.   Sir, blow your nose.
I dare not for the world. No, she is kept
By a great Don, Vitelli.

Bobadilla.   How?

Piorato.   'Tis true.

Bobadilla. See, things will veer about: this Don Vitelli   70
Am I to seek now to deliver letters
From my young mistress Clara. And I tell you
Under the rose—because you are a stranger,
And my special friend—I doubt there is
A little foolish love betwixt the parties,   75
Unknown unto my lord.

Piorato. [*Aside*]   Happy discovery.
My fruit begins to ripen. [*To Bobadilla*] Hark you, sir.
I would not wish you now to give those letters.
But home and ope this to Madonna Clara,
Which, when I come, I'll justify and relate   80
More amply and particularly.

Bobadilla.   I approve

---

63. señor] *F (Signior).*   64. señor] *F (Sgnior).*   65. Ha!] *F (Hauh—).*
66. I am steward] I am a Steward *F2;* I'm a *TSS.*   74. special] especial
Weber.   76. SD] *Weber.*   77. SD] *this edn.*

---

64. *not ... in't*] in a sexual sense, 'not to penetrate her'.

67. *blow your nose*] perhaps in a sexual sense, 'lose your erection'; the
length of noses and penises seems to have been linked in the period (see
5.3.204 n.).

68. *kept*] maintained.

73. *Under the rose*] in secret, in strict confidence; it occurs several times
in scene 2.3 of *Bush.*

73–4. *because ... friend*] a comical paradox.

75. *foolish*] unadvised (see 2.2.166).

76. *my lord*] my master, Álvarez.

79. *home*] go home.
ope this] reveal this (i.e., that Vitelli maintains a courtesan; see 3.4.3–4).

79. *Madonna*] Mock-respectful Italian title for 'my lady'; cf. Feste
addresses Countess Olivia with this title in Shakespeare's *TwN,* 5.2.1.

Your counsel and will practise it. *Beso las manos.*
Here's two chores chored. When wisdom is employed
'Tis ever thus. Your more acquaintance, señor.
I say not better, lest you think I thought not   85
Yours good enough.
Piorato.   Your servant, excellent steward.

                              Exit [*Bobadilla*].

Would all the Dons in Spain had no more brains.

                    Enter [*the*] ALGUAZIR.

Here comes the Alguazir. [*To him*] *Dieu vous garde,*
    monsieur.
Is my coz stirring yet?
Alguazir.   Your coz, good cousin?
A whore is like a fool, a kin to all   90
The gallants of the town. Your coz, good señor,

---

82. *Beso las manos*] *Weber; bazilos manos F; bazi los manos | Colman;* Baxilos manos *Mitchell.* 83. chores chored] *F (*chewres chewrd*); chewres chewr'd F2.* 84. señor] *F (*Signior*).* 86. SD] *Dyce.* 88. SD] *this edn.* Dieu vous garde] *F (*dieu vous gard*).* 90. a kin] *F2;* akin *F.* 91. señor] *F (*Signior*).*

---

82. *Beso las manos*] Spanish for 'I kiss your hands'; the F spelling, '*bazilos manos*', is a thin disguise. The grammatical gender of the word *manos* (feminine) was confused due to its seemingly masculine ending, and was rendered as *los manos*; *bazi* probably resulted from a confusion with the Italian imperative *baci*. The phrase is recorded in *DRAE* as a 'written or spoken formula of courtesy' (my translation). The formula was current in formal correspondence, and it was particularly associated with the proverbially ceremonious affectation of Spaniards.

83–4. *Here's ... thus*] This may be an aside.

83. *two chores chored*] two tasks accomplished; the original reading, 'chewres chewrd', is listed in the *OED* as example of the archaic use of the verb *chare* (def. 4). The noun *chare* is now usually employed in its Americanised phonetic variant, *chore*, applied to small domestic tasks (*OED*, *chare*, n.1, def. II. 5; *chore*, n.2). The correct modernisation is strictly 'two chares chared', but it is less recognisable in present-day English than this coinage, even if *chore* as a verb is not recorded in the *OED*.

86–7.] Bobadilla exits almost as the Alguazir appears, probably using opposite doors in the original staging.

87. *Dieu ... monsieur*] French for 'God save you, sir.'

89. *coz*] cousin, as a term of endearment.

90. *a kin*] related by blood, but with an obvious sexual connotation: all the gallants of the town call their whores 'cousin'.

Is gone abroad, sir, with her other cousin,
My lord Vitelli. Since when there hath been
Some dozen cousins here to enquire for her.
Piorato. She's greatly allied, sir.
Alguazir.   Marry, is she, sir,   95
Come of a lusty kindred. The truth is
I must connive no more. No more admittance
Must I consent to. My good lord has threatened me,
And you must pardon.
Piorato.   Out upon thee, man,
Turn honest in thine age, one foot i'th' grave?   100
Thou shalt not wrong thyself so for a million.
Look, thou three-headed Cerberus—for wit
I mean—here is one sop, and two, and three,
                              [*He gives him money.*]
For every chop a bit.
Alguazir.   Ay, marry, sir.
Well, the poor heart loves you but too well.   105
We have been talking on you, 'faith, this hour.
Where, what I said, go to. She loves your valour,
O, and your music most abominably.
She is within, sir, and alone. What mean you?

---

103. SD] *this edn.*   104. chop] chap *Colman.*   105. too] too too *TSS.*

95–6. *greatly ... kindred*] cf. Lucio in Shakespeare's *MM*: 'the vice [i.e., lust] is of a great kindred; it is well allied' (3.1.366–7).
97.] Cf. 3.1.23 n.
100. *one ... grave*] at an advanced age, almost ready to die; proverbial (Tilley, F569; a variant of 'To have one's foot in Charon's boat').
102. *Cerberus*] The mythological three-headed hound that guarded the gates of the Underworld. Piorato offers the Alguazir a morsel (a coin) for each of the three heads; he implies that the Alguazir's house, where he keeps the courtesan Malroda, is like hell, and that the pander acts as its canine gatekeeper. In a similar role, Cerberinus is the procurer and brothel's gatekeeper in the academic play *Zelotypus* (St John's College, Cambridge, 1605); see 3.3.23 n.
103. *sop*] a morsel; literally, a piece of bread dipped in water or wine.
104. *for ... bit*] 'for every mouth a bite'.
106. *on*] of.
107. *Where ... to*] 'Never mind where and what I said.'
109. *What ... you?*] This may indicate that Piorato tries to go in and the Alguazir physically stops him. TSS added the SD 'Piorato *changes sides*'.

Piorato. That is your sergeant's side, I take it, sir;   110
　　Now, I endure your constable's much better:
　　There is less danger in't. For one, you know,
　　Is a tame harmless monster in the light;
　　The sergeant's savage both by day and night.
Alguazir. I'll call her to you for that.
Piorato.　　　　　　　　No, I will   115
　　Charm her.

　　　　　　　Enter MALRODA.

Alguazir.　　She's come.
Piorato.　　　　　　My spirit!
Malroda.　　　　　　　　O my sweet!
　　Leap hearts to lips, and in our kisses meet.
Piorato. [*Singing*] *Turn, turn thy beauteous face away.*
　　How pale and sickly looks the day
　　　　　In emulation of thy brighter beams!   120
　　O envious light, fly, fly, be gone;
　　Come night, and piece two breasts as one;
　　　　　When what love does, we will repeat in dreams.
　　　Yet—thy eyes open—who can day hence fright?
　　　Let but their lids fall, and it will be night.   125
Alguazir. Well, I will leave you to your fortitude;

---

114. sergeant's savage] *this edn;* Sergeant salvage *F;* Sergeant, salvage *TSS;*
sergeant savage *Mitchell.*　115. I'll] I will *Colman.* I will] I'll *Colman.*
115–16. I will / Charm her] *lineation, Colman; one line, F.*　118. SD] *Dyce.*
Turn, turn] Turne, turne, turne *CA, MSB, MSE, MSR. away.*] away,
Song. *F.*　121. *fly, fly*] fly hence *MSR.*　122. *piece ... as*] joyne ... in *CA,
MSB, MSE, MSR.*　123. *When*] And *MSR. does*] dooth *MSR.*　124. *Yet*]
keepe *MSR. thy*] thine | *Weber, CA, MSE, MSR.*　125. *their*] thy *MSR.*

110–11.] see 2.1.130–3 n. and 3.1.49; the sergeant can be an arresting
officer at any time, while the constable is only active during the night.
　115–16.] This relineation renders both lines as perfect pentameters; it
seems the logical division, since lines 116 and 117 must form a rhyming
couplet.
　118–25.] The original musical setting for this song by John Wilson survives
in several sources (see Appendix 4, 235–7). The song was probably original
to the play, rather than a later insertion, as some of its ideas (the union of
lovers in one body, the blending of night into day) are immediately taken up
by the Alguazir in lines 128–9.
　126. *I ... fortitude*] Perhaps directed at Piorato, on account of his physical
strength (probably in a sexual sense); see 1.3.103 n.

And you to temperance. Ah, ye pretty pair,
'Twere sin to sunder you. Lovers being alone
Make one of two, and day and night all one.
But fall not out, I charge you, keep the peace;   130
You know my place else.   *Exit.*
Malroda.   No, you will not marry.
    You are a courtier, and can sing, my love,
    And want no mistresses. But yet I care not,
    I'll love you still, and when I am dead for you,
    Then you'll believe my truth.
Piorato.   You kill me, fair.   135
    It is my lesson that you speak. Have I
    In any circumstance deserved this doubt?
    I am not like your false and perjured Don
    That here maintains you, and has vowed his faith,
    And yet attempts in way of marriage   140
    A lady not far off.
Malroda.   How's that?
Piorato.   'Tis so.
    And therefore, mistress, now the time is come
    You may demand his promise, and I swear
    To marry you with speed.
Malroda.   And with that gold
    Which Don Vitelli gives, you'll walk some voyage,   145
    And leave me to my trade, and laugh, and brag,
    How you o'erreached a whore and gulled a lord.
Piorato. You anger me extremely. Fare you well.
    What should I say to be believed? Expose me

---

129. night] might *F2*.

127. *And ... temperance*] Perhaps directed at Malroda, ironically: temperance was the cardinal virtue associated with self-control and the moderation
of the physical appetites.
    131. *place*] duty, i.e., arising from his official position.
    134. *I am*] pronounced as one syllable, 'I'm'.
    136–7. *It ... doubt*] 'you are rebuking me, but I am not the one you should
be rebuking'.
    143. *his promise*] We never find out more about Vitelli's promise for liqui-
dating his relationship with Malroda. We must infer that it is an economic
settlement by which he will maintain her for his own sexual entertainment
at the Alguazir's house until he discharges her from that obligation with a
sum of money; she will then be free to marry Piorato (see 5.3.260).

To any hazard, or like jealous Juno—   150
Th' incensèd stepmother of Hercules—
Design me labours most impossible;
I'll do 'em, or die in 'em, so at last
You will believe me.

Malroda.   Come, we are friends; I do.
I am thine, walk in. My lord has sent me outsides,   155
But thou shalt have 'em, the colours are too sad.

Piorato. 'Faith, mistress, I want clothes indeed.

Malroda.   I have
Some gold too for my servant.

Piorato.   And I have
A better mettle for my mistress.

                                    Exeunt.

SCENE 3

Enter VITELLI *and* [*the*] ALGUAZIR *at several doors.*

Alguazir. [*Apart, seeing Vitelli*] Undone—wit, now or never
    help me: my master!
He will cut my throat; I am a dead constable;
And he'll not be hanged either, there's the grief.

SCENE 3] *F* (*Scena tertia.*). 1. SD] *this edn.*

150–2. *or ... impossible*] Juno was the Roman equivalent of Hera, Zeus'
wife, who was permanently angered by her husband's infidelities. Zeus
impregnated a mortal woman, Alcmene, who would give birth to Hercules,
and towards whom Hera would bear a mortal hatred (cf. 2.1.87). However,
she was only indirectly responsible for setting him upon the Twelve Labours,
but did not design them. Piorato fashions himself after the Greek hero who
metaphorically tamed Cerberus (lines 102–4): Hercules' twelfth labour was
to capture Cerberus alive.

152. *labours most impossible*] Sympson in *TSS* suggested that this paradoxical phrase should be modernised as 'labours 'most [i.e., almost]
impossible'.

155. *outsides*] outer garments (*OED* 3b; this instance is listed as one of
the examples).

157. *want*] lack.

159. *mettle*] sexual vigour (*OED* 2b), punning on the metal of his sword
as a phallic symbol.

3.3.0.] Location: '*A room in the same*' (Weber).

[*Aloud*] The party, sir, is here.

Vitelli.   What?

Alguazir.   He was here,
    I cry your lordship mercy. But I rattled him;   5
    I told him here was no companions
    For such debauched and poor-conditioned fellows;
    I bid him venture not so desperately
    The cropping of his ears, slitting his nose,
    Or being gelt.

Vitelli.   'Twas well done.

Alguazir.   Please your honour,   10
    I told him there were stews; and then at last
    Swore three or four great oaths, she was removed;
    Which I did think I might in conscience,
    Being for your lordship.

Vitelli.   What became of him?

Alguazir. 'Faith, sir, he went away with a flea in's ear,   15
    Like a poor cur, clapping his trindle tail

---

4. SD] *this edn.*   7. debauched] debauch'd *F2*; deboshd *F.*

4. *The party*] the other party, Piorato.

5. *rattled him*] (a) scolded him (*OED v.1* 4a); (b) shook him up (*OED v.1* 1b).

8. *venture*] expose himself to, put himself at risk of.

9–10. *cropping … gelt*] The Alguazir's imaginary threats to Piorato, though phrased as street-fight talk, are reminiscent of some punishments in the English legal system. Mutilation of the ears and the nose at the pillory, plus branding with a red-hot iron, were punishments imposed for forgery (*Statutes* 5 Eliz. c.14, 1562). However, emasculation was not the penalty for any crime, except in cases of high treason as part of being hanged, drawn, and quartered.

11. *stews*] brothels; cf. 2.1.189.

12. *she was removed*] she changed her accommodation, moved to another room.

13. *might*] might do.

15. *flea … ear*] proverbial (Tilley, F354; Tilley records this particular quotation).

16. *trindle tail*] the distinctly curly tail of this breed of dog; trindle-tails (or trundle-tails) were low-bred dogs of inferior value (*OED* 2 cites this passage); cf. Sir Francis Acton in Heywood's *Kindness*: 'Ay, and your dogs are trundle-tails and curs' (3.28).

Betwixt his legs—a chi ha, a chi ha, a chi ha—[*Aside*]
Now, luck.

Enter MALRODA and PIORATO.

Malroda. [*Apart to Piorato*] 'Tis he. Do as I told thee.
                     [*Piorato stands apart.*]
            [*To the Alguazir*] 'Bless thee, señor.
  [*To Vitelli*] O my dear lord.
Vitelli.   Malroda, what, alone?
Malroda. She never is alone that is accompanied   20
With noble thoughts, my lord; and mine are such,
Being only of your lordship.
Vitelli.   Pretty lass.
Malroda. O my good lord, my picture's done, but 'faith
It is not like. Nay, this way, sir, [*She shows him a*
   the light   *portrait, and takes*
Strikes best upon it here.   *him apart.*]
Piorato. [*Apart*]   Excellent wench.   *Exit.* 25
Alguazir. [*Aside*] I am glad the danger's over.   *Exit.*
Vitelli.   'Tis wondrous like,
But that art cannot counterfeit what nature
Could make but once.
Malroda. [*Aside*]   All's clear. Another tune

---

17. SD1] *Dyce.* Now, luck] now look *Mitchell.* 18. SD1] *this edn.* SD2]
GWW. SD3] *this edn.* señor] *F* (*Signior*). 19. SD] *GWW.* 23. SD]
this edn. 25. SD1 *Apart*] *this edn;* [*aside*] *GWW.* 26. SD1 *Aside*] *GWW.*
28. SD] *GWW.*

17. *a chi ha*] As Weber suggests, probably 'the imitation of sneezing, the
signal to Malroda and Piorato that Vitelli is in the house'; alternatively, the
sound of a dog retreating.
18–26.] The staging of this passage is insufficiently indicated in F; see
longer note.
18. *'Bless thee*] abbreviation of 'God bless thee'.
23. SD] Malroda shows Vitelli her portrait as a subterfuge to get him out
of the way and enable Piorato's exit, perhaps using one of the doors if he
had been hiding behind the curtain in the central discovery space; see longer
note.
24. *not like*] not a good likeness.
26. SD1 *Aside*] As the Alguazir is presumably not hidden from the other
characters, he speaks aside, rather than apart.
27. *But that*] except that.

You must hear from me now. [*Aloud*] Vitelli, thou'rt
A most perfidious and a perjured man,   30
As ever did usurp nobility.
Vitelli. What mean'st thou, Mal?
Malroda.   Leave your betraying smiles,
And change the tunes of your enticing tongue
To penitential prayers; for I am great
In labour even with anger, big with child   35
Of woman's rage, bigger than when my womb
Was pregnant by thee. Go, seducer, fly
Out of the world, let me the last wretch be
Dishonoured by thee. [*He advances towards her.*] Touch
    me not, I loathe
My very heart, because thou lay'st there long;   40
A woman's well helped up that's confident
In e'er a glittering outside on you all.
Would I had honestly been matched to some
Poor country-swain ere known the vanity
Of court. Peace, then, had been my portion,   45

---

32. *Mal*] an affective form of the name, normally of 'Mary'. Mary Frith,
the real-life model for the protagonist of *The Roaring Girl*, was known as
Moll or Mal Cutpurse; perhaps the outspoken Malroda is here linked with
the iconic cross-dressed character who had first appeared on stage a few
years before. Maria in *Walkers* is also addressed as 'Mal' (1.5.21).

34–7. *I ... thee*] Malroda's choice of imagery compares her anger with the
process that she underwent when she was pregnant with Vitelli's child (see
3.1.39 n.).

38–9. *let ... thee*] 'let me be the last unfortunate woman you defile'; presumably Vitelli has had more mistresses.

41–2. *A ... all*] An obscure phrase, approximately equivalent to 'a woman
is doomed ('well helped up'; perhaps alternatively 'made pregnant'?) if she
is fooled ('is confident', *OED* I.1) by the outward appearance of a gentleman'; *helped up* is not recorded in the *OED*.

42. *glittering*] pronounced as two syllables, 'glitt'ring'.

43–5. *Would ... court*] Cf. Vittoria's dying speech in *White Devil*: 'Oh,
happy they that never saw the court, / Nor ever knew great men but by
report!' (5.6.60–1).

45. *portion*] dowry (*OED* 1d).

Nor had been cozened by an hour's pomp
To be a whore unto my dying day.   [*She weeps.*]
Vitelli. [*Aside*] O, the uncomfortable ways such women have,
    Their different speech and meaning, no assurance
    In what they say or do. Dissemblers   50
    Even in their prayers, as if the weeping Greek
    That flattered Troy afire had been their Adam;
    Liars, as if their mother had been made
    Only of all the falsehood of the man,
    Disposed into that rib. Do I know this,   55
    And more, nay, all that can concern this sex
    With the true end of my creation?
    Can I with rational discourse sometimes
    Advance my spirit into heaven before
    'T has shook hands with my body, and yet blindly   60
    Suffer my filthy flesh to master it,
    With sight of such fair frail beguiling objects?
    When I am absent, easily I resolve
    Ne'er more to entertain those strong desires

---

47. SD] *this edn.*   48. SD] *Dyce.*

46. *an hour's pomp*] an hour of ostentatious public display (*pomp*, *OED* *n.*[1] 1a).

47. SD] Vitelli's vitriolic misogynistic speech responds to Malroda's outburst of weeping. Cf. Petruccio to Maria in *Prize* in the middle of a row: 'Thou most poor, paltry, spiteful whore. Do you cry?' (4.2.108).

48. *uncomfortable*] (a) disquieting (*OED* 1); (b) inconsolable (*OED* 2).

51–2. *weeping ... Troy*] As told by Virgil in the *Aeneid*, Sinon tricked Priam and the Trojans with 'wiles and forced tears' into bringing the wooden horse into Troy, precipitating the fall of the city (Book II, 196). Vitelli interprets Malroda's tears, and therefore all women's, as being as false (and potentially as dangerous) as Sinon's. The epic reference contrasts with the triviality of the situation: a man quarrelling with a prostitute.

52. *their Adam*] their father, their first origin.

53. *Liars*] punning on two senses, 'those who are deceitful' and 'those who lie down in bed'.

56. *this sex*] Vitelli generalises his ideas about loose women ('such women', line 48) to all women.

57. *true ... creation*] The ultimate purpose of man's creation is to beget children with women (Genesis 9:7).

end] purpose.

60. *shook hands*] said farewell; cf. Ferdinand in *Malfi*: 'You have shook hands with Reputation, / And made him invisible' (3.2.135–6).

That triumph o'er me, even to actual sin.   65
Yet, when I meet again those sorcerer's eyes,
Their beams my hardest resolutions thaw,
As if that cakes of ice and July met,
And her sighs, powerful as the violent North,
Like a light feather twirl me round about,   70
And leave me in mine own low state again.
[Aloud] What ail'st thou? Prithee, weep not. O, those
    tears
If they were true, and rightly spent, would raise
A flow'ry spring i'th' midst of January.
Celestial ministers with crystal cups   75
Would stoop to save 'em for immortal drink.
But from this passion, why all this?
Malroda.   Do ye ask?
You are marrying. Having made me unfit
For any man, you leave me fit for all.
Porters must be my burdens now to live,   80
And, fitting me yourself for carts and beadles,
You leave me to 'em. And who of all the world
But the virago, your great arch-foe's daughter?

---

72. SD] *this edn.*   73. rightly] *F2;* righly *F*   77. Do ye] *F* (Do'ye); D'ye
TSS; D'you *Colman;* Do you *Weber.*

---

65. *actual sin*] sexual intercourse, rather than unfulfilled desire.

66–8. *Yet ... met*] The radiance of Malroda's eyes is here compared to
the summer sun that melts Vitelli's icy resolutions. Piorato used a similar
image in his song (see 3.2.118–25).

68. *cakes of ice*] masses of compressed ice in a flattened form (*cake*, OED
4).

72–3. *those ... true*] Tilley records the proverb 'The courtesan weeps with
one eye, the wife with two, and the nun with four' (C729).

78–9. *Having ... all*] 'Having ruined my prospects of marrying respectfully, you have turned me into a prostitute.'

80. *Porters ... live*] She will have to bear (sexually) any low-class porter.
Her porter is now the Alguazir, who had been compared with Cerberus, the
porter of hell (3.2.102).

81. *carts and beadles*] As a common penalty for practising or facilitating
prostitution, whores and bawds would be whipped at the cart's tail by the
beadle (see also 4.3.99–100).

83. *virago*] manly or heroic woman, a female warrior (*OED* 2a); Malroda
implicitly suggests that Clara is now well known in Seville.

But on. I care not this poor rush. 'Twill breed
An excellent comedy. Ha, ha! 'T makes me laugh;   85
I cannot choose. The best is, some report
It is a match for fear, not love o' your side.
Vitelli. [*Aside*] Why, how the devil knows she that I saw
   This lady? Are all whores pieced with some witch?
   I will be merry. [*Aloud*] 'Faith, 'tis true, sweetheart,   90
   I am to marry!
Malroda.   Are you? You base lord!
   I swear I'll pistol thee!   [*She attacks him.*]
Vitelli.   A roaring whore?
   Take heed: there's a correction house hard by.
   You ha' learned this o' your swordman; that I warned
     you of:
   Your fencers and your drunkards. But, whereas   95
   You upbraid me with oaths, why, I must tell you
   I ne'er promised you marriage, nor have vowed,

---

84. poor] *F2*; poorc *F.* 88. SD] *Dyce.* 90. SD] *this edn.* 92. I swear]
this edn; by — *F*; by Heav'n *Colman.* SD] *this edn.*

---

84. *But on*] But carry on.
   I ... rush] 'I care not a bit' (a ready-made phrase; *OED* P2).
   86. *I ... choose*] 'I cannot choose but laugh at the idea of seeing you paired
up with a manly woman.'
   86–7. *some ... side*] Even if the existence of Álvarez's manly daughter
Clara seems to be known in Seville, this claim cannot be true: she has heard
that Vitelli feels something for Clara through Piorato, who found out via
Bobadilla (3.2), but it can hardly be commonly known.
   89. *pieced with*] consorted with (*OED* 3).
   90. *I ... merry*] 'I will jest with her.'
   92. *pistol thee*] 'shoot at thee with my pistol'; whether she produces a pistol
or the attack is solely ver+al is unclear.
   roaring whore] perhaps echoing the title of *The Roaring Girl* (see lines 32
n. and 47 SD n.). It is also reminiscent of Petruccio and Maria's row in *Prize*:
'Thou most poor, paltry, spiteful whore. Do you cry? / I'll make you roar
before I leave' (4.2.108).
   93. *correction house*] a house for the social re-education of prostitutes, such
as the one that existed in London at the former Bridewell Palace. That building adjoined the Blackfriars precinct where the King's Men had their indoor
playhouse; if *LC* was performed in the Blackfriars, the line would have been
particularly resonant.
   94. *learned ... swordman*] learned of Vitelli's amorous intentions towards
Clara from Piorato.
   96. *upbraid me*] censure me.
   97–100. *I ... know*] see 3.2.143 n.; Vitelli has not promised to marry
Malroda, as she is far below his social status; instead he appears to have

But said I loved you, long as you remained
The woman I expected, or you swore;
And how you have failed of that, sweetheart, you know.   100
You fain would show your power, but fare you well:
I'll keep no more faith with an infidel.

Malroda. Nor I my bosom for a Turk. Do ye hear?
Go, and the devil take me if ever
I see you more. I was too true.

Vitelli.   Come, pish.   105
That devil take the falsest of us two.

Malroda. Amen.

Vitelli.   You are an ill clerk, and curse yourself.
Madness transports you. I confess I drew you
Unto my will. But, you must know, that must not
Make me dote on the habit of my sin.   110
I will, to settle you to your content,
Be master of my word. And yet he lied

---

98. I loved] I'd love *TSS;* I love *Weber.*   103. Do ye] *F* (do'ye)*; d'ye *F2;*
Do you *Dyce.*

---

settled that she will remain at the Alguazir's house at his sexual disposal until
he chooses to discharge her by paying her a sum of money. She has failed
to fulfil the agreement, as she has been receiving other gentlemen, including
Piorato (cf. 3.2.90–4).

98. *long as*] so long as.

100. *of*] on.

101–2. *You ... infidel*] Vitelli bids her farewell with a couplet, signifying
that he is bringing the conversation to a close (and he is probably moving
to exit the stage); couplets were conventional indications of the end of scenes
(see 1.1.129–30).

102. *I'll ... infidel*] 'I will not share my religion with an unbeliever', figuratively alluding to their relationship. Though sometimes applied to Jews
and pagans, the term *infidel* was particularly used to denote Muslims, as
Malroda's retort makes clear.

103. *Nor ... Turk*] 'Nor will I preserve my love for another infidel'; the
Ottoman Turks were the constant enemies of Christendom in the
Mediterranean and a rich source of literary material, particularly with respect
to Western renegades who gave up their Christian faith and embraced Islam
while in captivity. Robert Daborne dramatised the story of a real-life English
pirate and renegade, John Ward, in his 1612 play *A Christian Turned Turk,*
and Massinger, based on Cervantes, would exploit the theme in *Renegado.*

107. *You are*] pronounced as one syllable, 'you're'.

108–9. *I ... will*] 'I persuaded you to comply with my wishes', but also
with a sexual connotation (punning on *will*, genitalia).

112. *master ... word*] Again alluding to his promise to Malroda (see
3.2.143 n.).

That told you I was marrying, but in thought.
But will you slave me to your tyranny
So cruelly, I shall not dare to look   115
Or speak to other women? Make me not
Your smock's monopoly. Come, let's be friends.
Look, here's a jewel for thee. [*He gives her one.*] I will
    come
At night, and—
Malroda.   What, i' faith? You shall not, sir.
Vitelli. 'Faith, and troth, and verily, but I will.   120
Malroda. Half drunk, to make a noise, and rail?
Vitelli.   No, no,
Sober and dieted for the nonce. I am thine,
I have won the day.
Malroda. [*Aside*]   The night, though, shall be mine.
                              Exeunt [*severally*].

SCENE 4

Enter CLARA *and* BOBADILLA *with letters.*

Clara. What said he, sirrah?
Bobadilla. Little or nothing. 'Faith, I saw him not,
    Nor will not. He doth love a strumpet, mistress;
    Nay, keeps her spitefully, under the constable's nose.

---

118. here's] *F* (her's). SD] *this edn.* 120. 'Faith] I'faith *TSS;* Faith
Dyce. 123. SD1] *this edn.* SD2] *Dyce.*

SCENE 4] *F* (*Scæna quarta.*).

---

122. *Sober ... nonce*] abstinent for the particular purpose.

3.4.0.] Location: '*A room in Álvarez's house*' (Weber). This scene echoes
Shakespeare's *R&J*: Clara questions Bobadilla about her lover, an enemy to
her family (as Juliet does with the Nurse in 2.4), while Sayavedra's courtship,
consented to by Clara's mother, echoes that of Count Paris with the Capulets'
encouragement (3.4 and 3.5).

0. SD *letters*] As at the beginning of 3.2, the letters from Clara that
Bobadilla never delivered to Vitelli (see line 7).

3. *Nor will not*] i.e., Nor will I see him.

2–12.] This speech is lined as verse in all editions, but the metre is irregular and could arguably be rendered as prose.

It shall be justified by the gentleman,   5
Your brother's master that is now within
A-practising. There are your letters. [*He gives her back*
   the letters.] Come,
You shall not cast yourself away while I live,
Nor will I venture my right worshipful place
In such a business—

            Enter EUGENIA *and* SAYAVEDRA

              Here's your mother. Down.   10
And he that loves you: an othergates fellow,
   Iwis. If you had any grace—
Clara.   Well, rogue.
               [*She sits down to embroider.*]
Bobadilla. I'll in to see Don Lucio manage. He'll make
   A pretty piece of flesh, I promise you;
   He does already handle his weapon finely.   *Exit.*   15

---

7. SD] *this edn.* 10. SD] *placement, this edn; indicated on the margin at lines
9–12, F; after 'grace' at line 12, F2; after line 15, TSS; after 'Down' at line 10,
Mitchell.* 11–12.] *lineation, Weber;* F *lines* I wish / rogue. 11. he] ye
Langbaine. 12. Iwis] *Dyce;* I wish *F.* SD] *this edn.* 12–13.] rogue / *Bob.*
Ile in to *F;* rogue. *Bob.* I'll in / To *TSS.* 13. He'll] *F;* He will *TSS.*

---

   5. *the gentleman*] Piorato.
   8. *cast yourself away*] (a) waste yourself; (b) give up on becoming a
woman.
   9. *right worshipful place*] office as steward; the title is comically
exaggerated.
   10. SD] The entrance is indicated marginally in F.
   Down] i.e., 'sit down to your work'; Sayavedra questions her about her
work in line 25.
   11–12.] The lineation of F was emended by Weber to regularise the metre.
   11. *an othergates fellow*] a fellow of another fashion, of a different kind
(*OED* B); Bobadilla compares Sayavedra favourably to Vitelli, who may be
younger and more handsome, but keeps a prostitute as his mistress, as
Bobadilla has reported to Clara.
   12. *Iwis*] certainly; first emended by Dyce, based on Heath.
   grace] charm, refinement (*OED* 1).
   13. *manage*] handle his sword (*OED* 5a).
   14. *A ... flesh*] a proper man, in a sexual sense; cf. Samson in Shakespeare's
R&J: 'Me they shall feel while I am able to stand, and 'tis known I am a
pretty piece of flesh' (1.1.27–8).
   15. *handle ... finely*] with a sexual connotation, probably ironic (*weapon*
for 'penis').

Eugenia. She knows your love, sir, and the full allowance
 Her father and myself approve it with;
 And, I must tell you, I much hope it hath
 Wrought some impression by her alteration.
 She sighs, and says 'forsooth', and cries 'heigh-ho';   20
 She'll take ill words o'th' steward and the servants,
 Yet answer affably and modestly;
 Things, sir, not usual with her. There she is;
 Change some few words.
Sayavedra.   Madam, I am bound to ye.
            [Eugenia stands apart.]
 [*To Clara*] How now, fair mistress, working?
Clara.   Yes, forsooth, 25
 Learning to live another day.
Sayavedra.   That needs not.
Clara. No, forsooth? By my truly, but it does:
 We know not what we may come to.
Eugenia. [*Apart*]   'Tis strange.
Sayavedra. Come, I ha' begged leave for you to play.
Clara.   Forsooth,
 'Tis ill for a fair lady to be idle.   30
Sayavedra. She had better be well-busied, I know that.

---

24. to ye] *F* (to'ye)*;* t'ye *F2;* t'you *Colman;* to you *Weber.* SD] *GWW.*
25. SD] *this edn.* 28. know] knew *F2.* SD] *GWW.*

---

20. *'forsooth' ... 'heigh-ho'*] Both expressions were perceived as signs of
feminine affectation; cf. in *Amends for Ladies*, Bold disguises himself as a
waiting woman, and tries to impersonate feminine speech by using both
(1.1).
 forsooth] in truth.
 heigh-ho] an audible sigh.
20–3. *She ... her*] According to Eugenia, Clara is trying to behave like a
modest lady, using feminine interjections and dealing with ill-mannered
servants, including Bobadilla, with graceful responses (by contrast with her
behaviour in 2.2).
 24. SD] Eugenia remains on stage to chaperone the meeting between her
daughter and her suitor, standing apart within earshot.
 25. *working*] embroidering.
 26. *That needs not*] 'You don't need to work to make a living.'
 27. *By my truly*] assuredly (*OED truly* B1).
 29. *play*] probably with a sexual connotation, as *well-busied* in line 31.

Turtle, methinks you mourn. Shall I sit by you?

[*He sits down by her.*]

Clara. If you be weary, sir, you had best be gone;
    I work not a true stitch, now you're my mate.
Sayavedra. If I be so, I must do more than side you.   35
Clara. Ev'n what you will, but tread me.
Sayavedra.   Shall we bill?
Clara. O, no, forsooth.
Sayavedra.   Being so fair, my Clara,
    Why do ye delight in black work?
Clara.   O, white, sir,
    The fairest ladies like the blackest men.
    I ever loved the colour: all black things   40
    Are least subject to change.
Sayavedra.   Why, I do love
    A black thing too. And the most beauteous faces
    Have oft'nest of them: as the blackest eyes,
    Jet archèd brows, such hair. I'll kiss your hand.

---

32. SD] *this edn.* 38. do ye] *F* (do'ye)*;* d'ye *F2;* d'you *Colman;* do you
Weber.

32–6. *Turtle ... bill*] The conceit around birds (*turtle, mate, tread,* and *bill*)
is initiated by Sayavedra in response, perhaps, to a groan of contempt from
Clara, interpreted by the gentleman (literally or ironically) as the 'mourn' of
a turtle dove. This birding conceit is also used by the Alguazir in 4.2.1–2,
speaking to Malroda.

32. *Turtle*] turtle dove, as a term of endearment between lovers; turtle
doves live in pairs.

34. *mate*] (a) companion (*OED* I.1a; Clara's meaning); (b) either of a
mating pair of birds (*OED* III.6b; Sayavedra's interpretation); Clara declares
that she has no room to work now that Sayavedra is sitting by her.

35. *If ... so*] 'If I am your sexual partner.'
    side you] be at your side, sit by you (*OED* 8a).

36. *but tread me*] 'but not to copulate with me' (as the male bird with the
female; *OED* 8a).
    bill] caress, make show of affection (*OED v.*^{2} 3).

38. *black work*] see 2.2.9 n.

39. *fairest ... blackest men*] For example, cf. Desdemona and Othello in
Oth., Bellamira and Ithamore in *Jew*, and Tamora and Aaron in *Tit.*

42. *black thing*] probably with a sexual connotation, referring to female
genitalia (*thing, OED* 11c).

44. *Jet archèd*] of a glossy deep black colour (*OED* B, 2) and formed into
an arch.

Clara. 'Twill hinder me my work, sir; and my mother   45
    Will chide me if I do not do my task.
Sayavedra. Your mother, nor your father shall chide. You
    Might have a prettier task, would you be ruled,
    And look with open eyes.
Clara.   I stare upon you,
    And broadly see you: a wondrous proper man;   50
    Yet 'twere a greater task for me to love you
    Than I shall ever work, sir, in seven year.
    [*Aside*] Pox o' this stitching, I had rather feel
    Two than sew one. This rogue has giv'n me a stitch
    Clean 'cross my heart. [*Aloud*] Good faith, sir, I shall
    prick you.   55
Sayavedra. In gooder faith, I would prick you again.
Clara. Now you grow troublesome. [*Aside*] Pish, the man is
    foolish.
Sayavedra. Pray wear these trifles.   [*He offers her a gift.*]
Clara.   Neither you, nor trifles;
    You are a trifle: wear yourself, sir, out,

---

45. me my work] *F2*; me work my *F.*   53. SD] *Dyce.* Pox o'] *Dyce;*
Plague o' Colman; — o' F.   55. SD] *this edn.*   55–6. Good ... again] *not
in F2.*   57. SD] *this edn.*   58. SD] *this edn.*

---

48. *prettier task*] by implication, in a sexual sense; cf. Pinac in *Chase*: 'I
have a pretty task, if she be thus curious' (2.2.35).

53–4. *I ... one*] probably with a military connotation, 'I had rather feel
two wounds in battle (or, more literally, the surgical stitches used to close a
wound), than sew one more.'

54–5. *This ... heart*] 'With his behaviour, this rogue [i.e., Sayavedra] has
managed to annoy me exceedingly'; alternatively, if she has Vitelli in mind,
she could be referring to the proverbial wound inflicted by Cupid's arrow
on a lover's breast.

55. *'cross*] across, through.

prick you] i.e., with the needle, which is the only weapon that Clara has
at her disposal to stop Sayavedra's advances.

56. *prick you again*] (a) 'I would try to make my advance again'; (b) 'I
would prick you in return', with an obvious sexual connotation in either
case.

57. *troublesome*] annoying, distressing (*OED* 3).

58. *trifles*] knick-knacks, trinkets (*OED* 3); Sayavedra may give Clara
some small item of clothing or jewellery to wear in token of his love for her;
the SD cannot be more specific as to what prop is being offered.

59. *You ... trifle*] 'You are a worthless person' (*OED* 2c, citing this
passage).

And here no more trifle the time away.   60

Sayavedra. Come, you're deceived in me. I will not wake,
      Nor fast, nor die for you.

Clara.   Goose, be not you deceived,
      I cannot like, nor love, nor live with you,
      Nor fast, nor watch, nor pray for you.

Eugenia. [*Apart*]   Her old fit.

Sayavedra. [*Aside*] Sure this is not the way. [*Aloud*] Nay, I
      will break   65
      Your melancholy.

Clara.   I shall break your pate, then.
      Away, you sanguine scabbard   [*She attacks Sayavedra.*]

Eugenia. [*To Clara*]   Out upon thee,
      Thou'lt break my heart, I am sure.

Sayavedra.   She's not yet tame.

      Enter ÁLVAREZ, PIORATO [*fencing with*] LUCIO,
              and BOBADILLA

---

64. SD] *GWW.* 65. SD1] *Weber.* SD2] *this edn.* 67. SD1] *this edn.*
SD2] *this edn.* 68. SD] *GWW; placed here in F; delayed to before 'She's not
yet tame' in F2; delayed to after 'She's not yet tame' in Weber.*

---

60. *And ... away*] 'And cease to waste your time here in a trifling business' (*trifle* is used as a verb; *OED* 4).

61–2. *Come ... for you*] Losing sleep, fasting, and dying are proverbially
associated with young, infatuated lovers.

62. *Goose*] Clara resorts again to the birding imagery, but changes the
tender *turtle* used by Sayavedra for the deprecatory *goose*, implying foolishness (cf. line 57).

64. *fit*] 'a paroxysm of lunacy (formerly viewed as a periodic disease)'
(*OED* 3b); cf. Young Lucius on Lavinia in *Titus Andronicus*: 'Unless some
fit or frenzy do possess her' (4.1.17).

67. *sanguine scabbard*] A sanguine complexion produced by a predomi-
nance of the blood over the other humours would cause a person to have
an excessive amorous disposition (*sanguine, OED* 3a); the term *scabbard* may
refer to someone who has scabs (associated with sexual desire in 3.1.86; see
also 2.1.101 n.) or, figuratively, to someone who is thin, long, and hollow as
a sword's sheath.

68. SD] As indicated by the marginal placing of this entrance SD in F
(after 'Out upon thee'), the brief comical squabble between Clara and
Sayavedra, in which Eugenia intervenes, and the entrance of Piorato fencing
with Lucio may overlap. The fight would put both siblings in immediate
visual contrast with one another: Clara with her needle is naturally more
effective against Sayavedra than Lucio with his sword against the professional
swordsman Piorato.

Álvarez. [*To Lucio*] On, sir; put home, or I shall goad you
        here
    With this old fox of mine, that will bite better.   70
    O, the brave age is gone; in my young days
    A chevalier would stock a needle's point
    Three times together. Straight i'th' hams!
    Or shall I give ye new garters?
Bobadilla.   'Faith, old master,
    There's little hope. The linen sure was dank   75
    He was begot in: he's so faint, and cold.
    Ev'n send him to Toledo, there to study,
    For he will never fadge with these Toledos.
    [*To Lucio*] Bear ye up your point there, pick his teeth.
        O, base.
Piorato. Fie, you are the most untoward scholar. Bear   80

---

69. SD] *this edn.*   72. needle's] *F (needles);* needless *F2.*   74. ye] you
Colman.   76. cold] *F2;* cold: 2 Torches / ready. *F*   79. SD] *this edn.* ye]
y' *TSS;* you *Dyce.*

69–74. *On ... garters?*] Álvarez instructs Lucio to respond to Piorato's
fencing lesson.
    69. *put home*] deliver a thrust at your opponent.
    goad you] prick you (*OED* 1); cf. The First Soldier in *FalseO*: 'Goad him
on with thy sword' (5.3.69).
    70. *old fox*] Álvarez's old sword; a *fox* was an English sword whose blade
had been engraved with a mark in the shape of a wolf, regularly mistaken
for a fox. (See *OED*, II.6; also, *White Devil* 5.6.234.)
    71–3. *in ... together*] 'When I was young, gallants would be trained to hit
the tip of a needle with a thrust of their swords three consecutive times'; the
precision required to do this would be enormous, qualifying those gentlemen
as consummate fencers.
    72. *stock*] strike with the thrust of a sword (*OED* 1, citing only this
passage).
    73. *Straight ... hams!*] 'Straighten your legs!' Piorato also comments on
the unsuitability of Lucio's posture (lines 80–1).
    74. *Or ... garters*] Knowing his son's keenness on fashion (see 1.2.1–2 and
111–13), Álvarez mockingly offers to buy Lucio a pair of new garters so that
he will be more disposed to straighten his legs to show them off.
    75. *dank*] wet; see 2.2.155–6 n.
    76.] At this point, F adds the marginal SD '2 Torches ready', preparing the
entrance of the two pages with lights at the beginning of 4.1, 62 lines and
an act break later (see Introduction, 30).
    77. *Toledo*] see 1.2.44 n.
    78. *fadge*] fit in with (*OED* 1); cf. 2.2.69.
    79. *point*] sword's tip.
    pick his teeth] 'aim at his face'.

Your body gracefully. What a posture's there?
You lie too open-breasted.
Lucio.   O!
Piorato.   You'd never
Make a good statesman.
Lucio.   Pray, no more.
I hope to breathe in peace, and therefore need not
The practice of these dangerous qualities;   85
I do not mean to live by't, for I trust
You'll leave me better able.
Álvarez.   Not a button.
Eugenia, let's go get us a new heir.
Eugenia. Ay, by my troth. Your daughter's as untoward.
Álvarez. [*To Lucio*] I will break thee bone by bone, and
bake thee,   90
Ere I'll ha' such a wooden son to inherit.
[*To Piorato*] Take him a good knock; see how that will
work.
Piorato. Now for your life, señor.   [*He attacks Lucio.*]
Lucio.   O, alas, I am killed,
My eye is out. Look, father. Sancho—
I'll play the fool no more thus; that I will not.   95
Clara. 'Heart! Ne'er a rogue in Spain shall wrong my
brother

---

88. Eugenia] *not in F2.* 90. SD] *this edn.* 92. SD] *GWW.* 93. señor]
F (Signior). SD] *this edn.* 94. Sancho—] *F;* Zancho! [Pox] *Dyce.*

---

82. *You ... open-breasted*] 'You are exposing your breast too much', which
facilitates receiving a wound from the opponent.
83. *statesman*] A statesman should be more secretive, and therefore, figuratively, not 'open-breasted'.
86–7. *I ... able*] 'I do not intend to fence professionally, as I hope my
inheritance will provide enough funds to live on.' Cf. Sayavedra seems to
have suggested to Clara earlier in this scene (26) that she will not need to
work to earn a living.
87. *Not ... button*] 'I will not leave you anything'; perhaps there is a hint
at the button, or protective metal ball that covers a sword's tip for fencing
practice.
89. *untoward*] ill-disposed (*OED*).
90. *I'll ... thee*] cf. Álvarez's threat in 4.3.25–6.
91. *wooden*] (a) stiff; (b) block-headed.
96. *'Heart*] Euphemistic form of 'God's heart' (usually *'Sheart*), a strong
oath.

Whilst I can hold a sword.   [*She attacks Piorato.*]
Piorato.   Hold, madam, madam!
Álvarez. Clara!
Eugenia.   Daughter!
Bobadilla.   Mistress!
Piorato.   Bradamante,
    Hold, hold, I pray!
Álvarez. The devil's in her o'th' other side, sure.   100
    [*To Piorato*] There's gold for you. [*He gives him money.*]
        [*Aside*] They have changed what-ye-call-'ts:
    Will no cure help? Well, I have one experiment,
    And if that fail, I'll hang him, then here's an end on't.
    [*Aloud to Eugenia*] Come you along with me, [*to Lucio*]
        and you, sir.
Bobadilla. [*To Lucio*] Now are you going to drowning.   105
            Exeunt Álvarez, Eugenia, Lucio, and Bobadilla.
Sayavedra. I'll ev'n along with ye. She's too great a lady
    For me, and would prove more than my match.   *Exit.*
Clara. You're he spoke of Vitelli to the steward?
Piorato. Yes, and I thank you; you have beat me for't.
Clara. But are you sure you do not wrong him?
Piorato.   Sure?   110
    So sure, that if you please venture yourself
    I'll show you him and his cockatrice together,

---

97. SD] *this edn.*   101. SD1] *GWW.* SD2, SD3] *this edn.*   104. SD1,
SD2] *this edn.*   105. SD1 *To Lucio*] *this edn.* SD2 *Exeunt*] *F2; Exit F.*

98. *Bradamante*] a legendary female warrior; she is Rinaldo's sister in
Boiardo's *Orlando innamorato* and Ariosto's *Orlando furioso.*

100. *The ... side*] 'The devil is backing her.'

101. *They ... what-ye-call-'ts*] Euphemistically, 'they have exchanged
their genitalia'. Álvarez starts to despair that the transformation operated by
custom on his children's behaviour may have changed their physiological sex
as well.

105. *Now ... drowning*] Either Bobadilla has overheard Álvarez's aside, or
he supposes that Lucio is in trouble.

108. *he*] he who.

112. *cockatrice*] i.e., Malroda. The cockatrice was a lethal mythical serpent
said to be hatched from a cock's egg that could kill by its mere glance; it
was depicted in heraldry as a hybrid monster with head and wings, but with
the legs of a cock and a serpent's barbed tail (*OED* 1a, 1c); cf. 2.1.34–8.

And you shall hear 'em talk.

Clara.   Will you? By heav'n, sir,
      You shall endear me ever, and I ask
      You mercy.

Piorato.   You were somewhat boisterous.   115

Clara. There's gold to make you amends. [*She gives him*
      money.] And for this pains,
      I'll gratify you further. I'll but mask me,
      And walk along with ye. 'Faith, let's make a night on't.
                                            [*Exeunt.*]

SCENE 5

Enter [the] ALGUAZIR, PACHECO, MENDOZA,
      METALDI, [*and*] LAZARILLO.

Alguazir. Come on, my brave water-spaniels; you that hunt
      ducks in the night, and hide more knavery under your
      gowns than your betters. Observe my precepts and edify
      by my doctrine. At yond corner will I set you; if drunkards

---

113. By heav'n] *Colman (*By Heaven*);* by — *F.* 115. You mercy] Your
mercy *Langbaine.* 116. you] y' *TSS;* ye *Weber.* SD] *this edn.* 117.
further] farther *F2.* 118. with ye] w'ye *TSS;* with you *Dyce.* SD]
Langbaine; Exit F.

SCENE 5] *F (Scæna quinta.).*

---

115. *boisterous*] rough, violent.

117. *mask*] Clara plans to adopt a disguise to walk about the streets at
night. If taken literally, she would be wearing a lady's mask when she reap-
pears in 4.2; it was not uncommon for ladies to appear in public wearing
masks to conceal their identity. As Vitelli instantly recognises her, however,
it is likely that her face remains uncovered and that she adopts the masculine
clothes she was wearing in her first appearance (as in the 2013 BADA
production).

3.5.0.] Location: '*Night. A street*' (Weber). The four rogues turned false
watchmen and led by the Alguazir, a corrupt constable, are reminiscent of
the watch led by Dogberry in Shakespeare's *MAdo* (3.3). The situation is
similar to some of the other plays in the repertory of the King's Men featuring the Gang of Four Plus One (see Introduction, 6–8); cf. Latrocinio
leading four thieves in Middleton's *Widow* (c. late 1615).

1. *water-spaniels*] dogs used for retrieving game in hunting.

2. *ducks*] figuratively, the fowl to be hunted, i.e., gulls, victims for robbery.

molest the street and fall to brabbling, knock you down   5
the malefactors, and take you up their cloaks and hats,
and bring them to me. They are lawful prisoners, and
must be ransomed ere they receive liberty. What else you
are to execute upon occasion, you sufficiently know, and
therefore I abbreviate my lecture.   10

Metaldi. We are wise enough, and warm enough.

Mendoza. Vice this night shall be apprehended.

Pacheco. The terror of rug gowns shall be known, and our bills
discharge us of after-reckonings.

Lazarillo. I will do anything so I may eat.   15

Pacheco. Lazarillo, we will spend no more; now we are grown
worse, we will live better. Let us follow our calling
faithfully.

Alguazir. Away, then; the commonwealth is our mistress. And
who would serve a common mistress, but to gain by her?   20

                                        Exeunt.

13–14.] *F lines in verse,* bils / recknings. /; *Colman lines* rug-gowns / us / after-reckonings. /.   13. bills] Bliss *Langbaine.*   14. after-reckonings] *F (*after recknings*).*   19–20.] *F lines in verse,* who / her? /; *Colman lines* then! / serve / her? /.

---

5. *brabbling*] quarrelling noisily, brawling.

6. *take ... hats*] cf. 4.3.1.

13. *rug gowns*] see 2.1.162 n.

13–14. *our ... after-reckonings*] 'may our bills (as symbols of our office) save us from paying the reckoning'; the four rogues have been appointed by the constable as unofficial watchmen to patrol the streets, though they intend to use their office unlawfully. Pacheco may also imply that, as they are officials of the state, and their actions respond to commands and are not therefore their own choices, they may get off lightly at the ultimate reckoning, i.e., the Last Judgment.

13. *bills*] (a) a type of weapon, usually carried in the period by constables of the watch, consisting of a curved blade supported by a long wooden staff; (b) the reckoning.

14. *after-reckonings*] later or subsequent reckonings.

17. *calling*] vocation; cf. Falstaff's opinion of the divine lawfulness of his thieving activity in *1H4*: ''Tis no sin for a man to labour in his vocation' (1.2.104–5).

19. *commonwealth*] see 2.1.104 n.

20. *common mistress*] a prostitute; the state is corrupt when unscrupulous constables and watchmen can take advantage of their offices.

ACT 4

SCENE I

Enter VITELLI, LAMORAL, GENEVORA,
ANASTRO, *and two pages with lights.*

Lamoral. I pray you see the masque, my lord.
Anastro. 'Tis early night yet.
Genevora. [*To Vitelli*] O, if it be so late take me along.
    I would not give advantage to ill tongues
    To tax my being here, without your presence   5
    To be my warrant.
Vitelli.   You might spare this, sister,
    Knowing with whom I leave you; one that is,
    By your allowance, and his choice, your servant,
    And, may my counsel and persuasion work it,
    Your husband speedily. [*To Lamoral*] For your
      entertainment,   10
    My thanks; I will not rob you of the means
    To do your mistress some acceptable service

SCENE 1] F (*Actus quartus. Scæna prima.*).　3. SD] *this edn.*　10. SD]
GWW.

    4.1.0.] Location: 'A street' (Weber).

    0. SD] The presence of two pages with torches, who reappear in 4.3.44 accompanying again Lamoral, Anastro, and Genevora, indicates that Act 4 takes place in the streets of Seville at night.

    1. *masque*] the Jacobean and Caroline dramatic entertainment. The four characters and the pages are on their way to attend a masque and a banquet at Lamoral's house (see 4.3.47), but Vitelli plans to visit Malroda instead. In the 2013 production, Watts changed this slightly and opened the second half of the performance with Vitelli, Genevora, and Lamoral sitting with their backs to the audience, as if watching the masque, listening to a song performed by the rest of the cast offstage.

    6. *warrant*] chaperone.

    8. *servant*] devoted admirer.

    9–10. *And ... speedily*] Perhaps an aside; we never discover whether Vitelli's intention to marry his sister to his friend Lamoral is known to her.

In waiting on her to my house.

Genevora.   My lord—

Vitelli. As you respect me, without further trouble

Retire, and taste those pleasures prepared for you,   15

And leave me to my own ways.

Lamoral.   When you please, sir.

Exeunt [severally].

SCENE 2

Enter MALRODA *and* [*the*] ALGUAZIR.

Malroda. You'll leave my chamber?

Alguazir.   Let us but bill once,

My dove, my sparrow, and I, with my office,

Will be thy slaves forever.

Malroda.   Are you so hot?

Alguazir. But taste the difference of a man in place:

You'll find that, when authority pricks him forward,   5

14. further] farther *F2.*   16. SD] *GWW.*

SCENE 2] *F (Scæna secunda.).*

---

14. *trouble*] protestation.

15. *those pleasures*] (a) the performance of the masque and the supper; (b) the pleasures derived from Lamoral's company.

4.2.0.] Location: '*A room in the Alguazir's house with a gallery*' (Weber). Clara uses the above space overlooking the stage to overhear Vitelli's dealings with Malroda.

1. *bill*] cf. the birding imagery associated with Sayavedra's amorous exchanges with Clara in his courtship of her in 3.4.32–6.

2. *dove*] turtle dove, romantic term of endearment; see 3.4.32.

sparrow] Also used as a term of endearment, but with a sexual connotation: sparrows were notorious for their promiscuity; cf. Lucio in Shakespeare's *MM*: 'Sparrows must not build in his house-eaves, because they are lecherous' (3.1.434–5).

3. *slaves*] the office and him.

hot] sexually aroused.

4. *man in place*] man in office.

5–8. *when ... right*] (a) when he is officially commanded to assist a lady, no one can better him; (b) when sexual arousal provokes him, no one will satisfy a lady better.

Your Don, nor yet your diego, comes not near him
To do a lady right. No men pay dearer
For their stol'n sweets than we: three minutes trading
Affords to any sinner a protection
For three years after; think on that. I burn,   10
But one drop of your bounty—

Malroda.   Hence, you rogue,
Am I fit for you? Is't not grace sufficient
To have your staff a bolt to bar the door
Where a Don enters, but that you'll presume
To be his taster?

Alguazir.   Is no more respect   15
Due to this rod of justice?

Malroda.   Do you dispute?
Good doctor of the dungeon, not a word more;
Pox! If you do, my lord Vitelli knows it.

Alguazir. Why, I am big enough to answer him,

---

6. nor yet] *F;* not yet *Langbaine;* nor *TSS.* 8. stol'n] *F* (stolne); stolen
Weber. 9. sinner] finner *F2.* 16. this] his *F2.* 18. Pox! If] *Colman;* —
if *F*

---

6. *Don ... diego*] presumably Vitelli and Piorato, though it could be a
general statement.

7–10. *No ... after*] No one pays better for a prostitute's services than
officers: in exchange for three minutes of sexual intercourse, they offer her
three years of protection.

8. *stol'n sweets*] unpaid sexual favours.

9. *sinner*] in this instance, specifically a prostitute.

10. *burn*] with sexual desire; cf. line 3.

11. *drop ... bounty*] 'a minimal part of your sexual favours' (taking only
three minutes).

13. *a bolt*] used as a bolt.

bar the door] (a) physically bolting it with the staff; (b) figuratively, guard-
ing it while the Don is with her.

15. *taster*] domestic officer who tasted food and drink before it was served
to his master to verify its quality or to detect poison (*OED* 2); in this instance,
figuratively, the Alguazir has been Vitelli's taster in enjoying Malroda's sexual
favours before the master arrives.

16. *rod ... justice*] the Alguazir's bill or staff of office, with a pun on his
penis.

19. *big*] (a) physically large, strong (perhaps with an allusion to the size
of his penis, his 'rod of justice'); (b) important, officially powerful.

Or any man.

Malroda.   'Tis well.

Vitelli. (*Within*)   Malroda.

Alguazir.   How?   20

Malroda. You know the voice, and now crouch like a cur
    Ta'en worrying sheep. I now could have you gelded
    For a bawd rampant. But on this submission
    For once I spare you.

Alguazir.   I will be revenged—

[*Enter* VITELLI.]

My honourable lord.

Vitelli.   There's for thy care.   25

                  [*He gives him money.*]

Alguazir. [*Aside*] I am mad, stark mad. Proud pagan; scorn
    her host?
    I would I were but valiant enough to kick her;

Enter PIORATO *and* CLARA, *above.*

I'd wish no manhood else.

Malroda.   What's that?

Alguazir. [*Aloud*]   I am gone.   *Exit.*

        [*Malroda and Vitelli talk apart.*]

Piorato. [*Above*] You see I have kept my word.

Clara. [*Above*]   But in this object

---

20. well. / *Vitelli.* (*Within*) Malroda] *F* (well. *Vitelli within.* / *Vit. Malroda.*).
23. rampant] *F2*; rampani *F.*   24. SD] *F2*; not in *F.*   25. SD] *this edn.*
26. SD] *Weber.*   27. I would I] Would I *TSS.*   28. I'd] *TSS*; I'ld *F*; I'll
F2; I would *Weber.*   SD1] *this edn.*   SD3] *GWW.*   29. SD1 *and* SD2] *this
edn.*

---

22. *worrying*] killing or injuring by biting and shaking, as dogs or wolves
might do (*OED* vb. 3a).

23. *bawd rampant*] lustful pander (*rampant, OED* 3, usually applied to
women); a rampant animal stands with its forepaws in the air in a threatening
manner (*OED* 1).

    submission] admission, confession (*OED* III.5).

24. *I ... revenged*] Perhaps an aside.

26. *Proud ... host?*] 'Arrogant unbeliever; does she mock her keeper?'

27. SD] Another instance of an anticipated entrance in *F*; later editions
delay it one line.

29. *object*] the vision of Malroda and Vitelli together.

Hardly deserved my thanks.

Piorato. [*Above*]   Is there aught else   30
   You will command me?

Clara. [*Above*]   Only your sword,
   Which I must have. Nay, willingly; I yet know
   To force it, and to use it.

Piorato. [*Above*]   'Tis yours, lady.
                    [*He gives her his sword.*]

Clara. [*Above*] I ask no other guard.

Piorato. [*Above*]   If so, I leave you.
   [*Aside*] And now, if that the Constable keep his word,   35
   A poorer man may chance to gull a lord.   *Exit.*

Malroda. By this good light, you shall not.

Vitelli.   By this light,
   I must, and will, Malroda. What, do you make
   A stranger of me?

Malroda.   I'll be so to you,
   And you shall find it.

Vitelli.   These are your old arts   40
   T'endear the game you know I come to hunt for,
   Which I have borne too coldly.

Malroda.   Do so still,
   For if I heat you, hang me.

Vitelli.   If you do not,
   I know who'll starve for't. Why, thou shame of women,
   Whose folly or whose impudence is greater   45
   Is doubtful to determine; this to me

---

30. SD] *this edn.*   31. SD] *this edn.*   33. SD1 *and* SD2] *this edn.*   34.
SD1 *and* SD2] *this edn*   35. SD] *this edn.*   37. good light] *Dyce;* good kiss
Colman; good — *F.*   this light] *Dyce;* this kiss *Colman;* this — *F.*

---

37. *good light*] euphemistic expression for 'God's light' censored in F (see
Appendix 3, 234).

41. *T'endear ... for*] 'To make your sexual favours more appealing by
delaying physical intercourse.'

42. *coldly*] indifferently.

43. *heat*] excite you sexually.

44. *who'll starve*] Vitelli threatens Malroda and, consequently, her offspring with starvation by vowing to stop her allowance if she denies him
immediate access to her sexual favours. Coming from the father of Malroda's
child (see 3.1.39 n.), this threat is particularly unpleasant.

That know thee for a whore.
Malroda.   And made me one,
    Remember that.
Vitelli.   Why, should I but grow wise
    And tie that bounty up, which nor discretion
    Nor honour can give way to, thou wouldst be   50
    A bawd ere twenty, and within a month
    A barefoot, lousy, and diseasèd whore,
    And shift thy lodgings oft'ner than a rogue
    That's whipped from post to post.
Malroda.   Pish! All our college
    Know you can rail well in this kind.
Clara. [*Above*]   For me   55
    He never spake so well.
Vitelli.   I have maintained thee
    The envy of great fortunes; made thee shine
    As if thy name were glorious; stuck thee full
    Of jewels, as the firmament of stars;
    And in it made thee so remarkable   60
    That it grew questionable whether virtue poor
    Or vice so set forth as it is in thee
    Were even by modesty's self to be preferred;

---

47. whore.] *F;* whore? *Langbaine.*   55. SD] *this edn.*   For] 'Fore *TSS.*

47. *made me one*] cf. 3.3.32–47.
49. *tie ... up*] give up enjoying your sexual favours (*OED* 6 lists the first recorded instance of this sense in 1760); see line 11 n.
49–50. *nor ... Nor*] neither ... Nor.
50. *way*] access.
54. *from ... post*] from the boundary of one parish to the next; as well as serving as public notice boards where notices could be pasted, posts were used as boundary markers and as places where criminals could be tied up and whipped as public punishment (*OED* II.5b).
   college] (a) presumably jocular, the professional fellowship of prostitutes; (b) women whom Vitelli has seduced. Vittoria in *White Devil* protests at being condemned for harlotry: 'A house of penitent whores? Who sent me to it? / Who hath the honour to advance Vittoria / To this incontinent college?' (4.2.112–4). See also 3.3.93 n.
55. *For me*] Sympson and Seward emended for ''Fore [i.e., Before] me', which is also a plausible reading; note that Clara's response (perhaps ironic) to Vitelli's abusive language against Malroda is to say that he speaks 'well'.
60. *remarkable*] noteworthy.
62. *set forth*] exposed, notorious (see *set OED vb.*¹ 10).

And am I thus repaid?

Malroda.   You are still my debtor;
Can this, though true, be weighed with my lost honour,   65
Much less my faith? I have lived private to you,
And, but for you, had ne'er known what lust was,
Nor what the sorrow for't.

Vitelli.   'Tis false.

Malroda.   'Tis true,
But how returned by you, thy whole life being
But one continued act of lust, and shipwreck   70
Of women's chastities.

Vitelli.   But that I know
That she that dares be damned dares anything,
I should admire thy tempting me. But presume not
On the power you think you hold o'er my affections;
It will deceive you. Yield, and presently,   75
Or by the inflamèd blood which thou must quench,
I'll make a forcible entry.

Malroda.   Touch me not,
You know I have a throat. Pox, if you do
I will cry out a rape, or sheathe this here,
                    [*She threatens to stab herself.*]
Ere I'll be kept and used for julep water   80
T'allay the heat which luscious meats and wine,
And not desire, hath raised.

Vitelli. [*Aside*]   A desperate devil;

---

64. SP] *F2; not in F.* 78. Pox] *Dyce;* by Heaven *Colman;* — *F.* 79.
SD] *this edn.* 82. SD] *Weber.*

---

66. *private*] offering you my sexual favours exclusively (which, according
to the Alguazir, is not true; see 3.2.93–4).

75. *presently*] straightaway.

76. *the inflamèd*] scans as three syllables, 'th'inflamèd'.

78. *You .. throat*] 'You know I can shout loudly'.

Pox] The censored expression in F could be another one-syllable oath
('*Sdeath, 'Slight, 'Swounds,* etc.); cf. *'Heart* in 3.4.96 (see Appendix 3, 232–3).

80. *julep water*] a sweetened drink administered to assuage passionate
feelings (*OED* 1 and 2).

81–2. *heat ... raised*] As already stated by Piorato (see 3.2.23 n.), a diet
based on certain meats (and wine, in this case) can produce an imbalance in
the bodily humours, generating an excess of choler, the hot and dry humour.
Malroda states that Vitelli's diet is the cause of his voracious sexual appetite,

My blood commands my reason. I must take
Some milder way.
Malroda. [*Aside*]   I hope, dear Don, I fit you.
The night is mine, although the day was yours.   85
You are not fasting now. This speeding trick—
Which I would as a principle leave to all
That make their maintenance out of their own Indies,
As I do now—my good old mother taught me:
'Daughter', quoth she, 'contest not with your lover,   90
His stomach being empty; let wine heat him,
And then you may command him.' 'Tis a sure one.
His looks show he is coming.
Vitelli.   Come, this needs not,
Especially to me. You know how dear
I ever have esteemed you—
Clara. [*Above*]   Lost again.   95
Vitelli. That any sigh of yours hath power to change
My strongest resolution, and one tear
Sufficient to command a pardon from me,
For any wrong from you, which all mankind

---

84. SD] *Weber.*   95. SD] *this edn.*   96. sigh] *Colman (conj. Sympson);*
sight *F*

---

and not his amorous attraction to her (*desire* in its emotional sense, *OED*
1a). Alternatively, *not desire* could be a misprint for *hot desire*, in which case
she would imply that lust would add to the heat caused by meat and drink.
    83. *My ... reason*] cf. *Oth.*: 'My blood begins my safer guides to rule, /
And passion, having my best judgment collied, / Essays to lead the way'
(2.3.198–200).
    84. *fit you*] give you your just punishment (*OED v.*[1] 12).
    85. *night ... yours*] as she had predicted at the end of 3.3.
    86. *fasting*] perhaps referring to Vitelli's intention to return to her 'dieted
for the nonce' (3.3.122).
    88. *own Indies*] Malroda is the source of her own wealth through prostitu-
tion; cf. her earlier characterisation of the source of her gold in 'a fertile
island' of her own (3.1.60–1) and Piorato comparing her to a 'wealthy mine'
(3.2.60). All these images – the island, the mine, and the Indies – refer to
her genitalia.
    92. *sure one*] a reliable maxim.
    93. *coming*] In Middleton's *Maiden's T*, Leonella stops the sexual advances
of Votarius with 'Back! You're too forward, sir. There's no coming for you'
(5.1.83), which Wiggins annotates as 'possibly with secondary meaning
"orgasm" (the usage is first recorded in 1650)'.

Should kneel in vain for!
Malroda.   Pray you pardon those   100
    That need your favour, or desire it.
Vitelli.   Prithee,
    Be better tempered. I'll pay as a forfeit
    For my rash anger this purse filled with gold.
                            [*He offers her a purse.*]
    Thou shalt have servants, gowns, attires, what not—
    Only continue mine.
Malroda. [*Aside*]   'Twas this I fished for.   105
Vitelli. Look on me, and receive it.
Malroda.   Well, you know
    My gentle nature, and take pride t'abuse it.
    You see a trifle pleases me; we are friends.
    This kiss, and this, confirms it.   [*She kisses him.*]
Clara. [*Above*]   With my ruin.
Malroda. I'll have this diamond and this pearl.
                            [*She takes the jewels from the purse.*]
Vitelli.   They are yours.   110
Malroda. But will you not, when you have what you came
        for,
    Take them from me tomorrow? 'Tis a fashion
    Your lords of late have used.
Vitelli.   But I'll not follow.
Clara. [*Above*] That any man at such a rate as this
    Should pay for his repentance.
Vitelli.   Shall we to bed now?   115
Malroda. Instantly, sweet. Yet, now I think on't better,
    There's something first that in a word or two
    I must acquaint you with.   [*They talk apart.*]
Clara. [*Above*]   Can I cry 'Ay me'
    To this against myself? I'll break this match,

---

103. SD] *this edn.*   105. SD] *Weber.*   109. SD1 *and* SD2] *this edn.*   110.
SD] *this edn.*   114. SD] *this edn.*   118. SD1] *GWW.*   SD2] *this edn.*

108. *trifle*] cf. Sayavedra's *trifles* in 3.4.58–60.
    110. *diamond ... pearl*] Malroda presumably extracts the two jewels from
the purse if it contains more than gold (103), although Vitelli could be
wearing them on his person.
    113. *Your ... late*] a generalisation.

Or make it stronger with my blood.   [*She*] *descends.*

Enter [*the*] ALGUAZIR, PIORATO, PACHECO,
METALDI, MENDOZA, [*and*] LAZARILLO, [*and they
stand apart.*]

Alguazir. [*To Piorato*]   I am yours;   120
  A Don's not privileged here more than yourself;
  Win her and wear her.
Piorato.   Have you a priest ready?
Alguazir. I have him for thee, lad. [*Aside*] And when I have
  Married this scornful whore to this poor gallant,
  She will make suit to me; there is a trick   125
  To bring a high-priced wench upon her knees.
  [*Aloud*] For you, my fine, neat harpies, stretch your
    talons
  And prove yourselves true night-birds.
Pacheco.   Take my word
  For me and all the rest.
Lazarillo.   If there be meat,
  Or any banquet stirring, you shall see   130
  How I'll bestow myself.
Alguazir.   When they are drawn,
  Rush in upon 'em. All's fair prize you light on.

---

120. SD2 *and they stand apart*] *Dyce, subst.; &c. F; and others* | *GWW.*
SD3 *To Piorato*] *this edn.* 123. SD] *GWW.* 126. high-priced] *Colman;*
high-priz'd *F;* high-pris'd *F2.* 127. SD] *Dyce.*

---

120. SD1] Clara exits from the above space into the 'tiring house before
re-entering at line 144.

SD2] F adds '&c.'; Williams emended for '*and others*'. However, as Dyce
noticed, there is no justification for other characters to appear at this point:
this is exactly the group of characters that re-enter at the beginning of the
following scene (4.3).

122. *Win ... her*] proverbial (Tilley, W408).

126. *high-priced wench*] expensive prostitute; this is a better modernisation
than *high-prized*, since the two verbs were not formally differentiated in the
period, and in this instance it seems to refer to the monetary value of the
courtesan's services (which the Alguazir profits from), rather than her general
worth.

127. *harpies*] In classical mythology, rapacious and filthy monsters with
women's bodies and bird's wings and claws, supposed to act as ministers of
divine vengeance (*OED* 1; cf. 2.2.193 n.); in transferred sense, thieves,
plundering people (*OED* 2).

I must away. Your officer may give way
To the knavery of his watch but must not see it.
You all know where to find me.
Metaldi.   There look for us.   135

                             Exit [the Alguazir].

Vitelli. [*To Malroda, noticing Piorato*] Who's that?
Malroda. [*Moving away from Vitelli*]   My Piorato,
                             welcome, welcome.
'Faith, had you not come when you did, my lord
Had done I know not what to me.
Vitelli. [*Aside*]   I am gulled;
First cheated of my jewels, and then laughed at.
[*To Piorato*] Sirrah, what make you here?
Piorato.   A business brings me,   140
More lawful than your own.
Vitelli.   How's that, you slave?
Malroda. He's such that would continue her a whore
Whom he would make a wife of.
Vitelli.   I'll tread upon
The face you dote on, strumpet.   [*He attacks Piorato.*]

       Enter CLARA [*with Piorato's sword*].

Pacheco. [*Coming forward*]   Keep the peace there.
          [*The watchmen attack Vitelli.*]
Vitelli. A plot upon my life too?
Metaldi.   Down with him.   145
Clara. [*To Vitelli*] Show your old valour and learn from a
    woman.

---

135. SD] *GWW.*   136. SD1 *and* SD2] *this edn.*   138. SD] *GWW.*   140.
SD] *this edn.*   make] makes *F2.*   142. her] *F2;* his *F.*   143. upon] on
TSS.   144. SD1, SD2, SD3, *and* SD4] *this edn.*   146. SD] *this edn.*

139. *jewels*] punning on *testicles.*
142–3. *He's ... of*] Perhaps directed at Pacheco and his gang before they
attack Vitelli: 'He (Vitelli) is a man who would keep her (Malroda) as a
prostitute, while he (Piorato) would marry her.'
142. *continue*] (a) cause to remain a prostitute (*OED* 2); (b) keep on,
retain as his own (*OED* 3a).
144. SD2] Another anticipated entrance in F, which other editors post-
pone until just before her first line.

One eagle has a world of odds against
A flight of daws, as these are.
              [Clara attacks Piorato and the watchmen.]
Piorato. [*To the watchmen*]   Get you off,
   I'll follow instantly.
Pacheco.   Run for more help there.
                  Exeunt all but Vitelli and Clara.
Vitelli. [*Aside*] Loss of my gold and jewels, and the wench too,   150
   Afflicts me not so much as th' having Clara
   The witness of my weakness.   *[He moves away.]*
Clara. [*Aside*]   He turns from me,
   And yet I may urge merit, since his life
   Is made my second gift.
Vitelli. [*Aside*]   May I ne'er prosper
   If I know how to thank her.
Clara. [*Aloud*]   Sir, your pardon   155
   For pressing thus beyond a virgin's bounds
   Upon your privacies. And let my being
   Like to a man, as you are, be th' excuse
   Of my soliciting that from you which shall not
   Be granted on my part although desired   160
   By any other. Sir, you understand me,
   And 'twould show nobly in you to prevent
   From me a farther boldness which I must
   Proceed in, if you prove not merciful,
   Though with my loss of blushes and good name.   165
Vitelli. Madam, I know your will, and would be thankful
   If it were possible I could affect

---

148. SD1 *and* SD2] *this edn.*   150. SD] *Dyce.*   152. SD1] *this edn.*   SD2]
Dyce.   154. SD] *Dyce.*   155. SD] *this edn.*   163. farther] further *Colman.*
164. merciful] *F2* (mercifull); mercifuil *F.*

---

147. *eagle*] the noblest of birds, as opposed to the daws.
148. *daws*] small black birds of the crow kind (*OED* 1); in figurative sense
the term was often applied contemptuously to people (*OED* 2).
154. *second gift*] (a) his life, that she has saved for a second time (the first
being in 1.3); (b) her gift after the sword she gave him in 2.2.246.
156. *pressing*] trespassing, interfering.
157. *privacies*] (a) private affairs; (b) private parts, genitalia.
159–61. *soliciting ... other*] 'requesting that you give me what I would
refuse to grant to anyone else (i.e., love, a kiss)'.
167. *affect*] feel affection for, love.

The daughter of an enemy.

Clara.   That fair false one
  Whom with fond dotage you have long pursued
  Had such a father; she to whom you pay   170
  Dearer for your dishonour than all titles
  Ambitious men hunt for are worth.

Vitelli.   'Tis truth.

Clara. Yet, with her as a friend, you still exchange
  Health for diseases, and to your disgrace
  Nourish the rivals to your present pleasures   175
  At your own charge, used as a property
  To give a safe protection to her lust,
  Yet share in nothing but the shame of it.

Vitelli. Grant all this so, to take you for a wife
  Were greater hazard, for should I offend you—   180
  As 'tis not easy still to please a woman—
  You are of so great a spirit that I must learn
  To wear your petticoat, for you will have
  My breeches from me.

Clara.   Rather from this hour
  I here abjure all actions of a man,   185
  And will esteem it happiness from you
  To suffer like a woman. Love, true love,
  Hath made a search within me, and expelled
  All but my natural softness, and made perfect

---

168. *That ... one*] i.e., Malroda.

170. *father*] Malroda's father seems to have been an enemy of Vitelli, or of Spain, but this is unclear, as no further reference to him is made in the play. (It is curious to note that Malroda has figuratively adopted the Alguazir and his wife as parents; see 3.1.57–8.)

174. *diseases*] (a) in a bodily sense, specifically venereal infections transmitted by prostitutes; (b) in moral terms, depravity, moral disgrace (*OED* 3; in this case, *health* means 'spiritual, moral, or mental soundness or well-being', *OED* 4).

182–4. *You ... me*] Vitelli echoes the women's song in Fletcher's *Prize*: 'For the good of the Commonweal / The woman shall wear the breeches' (2.6.49–50).

184–93. *Rather ... able*] This speech articulates the thematic core of the play to which the main title alludes: the power of love to transform the rebellious, masculine Clara into an affectionate and submissive wife.

That which my parents' care could not begin.   190
I will show strength in nothing but my duty,
And glad desire to please you, and in that
Grow every day more able.
Vitelli. [*Aside*]   Could this be,
What a brave race might I beget? I find
A kind of yielding, and no reason why   195
I should hold longer out. She's young, and fair,
And chaste for sure, but with her leave the devil
Durst not attempt her. [*Aloud*] Madam, though you have
A soldier's arm, your lips appear as if
They were a lady's.
Clara.   They dare, sir, from you   200
Endure the trial.   [*He kisses her.*]
Vitelli.   Ha! Once more I pray you.
                                        [*He kisses her.*]
[*Aside*] The best I ever tasted, and 'tis said
I have proved many; 'tis not safe, I fear,
To ask the rest now. Well, I will leave whoring,
And luck herein send me with her. [*Aloud*] Worthiest
     lady,   205
I'll wait upon you home, and by the way—
If e'er I marry, as I'll not forswear it—
Tell you, you are my wife.
Clara.   Which if you do,
From me all mankind women learn to woo.
                                        Exeunt.

---

193. SD] *Weber.*   198. SD] *this edn.*   201. SD1 *and* SD2] *GWW.*   202.
SD] *Dyce.*   205. herein] *F;* heaven *Dyce.*   SD] *this edn.*

197–8. with … her] 'the devil himself would not attempt to make amorous
advances on her, even if she encouraged him to do so'.

203. *proved*] tried (*OED* 6).

204. *the rest*] sexual intercourse; this attitude contrasts with the analogous
situation in *La fuerza*, which is reported by Hipólita as a full sexual encounter
forced by Luis (see Introduction, 25–6); cf. Genevora's attitude to premarital
sex expressed in 5.2.53.

205. *herein*] Dyce and Williams emended to *heaven*, implying that the line
can be paraphrased as 'may God send me luck with her'; but the F reading
stresses the more mundane, perhaps cynical side of Vitelli's character.

209. *mankind*] (a) masculine (*OED adj.*² 3); (b) furious, fierce, mad
(*OED adj.*¹).

SCENE 3

Enter [the] ALGUAZIR, PACHECO, METALDI,
MENDOZA, [*and*] LAZARILLO.

Alguazir. A cloak? Good purchase. And rich hangers? Well,
   We'll share ten pistolets a man.
Lazarillo.   Yet still
   I am monstrous hungry. Could you not deduct
   So much out of the gross sum as would purchase
   Eight loins of veal and some two dozen of capons?   5
Pacheco. O, strange proportion for five.
Lazarillo.   For five? I have
   A legion in my stomach that have kept
   Perpetual fast these ten years. For the capons
   They are to me but as so many blackbirds.
   May I but eat once and be satisfied,   10

SCENE 3] *F (Scæna Tertia.).*   0. SD LAZARILLO] *F2; Lararillo F.*   4.
sum] *F2;* some *F.*

4.3.0.] Location: '*Night. A street*' (Weber).
   1. *cloak … hangers*] The Alguazir comments on the booty that the band
of false watchmen have managed to get hold of, probably during the preceding squabble with Vitelli (4.2.144).
   hangers] ornamented strap on a sword-belt from which the sword was
hung (*OED n.*[2] 4b).
   2. *pistolets*] Spanish gold escudos.
   6. *proportion*] portion of food, excessive for only five people on stage.
   7. *legion*] perhaps reminiscent of the Gerasene demoniac in Mark 5:9 (see
1.3.78 n.)
   8. *these ten years*] the past ten years.
   9. *blackbirds*] small in comparison to a capon; it seems to be a reference
to the 'four and twenty blackbirds' (the two dozen in line 5) of the English
nursery rhyme: 'Sing a song o' sixpence / A pocket full of rye; / Four and
twenty blackbirds, / Bakèd in a pie. // When the pie was opened, / The birds
began to sing; / Was not that a dainty dish, / To set before the king?' The
rhyme seems not to be recorded in print until 1744, but it must have been
in oral circulation before then. One of the theories is that the king it mentions is Henry VIII and the blackbirds represent the monks of a soon-to-be-
dissolved monastery (Opie, 194–5). The rhyme is referred to in Fletcher's
Bonduca when Petillius exclaims 'Whoa! Here's a stir now: sing a song o' six
pence' (5.2.35).

Let the fates call me when my ship is fraught,
And I shall hang in peace.
Alguazir.   Steal well tonight,
And thou shalt feed tomorrow. So now you are
Yourselves again, I'll raise another watch
To free you from suspicion. Set on any   15
You meet with boldly. I'll not be far off
T'assist you and protect you.   *Exit.*
Metaldi.   O brave officer.

Enter ÁLVAREZ, LUCIO, [*and*] BOBADILLA.

Pacheco. Would every ward had one but so well given,
And we would watch for rug in gowns of velvet.
Mendoza. Stand close. A prize.
Metaldi.   Satin and gold lace, lads.   20
                                    [*They stand apart.*]
Álvarez. Why dost thou hang upon me?
Lucio.   'Tis so dark
I dare not see my way. For heaven's sake, father,
Let us go home.
Bobadilla.   No, ev'n here we'll leave you.
Let's run away from him, my lord.
Lucio.   O 'las.
Álvarez. Thou hast made me mad. And I will beat thee
        dead,   25
Then bray thee in a mortar, and new mould thee,
But I will alter thee.
Bobadilla.   'Twill never be.

---

20. SD] *GWW.*   26. thee in] *F* (the in).   new] *F2;* now *F*

11–12. *Let ... peace*] 'Wedding and hanging go by destiny' was proverbial (Tilley, W232).
    11. *fraught*] freighted as a ship, in this case with food (*OED* adj. 1).
    14. *another watch*] a second watch that will appear with the Alguazir later in the scene.
    18. *ward*] an administrative division or district under the jurisdiction of a constable (*OED* 19a).
    19. *rug*] see 2.1.162 n.; if there were such a corrupt officer in every district, thieving watchmen robbing rug gowns would be rich enough to buy rich velvet clothes for themselves.
    25–6. *beat ... thee*] see 2.2.150 n. and cf. Álvarez's threat in 3.4.90.

He has been three days practising to drink,
Yet still he sips like to a waiting woman,
And looks as he were murd'ring of a fart   30
Among wild Irish swaggerers.
Lucio.   I have still
Your good word, Sancho. Father.
Álvarez.   Milksop, coward;
No house of mine receives thee. I disclaim thee:
Thy mother on her knees shall not entreat me
Hereafter to acknowledge thee.
Lucio. [*To Bobadilla*]   Pray you, speak for me.   35
Bobadilla. I would, but now I cannot with mine honour.
Álvarez. There's only one course left that may redeem thee,
Which is to strike the next man that you meet,
And if we chance to light upon a woman,
Take her away and use her like a man,   40
Or I will cut thy hamstrings.
Pacheco. [*Apart to the other watchmen*] This makes for us.

---

30. murd'ring] *F* (murdring); murdering *F2*.   35. SD] *this edn.*   41. SD]
this edn.

---

30. *murd'ring of*] containing, stifling.
31. *wild Irish swaggerers*] The Irish were thought to have a proverbial
dislike of flatulence. Lucio is described as if he were containing his wind,
afraid to let it out in the presence of a band of dangerous Irishmen who will
take offence and attack him. In *Pierce Penniless* (1592) Thomas Nashe commented: 'The Irishman will draw his dagger and be ready to kill and slay if
one break wind in his company' (sig. D1ᵛ). In Marston's *Malcontent* there is
an exchange alluding to the same belief: '*Mendoza.* The Duke hates thee. /
Malevole. As Irishmen do bum-cracks' (3.3.49–50).
32. *Milksop, coward*] Perhaps a Chaucerian echo from 'The Prologue to
the Monk's Tale' in *The Canterbury Tales*: '"Allas," she seith, "that evere I
was shape / To wedden a milksop, or a coward ape"' (Chaucer, 240). See
as well 2.2.64 n. In *Malta*, Norandine rebukes a soldier for his concern about
his bleeding wounds: ''Tis but the sweat of honour, alas, thou milksop, /
Thou man of marchpane' (2.1.54–5).
33. *No … thee*] cf. Capulet to his daughter in *R&J*: 'hang, beg, starve,
die in the streets, / For, by my soul, I'll ne'er acknowledge thee, / Nor what
is mine shall never do thee good' (3.5.192–4).
34–5. *Thy … thee*] cf. The Duchess of York pleading for her son's life in
R2 5.3.85 onwards.
39. *light upon*] come across (*OED light v.*¹ 10d).
40. *use … man*] Álvarez instructs his son to rape the first woman he comes
across.

Álvarez. What dost thou do now?

Lucio.   Sir, I am saying my prayers;
    For being to undertake what you would have me,
    I know I cannot live.

             Enter LAMORAL, GENEVORA, ANASTRO,
                and [two] pages with lights.

Lamoral.   Madam, I fear
    You'll wish you had used your coach: your brother's
      house   45
    Is yet far off.

Genevora.   The better, sir. This walk
    Will help digestion after your great supper,
    Of which I have fed largely.

Álvarez. [*To Lucio*]   To your task,
    Or else you know what follows.

                      [*Álvarez and Bobadilla stand apart.*]

Lucio. [*Aside*]   I am dying.
    Now, Lord, have mercy on me. [*To Lamoral*] By your
      favour,   50
    Sir, I must strike you.

Lamoral.   For what cause?

Lucio.   I know not.
    And I must likewise talk with that young lady
    An hour in private.

Lamoral.   What you must is doubtful,
    But I am certain, sir, I must beat you.   [*He hits him.*]

---

42. do] *not in TSS.*   Sir, I am saying] I'm saying, Sir *TSS*; Sir, I'm saying
Colman.   48. SD] *this edn.*   49. SD1 *and* SD2] *this edn.*   50. SD] *this
edn.*   54. sir, I] Sir, that I *TSS.*   SD] *this edn.*

---

    42. *What ... now?*] Lucio has started to pray, maybe kneeling down, or
just joining his hands in prayer.

    44. SD [*two*] *pages*] i.e., the two pages who appeared in 4.1.

    47. *your great supper*] The masque, followed by a banquet, has taken place
at Lamoral's house.

    52. *talk*] Lucio is ignorant of what his father means by using Genevora
'like a man' (line 40), and he supposes that talking to the lady is sufficient;
in the next scene he sets out simply to kiss her (see 4.4.3).

Lucio. Help, help!

Álvarez.   Not strike again?

Lamoral.   How, Álvarez?   55

Anastro. This for my lord Vitelli's love. [*He attacks Álvarez.*]

Pacheco. [*Apart to the other watchmen*] Break out,
        And like true thieves make prey on either side,
        But seem to help the stronger.

Bobadilla.   O my lord;
        They have beat him on his knees.

Lucio.   Though I want courage,
        I yet have a son's duty in me, and   60
        Compassion of a father's danger; that,
        That wholly now possesses me.
                          [*He attacks Anastro and Lamoral.*]

Álvarez.   Lucio.
        This is beyond my hope.

Metaldi. [*Apart*]   So, Lazarillo,
                          [*He sets Lazarillo to steal from Anastro.*]
        Take up all, boy. Well done.

Pacheco. [*Apart*]   And now steal off
        Closely, and cunningly.

Anastro.   How? [*To Lazarillo*] Have I found you?   65
        Why, gentlemen, are you mad to make yourselves
        A prey to rogues?

Lazarillo. [*Aside*]   Would we were off.

Bobadilla.   Thieves, thieves!

---

56. Vitelli's] *F2*; *Vitell's F*   SD1 *and* SD2] *this edn.*   57. prey] *F2*; pray *F*
58. stronger] *GWW*; stranger *F*   62. SD] *this edn.*   63. SD1 *and* SD2]
this edn.   64. SD] *this edn.*   65. SD] *this edn.*   67. SP] *Dyce; Lam. F*
SD] *this edn.*

---

55. *strike again*] hit back (see *again, OED* A. I. 1a).

56. *Break out*] come forward.

58. *seem ... stronger*] Williams's emendation (see collation) resolves the apparent incongruity of the line by interpreting that the watchmen will take advantage of the fight to mingle with the two factions, steal from both, and then take the winning side to avoid being caught.

my lord] Álvarez.

62. SD] Lucio may attack Anastro first, as he seems to have started the fight with his father; by line 68 Lamoral is clearly fighting as well, presumably leaving Genevora to the care of the two pages.

Lamoral. Defer our own contention, and down with them.

                         [*They attack the watchmen.*]

Lucio. I'll make you sure.

Bobadilla.   Now he plays the devil.

Genevora. This place is not for me.   *Exit* [*with the pages.*]

Lucio.   I'll follow her;   70

    Half of my penance is past o'er.   *Exit.*

          Enter [*the*] ALGUAZIR [*with the*] ASISTENTE
          [*disguised as a watchman*], *and other watches.*

Alguazir.   What noise?

    What tumult's there? Keep the King's peace, I charge
        you.

Pacheco. [*Aside*] I'm glad he's come yet.

Álvarez. [*To the Alguazir*]   O, you keep good guard
    Upon the city when men of our rank
    Are set upon in the streets.

Lamoral. [*To the Alguazir*]   The Asistente   75

    Shall hear of't, be assured.

Anastro. [*To the Alguazir*]   And if he be
    That careful governor he is reported,
    You will smart for it.

Alguazir.   Patience, good señors.

    Let me survey the rascals. O, I know them,
    And thank you for them. They are pilf'ring rogues   80
    Of Andalusia that have perused

---

68. SD] *Dyce, subst.* 70. SD] *this edn.* 71. SD2 *Enter*] *F2; Entes F.*
SD2 *disguised … watchman*] *this edn.* SD2 *watches*] *F2; Watchcs F.*
73. SD1 *and* SD2] *this edn.* 75. SD] *this edn.* Asistente] *Dyce; Assistente*
| *GWW*; Assistant *Langbaine*; assistant *Weber*; assistance *F*; assistants *F2*.
76. of't] *F;* of it *Weber;* on't *F2.* SD] *this edn.* 78. señors] *F (Signiours)*.
80. pilf'ring] *F (pillfring)*; pilfering *Q.* 81. Andalusia] *Weber; Andaluzia
F; Andaluza F2.*

---

71. *half of my penance*] fighting against the first man they come across
(line 38); the second half is pursuing Genevora.

73. *yet*] so soon, already (*OED* 3b); see 1.2.64 n.

78. *will smart*] will be punished (*OED* 3b).

81. *Andalusia*] The large southern region of Spain in which Seville is
actually located.

All prisons in Castile. I dare not trust
The dungeon with them. No, I'll have them home
To my own house.

Pacheco.   We had rather go to prison.

Alguazir. Had you so, dogbolts? Yes, I know you had.   85
    You there would use your cunning fingers on
    The simple locks; you would. But I'll prevent you.

Lamoral. My mistress lost? Good night. *Exit [with Anastro].*

Bobadilla. [To Álvarez]   Your son's gone too,
    What should become of him?

Álvarez.   Come of him what will.
    Now he dares fight, I care not. I'll to bed.   90
    Look to your prisoners, Alguazir.   *Exit with Bobadilla.*

Alguazir.   All's cleared.
    Droop not for one disaster. Let us hug,
    And triumph in our knaveries.

Asistente. [Aside]   This confirms
    What was reported of him.

Metaldi.   'Twas done bravely.

Alguazir. I must a little glory in the means   95
    We officers have to play the knaves, and safely.
    How we break through the toils pitched by the law,
    Yet hang up them that are far less delinquents.
    A simple shopkeeper's carted for a bawd

---

88. SD1] *GWW.* SD2] *this edn.* too] *F (*to*); not in Langbaine, Q.* 93.
SD] *this edn;* [apart] *GWW.*

---

82. *Castile*] The dominant nation under the rule of the King of Spain,
extending in this period over most of the Iberian Peninsula, including
Andalusia; see 1.1.23 n.

85. *dogbolts*] dogsbodies, knaves; a term of abuse for a menial person
(*OED* 1).

88. *My ... lost?*] Lamoral has realised that Genevora and the pages have
disappeared in the tumult; the line is not an aside, as Bobadilla immediately
responds to it by noticing that Lucio has left as well.

92. *Droop not*] despair not.

93–4. *This ... him*] The Asistente is in disguise as a member of the second
group of watchmen under the Alguazir's command; it may be a confusing
moment for the audience, as they cannot know who he is until he discloses
his identity at line 115. (See longer note.)

97. *toils*] nets forming an enclosure in which to catch game in a hunt
(*OED n.*[2] 1).

99. *carted ... bawd*] see 3.3.81 n.

For lodging—though unwittingly—a smock-gamester;   100
Where, with rewards and credit, I have kept
Malroda in my house as in a cloister,
Without taint or suspicion.
Pacheco.   But suppose
The Governor should know't?
Alguazir.   He? Good gentleman,
Let him perplex himself with prying into   105
The measures in the market, and th' abuses
The day stands guilty of; the pillage of the night
Is only mine, mine own fee-simple,
Which you shall hold from me, tenants at will,
And pay no rent for't.
Pacheco.   Admirable landlord.   110
Alguazir. Now we'll go search the taverns, commit such
As we find drinking, and be drunk ourselves
With what we take from them. These silly wretches,
Whom I for form's sake only have brought hither,
Shall watch without, and guard us.
Asistente. [*Coming forward.*]   And we will   115
See you safe lodged, most worthy Alguazir,
With all of you, his comrades.
Metaldi.   'Tis the Governor.
Alguazir. We are betrayed!
Asistente.   My guard there! Bind them fast.
           [*The watch seize them.*]

---

115. SD] *Dyce.*   118. SD] *this edn; Enter Guard | TSS.*

100. *smock-gamester*] a prostitute, one who plays tricks in her undergarments; *smock* was often used in a derogatory way to refer to women: cf. Andrew in *Elder Brother*: 'these smock vermin, / How eagerly they leap at old men's kisses.' (3.2.37–8).

102. *cloister*] in secret, as in a nunnery, but also alluding to a brothel.

105–6. *prying ... market*] The Clerk of the Market was an officer in London responsible for verifying weights and measures (*clerk, OED*).

108. *fee-simple*] exclusive inheritance (*OED* a).

109. *tenants at will*] those who hold a property (here metaphorically the right to pillage in the night) at the pleasure of the rightful lessor (*OED*).

113. *silly wretches*] the second watch, including the disguised Asistente.

118. *My guard there!*] TSS assumed that the Asistente calls for reinforcements, and indicated the entrance of his guard. This would complicate the

How men in high place and authority
Are in their lives and estimation wronged   120
By their subordinate ministers! Yet such
They cannot but employ, wronged justice finding
Scarce one true servant in ten officers.
T' expostulate with you were but to delay
Your crimes' due punishment, which shall fall upon you   125
So speedily and severely that it shall
Fright others by th' example, and confirm
However corrupt officers may disgrace
Themselves, 'tis not in them to wrong their place.
Bring them away.

Alguazir.   We'll suffer nobly yet,   130
And like to Spanish gallants.

Pacheco.   And we'll hang so.

Lazarillo. I have no stomach to it, but I'll endeavour.

Exeunt.

SCENE 4

Enter LUCIO *and* GENEVORA.

Genevora. Nay, you are rude; pray you forbear; you offer
        now
    More than the breeding of a gentleman
    Can give you warrant for.

Lucio.   'Tis but to kiss you,

120. estimation] *F;* estimations *F2.*   125. upon] on *TSS.*

SCENE 4] *F (Scæna Quarta.).*   1. you offer] *F2;* your offer *F*

---

staging unnecessarily, as it would require at least two more supernumeraries
(or actors playing other roles). It would also imply that the other watches
accompanying him, and already present on stage, are not employed in the
arrest. The only other mention of a guard is in the final scene, when all these
malefactors re-enter accompanied by the guard (5.3.229 SD). The likeliest
possibility, for reasons of economy of staging, is that the Alguazir's second
watch are actually the Asistente's personal guard, perhaps also in disguise.
    122. *cannot but*] have no choice but.
    129. *place*] office.
    132. *endeavour*] attempt strenuously (*OED* 3).

    4.4.0.] Location: '*Another street*' (Weber).

And think not I'll receive that for a favour
Which was enjoined me for a penance, lady.   5
Genevora. You have met a gentle confessor, and for once—
So then you will rest satisfied—I vouchsafe it.
Lucio. Rest satisfied with a kiss? Why, can a man
Desire more from a woman? Is there any
Pleasure beyond it? May I never live   10
If I know what it is.
Genevora. [*Aside*]   Sweet innocence.   [*They kiss.*]
Lucio. What strange new motions do I feel? My veins
Burn with an unknown fire. In every part
I suffer alteration. I am poisoned,
Yet languish with desire again to taste it,   15
So sweetly it works on me.
Genevora. [*Aside*]   I ne'er saw
A lovely man till now.
Lucio.   How can this be?
She is a woman, as my mother is,
And her I have kissed often, and brought off
My lips unscorched; yours are more lovely, lady,   20
And so should be less hurtful. Pray you vouchsafe
Your hand to quench the heat ta'en from your lip;
Perhaps that may restore me.
Genevora.   Willingly.

[*He kisses her hand.*]

---

11. SD1] *Dyce.* SD2] *GWW.* 16. SD] *Dyce.* 21. you] *not in TSS.* 23.
SD] *this edn.*

---

5. *enjoined*] imposed as a task or obligation (*enjoin*, OED 2a).

6. *gentle confessor*] i.e., herself.

11. *Sweet innocence*] Perhaps an aside (as Williams indicates); the kiss may occur before or after this line.

12. *strange new motions*] unknown passions (*motion*, OED n. II. 12); cf. Iago in *Oth.*: 'we have reason to cool our raging motions, our carnal stings, our unbitted lusts' (1.3.329–31); also, presumably, an erection; see 1.2.27 n.

12–13. *My ... fire*] Feeling an unknown internal fire is a logical symptom of having been poisoned; cf. the poisoned Emperor in *Val.*: 'Oh villain! I grow hotter, hotter' (5.2.77).

17. *lovely*] loveable (*OED* 2).

17–20. *How ... unscorched*] This is phrased as an aside, but the direct address immediately following ('yours are more lovely, lady') necessarily implies that the previous lines have been heard by Genevora.

Lucio. The flame increases. If to touch you burn thus,
    What would more strict embraces do? I know not,   25
    And yet methinks to die so were to ascend
    To heaven through Paradise.
Genevora. [*Aside*]   I am wounded too,
    Though modesty forbids that I should speak
    What ignorance makes him bold in. [*Aloud*] Why do
        you fix
    Your eyes so strongly on me?
Lucio.   Pray you stand still.   30
    There is nothing else that is worth the looking on.
    I could adore you, lady.
Genevora.   Can you love me?

---

27. SD] *Dyce.* 29. SD] *this edn.* 30. strongly] *F* (*stronglie*)*; stranglie
GWW.* you] *not in TSS.*

25. *strict embraces*] closer physical contact (i.e., sexual intercourse); it is
etymologically related to *strait* (*OED* 1c: 'Of an embrace: close').

26. *to die so*] to burn in the metaphorical fire caused by Genevora's touch,
but also to experience an orgasm (*OED* 7d).

26–7. *ascend ... Paradise*] The echo of Dante's *Comedia* is clear: after
traversing the seven terraces of Purgatory guided by Virgil, the poet arrives
in the garden of Eden, or Earthly Paradise (*Purgatorio*, canti XXVIII–
XXXIII), in which, according to Genesis, Adam and Eve first lived in
innocence, free of all cares and wants. Subsequently guided by the spirit of
his beloved Beatrice, Dante travels through the nine spheres of heaven – corresponding to the seven planets (the Moon, Mercury, Venus, the Sun, Mars,
Jupiter, and Saturn), the fixed stars, and the Primum Mobile inhabited by
the angelic choirs – to reach the Empyrean Heaven which God inhabits
(*Paradiso*, canto XXXIII). Lucio implies an elevating journey through a
blissful space that leads to absolute goodness in the contemplation of God.
The context is quite openly blasphemous, as Lucio applies a familiar religious paradigm to his disconcerting sexual awakening.

27. *wounded*] Conventionally lovers start feeling affection when wounded
by Cupid's arrows.

30. *strongly*] fixedly, intensely; Williams's emendation to *strangely* makes
sense but seems unnecessary.

32. *adore*] Again, there is a religious undertone to the love that Lucio
experiences, elaborating on the Dantean imagery of lines 26–7, which goes
as far as regarding Genevora's glove as 'divine' (line 34); this sense will be
elaborated in 5.2.42–3. In the absence of prior erotic experience, the character may be applying the more familiar patterns of religious thinking with
which he must have been brought up.

love] Genevora asks whether Lucio can love her in a more mundane way.

Lucio. To wait on you in your chamber, and but touch
    What you, by wearing it, have made divine,
    Were such a happiness. I am resolved;   35
    I'll sell my liberty to you for this glove,
    And write myself your slave.

Enter LAMORAL.

Genevora.   On easier terms,
    Receive it as a friend.   [*She offers Lucio her glove.*]
Lamoral.   How? Giving favour!
    I'll have it with his heart.   [*Lamoral takes the glove.*]
Genevora.   What will you do?
Lucio. As you are merciful, take my life rather.   40
                [*Lucio kneels, and Lamoral starts to leave.*]
Genevora. Will you depart with't so?
Lamoral.   Does that grieve you?
Genevora. I know not. [*To Lucio*] But even now you
    appeared valiant.
Lucio. 'Twas to preserve my father. In his cause
    I could be so again.
Genevora.   Not in your own?
    Kneel to thy rival and thine enemy?   45
    Away, unworthy creature; I begin
    To hate myself for giving entrance to
    A good opinion of thee. For thy torment,
    If my poor beauty be of any power,

---

35. resolved] *F2;* resov'd *F.*   38. SD] *this edn.*   39. SD] *this edn.*   40.
SD] *this edn.*   41. SP *Lamoral.*] *F;Luc.TSS.*   42. SD] *this edn.*   appeared]
Langbaine; appeare *F.*   44–5. Not ... enemy?] *lineation, TSS; one line in F.*

36. *this glove*] Presumably Lucio is holding Genevora's hand. Women's
gloves had a strong erotic suggestiveness in the period; cf. De Flores intro-
ducing his fingers into Beatrice's glove in *Chang.*, 1.1.236–8. See Stallybrass
and Jones.
40. SD] Lucio must be kneeling at this point, as Lamoral refers to this
moment in 5.1.5–6.
41. SP *Lamoral*] The line was reassigned to Lucio in TSS and all subsequent editions, but the original reading does make sense as a reproachful
retort to Genevora's line.
45. *Kneel*] Alternatively, Lucio may kneel at this point.
47. *giving entrance to*] allowing myself to form.

Mayst thou dote on it desperately. But never   50
Presume to hope for grace till thou recover
And wear the favour that was ravished from thee.
Lamoral. He wears my head too, then.
Genevora.   Poor fool, farewell.
                              Exit [with Lamoral.]
Lucio. My womanish soul, which hitherto hath governed
This coward flesh, I feel departing from me;   55
And in me by her beauty is inspired
A new and masculine one, instructing me
What's fit to do or suffer. Powerful love,
That hast with loud and yet a pleasing thunder
Roused sleeping manhood in me, thy new creature,   60
Perfect thy work so that I may make known
Nature, though long kept back, will have her own.
                                    Exit.

---

53. SD] *this edn.*   62. SD] *Colman; Exeunt F.*

---

51. *grace*] favour (*OED* 2b), but alluding to Lucio's quasi-religious adoration for her (see lines 32 and 34).

52. *favour*] physical token of affection, i.e., the glove; see 2.2.218 n.

ravished] stolen forcibly (but with a sexual connotation).

53. *wears ... head*] Lamoral has placed the glove in his hatband (as implied in 5.1) at some point after he snatched it from Genevora and Lucio; however, it is not possible to determine the exact point at which he does this.

SD] Williams interpreted that Lamoral leaves after speaking his line, and then Genevora after hers; however, since Vitelli commissioned his friend to take his sister back to their home after the evening's entertainments (4.1.12–3), it is perhaps more likely that they leave the stage together.

54–62. *My ... own*] This speech is analogous to Clara's in 4.2.184–93, signalling Lucio's final assumption of his expected social gender through the power of love (as Vitelli will summarise in his concluding speech, 5.3.264–9).

60. *Roused sleeping manhood*] quite literally, as Genevora has provoked his first erection.

new creature] newly created being.

62. *Nature ... own*] Translated from Horace, *Epistles* I.10.24: 'Naturam expelles furca, amen usque recurret' ('You may drive out Nature with a pitchfork, yet she will ever hurry back'; Horace, 317).

ACT 5

SCENE I

Enter LAMORAL [*with Genevora's glove in his hat*]
and LUCIO.

Lamoral. Can it be possible that in six short hours,
    The subject still the same, so many habits
    Should be removed? Or this new Lucio be
    That yesternight was baffled and disgraced,
    And thanked the man that did it, that then kneeled   5
    And blubbered like a woman, should now dare

SCENE 1] F (*Actus Quintus. Scæna prima.*). 0. SD] *GWW.*

5.1.0.] Location: '*A street*' (Weber). The scene occurs the following morning, six hours after 4.4.

0. SD] They may both appear at separate doors, or alternatively following each other through the same doorway. In the 2013 BADA production, Lamoral spoke the first speech as a soliloquy to the audience, with Lucio coming on through a different door and overhearing the last few lines before confronting him.

glove ... hat] This was a sign of defiance to an opponent; the soldier Michael Williams wears the glove of Harry Le Roy (the disguised King) in his cap as a challenge in *H5* 4.1.212–14.

2. *habits*] (a) clothing, physical appearance (*OED* 1a); (b) demeanour, behaviour (*OED* 4); (c) customs (*OED* 9b). Cf. Duke Francisco in *White Devil*: 'See: a good habit makes a child a man, / Whereas a bad one makes a man a beast' (2.1.136–7).

3. *removed*] (a) altered, changed (*OED* 9); (b) taken away, taken off (*OED* 4a).

4. *baffled*] subjected to public disgrace or infamy after a combat (*OED* 3); cf. Longueville in *Fortune*: 'Have his disgrace talk for tobacco shops, / His picture baffled' (3.2.90–1).

5. *kneeled*] Lucio did kneel in front of Lamoral in the previous scene; see 4.4.40 n. and 45 n.

6. *blubbered*] wept effusively and unrestrainedly; the expression is generally used to ridicule the one who weeps (*blubber*, *OED* 3).

On terms of honour seek reparation
For what he then appeared not capable of?
Lucio. Such miracles men that dare do injuries
    Live to their shames to see for punishment   10
    And scourge to their proud follies.
Lamoral.   Prithee, leave me.
    Had I my page or footman here to flesh thee,
    I durst the better hear thee.
Lucio.   This scorn needs not,
    And offer such no more.
Lamoral.   Why, say I should;
    You'll not be angry?
Lucio.   Indeed I think I shall.   15
    Would you vouchsafe to show yourself a captain,
    And lead a little further to some place
    That's less frequented.
Lamoral. [*Aside*]   He looks pale.
Lucio.   If not,
    Make use of this.   [*He indicates his sword.*]
Lamoral. [*Aside*]   There's anger in his eyes too.
    His gesture, voice, and behaviour, all new fashioned.   20
    [*Aloud*] Well, if it does endure in act the trial
    Of what in show it promises to make good,

---

7. On terms] *F2;* One terme *F.*   seek] *F;* to seek *TSS.*   10. for] *TSS;* and
for *F.*   17. further] *F;* farther *F2.*   18. SD] *this edn.*   19. SD1 *and*
SD2] *this edn.*   21. SD] *this edn.*

---

7. *On ... honour*] 'On the basis of restoring his honour.'
    9–11. *Such ... follies*] 'Injurious men live in shame to see such prodigies
as punishment for their own arrogant stupidities.'
    12. *flesh*] to expose you to violence for the first time (*OED* 2a).
    13. *needs not*] is unnecessary.
    16. *captain*] one who leads others to do something (*OED* 1a).
    17–18. *place ... frequented*] Duels would typically take place in remote
locations, as they were illegal in public places (see Introduction, 11–12).
    20. *new fashioned*] transformed, modified (*fashioned, OED* 4a).
    21. *it*] Lucio's sword, as a visual referent to *this* in line 19.
    in act] in action, in actual use.

Ulysses' Cyclops, Io's transformation,
Eurydice fetched from Hell, with all the rest
Of Ovid's fables, I'll put in my creed;   25
And for proof all incredible things may be,
Write down that Lucio, the coward Lucio,
The womanish Lucio, fought.
Lucio.   And Lamoral,
The still-employed, great duellist Lamoral,
Took his life from him.
Lamoral.   'Twill not come to that, sure.   30
Methinks the only drawing of my sword
Should fright that confidence.
Lucio.   It confirms it, rather.
To make which good, know you stand now opposed
By one that is your rival, one that wishes

---

24. fetched] *F (*fetcht*);* fetch *F2.*   25. my] *TSS;* your *F.*   27. Write] *F2;*
Writ *F.*

23–5. *Ulysses ... creed*] Lamoral states that the possibility of Lucio bringing himself to fight against him is as improbable as the fictions retold in
Ovid's *Metamorphoses*.

23. *Ulysses' Cyclops*] Race of one-eyed giants; the most savage of them,
Polyphemus, is tricked by Odysseus (Ulysses in his Roman name) into
enabling his escape in the *Odyssey*. Ovid recounted the love story of
Polyphemus and the nymph Galatea, referencing the Cyclops's blinding by
Ulysses, in *Metam.*, XIII, 738–897.

Io's transformation] Io was a priestess of Hera with whom Zeus was in love;
to save her from Hera's jealousy, Zeus transformed Io into a white heifer.
Ovid retold the story in *Metam.*, I, 601–21.

24. *Eurydice ... Hell*] Orpheus, grieving for his wife Eurydice's sudden
death on their wedding day when she was bitten by a snake, decided to travel
to the Underworld to bring her back from the dead. He was allowed to do
so on condition that he would not look back at her until they had left Hades,
but he faltered and she was lost forever. Ovid included the story in *Metam.*,
X, 1–85.

25. *creed*] principles (normally of faith) that are held as the absolute truth
(*OED* 2b).

26. *be*] happen.

29. *still-employed*] (a) continuously employed; (b) employed for the time
being (perhaps until he loses this duel).

34. *wishes*] The verb governs the ensuing accumulation of clauses (lines
35–46).

Your name and title greater to raise his;   35
The wrong you did, less pardonable than it is,
But your strength to defend it, more than ever
It was when justice friended it; the lady
For whom we now contend, Genevora,
Of more desert (if such incomparable beauty   40
Could suffer an addition); your love
To Don Vitelli multiplied; and your hate
Against my father and his house increased;
And, lastly, that the glove which you there wear
To my dishonour, which I must force from you,   45
Were dearer to you than your life.

Lamoral.   You'll find
It is, and so I'll guard it.

Lucio.   All these meet, then,
With the black infamy to be foiled by one
That's not allowed a man. To help your valour,
That, falling by your hand, I may or die   50
Or win in this one single opposition
My mistress and such honour as I may
Enrich my father's arms with.

Lamoral.   'Tis said nobly;
My life with them are at the stake.

Lucio.   At all, then.

> [*They*] *fight* [*and Lucio takes Lamoral's sword and
> hat with Genevora's glove.*]

---

43. Against] *F2;* Aagainst *F.*   47. meet] must meet *F2.*   54. SD] *this
edn.*

---

35. *Your ... his*] Lucio wishes Lamoral to be more honourable, as by
beating him in a duel he will metaphorically transfer all that honour to
himself.

40. *desert*] excellence, worth (*OED n.*[1] 1b).

44. *there*] i.e., in his hatband.

49. *allowed*] acknowledged to be (*OED* II).

50–1. *or ... Or*] either ... Or.

51. *opposition*] duel, confrontation.

53. *Enrich ... arms*] (a) increase the family's honour and reputation; (b)
add new elements to the family's coat of arms (presumably by marriage).

54. *at the stake*] placed at hazard (*OED n.*[2] 1).

At all, then] The duel is not at first blood or to determine who will possess
the glove: everything is at stake, including the duellists' lives.

Lamoral. She's yours. This, and my life too, follow your
    fortune,   55
    And give not only back that part the loser
    Scorns to accept of—
Lucio.   What's that?
Lamoral.   My poor life,
    Which do not leave me as a further torment,
    Having despoiled me of my sword, mine honour,
    Hope of my lady's grace, fame, and all else   60
    That made it worth the keeping.
Lucio.   I take back
    No more from you than what you forced from me,
    And with a worser title. Yet think not
    That I'll dispute this as made insolent
    By my success, but as one equal with you;   65
    If so, you will accept me that new courage,
    Or call it fortune if you please, that is
    Conferred upon me by the only sight
    Of fair Genevora, was not bestowed on me
    To bloody purposes. Nor did her command   70
    Deprive me of the happiness to see her
    But till I did redeem her favour from you,
    Which only I rejoice in, and share with you
    In all you suffer else.
Lamoral.   This courtesy
    Wounds deeper than your sword can, or mine own.   75
    Pray you make use of either and dispatch me.

---

55. life too] *F2;* life, to *F*   56. loser] *Langbaine;* looser *F*   58. further]
farther *F2.*   70. purposes] purpose *TSS.*

---

    55. *This ... fortune*] An alternative modernisation (following F and Q) is
'This, and my life, to follow your fortune'.
    63. *title*] entitlement, legitimate right (*OED* 6); Lamoral was not entitled
to Genevora's glove, as it was given to Lucio.
    72. *her favour*] Genevora's glove.

Lucio. The barbarous Turk is satisfied with spoil,
    And shall I, being possessed of what I came for,
    Prove the more infidel?
Lamoral.   You were better be so
    Than publish my disgrace, as 'tis the custom,   80
    And which I must expect.
Lucio.   Judge better on me.
    I have no tongue to trumpet mine own praise
    To your dishonour. 'Tis a bastard courage
    That seeks a name out that way, no true-born one.
    Pray you be comforted, for by all goodness   85
    But to her virtuous self, the best part of it,
    I never will discover on what terms
    I came by these. Which yet I take not from you,
    But leave you in exchange of them mine own
    With the desire of being a friend; which, if   90
           [He gives Lamoral his own hat and sword.]
    You will not grant me but on further trial
    Of manhood in me, seek me when you please,
    And though I might refuse it with mine honour,
    Win them again and wear them. So good morrow.
                                 Exit.

Lamoral. I ne'er knew what true valour was till now,   95
    And have gained more by this disgrace than all
    The honours I have won. They made me proud,
    Presumptuous of my fortune, a mere beast
    Fashioned by them only to dare and do,

---

81. on] of *TSS.*   90. SD] *this edn.*   91. further] farther *F2.*

77–9. *Turk ... infidel*] The Turks would take hold of the material spoil
from an enemy ship, but they would also request a substantial ransom for
the prisoners taken alive; in this sense, as Lucio implies, they did not seek
to kill their enemies but to profit economically from them. However, Lucio,
perhaps not well informed, is mistaken if the suggestion is that the Turks
would leave behind their prisoners and only take their material belongings,
as this was not true; Massinger, based on Cervantes, would elaborate on this
theme in *Renegado*. Cf. Vitelli and Malroda in 3.3.102–3.

80. *custom*] see 1.2.51 n.; if the opponents' lives were at stake, the rules
of duelling dictated that one had to die; if he survived, Lamoral fears he
would see his reputation disgraced.

94. *win ... wear*] proverbial; see 4.2.122.

Yielding no reasons for my wilful actions   100
But what I stuck on my sword's point, presuming
It was the best revenue. How unequal
Wrongs well maintained makes us to others, which
Ending with shame teach us to know ourselves.
I will think more on't.

Enter VITELLI.

Vitelli.   Lamoral.
Lamoral.   My lord?   105
Vitelli. I came to seek you.
Lamoral.   And unwillingly
    You ne'er found me till now. Your pleasure, sir?
Vitelli. That which will please thee, friend. Thy vowed love
    to me
    Shall now be put in action. Means is offered
    To use thy good sword for me, that which still   110
    Thou wear'st as if it were a part of thee.
    Where is it?
Lamoral.   'Tis changed for one more fortunate.
    Pray you enquire not how.
Vitelli.   Why, I ne'er thought
    That there was music in't, but ascribed

---

103. makes] make *Colman.*   107. till] tell *F2.*   109. is] are *Weber.*   111.
thee] that *Langbaine.*   114. music] *F* (musick); magic *TSS.*   ascribed]
TSS; ascribe *F.*

---

102. *unequal*] disposed to act unjustly (*OED adj.* 4b).
103. *Wrongs well maintained*] Injuries firmly held.
105. *I ... on't*] This phrase and the preceding soliloquy (lines 1–8) are important to the characterisation of Lamoral as a reflective man.
106–7. *And ... now*] Perhaps an aside.
113–14. *I ... in't*] 'I never thought that there was anything special about it.' The expression sounds unfamiliar in English, as Sympson commented: 'My reader, no doubt, will be surprised with the music of a sword.' Probably by chance, it coincides with a colloquialism current in Spanish, used when an item on sale is overpriced: *¡Ni que tuviera música!* ('One would say it had music in it!') However, this phrase is not in any of the Spanish sources with which Fletcher and Massinger were familiar. The 2013 BADA production, following TSS, substituted the word 'music' with 'magic'.

The fortune of it to the arm.

Lamoral.   Which is   115
Grown weaker, too. I am not, in a word,
Worthy your friendship. I am one new vanquished,
Yet shame to tell by whom.

Vitelli.   But I'll tell thee
'Gainst whom thou art to fight, and there redeem
Thy honour lost, if there be any such.   120
The King, by my long suit, at length is pleased
That Álvarez and myself, with either's second,
Shall end the difference between our houses,
Which he accepts of. I make choice of thee,
And where you speak of a disgrace, the means   125
To blot it out, by such a public trial
Of thy approvèd valour, will revive
Thy ancient courage. If you embrace it, do;
If not, I'll seek some other.

Lamoral.   As I am
You may command me.

Vitelli.   Spoke like that true friend   130
That loves not only for his private end.

                                                    Exeunt.

SCENE 2

Enter GENEVORA *with a letter, and* BOBADILLA.

Genevora. This from Madonna Clara?
Bobadilla.   Yes, an't please you.

---

115. the] thy *TSS.*   115–16. Which ... word] *lineation, TSS; one line in F.*

SCENE 2] *F (Scæna secunda.).*   1. an't] *F2;* and't *F.*

---

117. *new*] newly.
122. *second*] a man who acts as a representative of one of the two fighters
in a duel, in charge of delivering the challenge, arranging the locality, and
verifying the weapons (*OED adj.* and *n.*[2] 9b). In 5.3 Lamoral will be Vitelli's
second, while Lucio will act as his father's.
131. *private*] own, personal.

5.2.0.] Location: 'Another street' (Weber).
1. *Madonna*] see 3.2.79 n.

Genevora. Álvarez' daughter?
Bobadilla.   The same, lady.
Genevora.   She,
    That saved my brother's life?
Bobadilla.   You are still in the right;
    She willed me wait your walking forth. And knowing
    How necessary a discreet wise man   ·   5
    Was in a business of such weight, she pleased
    To think on me. It may be in my face
    Your ladyship, not acquainted with my wisdom,
    Finds no such matter. What I am, I am;
    Thought's free, and think you what you please.
Genevora.   'Tis strange—   10
Bobadilla. That I should be wise, madam?
Genevora.   No, thou art so.
    There's for thy pains. [*She gives him money.*] And
       prithee tell thy lady
    I will not fail to meet her. I'll receive
    Thy thanks and duty in thy present absence.
    Farewell, farewell; I say now thou art wise.   15
                        Exit Bobadilla.
    She writes here she hath something to impart
    That may concern my brother's life. I know not
    But general fame does give her out so worthy
    That I dare not suspect her, yet wish Lucio

           Enter LUCIO.

---

2. same, lady] same Lady *Langbaine.*   10. strange—] *TSS;* ~, *F;* ~. *Lang-*
baine.   12. SD] *this edn.*

---

    4. *willed*] wished; cf. 1.1.128 n.
    wait] to await.
    7–9. *It ... matter*] Bobadilla comments again on his unbecoming face; cf.
2.2.87 n.
    7. *may be*] may be that.
    9. *What ... am*] echoing Exodus 3:14: 'And God said unto Moses, I AM
THAT I AM.' By echoing God's own words in a secular context, Bobadilla's
expression is openly blasphemous.
    18. *give her out*] publicly proclaim; for Clara's public reputation in Seville,
see 3.3.83.

Were master of her mind. But fie upon't;   20
Why do I think on him?   [*She notices Lucio.*]
                   See, I am punished for it
In his unlooked-for presence. Now I must
Endure another tedious piece of courtship
Would make one forswear courtesy.
Lucio.   Gracious madam,
                             [*He kneels.*]

The sorrow paid for your just anger towards me   25
Arising from my weakness, I presume
To press into your presence and despair not
An easy pardon.
Genevora. [*Aside*]   He speaks sense. O, strange.
Lucio. And yet believe that no desire of mine,
Though all are too strong in me, had the power   30
For their delight to force me to infringe
What you commanded, it being in your part
To lessen your great rigour when you please,
And mine to suffer with an humble patience
What you'll impose upon it.
Genevora. [*Aside*]   Courtly too.   35
Lucio. Yet hath the poor and contemned Lucio, madam—
Made able only by his hope to serve you—

---

21. SD] *this   edn.*   24. SD] *TSS.*   28. SD] *Dyce.*   29. desire] desires
Colman.   31. infringe] *F2;* iufringe *F.*   34. with] *F2;* wirh *F.*   35. SD]
Dyce.

20–4. *Were … courtesy*] Though it is unclear, Lucio probably does not
overhear her words; if so, she does not actually speak to him until line 50
after a long succession of asides. The precise point at which he enters – which
most editors delay two lines – is also uncertain.

24–49. *Gracious … creature*] Lucio's four speeches form in fact a long,
elaborate piece of rhetoric, only interrupted by Genevora's brief asides,
which is perhaps meant to give the impression that it has been carefully
scripted to impress the lady.

27. *despair not*] do not despair from achieving.

29–35. *And … it*] As Genevora immediately states, this is the language of
courtly love: contrived, embellished, and convoluted. What Genevora had
commanded was, of course, the recovery of the glove (4.4.50–2); Lucio, like
a knight-errant, offers to suffer any penance that his lady might request him
to undergo.

36. *contemned*] treated with contempt, despised.

Recovered what with violence, not justice,
Was taken from him, and here at your feet
With these he could have laid the conquered head   40
        [*He lays Lamoral's sword and hat at her feet.*]
Of Lamoral—'tis all I say of him—
For rudely touching that, which as a relic
I ever would have worshipped, since 'twas yours.

Genevora. [*Aside*] Valiant, and everything a lady could
  Wish in her servant.

Lucio.   All that's good in me,   45
That heavenly love (the opposite to base lust)
Which would have all men worthy, hath created;
Which, being by your beams of beauty formed,
Cherish as your own creature.

Genevora. [*Aside*]   I am gone
Too far now to dissemble. [*Aloud*] Rise, or sure   50
I must kneel with you too. Let this one kiss
        [*She raises and kisses him.*]

---

38. what] that *Langbaine.*   40. SD] *this edn.*   44. SD] *Dyce.*   46. heavenly] havenly *F2.*   49. SD] *Weber.*   50. SD] *this edn.*   51. SD] *this edn.*

---

40. SD] Presumably Lucio keeps the glove and offers Lamoral's hat and sword as proof of having vanquished him.

42–3. *For … yours*] Lucio recovers the religious sentiments expressed in 4.4.32–5.

42. *that*] Genevora's glove.

relic] in a Catholic context, the physical remains of a saint (the whole body or part of it), or a personal item that belonged to them, preserved as an object of veneration (*OED* 1a). The veneration of relics was a matter of contention in Protestant contexts.

45–9. *All … creature*] The complicated syntax reaches its climax in this speech with a succession of embedded clauses. The first sentence can be paraphrased as 'Everything that is good in me was created by that heavenly love which makes men worthy'; the second one can be approximated as 'Cherish that love as your own creation, because it was prompted by your beauty.' Lucio platonically identifies Genevora with the ideal on which was modelled the heavenly love that is, in its stead, the source of all goodness in Lucio. Cf. the Dantean imagery alluded to in 4.4.26–7.

50. *dissemble*] conceal my feelings.

51. SD] There are two possibilities for staging this moment: either she raises him at this point, or she kneels in front of him here, imposing the need for both actors to stand up later at an unspecified moment. The first seems the more likely possibility.

Speak the rest for me. 'Tis too much I do,
And yet, if chastity would, I could wish more.
Lucio. In overjoying me you are grown sad;
    What is it, madam? By my soul, I swear   55
    There's nothing that's within my nerves—and yet,
    Favoured by you, I should as much as man—
    But when you please, now or on all occasions
    You can think of hereafter, but you may
    Dispose of at your pleasure.
Genevora.   If you break   60
    That oath again, you lose me. Yet so well
    I love you, I shall never put you to't;
    And yet forget it not. Rest satisfied
    With that you have received now. There are eyes
    May be upon us; till the difference   65
    Between our friends are ended, I would not
    Be seen so private with you.
Lucio.   I obey you.
Genevora. But let me hear oft from you, and remember
    I am Vitelli's sister.
Lucio.   What's that, madam?

---

55. *By my soul, I swear*] *Dyce;* by Heav'n *Colman;* by — *F*   61. lose] loose
F2.

---

53. *if ... more*] Genevora's intention to remain a virgin until after her marriage contrasts with Vitelli's calculation in 4.2.203–4: he just assumes that it is not 'safe [...] to ask the rest now', as it will probably be denied, but not that it is improper. However, Genevora shares this determination with Clara, whose newly accepted gender identity, responding to social expectations around her sex and her rank, would preclude premarital intercourse.

54. *sad*] serious; perhaps she is crying as well.

55. *By ... swear*] This censored oath was reconstructed by Colman as 'by Heav'n', but four syllables are missing in order to complete the pentameter; Dyce's suggestion seems acceptable. (See Appendix 3, 234.)

56. *my nerves*] my sinews (*OED n.*[2]), the maximum compass of my strength (*OED sinew, n.*, 3).

57. *I ... man*] 'I would be able to accomplish as much as any man.'

65–6. *till ... ended*] From the street brawl on the previous night, Lucio is aware that Lamoral and Anastro are members of Vitelli's faction, and he assumes Genevora is close to them; but he does not know that she is Vitelli's sister.

68–9. *remember ... sister*] She mentions this fact, seemingly unknown to Lucio, in passing, and leaves the stage before he has registered her comment; however, he is fully aware of it by 5.3.130.

Genevora. Nay, nothing, fare you well. Who feels love's fire   70
    Would ever ask to have means to desire.

Exeunt [severally].

SCENE 3

Enter [the] ASISTENTE, SAYAVEDRA, ANASTRO,
[*a*] HERALD, [and] *attendants.*

Asistente. Are they come in?
Herald.   Yes.
Asistente.   Read the proclamation,
    That all the people here assembled may
    Have satisfaction what the King's dear love,
    In care of the republic, hath ordained.
    Attend with silence. [*To the Herald*] Read aloud.   5
Herald. (*Reading*) 'Forasmuch as our high and mighty master,

---

71. SD] *this edn.*

SCENE 3] *F (Scæna tertia.).*   5. SD] *this edn.*

70–1. *Who ... desire*] 'Whoever feels the effects of love would always demand (by right) to have the means to realise their desire'; *ask* could mean (a) to demand by right (*OED* 19a); or (b) to call for, to require (*OED* 23).

5.3.0.] Location: The Castle of Santiago. Weber indicates '*A court in the Castle of Santiago with a scaffolding in the background*'; Dyce adds the colourful '*filled with spectators*'.

1. *they*] the combatants, i.e., Álvarez and Lucio on one side, Vitelli and Lamoral on the other.

2. *people ... assembled*] presumably addressed to the audience in the playhouse.

3. *satisfaction*] information that dispels all doubts (*OED* 6a).
    what] as to what.

4. *republic*] from the Latin *res publica* ('public affairs', *Collins*); the State, the commonwealth (*OED* 1), rather than a country with no monarch.

6–33. *Forasmuch ... King*] The proclamation takes up the legal jargon and the syntactic complexity of actual Jacobean proclamations. A typical printed proclamation would open with the words 'By the King', followed by a descriptive title and an opening summary of the antecedents of the situation, and would conclude with a command and the characteristic 'God save the King'. However, Jacobean proclamations were phrased as the King's own words in the first person plural, while in this instance it reports the King's command through an official voice (also in the first person plural).

Philip, the potent and most Catholic King of Spain, hath
not only in his own royal person been long and often
solicited and grieved with the deadly and uncurable
hatred, sprung up betwixt the two ancient and most   10
honourably descended houses of these his two dearly and
equally beloved subjects, Don Ferdinando de Álvarez and
Don Pedro de Vitelli—all which in vain His Majesty hath
often endeavoured to reconcile and qualify—but that also
through the debates, quarrels, and outrages daily arising,   15
falling, and flowing from these great heads, his public
civil government is seditiously and barbarously molested
and wounded, and many of his chief gentry—no less
tender to His Royal Majesty than the very branches of
his own sacred blood—spoiled, lost, and submerged in   20
the impious inundation and torrent of their still-growing
malice; it hath therefore pleased His Sacred Majesty, out
of his infinite affection to preserve his commonwealth

---

9. uncurable] honorable *F2*.   11. honourably] uncurable *F2*.   12. Ferdi-
nando] Fernando *Dyce*.

---

7. *Philip*] presumably King Philip III of Spain; see 1.1.21 n.

Catholic ... Spain] 'His/Her Catholic Majesty' is the traditional title of the
kings and queens of Spain (*OED catholic* 7c). The title of 'Catholic Monarchs'
(*Reyes Católicos*) was granted by Pope Alexander VI in 1494 to Queen
Isabella I of Castile and her husband King Ferdinand II of Aragon, and has
remained a traditional title of the Spanish monarchy to the present day. The
etymological meaning of *Catholic* (from the ancient Greek καθολικός) is
'universal', which the Roman Church applies to itself; the Hispanic Monarchy
in this period also aimed to be universal by expanding its territory and political influence across the world.

11–12. *houses ... subjects*] Perhaps reminiscent of the first line of
Shakespeare's *R&J*: 'Two households, both alike in dignity' (Prologue.1).

12. *Ferdinando*] the Italian form of the name, perhaps perceived as a fuller
and more formal version of the correct Spanish *Fernando*, the name given
by Pacheco in 2.1.137.

16–17. *public civil government*] the state and its control of the civil institutions, but also, in this context, the preservation of public order.

17. *seditiously*] The offence to the crown is such as to constitute an act of
sedition, probably understood as a 'violent party strife' (*OED* 1), but also
hinting at a rebellion against the state (*OED* 2a and 2b).

molested] disturbed, vexed.

20. *blood*] offspring, descendants in the family tree.

23. *commonwealth*] see 2.1.104 n.

and general peace from farther violation—as a sweet and
heartily loving father of his people—and on the earnest   25
petitions of these arch-enemies, to order and ordain that
they be ready, each with his well-chosen and beloved
friend, armed at all points like gentlemen, in the Castle
of Santiago on this present Monday morning betwixt
eight and nine of the clock; where—before the combat-   30
ants be allowed to commence this granted duel—this to
be read aloud for the public satisfaction of His Majesty's
well-beloved subjects.' God save the King.

                                                    Drums within.
Sayavedra. Hark, how their drums speak their insatiate
          thirst
      Of blood, and stop their ears 'gainst pious peace,   35
      Who, gently whispering, implores their friendship!
Asistente. Kings nor authority can master fate.
      Admit 'em, then, and blood extinguish hate.

          Enter severally ÁLVAREZ *and* LUCIO, VITELLI
                    and LAMORAL.

---

24. farther] further *Colman.* a] *not in Langbaine.* 27. be] by *F2.* 29.
Santiago] St. Jago *F;* Saint Jago *Darley; St.* Iago *GWW.* 33. God save] *this
edn;* 'Save *F;* Save *Weber.* 34. how] *not in F2.*

    26. *order and ordain*] determine and command.
    28. *friend*] his second; see 5.1.122 n.
    28-9. *Castle of Santiago*] The building is not in Seville, where the play is
set, but in Sanlúcar de Barrameda, whose port is mentioned in 1.1.2 (see
n.).
    31. *granted duel*] a duel for which the King has given especial permission
(see Introduction, 11–12 and 36–7).
    31-2. *this to be*] this is to be.
    33. *God ... King*] The phrase in F was "Save the King'; the apostrophe
stands for the censored word *God.* (See Appendix 3, 233–4.)
    34. *their*] the combatants'.
    38. SD] The text indicates that the two opposing factions come on stage
through the two flanking doors at either side of the *frons scaenae,* presumably
standing at opposite ends of the platform, establishing a striking visual confrontation. The Asistente and his attendants, plus Sayavedra and Anastro
– all of whom are present to arbitrate in the duel – are probably meant to
occupy the central part of the stage.

Sayavedra. Stay. Yet be pleased to think, and let not daring—
    Wherein men nowadays exceed even beasts,   40
    And think themselves not men else—so transport you
    Beyond the bounds of Christianity.
    Lord Álvarez, Vitelli, gentlemen,
    No town in Spain, from our metropolis
    Unto the rudest hovel, but is great   45
    With your assurèd valours' daily proofs.
    O, will you then for a superfluous fame,
    A sound of honour—which in these times all
    Like heretics profess, with obstinacy
    But most erroneously—venture your souls?   50
    'Tis a hard task thorough a sea of blood
    To sail, and land at heaven!
Vitelli.   I hope not
    If justice be my pilot. But, my lord,
    You know if argument, or time, or love,
    Could reconcile, long since we had shook hands;   55
    I dare protest your breath cools not a vein

---

51. 'Tis] It is *Weber.*   thorough] through *F2.*

42. *Christianity*] Christian values; cf. 2.2.49. See also 1.1.41 n.

44. *No*] there is no.

metropolis] Madrid, the capital of the Spanish Monarchy since the mid-sixteenth century.

45–6. *great / With*] in this context, well acquainted with; figuratively, pregnant with, full of (*OED* 5b).

51–2. *'Tis ... heaven!*] The metaphor is powerful: the soul sails through the sea to its salvation (the pun *heaven/haven*), but if the waters are bloodied by homicide, then only repentance and penance (a 'hard task') can clear them and grant safe passage. The image seems to be associated to a certain extent with the classical myth of the river Styx that separated the world of the living from the Underworld, and which the souls of the deceased had to traverse on Charon's boat.

53. *justice*] Perhaps personified as the pilot of the ship/soul of the preceding metaphor; cf. Vitelli's invocation to Astrea in 1.1.115 (see n.).

53–75. *But ... lordship*] This exchange between the combatants, which verbalises the fight before it actually takes place, is in the tradition of the Anglo-Saxon *bēot*, the boastful threats pronounced by a hero before a battle.

54–5. *if ... reconcile*] 'if our differences could have been reconciled either by time or by love'.

56. *vein*] (a) course of action (*OED* 13a); (b) temporary state of mind (*OED* 14b).

In any one of us, but blows the fire
Which nought but blood reciprocal can quench.
Álvarez. Vitelli, thou sayst bravely, and sayst right,
And I will kill thee for't, I love thee so.   60
Vitelli. Ha, ha, old man. Upon thy death I'll build
A story with this arm for thy old wife
To tell thy daughter Clara seven years hence,
As she sits weeping by a winter fire,
How such a time Vitelli slew her husband   65
With the same sword his daughter favoured him,
And lives, and wears it yet. Come, Lamoral,
Redeem thyself.
Lamoral.   Lucio, Genevora
Shall on this sword receive thy bleeding heart
For my presented hat laid at her feet.   70
Lucio. Thou talkst well, Lamoral, but 'tis thy head
That I will carry to her to thy hat.
Fie, father, I do cool too much.
Álvarez.   O boy,
Thy father's true son.
Beat, drums. And so good morrow to your lordship.   75
                                        [*Drums.*]

Enter above EUGENIA, CLARA, [*and*] GENEVORA.

---

64. winter fire] *F* (wintet fire); winters fire *F2*.   75. SD1] *Weber.*

---

58. *blood reciprocal*] blood shed in return for that of Vitelli's uncle Don Pedro.

60. *And ... so*] 'And I love thee in such way that I will kill thee for it.'

62. *story*] Perhaps punning on building a *storey* in an unusual architectural metaphor: Vitelli's arm, causing Álvarez's death, will thus construct a new level of a metaphorical building (perhaps on top of the previous section, corresponding to his uncle's murder).

66. *favoured him*] gifted him with as a favour or token (*OED favour, v.,* 2c); see 2.2.218 n.

71–2. *'tis ... hat*] 'I will reunite your head with your hat by cutting it off and presenting it to Genevora.'

75. SD1] The drums, as before, may be heard within. However, since they were assumed earlier to be accompanying the combatants (line 33), the musicians might actually be visible; they may be in the gallery (yet leaving space for the four characters that will appear there next), or on the stage, perhaps entering with either party (though the space may be overcrowded).

Sayavedra. Brave resolutions.

Anastro.   Brave, and Spanish right.

Genevora. Lucio.

Clara.   Vitelli.

Eugenia.   Álvarez.

Álvarez.   How the devil
    Got these cats into th' gutter? My puss too?

Eugenia. Hear us.

Genevora.   We must be heard.

Clara.   We will be heard.
    Vitelli, look: see Clara on her knees   80
    Imploring thy compassion. [*Aside*] Heaven, how sternly
    They dart their emulous eyes, as if each scorned
    To be behind the other in a look!
    [*Aloud*] Mother, death needs no sword here. O my sister—
    Fate fain would have it so—persuade, entreat;   85
    A lady's tears are silent orators,
    Or should be so at least, to move beyond
    The honiest-tonguèd rhetorician.
    [*To Vitelli*] Why will you fight? Why does an uncle's death,
    Twenty year old, exceed your love to me   90
    But twenty days, whose forced cause and fair manner
    You could not understand, only have heard?
    Custom, that wrought so cunningly on nature

---

81. SD] *this edn.*   84. SD] *this edn.*   88. honiest-tonguèd rhetorician]
Colman (conj. TSS); honest tongu'd-Rethoritian *F.*   89. SD] *GWW.*

---

76. *Spanish right*] rightly, properly Spanish.

78. *gutter*] guttering along the edge of a roof (*OED* 2).

My puss] Eugenia.

80. *on her knees*] The three women kneel at unspecified points in this section; this prompts questions about visibility: presumably actors kneeling in the gallery above the stage, behind the railing, would still be perfectly visible. In the Shakespeare Institute and BADA productions, the women pleaded on the main stage between the opposing factions.

82. *emulous eyes*] rivalrous gazes.

83. *behind*] inferior to.

84. *sister*] sister-in-law, i.e., Genevora; Clara and Genevora declare later that they regard themselves as Vitelli's and Lucio's wives 'wanting but ceremony' (see, respectively, lines 170–1 and 175).

88. *honiest-tonguèd rhetorician*] the orator with the sweetest, most eloquent speech. The word *rhetorician* scans as four syllables. (See longer note.)

93. *Custom*] see 1.2.51 n.

In me that I forgot my sex, and knew not
Whether my body female were, or male,   95
You did unweave, and had the power to charm
A new creation in me, made me fear
To think on those deeds I did perpetrate.
How little power, though, you allow to me
That cannot with my sighs, my tears, my prayers,   100
Move you from your own loss, if you should gain.
Vitelli. I must forget you, Clara, till I have
Redeemed my uncle's blood, that brands my face
Like a pestiferous carbuncle. I am blind
To what you do, deaf to your cries, and marble   105
To all impulsive exorations.
When on this point I have perched thy father's soul,
I'll tender thee this bloody reeking hand
Drawn forth the bowels of that murderer.
If thou canst love me then, I'll marry thee,   110
And for thy father lost, get thee a son;
On no condition else.
Asistente.   Most barbarous.
Sayavedra. Savage.
Anastro.   Irreligious.

---

101. should] *F2;* shoule *F.*   107. on] in *F2.*

96. *unweave*] unravel, reveal.
98. *perpetrate*] performed (in a neutral sense; *OED* 1).
101. *Move you from*] Make you overcome.
    gain] win; if Vitelli is victorious in the combat, he will lose Clara's love.
103–4. *brands ... carbuncle*] Don Pedro's death, while unavenged, is dis-
honourable to his family, and thus Vitelli's face must be reddened by shame.
A carbuncle was a pustule on the face or nose associated with rosacea (*OED*
3b), a chronic skin disease that produced a persistent reddening of the face;
Vitelli characterises it as contagious (*pestiferous*; *OED* 2b), but later medical
knowledge revealed it was not.
104. *I am*] pronounced as monosyllabic, 'I'm'.
106. *exorations*] entreaties; pronounced as five syllables.
107. *this point*] his sword's tip.
110–11. *I'll ... son*] cf. King Richard to Queen Elizabeth on having killed
her children in Shakespeare's *R3*: 'But in your daughter's womb I bury them,
/ Where, in that nest of spicery, they will breed / Selves of themselves, to
your recomfiture' (4.4.354–6).

Genevora.   O Lucio!
   Be thou more merciful. Thou bear'st fewer years,
   Art lately weaned from soft effeminacy,   115
   A maiden's manners and a maiden's heart
   Are neighbours still to thee. Be then more mild,
   Proceed not to this combat; be'st thou desperate
   Of thine own life? Yet, dearest, pity mine.
   Thy valour's not thine own: I gave it thee,   120
   These eyes begot it, this tongue bred it up,
   This breast would lodge it. Do not use my gifts
   To mine own ruin. I have made thee rich;
   Be not so thankless to undo me for't.
Lucio. Mistress, you know I do not wear a vein   125
   I would not rip for you to do you service.
   Life's but a word, a shadow, a melting dream,
   Compared to essential and eternal honour.
   Why would you have me value it beyond
   Your brother? If I first cast down my sword   130
   May all my body here be made one wound,
   And yet my soul not find heaven thorough it.
Álvarez. [*To Eugenia*] You would be caterwauling too, but
     peace,
   Go, get you home, and provide dinner for
   Your son and me. We'll be exceeding merry.   135
   O Lucio, I will have thee cock of all
   The proud Vitellis that do live in Spain.

---

114. more] *not in F2*.   132. thorough] through *Weber*.   133. SD] *this edn.*

115. *weaned*] Bobadilla and Álvarez had called him *milksop* (2.2.64 and
4.3.32).
118. *desperate*] despairing, unhopeful (of saving his life; *OED* 1a).
125. *wear a vein*] An odd image (veins as external appendages rather than
internal to the body), seemingly unattested in other English texts of the
period.
127. *Life's ... dream*] cf. Shakespeare's *Macbeth*: 'Life's but a walking
shadow, a poor player / That struts and frets his hour upon the stage, / And
then is heard no more' (5.5.23–5).
132. *thorough*] Pronounced as one syllable, *through*.
136. *cock*] victor, vanquisher (*OED* 7a); akin to *cock of the game*, a dexter-
ous fighter (*OED gamecock* 2; see 2.2.56).

Fie, we shall take cold. Hunch. Pox, I am hoarse
Already.
Lamoral. [*To Vitelli*] How your sister whets my spleen!
I could eat Lucio now.
Genevora.   Vitelli, brother,   140
Ev'n for your father's soul, your uncle's blood,
As you do love my life, but last and most
As you respect your own honour and fame,
Throw down your sword. He is most valiant
That herein yields first.
Vitelli.   Peace, you fool.
Clara.   Why, Lucio,   145
Do thou begin; 'tis no disparagement.
He's elder and thy better, and thy valour
Is in his infancy.
Genevora. [*To Vitelli*] Or pay it me,
To whom thou ow'st it. O, that constant time
Would but go back a week: then, Lucio,   150
Thou wouldst not dare to fight.
Eugenia.   Lucio, thy mother,
Thy mother begs it: throw thy sword down first.

---

138. Pox, I am] *Dyce;* — I am *F;* by Heav'n I'm *Colman;* by Heav'n, I am
Weber. 139. SD] *GWW.* 140. now. / *Genevora.* Vitelli, brother] *F2;*
now: / *Gen. Lamorall;* you have often sworne / You'ld be commanded by me.
/ *Gen. Vitelli,* Brother *F.* 148. SD] *this edn.*

138. *Hunch*] a cough, as if something were sticking in his throat.
139. *spleen*] (a) courage, resolution (*OED* 5a); (b) passion, ill temper
(*OED* 7a). In humoral theory the spleen was the seat of melancholy, rather
than choler (the expected humour in an enraged fighter; see 3.2.23 n.).
140. *I ... now*] cf. Beatrice on Claudio in *MAdo*: 'I would eat his heart in
the market place' (4.2.307–8). The insertion at this point in F of a phrase
that is repeated in lines 153–4 ('Lamoral, / You have often sworn you'd be
commanded by me'), perhaps indicates a passage marked in the prompt
book to be cut in performance. The repetition of the phrase 'Your hearing
for six words' (Genevora in line 156 and Eugenia in line 179) may also be
an indicated cut; perhaps Genevora's line should be omitted, but as it is
assigned later to a different character, F2 and all editors except Williams
retained it. (See Introduction, 30.)
147–8. *valour ... infancy*] Lucio's newly found courage is yet immature;
cf. line 115.
149–50. *O ... week*] Cf. Salisbury in *R2*: 'O call back yesterday, bid time
return' (3.2.65); Frankford in *Kindness*: 'That it were possible / To undo
things done, to call back yesterday' (13.51–2).

Álvarez. I'll throw his head down after, then.
Genevora.   Lamoral,
     You have often sworn you'd be commanded by me.
Lamoral. Never to this. Your spite and scorn, Genevora,   155
     Has lost all power in me.
Genevora.   Your hearing for six words.
Asistente, Sayavedra, and Anastro. Strange obstinacy!
Álvarez, Vitelli, Lucio, and Lamoral. We'll stay no longer.
Clara. Then by thy oath, Vitelli,
     Thy dreadful oath thou wouldst return that sword   160
     When I should ask it: give it to me now,
     This instant I require it.
Genevora.   By thy vow,
     As dreadful, Lucio, to obey my will
     In any one thing I would watch to challenge,
     I charge thee not to strike a stroke. Now he   165
     Of our two brothers that loves perjury
     Best, and dares first be damned, infringe his vow.
Sayavedra. Excellent ladies.
Vitelli.   Pish, you tyrannise.
Lucio. We did equivocate.
Álvarez.   On.
Clara.   Then, Lucio,
     So well I love my husband—for he is so,   170

---

154. sworn] *Dyce;* swore *F* [*see 140. t.n.*].   156. in] on *TSS.* Your ...
words] *not in GWW.*

154. *You have*] pronounced as one syllable, 'You've'.
156. *Your ... words*] see line 140 n.
160. *dreadful*] awe-inspiring (*OED* 2a).
164. *watch*] wait expectantly for the occasion (*OED* 12b).
165–7. *Now ... vow*] As a challenge: 'After these reminders, let either
brother dare to damn himself for perjury.'
168. *Pish ... tyrannise*] There is no indication that Vitelli yields Clara's
sword, and he thus breaks the promise he implicitly made in 2.2.242.
169. *did equivocate*] made an ambiguous (and therefore invalid) promise
(*OED* 3a); the term was politically loaded in the wake of the 1605 Gunpowder
Plot, particularly after the trial of Father Henry Garnett (1555–1606), the
Superior of the Society of Jesus in England, who defended the use of equivo-
cation when being interrogated, and who was executed for high treason for
his supposed involvement in the plot.

Wanting but ceremony—that I pray
His vengeful sword may fall upon thy head
Successfully for falsehood to his sister.
Genevora. I likewise pray, Vitelli, Lucio's sword—
   Who equally is my husband as thou hers—   175
   May find thy false heart, that durst gage thy faith,
   And durst not keep it.
Asistente.   Are you men or stone?
Álvarez. Men, and we'll prove it with our swords.
Eugenia. Your hearing, for six words, and we have done,
   Sancho come forth—we'll fight our challenge too.   180

     Enter BOBADILLA [*above*] *with two swords and a pistol.*
     [*He gives the swords to Clara and Genevora.*]

   Now speak your resolutions.
Genevora.   These they are:
   The first blow given betwixt you sheathes these swords
   In one another's bosoms.
Eugenia. [*To Bobadilla*]   And, rogue, look
   You at that instant do discharge that pistol
   Into my breast. If you start back or quake,   185
   I'll stick you like a pig.
Álvarez.   Hold! You are mad.
Genevora. This we said. And by our hope of bliss
   This we will do. Speak your intents.
Clara and Genevora.   Strike.
Eugenia.   Shoot.
Álvarez, Vitelli, Lucio, and Lamoral.
   Hold, hold! All friends.
Asistente.   Come down.
         [*Exeunt those above.*]

---

177. stone] *F;* stones *TSS.*   180. SD] *this edn.*   183. SD] *this edn.*   186.
Hold!] *F (—* hold:*); By Heaven! Hold! Weber.*   187. we] we have *TSS.*
189. SD] *GWW.*

---

  171. *Wanting but*] Lacking only.
  176. *gage*] (a) stake, wager (*OED* 2a); (b) engage ('gage).
  177. *men or stone*] Stones are immovable, while men are subject to be
emotionally moved.
  182–6. *The ... pig*] This triple assisted suicide is reminiscent of the final
scene of Webster's *White Devil.* (See longer note on the staging.)
  186. *stick*] stab.

Álvarez.   These devilish women
   Can make men friends and enemies when they list.   190
Sayavedra. A gallant undertaking, and a happy,
   Why, this is noble in you, and will be
   A welcomer present to our master Philip
   Than the return from his Indies.

      Enter [below] CLARA, GENEVORA, EUGENIA,
          and BOBADILLA.

Clara. Father, your blessing.
Álvarez. [*To Vitelli*]   Take her. If ye bring not   195
   Betwixt you boys that will find out new worlds
   And win 'em too, I'm a false prophet.
Vitelli. [*To Lucio*]   Brother,
   There is a sister. Long divided streams
   Mix now at length by fate.
Bobadilla. I am not regarded. I was the careful steward that   200
   provided these instruments of peace. [*To Vitelli*] I put the
   longest weapon in your sister's hand, my lord, because
   she was the shortest lady; for likely the shortest ladies
   love the longest—— men. And for mine own part, I could

---

194. SD] *Weber.*   195. SD] *this edn.*   ye] *F2;* he *F.*   197. SD] *this edn.*
201. SD] *this edn.*   204. longest—] *long dash not in Colman.*

---

  189. *devilish*] pronounced as two syllables, *dev'lish.*
  193. *master Philip*] the King of Spain (see line 7 n.).
  194. *return ... Indies*] 'the income generated by his colonies in the West
Indies' (*return, OED n.* 2a).
  197. *false prophet*] One whose prophecies prove to be mistaken; in
Matthew 7:15 Jesus warns against false prophets.
  198–9. *Long ... fate*] 'Destiny has blended two sundered bloodlines into
a durable one.'
  200. *I ... regarded*] Cf. in Shakespeare's *1H6*, the Bishop of Winchester is
left alone on stage: 'Each hath his place and function to attend: / I am left
out; for me nothing remains' (1.1.173–4).
  201–4. *I ... men*] An extended sexual metaphor: ladies of short stature
are said to be attracted to men who carry long weapons (i.e., men who have
large penises).
  204. *longest*——] The long dash may indicate a humorously meaningful
pause (or a cough?), suggestive of a missing word. If the sexual pun was
censored, the missing word must have been the past participle of a verb
qualifying men who are militarily well equipped, and metaphorically who
possess large penises. Given the context, a phrase like 'longest-weaponed'
or 'longest-provided' seem likely choices. However, it might have been 'the
longest-nosed men': in Middleton's *Maiden's T*, the Wife says: 'must you /
Give such bold freedom to your long-nosed fellow / That every room must

have discharged it: my pistol is no ordinary pistol, it has   205
two ramming bullets; but, thought I, why should I shoot
my two bullets into my old lady? If they had gone, I would
not have stayed long after. I would ev'n have died too,
bravely i' faith, like a Roman steward. Hung myself in
mine own chain, and there had been a story of Bobadilla   210
Spindola Sancho, for after ages to lament. Hum, I perceive I am not only not regarded, but also not rewarded.

Álvarez. Prithee, peace. 'Shalt have a new chain next Saint
Jacques' Day, or this new gilt.

Bobadilla. I am satisfied. Let virtue have her due. And yet I   215
am melancholy upon this atonement. Pray heaven the
state rue it not. I would my lord Vitelli's steward and I
could meet; they should find it should cost 'em a little
more to make us friends. Well, I will forswear wine and
women for a year, and then I will be drunk tomorrow,   220
and run a-whoring like a dog with a broken bottle at's
tail; then will I repent next day, and forswear 'em again
more vehemently; be forsworn next day again, and repent
my repentance. For thus a melancholy gentleman doth,
and ought to live.   225

---

216. melancholy] me- *Q*. 226. shall] stall *F2*.

---

take a taste of him?' (4.1.77–9), which Wiggins annotates as 'a long nose was considered a sign of a long penis'.

205–6. *pistol ... bullets*] Extended pun on the pistol and two bullets being Bobadilla's penis and testicles; cf. Pistol in *2H4* threatens to shoot at Mistress Quickly: 'I will discharge upon her, Sir John, with two bullets' (2.4.111–12).

209–10. *like ... chain*] Roman soldiers would commit suicide by letting themselves fall on their own swords; Bobadilla supposes Roman stewards would follow a similar process using the distinctive badge of their office, (ahistorically) their chains. (See also 2.2.122.)

213. *'Shalt*] Thou shalt.

213–14. *Saint Jacques' Day*] 25 July; Saint James the Apostle is the patron saint of Spain (see 1.2.6 n.).

214. *this*] your existing chain.

216. *atonement*] reunion, reconciliation (etymologically, becoming one, 'at-one-ment').

219–24. *Well ... repentance*] Echoing Sir John Falstaff's repeated intentions to amend his usual ways; e.g., 'I must give over this life, and I will give it over' (*1H4*, 1.2.95).

224–5. *For ... live*] Alternatively, without the comma: 'For thus a melancholy gentleman doth [live] and ought to live.'

Asistente. Nay, you shall dine with me. And afterward
    I'll with ye to the King. But first, I will
    Dispatch the castle's business, that this day
    May be complete. Bring forth the malefactors.

> *Enter [the]* ALGUAZIR, PACHECO, METALDI, MENDOZA,
>   LAZARILLO, PIORATO, MALRODA, *and [the] guard.*

    You, Alguazir, the ringleader of these   230
    Poor fellows, are degraded from your office.
    You must restore all stolen goods you received,
    And watch a twelvemonth without any pay.
    This, if you fail of, all your goods confiscate,
    You are to be whipped, and sent into the galleys.   235
Alguazir. I like all but restoring; that Catholic doctrine

---

232. restore] return *F2.*

---

226. *Nay ... me*] cf. Justice Clement at the end of Jonson's *EMI*: 'And now, to make our evening happiness more full, this night you shall be all my guests' (5.3.378–9). The character who was elated at the prospect of being invited to supper earlier in the play, Lazarillo, is about to make his final appearance; see 2.1.231–2 n.

228. *the Castle's business*] In the play, the Castle of Santiago, perhaps the Asistente's official residence or the seat of his government, is presumably being used as a prison where the Alguazir and his associates are being held for trial.

229. SD] At this point the stage is filled with the maximum number of actors required in the play: nineteen speaking characters and a minimum of four supernumeraries.

230–53. *You ... rows*] This section is reminiscent of the final scene of Jonson's *Volpone* (5.12.106–51), in which the four *avocatori* pronounce their sentence on the fate of the various characters. In *LC* the malefactors are taken off presumably guarded.

230. *ringleader*] chief instigator of a criminal activity (*OED* 1).

235. *You ... galleys*] Taken almost directly from the sentence pronounced on Mosca in *Volpone*: 'For which our sentence is, first thou be whipped; / Then live perpetual prisoner in our galleys' (5.12.113–14). The Alguazir has served a term in the galleys already (see 2.1.172–3 and 198–9).

236. *restoring*] Giving back stolen goods to their rightful owner was a typical condition for the absolution of the sin of robbery, and was associated with Catholicism, as Clocledemoy expresses in Marston's *Courtesan* (c. 1604): 'Restitution is Catholic' (1.2.8–9). The line is a reminder that the characters on stage are Spanish Catholics. If the Alguazir is, in fact, a converted Jew (see 2.1.170–1 n.), this line might be a reminder of the fact that he finds Christian doctrine objectionable. The phrase is also reminiscent of Falstaff: 'O, I do not like that paying back; 'tis a double labour' (*1H4*, 3.3.180–1).

I do dislike. Learn, all ye officers,
By this to live uprightly—if you can.   *Exit.*
Asistente. [*To Pacheco*] You, cobbler, to translate your
    manners new,
    Are doomed to th' cloister of the Mendicants   240
    With this your brother botcher there, for nothing
    To cobble and heel hose for the poor friars,
    Till they allow your penance for sufficient,
    And your amendment; then you shall be freed,
    And may set up again.
Pacheco.   Mendoza, come.   245
    Our souls have trod awry in all men's sight;
    We'll underlay 'em till they go upright.
                       Exeunt Pacheco and Mendoza.
Asistente. [*To Metaldi*] Smith, in those shackles you for your
    hard heart
    Must lie by th' heels a year.
Metaldi.   I have shod your horse, my lord.   *Exit.*
Asistente. Away. [*To Lazarillo*] For you, my hungry
    white-loafed face,   250
    You must to th' galleys, where you shall be sure
    To have no more bits than you shall have blows.

---

239. SD] *this edn.*   240. cloister] cloisters *F2.*   Mendicants] Mend cants
Langbaine.   243. your] you *F2.*   247. SD *Exeunt*] *F2. (Exe.); Enit F.*
248. SD] *this edn.*   250. SD] *this edn.*

---

240. *doomed*] sentenced.
    Mendicants] Mendicant friars, devoted to acts of charity and subsisting
exclusively on alms; cf. First Avocatore to Corbaccio in *Volpone*: 'We here
possess / Thy son of all thy estate, and confine thee / To the Monastery of
San' Spirito' (5.12.129–31).
    241. *for nothing*] for no payment.
    245. *set up again*] restart your business.
    246. *souls*] Pacheco puns again on the homophone *souls* and *soles*, as in
2.1.112.
    247. *underlay*] (a) give support to the souls (*OED* 1a); (b) provide shoes
with a new or extra sole (*OED* 1c); (c) debase them, humble them (approximately *OED* 2a, 'to place [something] beneath').
    252. *bits*] bites, morsels (*OED bit* 1a).
    blows] Malefactors convicted to row in the galleys would be regularly
whipped; see 2.1.173 n.

Lazarillo. Well, though herrings want, I shall have rows.

[*Exit.*]

Asistente. [*To Piorato*] Señor, you have prevented us, and
    punished

    Yourself severelier than we would have done: 255

    You have married a whore; may she prove honest.

Piorato. 'Tis better, my lord, than to marry an honest
    woman

    That may prove a whore.

Vitelli. [*Aside to Piorato*] 'Tis a handsome wench; an thou
    canst keep her tame,

    I'll send you what I promised.

Piorato.   Joy to your lordships.   260

Álvarez. Here may all ladies learn to make of foes

    The perfect'st friends, and not the perfect'st foes

    Of dearest friends, as some do nowadays.

---

253. though] tho' I *TSS*. SD] *Weber*. 254. SD] *this edn.* Señor] *F*
(*Signior*). 259. SD] *this edn.* an] *Colman; and F* 261. Here] Hear *F2*.

---

253. *want*] lack.

rows] punning on *roes*; the roe is the (edible) mass of eggs spawned by fish
and shellfish and generally carried by the female in her ovaries. Instead of
getting the meal he has been longing for, Lazarillo is sentenced to row in
the galleys, a physical activity that was particularly demanding and that
weaker individuals did not typically survive.

256. *married ... whore*] A comic inversion of a conventionally heinous fate.
In *Cupid*, the god of love causes the infatuation of Duke Leontius with a
prostitute, Bacha, so that he quickly proposes marriage to her; the social
grotesqueness of this situation is the basic dramatic conflict of the play. In
Shakespeare's *MM*, Lucio is condemned to marry a whore; he exits declaring
that 'Marrying a punk [...] is pressing to death, whipping, and hanging'
(5.1.521–2). As a newly-wed couple in a comedy, Piorato and Malroda may
remain on stage for the remainder of the scene after line 260.

259–60. *'Tis ... promised*] The aside is not marked in any previous edition.
If heard by the whole cast of characters, this speech would be strikingly
inappropriate; it would be extremely awkward for a gentleman like Vitelli to
praise the beauty of a prostitute in public, in front of his betrothed Clara,
her violent father, and the civic authority represented by the Asistente, or to
allude to a (private) pre-concerted promise to Piorato if he can keep Malroda
at bay (see 3.2.143 n.). The aside is an efficient way of resolving Malroda's
plot line. In the Shakespeare Institute production, Clara overheard the
speech and gave Vitelli a scathing look.

263. *as ... nowadays*] Perhaps a reference to the Overbury scandal. (See
2.2.159 n. and Introduction, 10–11.)

Vitelli. Behold the power of love: lo, nature lost
    By custom irrecoverably, past the hope   265
    Of friends restoring, love hath here retrieved
    To her own habit, made her blush to see
    Her so long monstrous metamorphoses.
    May strange affairs never have worse success.

                                                    Exeunt.

<hr>

264. lo, nature] *Dyce;* to nature *F; Nature,* tho' *Colman (conj. TSS);* So
Nature *Weber.*

<hr>

  265. *custom*] see 1.2.51 n.
  269. *success*] ending.

Epilogue

Our author fears there are some rebel hearts,
Whose dullness doth oppose love's piercing darts;
Such will be apt to say there wanted wit,
The language low, very few scenes are writ
With spirit and life; such odd things as these   5
He cares not for, nor ever means to please;
For if yourselves, a mistress, or love's friends,
Are liked with this smooth play, he hath his ends.

FINIS.

1. author] *F2; Auhor F.* rebel] Rebels *Beaumont.*

2. *dullness*] hardness that prevents love's proverbial arrows from penetrating the heart.
3. *apt*] disposed.
wanted] lacked.
5. *odd*] irregular (*OED* 8a).
8. *Are ... with*] Have enjoyed.
smooth] free of irregularities, well-crafted.
he ... ends] 'he will have achieved his target'.

A Prologue

Statues and pictures challenge price and fame
If they can justly boast and prove they came
From Phidias or Apelles. None deny
Poets and painters hold a sympathy,
Yet their works may decay and lose their grace,   5
Receiving blemish in their limbs or face.
When the mind's art has this pre-eminence,
She still retaineth her first excellence.
Then why should not this dear piece be esteemed
Child to the richest fancies that e'er teemed,   10
When not their meanest offspring that came forth
But bore the image of their fathers' worth?
Beaumont's and Fletcher's, whose desert outweighs
The best applause, and their least sprig of bays
Is worthy Phoebus; and who comes to gather   15

---

1. price] praise *Beaumont*.   4. painters] Picture Painters *Beaumont*.   14.
bays] Boyes *F2*.

---

0. reviving] revival.

3. *Phidias or Apelles*] respectively, celebrated and proverbial sculptor and
painter of classical antiquity.

4. *sympathy*] affinity.

7. *mind's art*] the product of artistic creation.

this pre-eminence] this privilege, i.e., survive in time.

9. *this dear piece*] i.e., the present play.

10. *fancies*] invention, wit.

teemed] gave birth, engendered.

11–12. *When … worth*] 'When even the lesser of their works attested the
greatness of the authors.'

13. *desert*] merit.

14. *bays*] bay leaves in a laurel wreath crowning poetic achievement.

15. *Is worthy Phoebus*] is as valuable as the sun.

Their fruits of wit, he shall not rob the treasure.
Nor can you ever surfeit of the plenty,
Nor can you call them rare though they be dainty.
The more you take, the more you do them right,
And we will thank you for your own delight.   20

---

16. *Their ... treasure*] The imagery is confusing: from sculptures and paintings, through a metaphor of human generation (works as the artists' children), the poem finally presents images of vegetation and material value that are not totally coherent with the previous lines.

19. *The ... right*] 'The more you appreciate them (by reading or, perhaps, performing them), the more justice you do them.'

Longer notes

1.2.51. *custom*] The word *custom* functions as a kind of verbal leit-motif in *LC*, recurring in 1.3.21, 174, and 180; in 2.2.99 and 145; in 5.1.80; and in 5.3.93 and 265. This insistence on the use of the term, equivalent to the Spanish *costumbre*, to emphasise the central theme of the play – the conflict between natural impulses and cultural constructions – was probably the keyword that prompted A. L. Stiefel in 1897 to identify *La fuerza de la costumbre* as the main narrative source of the play. Kathleen Jeffs encoded the duality between established behaviour and clothing in the title of her trans-lation of Guillén de Castro's play: *The Force of Habit*.

1.3.73–8.] The sequence in F is as follows: the sound of clashing swords starts as Álvarez begins to speak, Eugenia's next speech is interrupted, and Álvarez enquires about a voice that has just been heard. (See figure 8.) The lines spoken by Sayavedra and Vitelli offstage are printed immediately after with no speech prefixes. F2 interpreted that *voice* must have been a misprint for *noise*, refer-ring to the clashing swords, and gave the first two unassigned lines to Sayavedra (75–6) and the third to Vitelli (78). However, it still printed the SDs *Sayavedra within* and *Vitelli within* in the margin. GWW rephrased the first as *Sayavedra [calls] within* and placed it after the SD about the noise of the swords, thus justifying the F reading *voice*. However, there could be a simpler explanation: the F placing of the two marginal SDs indicates the position of the two speeches that were printed after Álvarez's line, rendering a logical sequence: Eugenia is interrupted by Sayavedra shouting within, Álvarez asks whose voice it is, and then Vitelli replies. This has been the interpretation followed in the present edition, thus justifying the F reading *voice* and the F position of the SD about the clashing of swords. We can only speculate that the copy MS was confusing at this point, perhaps lacking enough available space on the page to clarify the sequence of events. However, the position of the SD about the noise of the swords is still a point of contention, and could be the cause of the interruption of Eugenia's line, as Dyce first sug-

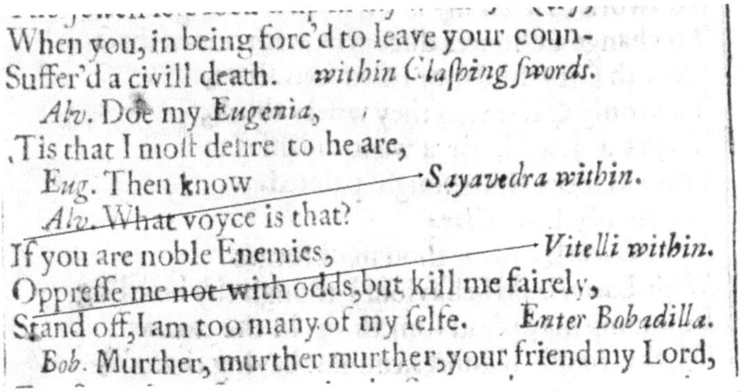
When you, in being forc'd to leave your coun-
Suffer'd a civill death. *within Claſhing ſwords.*
Alv. Doe my *Eugenia*,
,Tis that I moſt deſire to heare,
Eug. Then know *Sayavedra within.*
Alv. What voyce is that?
If you are noble Enemies, *Vitelli within.*
Oppreſſe me not with odds, but kill me fairely,
Stand off, I am too many of my ſelfe. *Enter Bobadilla.*
Bob. Murther, murther murther, your friend my Lord,

Figure 8 Typesetting problem in 1.3; F, sig. 5Q4^{v}, courtesy of Pennsylvania State University

gested, thus justifying the F2 reading *noise*. The passage, following Dyce, would alternatively appear as follows:

Eugenia. Then know— *Within clashing swords.*
Álvarez. What noise is that?
Sayavedra. (*Within*) If you are noble enemies,
Oppress me not with odds, but kill me fairly.
Vitelli. (*Within*) Stand off; I am too many of myself.

GWW (and Mitchell) chose to print Álvarez's line 'What voice is that?' (77) and Sayavedra's 'If you are noble enemies' (75) as one whole (twelve-syllable) line of verse.

3.3.18–26.] Malroda's first lines express a command ('Do as I told thee'), a formulaic salutation (''Bless thee, señor'), and a greeting to someone of higher social rank ('O my dear lord'). The first addressee must be Piorato and the third, Vitelli. The identity of the second, however, is not straightforward to determine. I have opted for the interpretation I think most plausible: Malroda instructs Piorato to hide from Vitelli (the first command), then comes forward acknowledging the presence of the Alguazir, and then speaks to Vitelli. Williams interpreted that the Alguazir '*stands apart*' before Malroda and Piorato's entrance, being thus invisible to the two of them and therefore requiring that her second sentence is necessarily addressed to Piorato as a formula of dismissal. This alternative option would appear as follows:

Alguazir. [*Aside*] Now, luck. [*He stands apart.*]
Enter MALRODA *and* PIORATO.

Malroda. [*Apart to Piorato*] 'Tis he. Do as I told thee. 'Bless thee, señor.
[*Piorato stands apart.*]
   [*to Vitelli*] O my dear lord.

However, there seems to be little dramatic justification for the
Alguazir to retreat or hide at the appearance of the courtesan and
the swordsman, as both parties know of each other's presence in the
house.

3.3.23 SD.] Malroda uses a portrait to distract Vitelli and enable
Piorato's exit. A hand-held miniature portrait would have been more
convenient to carry on stage, and cheaper to procure, than a full-
scale painting discovered behind the curtains of the discovery space.
In addition, a large portrait would need to resemble the actor playing
Malroda, as her features would be more readily visible than those
represented in a small portable picture. Weber added the slightly
confusing SD '*Shows a picture, behind which* PIORATO *steals out*',
while Dyce phrased it more clearly as '*While she shews* VITELLI *the
picture,* PIORATO *steals to the door*'. Portraits seem to have been
used to advertise the physical attributes of prostitutes. In *Zelotypus*
(St John's College, Cambridge, 1605), Cerberinus, the brothel gatekeeper, shows his gallery of portraits: 'Come here, my guest, and
inspect my wares. Here there is a fair display of the fairest girls' (3.7).

4.3.93–4.] The theme of the disguised ruler was particularly prominent in English drama at the turn of the seventeenth century. For
instance, King Henry appears in disguise among his soldiers in
Henry V (1599). It is the main plot device of a cluster of plays in
1603–04: Duke Altofronto as Malevole in *Malcontent*, Prince Phoenix
in Middleton's *The Phoenix*, Duke Ferneze in John Day's *Law-tricks*,
Duke Hercules as Faunus in Marston's *Fawn*, and Duke Vincentio
as Friar Lodowick in *MM* (see Wiggins, *Time*, 107–10, and Quarmby).
To avoid the confusion, in the 2012 Shakespeare Institute production the Asistente appeared above overhearing the scene, dressed in
full costume and wearing a chain of office indicating his status, and
descended at the appropriate point.

5.3.88. *honiest-tonguèd rhetorician*] Colman's reading responded to
Seward's and Sympson's proposed emendation. Seward spotted
the obvious incongruity in F: 'That there is no proper antithesis
between the *silent oratory of a lady's tears* and the *honesty of a rhetorician's tongue,* must be clear to any reader of common sense.' He
suggested that the antithesis would only be rendered if *honest* is

substituted with *loudest*, 'which is not far from the trace of the letters'. Sympson, however, proposed *honiest* as a less radical and more plausible reading, suggesting that 'our poets who were admirers of the classics, might possibly have had Nestor in their eye, who is thus described by Homer: "experienced Nestor is persuasion skilled; / Words sweet as honey from his lips distilled." (Mr. Pope's translation.)'

5.3.182–6. *The ... pig*] The plan to carry out an assisted triple suicide is similar to Flamineo's plot in the final scene of Webster's *White Devil*. Flamineo gives two pistols each to Vittoria and Zanche so that they can simultaneously shoot into each other's breasts and into his own. In the present case, the addition of a fourth agent, Bobadilla, is probably due to two practical considerations. On the one hand, since the women have tried to reason with the duellists first for a considerable space of time (just over one hundred lines, 75–180), the weapons are not needed until this point as they would give away their intentions; Bobadilla is the obvious servant of Eugenia's household to be employed in carrying them on stage. On the other hand, as the suicide is to be performed in the above playing space, it would be ineffective to attempt it with only three actors: Flamineo, Vittoria, and Zanche are necessarily required to stand on stage forming a triangle, whereas this would be impractical to accommodate in a gallery; the division of the available personnel into two pairs – Genevora and Clara on one side, Eugenia and Bobadilla on the opposite – presents a flatter, and therefore more effective, stage picture. In any case, Eugenia needs an extra weapon to make sure that Bobadilla will do as he has been told, by threatening to stab him (a proven coward) if he fails to shoot.

APPENDIX 1
Press variants in F

This edition has been prepared with two control copies of the 1647 folio at hand: the Bridgewater exemplar at the Houghton Library, Harvard University (Bdw) and the copy at the Thomas Fischer Rare Book Library, University of Toronto (Tnt). George Walton Williams collated 16 copies of the folio, marked below with an asterisk (*),[1] and I have collated a further 11 copies, which confirm his findings. These 27 copies are as follows:

Bdw (Houghton Library, Harvard University; HEW 7.11.5; Bridgewater copy), **Bhm¹** (Cadbury Research Library, University of Birmingham; Selbourne Coll q PR 2420-1647), **Bhm²** (Birmingham Central Library; AQ094/1647/6), *****Bodl** (Bodleian Library, Oxford; B.1.8.Art.), **Bro** (Brotherton Library, University of Leeds; BC Lt Quarto BEA), *****Camb¹** (Cambridge University Library; Aston a.Sel.19), *****Camb²** (Cambridge University Library; SSS.10.8), **ChII** (Brotherton Library, University of Leeds; BC Lt Quarto BEA; King Charles II's copy), *****CSmH** (Henry E. Huntington Library; 112111), *****DFo¹** (Folger Shakespeare Library; copy¹), *****DFo²** (Folger Shakespeare Library; copy²), **GHHB** (private copy, Brett Greatley-Hirsch; Greatley-Hirsch Hellfish Bonanza 70), **Hou¹** (Houghton Library, Harvard University; HOU 14421.3), **Hou²** (Houghton Library, Harvard University; HOU F 59S-368), **Hou³** (Houghton Library, Harvard University; HOU F 72-39), **Hou⁴** (Houghton Library, Harvard University; HOU F 14421.3.2), *****NCD** (Duke University), *****NCU** (University of North Carolina), *****NN¹** (New York Public Library; Berg Collection/Beaumont Copy¹), *****NN²** (New York Public Library; Berg Collection/Beaumont Copy²), *****NN³** (New York Public Library; Berg Collection/Beaumont Copy³), *****NN⁴** (New York Public Library; *KC/1647/Beaumont; Astor copy), *****NN⁵** (New York Public Library; Arents Collection 232, Acc. 3583), **Tnt** (Thomas Fischer Rare Book Library, University of Toronto; E-10 07451), *****TxU** (Harry Ransom Center, University of Texas; Ah/B 384/C647/copy²), *****ViU¹** (University of Virginia; 217972), *****ViU²** (University of Virginia; 570973).

These are the nine press variants that have been detected:

Quire Q *(outer sheet, inner forme)*
State *1:* TxU
State *2: the rest*

Sig. 5Q4ʳ

pagination 127] *state 2;* 128 *state 1*
1.2.96. *(left column, line 31)* which] *state 2;* whtch *state 1*
1.2.101. *(left, 36)* cooks,] *state 2;* ~, *state 1*
1.3.68. *(right, 66) Alvarez] state 2; Alvarezi state 1*
1.3.68. *catchword (right, 67)* Accompt] *state 2;* Accomp *state 1*

Quire R *(inner sheet, inner forme)*
State *1:* CSmH, Hou³
State *2: the rest*

Sig. 5R2ᵛ

2.2.186. *(left, 57)* Tis] *state 2;* Ti3 *state 1*

Quire R *(outer sheet, outer forme)*
State *1:* Bhm¹, Bro, Camb¹, DFo², GHHB, Hou³, NN³,⁵, Tnt, ViU¹,²
State *2:* Bdw, Bhm², Bodl, Camb², ChII, CSmH, DFo¹, Hou¹,²,⁴,
NCD, NCU, NN¹,²,⁴, TxU

Sig. 5R1ʳ

2.1.112. *(right, 50)* foule-menders] *state 2;* foule-members *state 1*

Quire S *(middle sheet, outer forme)*
State *1:* Bdw, Bhm¹,², Bro, Camb¹, ChII, CSmH, DFo², GHHB, Hou²,
NCD, NCU, NN¹⁻³, TxU, ViU²
State *2:* Bodl, Camb², DFo¹, Hou¹,³,⁴, NN⁴,⁵, Tnt, ViU¹

Sig. 5S2ʳ

4.2.124. *(left, 34)* gallant,] *state 2;* ~. *state 1*

Quire S *(outer sheet, inner forme)*
State *1:* Bhm¹, Bro, ChII, ViU²
State *2: the rest*

Sig. 5S1ᵛ

4.2.56. SP *(right, 12) Vit.]* state 2; ∀it. state 1

NOTE

1 See GWW, 'Press-variants in F1 (1647)', 97–8.

APPENDIX 2
Compositorial analysis and running titles

Williams's compositorial analysis was based on the unpublished work of Standish Henning. It indicated that the text was composed seriatim, that is, following the order of the manuscript from beginning to end for each play, rather than typesetting by formes. The division of the shares among the three compositors is as follows:[1]

Compositor			
A:	$Q4^v$, $R1^r$, $R1^v$, $R2^r$		$R4^v$, $S1^r$, $S1^v$
B:		$R2^v$, $R3^r$, $R3^v$, $R4^r$	
C: $Q3^r$, $Q3^v$, $Q4^r$			
A:		$S5^r$, $S5^v$, $S6^r$	
B:	$S3^v$, $S4^r$, $S4^v$		
C: $S2^r$, $S2^v$, $S3^r$			

The running titles follow a regular pattern:[2]

Verso:	I	$Q3^v$, $R4^v$	Loves Cure, or	Two spaces after the comma.
		$S5^v$	Loves Cure, &c.	Three spaces after 'Loves'.
	III	$Q4^v$, $R1^v$, $S2^v$, $S4^v$	Loves Cure,or	No space after the comma; the title is pied between quires Q and R, only 'Loves' remaining as initially typeset.
	V	$R2^v$, $R3^v$, $S1^v$, $S3^v$	Loves Cure, or	One space after the comma.
Recto:	II	$Q4^r$, $R4^r$, $S3^r$, $S5^r$	The Martiall Mayde.	
	IV	$R1^r$, $S1^r$, $S2^r$	The Martiall Maid.	
	VI	$R2^r$, $R3^r$, $S4^r$	The Martiall Maid.	

NOTES

1 Adapted from GWW, 10; see that page for further information about the linguistic preferences of the three compositors.
2 Adapted from GWW, 9.

APPENDIX 3
Censorship in F

The text of the play in the 1647 folio appears to have been expurgated of oaths and expressions of profanity, which were substituted with long dashes. Establishing at what point this censorship was effected is not straightforward: plays in Griffin's section 5 show varying degrees of censorship, but the elimination of certain words – particularly oaths appealing to God in a Christian context, and wishing the plague or the pox on someone or something – was not consistent throughout the sequence. Section 5 contains *The Sea Voyage, The Double Marriage, The Pilgrim, The Knight of Malta, The Woman's Prize, Love's Cure, The Honest Man's Fortune*, and the poem 'Upon an Honest Mans Fortune / By Mr. John Fletcher.' (sig. 5X4^v). These texts, as the rest of those in F, had not been printed before, and only one of them is extant in an alternative contemporary version: the undated Lambarde MS of *Prize*. The text of this play was relicensed for performance by Sir Henry Herbert, Master of the Revels, on 21 October 1633, 'purged of oaths, prophaness [*sic*], and ribaldry'.[1] F reproduces the censored text, while the Lambarde MS gives the original version, and it 'clearly descends from a copy-text that predates Herbert's censorship'.[2] These alterations may give us an idea of what is missing in *LC*. As the play appears not to have needed to be relicensed by Herbert, maybe Massinger eliminated these expressions in his revision to bring it into line with the decorum imposed by the Master of the Revels at the time. Even so, surely the prompt book used as copy for F offered a non-offensive alternative, as the actors could not be expected to verbalise a dash. It is probable, then, that the dashes were introduced in the printing house, or just before handing the copy over to the printer, in response to stricter censorship in the early years of the Cromwellian regime. Any attempt to reconstruct the suppressed phrases can only be an act of informed speculation. Colman proposed the first reconstructions, which Dyce mostly adopted, although he gave some other independent solutions.

Even if the case of *LC* is slightly different, Herbert's expurgation of *Prize* is a good indication of the kind of censorship effected on plays from the 1610s in revivals that occurred twenty years later.

Meg Powers gives a list of the censored words and phrases in the
Lambarde MS in her edition for the Malone Society Reprints
(Appendix B, xxiv–xxv). According to this list, the expressions of
ribaldry that Herbert objected to would not be detectable in F
without an alternative text, as they were simply omitted, or were
altered for tamer words. For example, the MS's 'pispots' was substituted with F's 'looking-glasses' (Bowers's edition, 4.2.2), while
passages such as 'for then old women are cool cellars' (3.2.37) were
excised altogether. Objectionable profanity was also altered in a
similar way. Three passages were cut out, while other phrases were
diluted: the MS's 'Christian' for F's 'certaine' (2.2.51), 'this creed'
for 'these Articles' (2.6.158), or 'religion' for 'adventure' (4.5.167).
All these instances represent irrecoverable phrases in the absence of
an alternative text, which is the case with *LC*. However, there are
other oaths and expressions of profanity that are relevant to this
discussion in which the censored phrase was substituted with the
familiar long dash. For example, the phrase 'O pox on't' in the MS
changed to 'A ——' in F, while a number of expurgated oaths are
immediately recognisable in *LC*. A single long dash, not preceded
by any other word, could encode 'Death' (as in *Prize* 1.3.278, implying 'God's death' or frequently ''Sdeath'), or 'troth' (4.5.183), or
even 'I vow' (1.3.290, 5.4.40). The expression 'by this hand' could
substitute 'by this light' (i.e. 'God's light'; 4.5.60). And, most inter-
estingly, the expurgated 'By ——' does not necessarily imply a
missing word, but a phrase censored altogether: 'By ——' in 5.4.72
reads 'I sweare' in the Lambarde MS.

We can examine the censored expressions in *LC* under four broad
categories:

1) Missing single words indicated by a long dash.
   '*Zancho:* —' (Lucio, 3.4.94; sig. 5S1^r, left column, line 41)
   '—— if you doe, my Lord *Vitelli* knowes it' (Malroda, 4.2.18; 5S1^v,
   left, 19)
   '—— if you doe / I will cry out a rape' (Malroda, 4.2.78–9; 5S1^v,
   right, 39)
   '—— I am hoarfe / Already' (Álvarez, 5.3.138–9; 5S5^r, left, 54)
   '—— hold: you are mad' (Álvarez, 5.3.186; 5S5^r, right, 52)

In 3.4.94, Dyce suggested that there is a missing word, and emended
for *pox*, though it could just be an interruption in the speech, as I
have assumed; all other editors printed the dash or omitted it altogether. Weber emended the last instance, 5.3.186, for 'By Heaven!

Hold!', but no other edition, including mine, has followed suit. In the other three cases, I have followed Dyce and have emended for *pox*. According to the Lambarde MS, these one-word censored oaths could also be *faith*, *troth*, or *death*, or even censored instances of *heav'n*.

2) Censored curses.
'a —— O' this filthie vardingale' (Clara, 2.2.69–70; 5R2ʳ, left, 58)
'the ——on your aphorifmes' (Malroda, 3.1.3; 5R3ʳ, left, 18)
'— o' this ftitching' (Clara, 3.4.53; 5R4ᵛ, right, 56)

The word missing here is surely *pox* or *plague*, though the editorial consensus has been to emend for *pox*, and only in one case, 3.4.53, did Colman choose *plague*. In Griffin's section 5, the word *pox* used as an oath appears three times in *Malta*, once in *Double* and six times in *Pilgrim*, so its censoring was probably not due to printing-house prudishness, but pre-printing censorship on the MS that served as copy. The word *plague*, generally more common than *pox* in Fletcher, appears as an oath twice in *Malta* and four times in *Pilgrim* (plus twice in *Prize* but not as an oath).

3) Censored oaths and invocations to the divine. This is the most complicated case, as the expurgated oaths could be missing a word, or they could be a substitution for a phrase such as 'I swear' (as in the Lambarde MS). These are the cases:
'come not on, by ——' (Clara, 1.3.143; 5Q4ᵛ, right, 21)
'Ile have you fearch'd, by ——' (Álvarez, 2.2.159; 5R2ᵛ, left, 26)
'By —— ile Pistoll thee' (Malroda, 3.3.92; 5R4ᵛ, left, 18)
'by —— fir, / You fhall endeere me ever' (Clara, 3.4.113–14; 5S1ʳ, left, 66)
'by ——, / There's nothing' (Lucio, 5.2.55–6; 5S4ʳ, right, 63)
''Save the King' (Herald, 5.3.33; 5S4ᵛ, left, 58)

I have deployed the Lambarde MS suggestion, 'I swear', to reinforce Álvarez's line 'I'll have you searched' and Malroda's 'I'll pistol thee'. This clearly would not work in 1.3.143, so in that instance, and in 3.4.113–14, this edition follows Colman's 'by heaven', which is consistent with the practice in the text of *Prize*. Other instances of 'by heaven' are included in the Griffin section: in *SeaV*, *Double*, *Malta*, and *Fortune*. It is used once in *LC*, though not as an oath (the Alguazir in 3.1.76–7: 'My free will / Left me by heaven'). In *LC* there are six other instances of *heaven* used as an indirect invocation:

Vitelli says 'I would to heaven' (2.1.150), and then simply 'would to heaven' (2.2.191); the Alguazir, 'O equal heaven' (3.1.68); Lucio, 'For heaven's sake' (4.3.22); Clara, simply invoking 'Heaven' (5.3.81); and Bobadilla, 'Pray heaven' (5.3.216). The phrase 'by heaven' may have been felt as more direct, and therefore requiring expurgation.

In 5.2.55–6, in which no fewer than four syllables are missing, this edition follows Dyce's 'by my soul, I swear', which is also consistent with the Lambarde MS readings (which Dyce may have consulted). In the last example, the word missing is clearly *God*, as 'God save the King' was the phrase invariably printed in Jacobean royal proclamations (see 5.3.6–33 n.); previous editors either printed the apostrophe or omitted it.

4) God's light.
'By this good —— [...] By this ——' (4.2.37; 5S1ᵛ, left, 51–2)

In this passage, Vitelli is trying to have sex with Malroda, so Colman suggested that the missing word is not an oath, but an objectionable amorous proposition: *kiss*. This seems too tame to have merited censorship, especially in a play containing a considerable number of quite direct sexual allusions. Dyce suggested instead that the missing word is *light*, though he did so with some reluctance: 'I am by no means certain that the word which I have inserted is the true one' (163). If the missing word is *light*, it would have been understood as an abbreviation of 'by God's light', a strong oath sometimes euphemistically given in plays of the period as ''Slight'. The expression 'by this light' is very common in plays of the Fletcher canon, including some chronologically close to *LC* such as *Wit without Money*, *Monsieur Thomas*, *The Mad Lover*, and *Prize*. The latter, together with *Pilgrim*, which also contains the expression 'by this light', were printed by Griffin in section 5, which again suggests that the expurgation probably took place before the MS arrived in the printing house.

NOTES

1 *Herbert*, 20.
2 Lambarde MS, xviii.

APPENDIX 4
Piorato's song

The music for Piorato's song (3.2.118–25) was composed by John Wilson (1595–1674), lutenist, composer, and Professor of Music at the University of Oxford from 1656 to 1661. By 1614 Wilson was composing regularly for the King's Men alongside Robert Johnson, although he could have been collaborating with the company as early as 1611. He would continue this partnership for the following fifteen years or so, providing musical arrangements and original work, particularly songs, for their performances at the Globe and Blackfriars playhouses, and at court. Fletcher plays containing Wilson's surviving songs from this period include, in chronological order, *Valentinian*, *Love's Cure*, *Beggars' Bush*, *The Mad Lover*, *The Queen of Corinth*, *Rollo, Duke of Normandy*, *The Loyal Subject*, *The False One*, *Women Pleased*, *The Wild-Goose Chase*, and *The Pilgrim*. Other plays from the repertory of the King's Men featuring extant songs by Wilson are Thomas Middleton's *The Witch* (*c.* 1616), John Ford's *The Lover's Melancholy* (1628), and Richard Brome's *The Northern Lass* (1629).[2]

The song in *LC* circulated independently in manuscript long before it was printed. The text appears in several privately owned collections and miscellanies from the 1630s: it was transcribed at the end of an MS of John Donne's poems;[3] it survives (headed 'To his Love') in a *c.* 1634 miscellany compiled by or for Thomas Finch, 2nd Earl of Winchilsea (MSR); in a MS collection of poems now owned privately by the Stoughton family in Warwick; and, headed 'Upon his Mistress's Eyes', in another miscellany now at the University of Newcastle-upon-Tyne.[4] As a song accompanied by Wilson's musical setting it also features in several extant manuscripts: a mid-seventeenth-century part-book owned by a member of the Filmer family of Kent;[5] a *c.* 1650s set of manuscript songbooks compiled by Edward Lowe;[6] and an autograph manuscript that John Wilson presented to the University of Oxford in 1656 (MSB). Wilson included a somewhat simplified version of the song in *Cheerful Airs* (Oxford: Printed by W. Hall for Richard Davis, 1659), sigs T2ᵛ–T3ʳ. The MSB version for vocal soloist and accompaniment has been recorded by Julianne Baird (soprano) and Ronn McFarlane (lute) on *The English Lute Song* (Dorian Recordings, 2005). The early music group English Ayres included an arrangement of the *Cheerful Airs* version for three voices (soprano, alto, and bass) plus lute on their album *The Laughing Cavalier* (Magnatune, 2010).

Figure 9 Piorato's song, edited by Jennifer Moss Waghorn

EDITED TRANSCRIPTION OF MSB BY
JENNIFER MOSS WAGHORN

This transcription reproduces the modernised spelling and punctuation used in this edition of the text. The only significant textual
variant is in bar 12. The modernised F text (given here) reads 'piece
two breasts as one'; the MS version reads 'Joyne two Brests in one'.

All quavers that share a crotchet beat have been written with
joined stems here for ease of reading, as some stems are not joined
in the MS ('beau-teous', bar 2; 'e-mu', bar 5; 'en-vious', bar 8;
'when what', bar 13; 'but their', bar 19). Slurs have been added to
clarify single syllables sung over multiple notes, where indications
of slurred notes are missing from the MS ('of', bar 6; 'two', bar 12;
'thy', bar 16; 'eyes', bar 16; 'it', bar 20). The *dal segno* sign at bar
16 is Wilson's usual method of denoting a repeat from this point to
the end of the piece in this MS. It has been kept here to avoid the
implication that the final repeated section is musically separate from
the rest of the song by using more clearly demarcated repeat bar
lines. There are minor rhythmic and pitch variants in the other
surviving settings of this song; the main difference of note is the
opening bar, which is written as two minims for 'Turn, turn' rather
than the more dynamic offbeat crotchets marked here. The other
settings are written for two or three voices instead of one; these
additional lines must have been added at a later date.

NOTES

1 See Wiggins, *Catalogue*, 1799 (*Bush*). Jennifer Moss Waghorn argues that
  'Wilson's involvement, though not his role as a composer, begins with the
  start of his apprenticeship on the 18th February 1611 (Guildhall Library
  MS 11571/9, fo. 385^v)'; private correspondence. As an apprentice, Wilson
  regularly performed as an actor with the company, playing small roles and
  usually required to sing on stage.
2 See Spink.
3 Trinity College, Cambridge, MS R. 3.12 (James 592), 243.
4 MS Bell-White 25, fos. 25^v–26^r; see Wiggins, *Catalogue*, 1779.
5 Now at the Yale Music Library at Yale University, New Haven, Misc. MS
  170, Filmer MS 4 (a) fo. 15^r, (b) fo. 11^r, (c) fo. 15^v.
6 Two out of the three volumes survive, both for treble: Bodleian Library,
  Oxford, MS Mus. d. 238, 76; and MSE.

APPENDIX 5
Disputed narrative sources

R. Warwick Bond suggested a connection between four passages in *Love's Cure* and an episode in *Gerardo the Unfortunate Spaniard* by Gonzalo de Céspedes y Meneses, which George Walton Williams accepted without verification.[1] The original book had been printed in Madrid in 1615 as *Poema trágico del español Gerardo*, and was only published in Leonard Digges's English translation in 1622.[2] As these two dates are obviously incompatible with the date of composition of *LC*, Bond's suggestion could only hold true if the play had been revised at a later stage to include the passages supposedly derived from *Gerardo*. As Hoy accepted the post-1625 revision by Massinger, including the sections in Act IV alluded to in Bond's theory, this might have been a possibility that would still allow for the retention of the topical allusions to the 1611–15 period in the extant, plausibly revised text.[3] However, Bond's identification of *Gerardo* as a source for *LC* does not stand closer scrutiny.

First, he traced the gulling of Vitelli by Malroda and her associates in 4.2, and the subsequent attack on the young gallant by the group of four rogues, to a passage in *Gerardo* in which the protagonist is ensnared into the private chambers of his beloved Clara, only to be attacked by her uncle and his servants. In his escape, after he has 'leaped out of the window into the street', Gerardo leaves behind 'hat, cloak and pistol as spoils',[4] which Bond linked to the cloak and 'rich hangers' that the Alguazir has been given at the beginning of the following scene (4.3.1). The objects left behind, and the motivation and unfolding of both dramatic situations, are substantially dissimilar. Clara and Gerardo have sexual intercourse before they are interrupted: as he narrates, 'being with her, without scruple [I] gave myself to her embraces, and those arms whose close culling made me mad with joy'.[5] Clara's strategy is to undress the young and naïve Gerardo to maximise his vulnerability, and to leave him defenceless against her uncle by stripping him of his pistol. Vitelli merely loses the hangers of his sword and not the weapon itself, and does not flee the scene, as he is saved, for the second time, by the Clara of *LC*. By contrast, Malroda's approach is based on a negation of further sexual intercourse with her old lover: in order to gull Vitelli out of his jewels before marrying Piorato, she effectively delays the moment of yielding to his advances. After a long conversation in which Vitelli has employed different strategies to try to work his way into her bed, the scene culminates in a final delay:

> *Vitelli.*   Shall we to bed now?
> *Malroda.* Instantly, sweet. Yet, now I think on't better,
>   There's something first that in a word or two
>   I must acquaint you with. (4.2.115–18)

As if this were the agreed signal, the Alguazir and the four rogues invade the scene at that point, eliminating any possibility of success for Vitelli. The difference between the two situations and the characters' motivations are only loosely reminiscent of one another through a commonplace resemblance.

Bond added that 'Clara [in *Gerardo*] excuses herself as urged by her kindred to compel his fulfilment of an alleged promise of marriage',[6] comparing this to *LC* 3.3.95 onwards, and 4.2.142–3. Both instances refer to Malroda's claim that Vitelli has promised to marry her, which the gallant disclaims in strong terms. The situations, however, are unconnected as the promised marriage in *Gerardo* merely serves as Clara's justification for her treachery, while Vitelli denies the betrothal when Malroda indignantly reacts to the rumour that he is marrying someone else. The second example is based on a misreading of the real sense of the lines: 'He's such that would continue [i.e. keep] her a whore / Whom he would make a wife of.' (142–3). The promise of marriage is Piorato's, and not Vitelli's.

Finally, Bond drew a comparison between a second night-time attack on Gerardo by his rival, Rodrigo, who supposedly corresponds here to Vitelli, with 'the second exploit of the Alguazir's crew' in 4.3. This is even more tenuous, as this scene does not even include Piorato, and the intention of the group of rogues is not to attack Vitelli again, but to steal from anyone they might come across at night.

Despite the use of the name Clara in both works, and the fortuitous recurrence of the phrase *in cuerpo* (*LC* 2.1.1), which appears only once in the English version of *Gerardo* (sig. O2ᵛ), and the surnames Sayavedra (only once on sig. N8ᵛ) and Mendoza (only once on sig. O3ᵛ, as *Mendosa*), the link between the Spanish novel and the English play can be safely dismissed.

LA CESAREA GONZAGA AS A POSSIBLE INDIRECT SOURCE

A. L. Stiefel noted that Castro's play might have borrowed some plot details from a prose comedy by Luca Contile (1505–74), printed in Milan by Francesco Marchesino in 1550 under the title *Comedia del Contile chiamata la Cesarea Gonzaga* (*Comedy by Contile called The Cesarea Gonzaga*; the name of the play refers to its dedicatee, Cesare Gonzaga, Duke of Ariano).[7] However, the differences outweigh the similarities, which perhaps suggests a minimal inspiration, or perhaps a fortuitous coincidence. The story involves not one, but two families. On the one hand, Petronio, a gentleman from Bologna, has two children, Lucanio and Cornelia, who has been cross-dressed as a boy named 'Ottavio' from birth, and whose real identity is only known to her father and her father's aunt, Angela. On the other hand, Sempronia, a lady from Sassatella, near Modena, has taken refuge in Bologna from her murdered husband's enemies with her daughter Camilla and her son Cesare, who has been disguised as a girl named 'Giulia' to protect him from their foes. Lucanio falls in love with 'Giulia' (Cesare); Cesare falls in love with 'Ottavio' (Cornelia); and Cornelia in her stead loves Lucanio, who hates 'Ottavio'. Lucanio manages to arrange to have sex in the dark with 'Giulia', only to find himself in bed with Camilla. Meanwhile, 'Ottavio' has arranged a nightly tryst with 'Giulia' at his uncle Alonzio's house. There they both discover their real identities. Cesare, who was in love with a man finds out that that man is, in fact, a woman. But they both fall in love; as Cesare confesses to the astonished Lucanio:

> Non sono io vostra moglie ma vostro cognato, ed è certissima cosa ch'amo vostro fratello come donna e moglie che ella m'è. (sig. O1ʳ)

> 'I am not your wife, but your brother-in-law, and it is most certain that I love your brother as a woman and as the wife that she is to me.'

In the final scene, in addition to the marriage of Cesare and Cornelia, the parents of each family, Sempronia and Petronio, marry each other; Lucanio marries Camilla; and Sempronia's steward Castruccio marries Angela.

The name 'Ottavio' might have been reused for the duellist Otavio in *La fuerza*; the presence of Ruberto, the tutor of Lucanio and 'Ottavio', corresponds to that of the *ayo* or Tutor; and Castruccio may broadly correspond to Galván (and therefore to Bobadilla). The case of double cross-dressing is, however, quite dissimilar, as they are not siblings and they end up marrying each other. Contile's play also contains obvious homoerotic overtones, while in the Spanish and English versions this theme is veiled at best.

Though it is intriguing that the name of Lucanio is closer to *LC*'s Lucio than to Castro's Félix, it is most likely a coincidence: Lucanio is the brother of a female cross-dresser, but he is not himself one. Another similarity with the English version is that Sempronia has specifically concealed her son from her enemies by dressing him up as a girl, fearing that he might be abducted. Eugenia has taken a similar measure in *LC*, though she is not afraid of abduction but plain murder, while Doña Costanza in *La fuerza* is herself hiding from her father's wrath, but has no other enemy, and her reason for dressing Félix in girl's clothes is to keep him at home, away from city brawls and the aggressive world of men. However, rather than trying to trace any kind of mutual literary influence, we can probably assume that these women's motherly protectiveness towards their sons has classical origins: Thetis disguised her son Achilles as a woman to protect him from mortal dangers, as Tirso de Molina dramatised in *El Aquiles*.[8] In addition, as Martin E. Erickson stated, 'the Italian play does not have a martial maid, as do both the Spanish and English plays'.[9] Finally, the whole confusion that drives the plot of the Italian play is based on the fact that only a few relatives know the actual identity of the two cross-dressers, whereas in *La fuerza* and *LC* cross-dressing never really addresses the disguise theme as it does not cause comic confusion (except briefly for Vitelli in I.3). Therefore, it seems safe to assume that, even if Contile's comedy had any influence on Castro, the remote similarities that we may find in *LC* would be due to their appearance in its Spanish literary precedent, and not a direct borrowing from the Italian play.

NOTES

1 See Bond, and GWW, 7.
2 For further information about the contemporary popularity of the novel around Europe, see Cucala Benítez. Fletcher used the novel as a narrative source in *SpCur*.
3 Hoy, 'Shares VI', 49.

4 *Gerardo*, sig. D8^v.
5 *Gerardo*, sig. D8^r.
6 Bond, 267.
7 See Stiefel, 'Nachahmung' 2, 282.
8 Bravo-Villasante, 76.
9 Erickson, 119.

Index

Achilles 2.1.87–8
Adam 3.3.52
*Adelantado 2.1.72
Aeneas 2.1.87–8
*after-reckonings 3.5.13–14
Alba, 3rd Duke of, pp. 3, 4, 65–7,
    Characters in the Play 6
    1.1.114, 2.1.137
Albert VII of Austria, Archduke
    pp. 3, 12–13, 1.1.7, 1.1.21,
    1.1.40, 1.1.102
Alemán, Mateo: *Guzmán de
    Alfaroche* pp. 22, 29, 66
*Alguazir Characters in the Play 17
Allen, William p. 59
*alone 1.1.22
Álvarez de Toledo y Pimentel,
    Fernando, *see* Alba 3rd Duke
    of
Anastro, Gaspar de p. 3,
    Characters in the Play 5
*anatomy 2.1.203
Andalusia 4.3.81
*andirons 3.1.55
*angle-rod 2.1.8
Anne of Austria, Infanta of Spain
    p. 13
Apelles A Prologue 3
*apish 1.3.9
*aquafortis 3.2.27
*aqua-vitae 3.2.28
Archduke, *see* Albert VII
Arias de Bobadilla, Francisco, 4th
    Count of Puñonrostro p. 4,
    Characters in the Play 11
*Asistente Characters in the
    Play 1
Astley, Sir John p. 9
*atonement 5.3.216

Bacon, Francis, Lord Verulam
    3.2.51
*bairn 3.1.39

Ball, Robert F. pp. xii, 50, 61
*Barbary 2.2.137
Barker, Robert p. 12
Barry, Lording: *The Family of Love*
    1.1.74
*bays A Prologue 14
Beaumont, Francis pp. 1, 4–6,
    14–19, 30, 32, 37, 47, 50, 52,
    54–5, 58, A Prologue 13
Bedell, Michael pp. 9, 53
Bel and the dragon 2.2.170
*Belgia 1.3.31
Benfield, Robert p. 59
*berayer 2.1.197
Berkenhead, Sir John p. 32
*bills 3.5.13
Birch, George pp. 8, 53
Bird, Theophilus p. 59
*bisognos 2.1.158
*blacks 1.2.96
*black work 2.2.9
*blister 3.1.37
*block 2.1.183
*blubbered 5.1.6
*boot-hose 1.2.113
*brabble 2.2.172
Bradamante 3.4.98
*bray 2.2.150
British American Drama Academy,
    BADA pp. viii, xiii, 50–1,
    1.1.0, 1.3.46, 2.2.75–9,
    2.2.152–4, 3.4.117, 5.1.0,
    5.2.113–14, 5.3.80
Brome, Richard: *The Northern Lass*
    p. 235
Buckingham, Duke of, *see* Villiers,
    George
*bull's pizzle 2.1.173
Burbage, Richard pp. 7–8
*butt 3.1.8

Carlell, Lodowick: *The Deserving
    Favourite* pp. 15, 54

Carleton, Sir Dudley p. 54
Carr, Robert, 1st Earl of Somerset pp. 10–11
*carrion 2.1.133
Castile 1.1.23, 1.1.53, 4.3.82
Castro, Guillén de pp. 4, 19–22, 45, 56–7
  El curioso impertinente p. 56
  Don Quijote de la Mancha p. 45
  La fuerza de la costumbre pp. 4, 19–26, 28, 56–7, Characters in the Play 2
  Los malcasados de Valencia p. 56
  Las mocedades del Cid pp. 20, 56
*Catholic Monarchs 5.3.7
*caviary 3.2.24
*cazzo 2.1.159
Cerberus 3.2.102
Cervantes, Miguel de pp. 1, 20, Characters in the Play 10, 3.3.103, 5.1.77–9
  Los baños de Argel p. 20
  Don Quijote de la Mancha p. 56, Characters in the Play 11
  Novelas ejemplares pp. 20, 22, 57, Characters in the Play 1
Céspedes y Meneses, Gonzalo de: *Gerardo* pp. 238–9, 242
Chamberlain, John pp. 53–4
*chandler 2.1.186
Charles, Prince of Wales p. 13
Chaucer, Geoffrey 4.3.32
*chilblains 2.1.101
*choler adust 3.2.25
*Christian 1.1.41
*church 2.1.190
Cid, Rodrigo Díaz de Vivar, the pp. 20, 45, 56
*cittern-head 2.2.112
Clark, Hugh p. 59
Clifton, Sir Gervase p. 52
Clifton, Lady Penelope p. 52
*clinch 2.1.128
*close 2.1.226
*closet 1.3.88
*cloy 1.3.67
*cobbler 2.1.66
*cock o' th' game 2.2.56
*cockatrice 3.4.112
*cod-piece 2.2.76

*coil 2.2.44
*college 4.2.54
*commonwealth 2.1.104
Condell, Henry p. 8
*congee 2.1.63
*constitution 2.2.170
Contarini, Piero p. 53
*contemned 5.2.36
*contend 1.3.182
Contile, Luca: *La Cesarea Gonzaga* pp. 240–1
Corneille, Pierre pp. 20, 45, 56
*correction house 3.3.93
*cotquean 2.2.6
*court lip 1.3.17
Cowley, Richard pp. 7, 8, 52
*coz 3.2.89
*crabbed blockhead 2.1.93
*craven chicken 2.2.56
*creed 5.1.25
cross-dressing pp. xii, 1, 21, 24, 25, 27, 37–40, 42, 47, 57, 240–1
Crosse, Nicholas pp. 9, 53
Crossley, Martha p. 50
*crudities 3.2.26
*cuerpo 2.1.2
*custom 1.2.51
Cyclops 5.1.23

Daborne, Robert: *A Christian Turned Turk* 3.3.103
*dag 2.2.135
*dank 3.4.75
Dante Alighieri: *Comedia* 4.4.26–7, 5.2.45–9
*daws 4.2.148
Day, John: *Law-tricks* p. 226
Dekker, Thomas p. 55
  Blurt p. 58, 3.1.3
  Match Me in London p. 58
  PMHW Characters in the Play 19
  The Roaring Girl p. 38, 3.3.32, 3.3.92
  Shoe Characters in the Play 13, 2.1.115
  Untrussing 2.1.64
*desert 5.1.40
*desperately 2.2.134
Devereux, Frances, Countess of Essex, *see* Howard, Frances

Devereux, Robert, 3rd Earl of Essex p. 10, 2.2.159
diablo 2.2.2
Diogenes 2.2.150
*dogbolts 4.3.85
Donne, John p. 235
Doran, Gregory pp. 45, 60
*dough-baked 2.1.73
*dread 1.3.156
*dreadful 5.3.160
duelling pp. 3, 11–12
*dullness Epilogue 2
Dutch Republic, *see* United Provinces

Ecclestone, William pp. 7–8
Egmont, Lamoraal, Count of p. 3, Characters in the Play 2, 4
Elwes, Sir Gervase pp. 10–11
*enjoined 4.4.5
*equinoctial 2.2.167
*equivocate 5.3.169
Ethiop 2.2.151
Eurydice 5.1.24
*exorations 5.3.106
*expositor 2.2.178

*fabulous 2.1.42
*fadge 2.2.69
*falchion 1.1.77
*fancies A Prologue 10
farce pp. 7, 36
*farthingale 2.2.70
*fashion 1.3.37
*favour 2.2.218
*fee-simple 4.3.108
Ferdinand II, King of Aragon, *see* Catholic Monarchs
Field, Nathan pp. 4–5, 14–15, 17–18, 20, 55
  Amends pp. 38, 60, 3.2.27
Finet, John p. 53
*fleers 2.2.25
Fletcher, John pp. xii, 1, 3–7, 9, 13, 14–22, 24–6, 29–30, 32–3, 37–9, 42, 44–5, 47, 50, 52–5, 57–60, Characters in the Play 1, 18
  4Plays p. 54
  Barnevelt 1.2.35–6

Bush pp. 19, 53, 55, 235, 237, 3.2.73
Chase pp. 32, 235, 3.4.48
Corinth pp. 19, 54–5, 57, 235
Cupid p. 39, Characters in the Play 18, 1.1.93–4, 5.3.256
The Devil of Dowgate p. 53
Double pp. 53, 231, 233
Elder Brother 4.4.100
FalseO pp. 59, 235, 3.4.69
FMI pp. 57, 59
Fortune pp. 5, 14–15, 39, 54, 231, 233, 5.1.4
Hater pp. 54, 58
H8 p. 14
LFrL p. 39, 1.2.10
Lieut 3.2.27
LP pp. 20, 39, 55, 57, 59, Characters in the Play 7
The Loyal Subject pp. 7, 39, 235
The Maid's Tragedy p. 39
Malta 231, 233, 4.3.32
Monsieur Thomas pp. 39, 234
Mill pp. 39, 53
Phil pp. 37, 39, 1.3.93
Pilgrim pp. 39, 231, 233–4, 235, 2.2.67–8, 3.1.86
Princess 2.1.176, 3.1.59–61
Prize pp. 33, 231–4, 2.2.104–5, 2.2.150, 2.2.151, 2.2.238–9, 3.3.47, 3.3.92, 4.2.182–4
Progress pp. 18, 53
Prophetess p. 53
Rollo pp. 7, 55, 235
The Scornful Lady p. 39
SeaV pp. 53, 231, 233, 3.1.59–61
SpCur pp. 53, 241, Characters in the Play 1, 17
T&T p. 55
Val pp. 5, 7, 14, 235, 2.1.181, 4.4.12–13
Walkers pp. 14–15, 39, 54, 3.3.32
Women Pleased 235
Ford, John pp. 4, 52
  Love's Sacrifice p. 55
  The Lover's Melancholy p. 235
  'Tis Pity 2.2.43–4, 2.2.117
*forgery 2.1.118
*forsooth 3.4.20
*fortitude 1.3.103

*fortune 1.1.5
*fraught 4.3.11
*freely 1.1.105
Frith, Mary, alias Moll Cutpurse p. 38, 3.3.32

*gage 5.3.176
*gait 2.2.25
*galleys 2.1.172
*gammons 3.2.23
*gelt 2.2.154
*gender 2.2.58
gender identity pp. 1, 37, 39–43, 51, 5.2.53
*genius 1.3.137
*gentle craft 2.1.115
Gerardo, see Céspedes y Meneses, Gonzalo de
*gingerly 2.2.27
*goad 3.4.69
Gondomar, see Sarmiento de Acuña, Diego
Gough, Robert pp. 8, 52
*grace 1.2.19
*grand 2.1.136
*Grandee 2.1.72
*gratified 2.1.156
Griffin, Edward pp. 33, 231, 233–4
Grimeston, Edward pp. 27, 57
*gutter 5.3.78

*habits 5.1.2
Hammerton, Stephen p. 59
*harpies 4.2.127
Harvey, Richard: Plain Perceval 2.1.66
*haunches 1.2.93
Haynes, Walter pp. 8, 53
*heigh-ho 3.4.20
Herbert, Sir Henry, Master of the Revels pp. 9, 18, 47, 53, 55, 60, 231–2, 234
Herbert, Philip, Earl of Pembroke and Montgomery p. 32
Hercules 2.1.87–8
Heywood, Thomas: Kindness 2.2.6–7, 3.3.16, 5.3.149–50, Love's Mistress p. 55
*hip-hap 2.2.70

*holp 1.2.30
Horace 4.4.62
*horoscope 2.2.169
*hose-heeler 2.1.65
Howard, Frances, Countess of Essex, then Countess of Somerset p. 10, 2.2.159

*Indian 1.2.32
Indies, West 1.2.32, 3.1.59–61, 4.2.88, 5.3.194
*indifferently 2.1.81
*industrious 2.1.176
*Infanta 1.1.20
*infidel 3.3.102
Inquisition 2.1.174
Io 5.1.23
*iron-pated 2.1.80
Isabella I, Queen of Castile, see Catholic Monarchs
Isabella Clara Eugenia, Infanta of Spain pp. 3, 12, 13, Characters in the Play 7, 8, 1.1.7, 1.1.20, 2.2.137
Islands 2.1.176
*itch 3.1.86
*iwis 3.4.12

*Jack-i'-th' box 3.1.35
*jades 2.2.140
*jakes-farmer 2.1.71
James I and VI, King of Great Britain pp. 9, 12, 37, 54, 1.3.93
*jet 3.4.44
Johnson, Robert p. 235
Jonson, Ben p. 55
    Alch. p. 8, 2.1.178, 3.2.34
    Bart. Fair pp. 38, 60
    The Devil Is an Ass p. 38
    Eastward Ho! 1.1.74
    EMI Characters in the Play 11, 5.3.226
    Epicene p. 38
    Volpone 5.3.230–53, 5.3.235, 5.3.240
*jostle 2.2.38
*julep water 4.2.80
Juno 3.2.150
*just wreak 1.1.118

*kennel 2.2.43–4
*kibed heels 2.1.101–2
King's Men pp. 5–8, 14–15, 18, 30,
    32–3, 46, 53, 55, 58–60, 235,
    Characters in the Play 13,
    3.3.93, 3.5.0
Kyd, Thomas: *SpT* 1.1.77

Lady Elizabeth's Men pp. 7–8,
    14–15, 18
Langbaine, Gerard pp. 34, 47, 48,
    60
Lazarillo de Tormes pp. 28–9,
    Characters in the Play 14,
    3.1.3
Livy 1.2.66
*lop off 2.2.62
Louis XIII, King of France p. 13
*love-knot 2.2.242
Lowin, John pp. 8, 59
Lyly, John: *Galatea* p. 42, 2.2.19,
    Love's Metamorphosis p. 55

Mabbe, James p. 22
    Exemplary Novels p. 57
    The Rogue pp. 30, 57–8
*Madonna 3.2.79
Madrid, pp. 13, 20–1, 56, 238,
    Characters in the Play 18,
    2.1.139, 3.1.55, 5.3.44
Maid's Metamorphosis, The p. 42
*manage 3.4.13
Maria Anna of Austria, Infanta of
    Spain p. 13
Marlowe, Christopher: *Jew* 3.4.39
*Marry 2.1.159
Mars 2.1.95
Marston, John
    Courtesan 5.3.236
    Eastward Ho! 1.1.74
    Fawn 4.3.93–4 (longer note)
    Histriomastix 1.1.74
    Malcontent Characters in the Play
        16, 1.2.24, 4.3.31, 4.3.93–4
        (longer note)
Massenet, Jules: *Le Cid* p. 56
Massinger, Philip pp. 1, 4–6, 13–19,
    21–2, 24–6, 29, 39, 42, 44, 46,
    52, 54–5, 231, 238, 5.2.113–14
    Bashful p. 60

BAYL p. 58
    The Bondman 3.2.51
    Milan p. 60, Characters in the
        Play 7
    RA 1.3.98
    Renegado p. 19–20, Characters
        in the Play 2, 3.3.103, 5.1.77–9
*massy 1.1.85
*mate 3.4.34
*meat 1.2.4
*mechanic 2.1.105
Mendicants 5.3.240
*metamorphosed 2.2.173
*mettle 2.1.62
Mexico 1.2.33
Middleton, Thomas p. 54
    Chang. p. 53, 3.2.30–1, 4.4.36
    Chaste Maid pp. 8, 52
    Maiden's T 4.2.93, 5.3.204
    The Nice Valour p. 52
    The Phoenix 4.3.93–4 (longer note)
    The Roaring Girl p. 38, 3.3.32,
        3.3.92
    The Triumphs of Truth p. 53
    The Widow pp. 7, 38, 3.5.0
    Wit at Several Weapons pp. 52,
        59
    The Witch p. 235
*milksop 2.2.64
*mittens 2.1.211
*modicum 3.2.20
*molested 5.3.17
Molina, Tirso de: *El castigo del
    penséque* p. 20
Moll Cutpurse, *see* Frith, Mary
*mollify 2.2.88–9
*mongrel 2.1.169
Moors p. 29, 2.1.179–80
Moseley, Humphrey pp. 4, 15,
    32–3, 46–7, 58
*Muscovite 2.2.155–6
*musketeers 1.1.55

Nashe, Thomas: *Pierce Penniless*
    4.3.31, *The Unfortunate
    Traveller* 2.1.102
Nassau, Maurice of pp. 13, 54,
    1.2.35–6
*nectar 1.3.48
*nightcap 1.2.94

Orange, William, Prince of p. 3, Characters in the Play 5
Orlerls, Jan Janszn p. 54
Ostend, siege of pp. 3, 6, 11, 13, 26–8, 36, Characters in the Play 7, 11, 1.1.7, 1.1.14, 1.1.21, 1.1.39, 1.1.40, 1.1.79, 1.1.96, 1.2.35–6, 1.3.31
*othergates 3.4.11
*outsides 3.2.155
Overbury, Sir Thomas pp. 10–11, 5.3.263
Ovid 5.1.23, 5.1.24

Paradise 4.4.27
Paul's, Children of pp. 14, 42, 54–5
*pease 2.1.55
*pee 2.1.184
*period 1.3.54
*perpetrate 5.3.98
*petronel 1.1.74
Phidias A Prologue 3
Philip II, King of Spain p. 3, Characters in the Play 2, 4, 7, 1.1.20, 1.1.21
Philip III, King of Spain pp. 12–13, Characters in the Play 7, 1.1.21, 5.3.7
*phlegmatic humour 3.2.26
Phoebus A Prologue 15
picaresque novel pp. 28–30
*pilchard 2.1.51
*pilfery 2.1.172
*pistolets 4.3.2
Playford, John 2.2.6–7
*point 3.4.79
*poise 2.2.230
Pollard, Thomas pp. 8, 59
*poor John 2.2.110
*portion 3.3.45
Portuguese p. 57, 2.1.179–80
*postern 1.1.63
*pottage 2.2.4
*precinct 3.1.48
*prepuce 2.2.75
*pressed 2.1.176
*probatum 3.2.39
*provant 2.1.55
*provided 1.2.26

*punklings 2.1.178
*punks 2.1.178

*qualify 2.2.89
*quality 2.1.77
Queen's Revels, Children of the pp. 14–15
*quiet 2.2.39
*quittance 2.1.226

*rampant 4.2.23
*rank 2.1.3
*rattled 3.3.5
*ravished 4.4.52
*red herring 2.1.46–7
*relic 5.2.42
*republic 5.3.4
*respectively 1.2.92
revenge tragedy pp. 3, 36
*ringleader 5.3.230
*ris 2.1.191
Robinson, Humphrey p. 32
Robinson, Richard pp. 8, 59
Rowland of Anglesey, David p. 28
Rowley, William: All's Lost by Lust p. 58, Wit at Several Weapons pp. 52, 59, Chang. see Middleton, Thomas
*royal 2.1.177
*rug 2.1.162
Rutter, Joseph: The Cid p. 20

*Saint Jacques 1.2.6
*sand-blind 2.1.229
*sanguine scabbard 3.4.67
Sanlúcar de Barrameda 1.1.2, 5.3.28–9
Santiago, Castle of 5.3.28–9
*sardine 2.1.52
Sarmiento de Acuña, Diego, Lord (and later Count) of Gondomar p. 13
*satisfaction 1.3.176
Saturn 2.1.88.
*scabs 2.1.101
*scallion-faced 2.1.75
Seneca 3.2.51
*Señor 2.1.4

Seville pp. 1, 13, 22, 29, 36,
    Characters in the Play 1, 2, 6,
    11, 1.1.0, 1.1.2, 1.1.10, 1.1.34,
    1.1.38, 1.2.24, 1.2.32, 1.2.53,
    1.3.57, 1.3.154, 2.1.4, 2.1.60,
    2.1.180, 2.2.46, 3.1.46, 3.2.60,
    3.3.83, 3.3.86–7, 4.1.0, 4.3.81,
    5.2.18, 5.3.28–9
*shads 2.2.133
Shakespeare, William pp. 1, 5, 14,
    47, 50
    A&C 2.1.130–3
    AYL 1. 2.14–15
    Cardenio pp. 14, 45, 60
    Cymbeline p. 38
    1H4 3.5.17, 5.3.219–24, 5.3.236
    2H4 2.1.9–10, 2.2.155–6,
        5.3.205–6
    H5 5.1.0
    1H6 5.3.200
    H8 p. 14
    JC 2.1.112
    Lear H 2.2.48
    Lear T 2.1.36–8
    Macbeth 5.3.127
    MAdo 3.5.0, 5.3.140
    MM 3.2.95–6, 4.2.2, 4.3.93–4
        (longer note), 5.3.256
    MND 2.1.170–97
    MV 2.1.229
    Oth. 3.4.39, 4.2.83, 4.4.12
    R2 4.3.34–5, 5.3.149–50
    R3 5.3.110–11
    R&J 2.2.29, 3.4.0, 3.4.14, 4.3.
        33, 5.3.11–12
    Tit. 3.4.39
    TwN 3.1.25, 3.2.79
Shakespeare Institute pp. xii–xiii,
    50, 1.3.46, 2.2.75–9, 2.2.152–4,
    4.3.93–4 (longer note), 5.3.80,
    5.3.259–60
Shank, John p. 8
Shirley, James: Love's Cruelty
    p. 55, The Opportunity
    p. 20, The Triumph of
    Peace 1.1.74, The Young
    Admiral p. 20
*skill 2.2.262
*skirred 2.2.130
*skulked 2.1.176

*small beer 3.2.47
*smock-gamester 4.3.100
*sop 3.2.103
*soul-menders 2.1.112
Spanish Netherlands pp. 3,
    12–13, 1.1.6, 1.1.7, 1.1.20,
    1.1.114, 1.3.31
*sparrow 4.2.2
*spinster 2.2.6
*spleen 5.3.139
*spoiled 2.2.141
*squiring 2.1.178
*stews 3.3.11
*stick 5.3.186
*stockfish 2.2.111
Stuart, Arabella p. 37
*success 1.1.82
Suett, Richard: The Female Duellist
    pp. 47, 60
Swanston, Eliard pp. 32, 59

*talons 2.1.211
*taster 4.2.15
Taylor, Joseph p. 59
*teemed A Prologue 10
*tenants at will 4.3.109
*tissue 1.3.14
*Toledo 1.2.44
Tooley, Nicholas pp. 7–8, 52
*traduction 3.1.74
tragicomedy pp. 5, 14–15, 37
transgender pp. 1, 40–4
*tread 3.4.36
*trifles 3.4.58
*trim 2.2.222
*trindle tail 3.3.16
Troy 3.3.52
Turk 3.3.103, 5.1.77
*turtle 3.4.32

Ulysses 5.1.23
*uncomfortable 3.3.48
*underlay 5.3.247
Underwood, John pp. 7–8,
    52
*unequal 5.1.102
United Provinces p. 26, 1.2.35–6
*untoward 3.4.89
*unweave 5.3.96
*upbraid 3.3.96

Valencia pp. 20, 45, 56
Vega, Félix Lope de: *El acero de Madrid* p. 57, *Don Lope de Cardona* p. 20
Venus p. 42, 2.1.94–5
*vicegerent 3.1.46
**videlicet* 2.1.101
Villiers, George 1st Duke of Buckingham, p. 13
*virago 3.3.83
Virgil 3.3.51–2, 4.4.26–7
Vitelli, Giovanni Luigi, 'Chiappino' p. 3, Characters in the Play 2
Vulcan 2.1.89

*waistcoat 3.1.18
*warrant 4.1.6
*water-spaniels 3.5.1
Watts, Graham pp. xiii, 50, 1.1.0, 4.1.1
*waxed 2.1.108
Webster, John pp. 4, 55
    Law Case p. 59, 3.2.15–21

Malfi pp. 6–8, 3.3.60
White Devil 1.1.15–17, 3.3.43–5, 3.4.70, 4.2.54, 5.1.2, 5.3.182–6 (and longer note)
*whiting-mops 2.2.96
Wilson, John pp. 235–7, 3.2.118–25
Wilson, Robert: *The Cobbler's Prophecy* 2.1.106–7
Winwood, Sir Raphe p. 54
*wooden 3.4.91
*woollen-witted 2.1.80
*worrying 4.2.22
*worshipful 2.1.206
*wresting 1.1.115
*wrought 1.2.111

*yet 1.2.64

Zelotypus 3.2.102, 3.3.23 SD (longer note)
Ziuzin, Aleksei Ivanovich pp. 9–10, 53, 2.2.155–6

CPSIA information can be obtained
at www.ICGtesting.com
Printed in the USA
LVHW081811270522
719945LV00004B/174